PATERNOSTER BIBLICAL MONOGRAPHS

C000162097

The Voice of Jesus

Studies in the Interpretation of Six Gospel Parables

Series Preface

One of the major objectives of Paternoster is to serve biblical scholarship by
providing a channel for the publication of theses and other monographs of high
quality at affordable prices. Paternoster stands within the broad evangelical tradition
of Christianity. Our authors would describe themselves as Christians who recognise
the authority of the Bible, maintain the centrality of the gospel message and assent to
the classical credal statements of Christian belief. There is diversity within this
constituency; advances in scholarship are possible only if there is freedom for frank
debate on controversial issues and for the publication of new and sometimes
provocative proposals. What is offered in this series is the best of writing by
committed Christians who are concerned to develop well-founded biblical
scholarship in a spirit of loyalty to the historic faith.

Series Editors

I. Howard Marshall, Honorary Research Professor of New Testament, University of
Aberdeen, Scotland, UK

Richard J. Bauckham, Professor of New Testament Studies and Bishop Wardlaw
Professor, University of St Andrews, Scotland, UK

Craig Blomberg, Distinguished Professor of New Testament, Denver Seminary,
Colorado, USA

Robert P. Gordon, Regius Professor of Hebrew, University of Cambridge, UK

Tremper Longman III, Robert H. Gundry Professor and Chair of the Department of
Biblical Studies, Westmont College, Santa Barbara, California, USA

PATERNOSTER BIBLICAL MONOGRAPHS

The Voice of Jesus

Studies in the Interpretation of Six Gospel Parables

Stephen I. Wright

Foreword by James D.G. Dunn

Copyright © Stephen I. Wright 2000
First published 2000 by Paternoster

Paternoster is an imprint of Authentic Media
9 Holdom Avenue, Bletchley, Milton Keynes, MK1 1QR, UK
and
P.O. Box 1047, Waynesboro, GA 30830–2047, USA

04 03 02 01 00   7 6 5 4 3 2 1

British Library Cataloguing in Publication Data
A catalogue record for this book is available from the British Library

ISBN-10 0–85364–975–8
ISBN-13 978–0–85364–975–5

Typeset by the Author
and printed and bound in Great Britain by
Nottingham Alphagraphics

For my parents
N.I.W. and R.W.

Contents

Foreword   **xi**

Acknowledgements   **xiii**

Chapter 1

The Voice and Figures of Jesus   **1**

1 The Idea of a Voice   1

2 Discerning a Voice: Figures of Speech   3

3 Figures, Tropes and Parables   6

4 Intention, Influence and Insight   11

    Intention   12

    Influence   14

    Insight   17

5 Texts   18

Notes   19

Chapter 2

Parables and Proclamation:

Luke's Interpretation of the Parables   **30**

1 Luke: the Intention to Interpret   30

2 Luke's Interpretative Key: Metonymy   31

3 Luke's Parable Interpretations   33

    The Six Parables   33

    Characters   35

    Wealth and Poverty   37

    Celebration and Friendship   41

    Compassion and Mercy   44

    Righteousness and Unrighteousness 45

    Life and Death   48

    Humiliation and Exaltation   50

4 From Influence to Insight: The Voice of Jesus in Luke 51

Notes   55

Chapter 3
The Age of Divine Meaning: Parable Interpretation
from the Fathers to the Reformers   **62**
1 A Heritage Misconstrued   62
2 The Intention of the Premodern Commentators   67
    Ambrose and Bede   68
    Bonaventure   71
    Calvin   73
3 The Premodern Commentators' Interpretative Keys:
The Range of Tropes   74
4 The Premodern Commentators' Parable Interpretations   76
    The Good Samaritan   76
    The Prodigal Son   79
    The Shrewd Steward   85
    The Rich Man and Lazarus   90
    The Judge and the Widow   95
    The Pharisee and the Customs Officer   96
5 From Influence to Insight: The Voice of Jesus in the
Premodern Commentators   97
Notes   100

Chapter 4
The Age of Historical Quest:
The Parable Interpretation of Adolf Jülicher   **113**
1 Jülicher and Historical Criticism   113
2 The Intention of Jülicher   114
3 Jülicher's Interpretative Key: Simile   115
4 Jülicher's Parable Interpretations   118
    The Good Samaritan   118
    The Prodigal Son   119
    The Shrewd Steward   122
    The Rich Man and Lazarus   124
    The Judge and the Widow   125
    The Pharisee and the Customs Officer   126
5 From Influence to Insight: The Voice of Jesus in Jülicher   127
Notes   141

Chapter 5
The Age of the Reader:
The Parable Interpretation of Bernard Brandon Scott **151**
1 The Escape from 'Severe History'   151
2 The Intention of Scott   155
3 Scott's Interpretative Key: Metaphor   158
4 Scott's Parable Interpretations   160
   The Good Samaritan   160
   The Prodigal Son   162
   The Shrewd Steward   166
   The Rich Man and Lazarus   167
   The Judge and the Widow   168
   The Pharisee and the Customs Officer   169
5 From Influence to Insight: The Voice of Jesus in Scott   170
Notes   177

Chapter 6
Parables and Persuasion:
The Voice of Jesus in his Contemporary Context **182**
1 The Synchronic Context of Jesus: Society and Faith   182
2 Inadequate Interpretative Keys   185
   Metaphor   185
   Metonymy   186
   Irony   187
   Hyperbole   187
3 Synecdoche as an Interpretative Key   193
   Whole to Part: world into story   195
   Part to Whole: story into world   201
4 The Voice of Jesus in Synchronic Perspective:
Gracious Wisdom   207
Notes   212

Chapter 7
Parables and Precursors:
The Voice of Jesus and the Voices of Scripture **227**
1 The Diachronic Context of Jesus: Scripture   227

2 The Parables' Continuity with Scripture   229
    Synecdoche and Wisdom   230
    Synecdoche and Sacred History   231
    Synecdoche and Law   232
    Synecdoche and Prophecy   234
    Jesus and 'Conventional Wisdom'   235
3 Interpretative Keys: The Parables' Troping of Scripture   235
    Irony and normality   236
    Synecdoche and narrativity   236
    Metonymy and brevity   237
    Hyperbole and humanity   237
    Metaphor and fictionality   238
    Metalepsis and allusiveness   238
4 The Voice of Jesus in Diachronic Perspective: New and Old   240
Notes   241

Chapter 8
The Story of a Voice   **246**
Notes   250

Bibliography   **253**

Index of Ancient Literature   **269**
    Old Testament   269
    Apocrypha and Pseudepigrapha   270
    New Testament   270
    Parables   273

Index of Greek Words   **274**

Index of Authors   **275**

Index of Subjects   **279**

FOREWORD

One of the things which have become clearer over the past few years is that biblical texts are like a sequence of extended musical chords, full of rich harmonies, resonating and reverberating with countless echoes of other chords and harmonies. Any great piece of literature has, by definition, a greater depth than often appears at first sight, and the history of its own reception has added further dimensions of depth. The intertextual echoes which someone like George Steiner can evoke and start resonating round a reader's or hearer's own memory makes one of his own performances (essays or lectures) memorable.

In New Testament studies it was a fresh approach to Jesus' parables in the past twenty or so years which began to bring this home to a new generation of readers and hearers. The new approach broke through what many had come to perceive as the three tyrannies: the tyranny of the 'parables have only one point of significance' approach; the tyranny of the 'parables only have meaning when locked into their historical context of origin' approach; and latterly, the tyranny of a 'text only' approach, which forgets that the parables were first spoken and heard and that still today they are more often heard than read. The dynamics of oral/aural retelling, rather than the clinical analysis of parable as written text, opens up different dimensions not adequately described by the term 'intertextuality'.

All this makes study of the parables much more exciting, but also much more demanding than before. Fortunately in Stephen Wright we have the necessary competence and breadth. As someone with a first class Honours degree in English Language and Literature from Oxford, as well as a PhD in New Testament from Durham, he is in an unusually good position to evaluate the strengths and weaknesses of both the traditional treatments of the parables and the most recent research on them. He has carried through his task with an awareness of and sensitivity to the nature of literary figure which is unsurpassed in anything I have read on this subject, or in any other literary readings of the New Testament. His research into the often despised traditional interpretations of the parables (so largely ignored in the wake of Jülicher) has shown how much of the standard criticism is unperceptive and undeserved. The result is a much more nuanced appreciation of the way parables function and of such descriptions as the 'radicality', 'originality' and 'subversiveness' of Jesus' own teaching through parables. The resulting thesis was first class and its publication should mark something of a milestone in the study of the parables.

James D. G. Dunn
University of Durham, April 2000

ACKNOWLEDGEMENTS

This book is a revised version of a thesis submitted for the degree of Doctor of Philosophy at the University of Durham in 1997. My supervisor was Professor James Dunn, to whom I owe a great debt of gratitude for his encouragement of my work and for the rich store of wisdom he shared with me over my three years under his tutelage. I am most grateful to him also for contributing the foregoing Foreword. I would like also to thank my examiners, Dr David Jasper of Glasgow and Dr Walter Moberly of Durham, for their careful reading and for the stimulating exchange which brought the process to a climax. The funding for the project, including a short study trip to Germany, was provided by the British Academy, and I am truly thankful to them for the opportunity thus opened up.

The academic community in Durham was a source of great support and intellectual invigoration. In the Department of Theology Dr Stephen Barton read some of my work and I benefited greatly from discussing it with him. I am grateful to him and to Dr Loren Stuckenbruck for their friendship and help. The collegiality of the Postgraduate New Testament Seminar and informal exchanges with fellow-members contributed indirectly in many ways to my work. In the Department of English Dr Seán Burke generously gave time at different stages to read and comment on my writing, opening up aspects of literary theory and, not least, pointing me to the wealth of material from the Patristic and medieval eras which can provide a starting-point for contemporary reflection on literary matters.

Others have played a part along the way, which I am glad to acknowledge. It was Dr Robert Young at Exeter College, Oxford in the late 1970's who introduced me to the writing of Harold Bloom; I daresay he would be surprised that his attempts to get me to understand this fascinating but difficult writer had eventually borne fruit (if indeed they have!). A few years later The Reverend John Sweet at Selwyn College, Cambridge, introduced me to academic study of the New Testament, including the parables, with memorable enthusiasm and warmth. Awareness of historical issues was sharpened further under the guidance of Dr Chip Coakley at Lancaster University in 1990-91.

It was then at a meeting in the University of Tübingen in 1993 that the seeds of the thesis were sown. Professor Gerd Jeremias assured me that there was work still to be done on the parables, the labours of his esteemed father and many since notwithstanding! Professor Hermann Lichtenberger suggested the special-Luke material as a fruitful field, and also most generously lent my family and me his house for three weeks in August 1996. This enabled me to plunder (metaphorically, of course) the treasures of that wonderful theological centre, insofar as the brevity of the stay allowed. As well as gaining a first-hand sense of some recent German scholarship, I came upon the otherwise rather inaccessible commentary of Bonaventure on Luke, in an exquisite sixteenth-century edition; the study of this turned out to be a high point of the whole project.

I have also valued conversations about the parables with Dr Ruth Etchells and The Reverend Theo Harman, in Durham; and Dr Alastair Campbell, The Reverend Peter Stevenson and Mr Arthur Rowe, current colleagues at Spurgeon's College, London, where it has been a privilege also to take part in various seminars related to the parables.

In the preparation of the book for publication - a challenge for information-technology skills as much as authorial ones - I have been greatly helped by Mr Jeremy Mudditt of Paternoster Publishing. I thank him for his patience. I am also most grateful to Dr John Welford for his help and keen eye in proofreading.

In all of this, members of my family have been significant players. My brother, Dr Tom Wright, has long encouraged me to academic endeavour - and possibly feels I have been dilatory in heeding his advice! His enthusiasm for Christian scholarship has been a great example to me; he also kindly made time to read a chapter of the original thesis at draft stage. It was at his suggestion that I set out on the path of full-time research. That I stayed the course is due in no small measure to the unfailing support of my wife, Linda, whose belief in me and daily nurturing of me have undergirded the whole adventure. Together with our children she has, often sacrificially, provided the atmosphere where study and thought were possible.   In addition, she brought her linguistic expertise to bear in checking my German translations in Chapter 4 and saving me from a number of errors. Any errors of any kind that remain, there or in any other part of the book, must of course be put down to my account.

Finally, it is fitting that a book dealing much with origins and influences should be dedicated with love to those who brought its author into the world and in countless ways have shaped who he is. For all their guidance and care over the years I am grateful to my parents, but above all for bringing me into the church of God, where the framework of 'divine meaning' remains real *and* the voice of Jesus of Nazareth can still be heard.

CHAPTER 1

The Voice and Figures of Jesus

Individuality must be intuited.[1]

There is no method other than yourself.[2]

1. The Idea of a Voice

'Voice' has been a significant term in the study of the parables of Jesus. Its meaning has interestingly modulated in accordance with general developments in gospel studies. In the late nineteenth century, Adolf Jülicher differentiated the 'voice of Jesus' from the 'voice of the Evangelists' to argue the necessity of 'source-criticism', the tracing of the sources from which the Evangelists obtained their material.[3] The goal of his work was to recover the parables of Jesus from the obfuscation which he believed they had suffered at the hands not only of later interpreters but also of the earliest Christians, including the Evangelists themselves. In the mid-twentieth century, Joachim Jeremias expressed the hope of returning to the 'actual living voice of Jesus'.[4] This would entail where possible the reconstruction of Jesus' original Aramaic,[5] and was to be fulfilled through the tools of 'form-criticism', the attempt to understand the 'forms' of New Testament literature with reference to the function they performed in the early church. Jeremias outlined ten 'principles of transformation' by which he believed the parables had been shaped since they were originally spoken by Jesus.[6]

Contemporary scholars have been more attuned to the elusiveness of the object and the sophistication required to approach it. Opening the 'Jesus Seminar', Robert W. Funk acknowledged the plurality of voices in the gospel texts[7] and the difficulty of isolating the voice of Jesus.[8] The idea of the 'voice' of the parables in particular is prominent in the work of a member of the Seminar, Bernard Brandon Scott.[9] Though continuing the Jülicher-Jeremias historical project of separating out the supposed original from the later accretions in which it is seen as embedded, he introduces the new criterion of *tone*. The 'authentic' Jesus is recognized by 'a tendency to play in minor keys',[10] an air of unconventionality which cuts against 'common wisdom'.[11] In contrast to Jeremias's Lutheran orthodoxy, Scott and others in the Jesus Seminar tend to identify the ecclesiastical mainstream with this 'common wisdom' over against a 'radical' Jesus. Moreover, Scott sees the 'originating structure' of the parables as a more significant and accessible goal than their original words (the object of Jeremias's quest).[12] A further exploration of the theme of Jesus as original and creative in his use of parables is found in Charles W. Hedrick's examination of the 'creative voice' of Jesus.[13]

I wish to examine what is involved in a quest for the 'voice' of Jesus, especially in relation to the parables, and suggest how such a quest may be advanced. I believe there can be no retreat to a pre-Jülicher stance in which the 'voices' of Jesus and the Evangelists remain undistinguished from each other. We have seen the imprint of tradition upon the texts and we cannot now pretend that we have not. Nevertheless, I believe the 'historical-critical' criteria which continue to be used to distinguish different 'voices' within the parables - including that of unconventionality - to be essentially arbitrary and flawed.[14] That does not mean, however, that an inquiry concerning 'the voice of Jesus' is without interest, value or potential results.[15] The new awareness of the importance of detecting tone and tenor above establishing original words, seen in the works of Scott and Hedrick, is a positive development. But the openness to different kinds of literary criticism visible in such writers has in one sense not yet gone far enough. The nature of the parables as figurative language has not been allowed to challenge the expectations and methods of historical inquiry which we have inherited from the rise of biblical criticism in the wake of the Enlightenment.[16]

My contention is that texts such as the parables of Jesus require interpreters to be creative, but that this does not imply that we can do no more than invest the parables with our own 'meanings'. To discern a 'voice' in the parables - whether that of Jesus or of the tradition or of the Evangelist - entails a creative response, but not the mere projection of the interpreter's wishes.[17]

I will both illustrate this from the history of interpretation and perform it in my own. My recounting of the history of interpretation will be more than conventional scene-setting, or elimination of 'flawed' interpretations in order to establish one's own as the sole credible option.[18] Rather, by studying earlier parable readings in some depth, I shall show how deeply influenced the contemporary interpreter is by the whole tradition of interpretation (such that claims to great novelty would be pretentious), and I will present my own proposals as one turn the story might take next (rather than as the closure or climax of the story). In contradistinction from modern suspiciousness with respect to tradition's distorting power, the feeling that a wedge must be driven between Jesus and all who came after, I want to suggest that the parables represent in acute form our *need* of tradition for understanding, not in the sense of a body of received wisdom so much as what Andrew Louth calls 'an inarticulate living of the mystery, the tacit dimension'.[19] If there can be no hearing of the voice of Jesus in the texts without a creative response to them, this need not throw the interpreter back into solipsism. Rather, it should lead us precisely to hear what others have heard, not to privilege a hermeneutic of privacy or novelty.

This naturally raises the question of my theological interests in this project. I write from a standpoint of orthodox Christian faith. However, I do not believe that this prejudges the kind of 'voice' that I am likely to hear in these parable texts. As we shall see, during the great period of 'orthodoxy' the issue of the tone and intention of Jesus of Nazareth was not a primary concern for exegetes. Christians who are concerned with these things today study them in a scholarly context that has been influenced by many currents of thought, whose relationship to Christian 'orthodoxy' is by no means uncomplicated or obvious.[20] There *is* no 'party line' on the parables to which the Christian interpreter will irresistibly be drawn. Further, the specifically philosophical questions of how a person believed to have risen from the dead and to transcend space and time may 'speak' through written texts today are beyond the scope of my inquiry;[21] so are the metaphysical links between theology and literature or history in themselves.[22]

My concern, then, is with the 'voice' of Jesus of Nazareth, as a metaphor for his stance, attitude, individuality, personal stamp.[23] It will be convenient to think of it in both a 'horizontal' or 'synchronic' dimension (his voice in relation to his contemporary context) and a 'vertical' or 'diachronic' dimension (his voice in relation to the tradition in which he stands). I propose that the chief means of discerning that voice is to make a creative response to his parables as figures of speech.

2. Discerning a Voice: Figures of Speech

Figures of speech are tokens of the individuality that points us to a particular 'voice'. To focus upon figures offers, as we shall see, a way to combine historical seriousness about the 'voice of Jesus' in the parables, a sense of the limits of historical inquiry on such a topic, and an awareness of the importance of literary sensitivity. It also provides a useful thread through the history of interpretation.

Pierre Fontanier defined figures as the 'more or less remarkable forms, features or turns, varyingly successful, through which discourse, as expression of ideas, thoughts or feelings, makes itself more or less different

from what would have been the simple or common expression'.[24] This
definition captures well the loose and conventional way in which the term
'figure of speech' is used. One can immediately notice the questions it begs.
Who is to decide what is remarkable expression, and what is common - and
on what grounds? Cannot all language be seen as 'figurative' in some
sense? May there be figures that are recognizable as such to a speaker or
writer, but not to the hearer or reader, and *vice versa?* If a figure becomes
simply a part of the common currency of language, so that it is universally
recognized and understood, does it thereby cease to be a figure, having lost
the air of deviancy?[25] What difference might *writtenness* make to a figure
of *speech*?[26] These questions simply point up the fact that the detection of
figures is precisely a matter of custom and of personal response, and not of
deciphering language according to an absolute set of rules. As a linguistic
signal a figure of speech is not simply translatable into 'normal' language,
for an essential aspect of its 'meaning' is to draw attention to itself and thus
indirectly to its maker.

Almost universally the parables have been treated as 'figures of
speech'[27] - whether or not the term has been explicitly used - for two main
reasons. First, for most of Christian history they have been read as part of a
highly significative sacred text.[28] In this period they were generally
regarded as no more or less 'figurative' than other parts of Scripture. Like
the surrounding text, they were seen as richly suggestive and uniquely
shaped by the divine author for his purposes. Second, since the rise of
historical criticism the parables have been regarded as figures in a narrower
sense.[29] Read in the context of the gospels, they strike an attentive reader
with a *prima facie* peculiarity or uniqueness not even possessed by the
surrounding texts, like peaks soaring above an already impressive
landscape. Scholars generally ready to mistrust the Evangelists' ascriptions
of words or deeds to Jesus have seen them as 'figures' that point to the
mind of an individual creator, distinct from the Evangelists, and have been
drawn irresistibly to identify that creator with Jesus. Queries about the
authenticity of this or that parable or part of a parable have not altered this
overwhelming verdict of modern scholarship.[30] John Drury's work,
however, exposes the fact that this argument is not watertight.[31] Do the
parables rise *so* high above the landscape that it is impossible simply to
read them as pointing to the individual artistry *of a writer such as Luke,*
rather than to the mind of Jesus?

So although there may be general agreement that a certain segment of
text constitutes a figure, a more or less striking linguistic token of
individuality, that does not tell us *whose* individuality. The truth in our
present case presumably lies somewhere between two extremes. At one end
of the range of possibility, Jesus may have been consistently individual and
'different' in his use of language, whereas the tradition and the Evangelists

tended to assimilate this difference to common wisdom. At the other end, Jesus may have enunciated things in a way that many others had enunciated them and were continuing to enunciate them, but the tradition and especially the Evangelists were very creative, even making their own 'figures' and ascribing them to Jesus. There is a large spectrum between these two extremes, and much seems to depend on personal judgement.

How then can the rhetorical category 'figure' possibly advance an investigation into the voice of Jesus? Paul de Man offers what may seem a counsel of despair: 'Far from constituting an objective basis for literary study, rhetoric implies the persistent threat of misreading.'[32] In fact, however, the category 'figure' may clarify the nature of our task and the mode in which it must be undertaken.

The slipperiness of rhetoric as a foundation for literary study, exposed by de Man, simply underlines the *de facto* element of individual human construal involved in comprehending figurative language. De Man sees the conditioning of humans by language as more fundamental than the conditioning of language by humans.[33] But rather than surrendering to this view and therefore despairing of rhetorical categories as a part of a deceitful web of language in which we are irretrievably enmeshed, it is possible to celebrate the personal element in the formation of, and response to language, and see rhetoric - above all the notion of 'figure' - simply as the indicator of language's irreducible humanity.

This notion of 'figure' reminds us that we are not dealing with language as just a conventionally-shaped entity; and that an *aesthetic* act is involved in the detection of an individual 'voice'.[34] Last century the form-critic Martin Dibelius denied the necessity for such a response in the case of the NT, by characterizing the NT literature as a 'sociological result'.[35] Since in his view 'the author's personality is of little importance'[36] in these writings, no 'aesthetic judgement of a personal and creative character'[37] needed to be made with respect to them: the field belonged, he thought, to historical-critical methods in a strict sense. But these judgements about the NT are themselves aesthetic ones, in the fundamental sense of 'perceptions'.[38] They have been challenged. Stephen Neill, for instance, has written that 'each of the evangelists is an author, and an author of genius, in his own right'.[39] Subsequent studies have celebrated the individual skill of the Evangelists.[40] Jesus himself has frequently been regarded as an (oral) 'author' of genius.[41] A properly nuanced view of the NT will be open to the possibility of its containing a mixture of conventionally- and personally-shaped material.[42] The central point is that historical data alone, though vital, will not be able to distinguish between those kinds of material for us. Both the initial recognition of the personal - the discernment of the voice - and its understanding and appraisal, are matters of personal, aesthetic response, with the implication that 'objective' standards of verification are simply inapplicable.[43]

The rigour of much modern historical criticism of the Bible has not been at ease with this fact. It has erected its apparatus for deciding how to distinguish Jesus-material from later accretions, and then, as a separate stage, interpreted what Jesus is supposed to have said. But the apparatus itself has been controlled by literary and interpretative judgements, thus making the process circular. To construe a figure, however, is *in the same moment* both to detect the individuality of the voice and to intuit what the speaker means.

In practice this means that parables exemplify in acute form the need for historical study and aesthetic construal to go hand in hand. The father of modern hermeneutics, Friedrich D.E. Schleiermacher, understood this clearly. Anthony Thiselton states Schleiermacher's position thus:

> To 'divine' without comparative philological or critical study is to become a hermeneutical 'nebulist'; to engage in comparative philological questions without a living, intuitive perception of the spirit of the subject-matter and its author is to remain a hermeneutical 'pedant'.[44]

To attend to the figurative nature of texts is simultaneously to engage in both activities that Schleiermacher saw to be necessary. Comparative historical study is required, because only so can our perceptions be saved from mere eccentricity; 'divination' or aesthetic response is also required, because otherwise there will always be a tendency to reduce the individual to the conventional, or at least to a readily analysable form of deviation from the conventional. The history of parable interpretation reveals at every stage the presence of a creative, imaginative perception of the spirit 'of the subject-matter and its author'. Equally, it reveals the importance of a sense of the historical location of the 'author'. My focus in this book is on the aspect of creative perception, but that is only because it has been the neglected or unacknowledged element in much scholarly parable interpretation over the last two centuries. I hope it will be clear throughout that I am not presenting this in *opposition* to historical study but as its indispensable complement.

3. Figures, Tropes and Parables

Interpreters make their creative construals of figures such as parables by labelling them - explicitly or implicitly - with the conventional name of a particular figure of speech, for example simile or metaphor.[45] The conventionality of all 'discourse about discourse' has been thoroughly exposed by Roland Barthes;[46] there is no 'correct' definition of particular figures. Since interpretation does not need to presume that the speaker or writer was conscious of using a particular figure, indeed would usually be foolish to presume this except in cases of the most carefully contrived rhetoric (few poets, prophets or preachers will have stopped to think 'now I will use a metaphor to get my point across to best effect'), we do not need to worry about using potentially 'anachronistic' definitions of figures in our interpretation of ancient texts.[47] We are not concerned with rhetorical systems with which Jesus might have been familiar, but with instinctive language patterns into which contemporary understandings of rhetoric may give us as much insight as ancient ones.

The most basic distinction that needs to be made is between a *figure* and a *trope*.[48] Though the terms are sometimes used interchangeably, it is helpful to keep 'figure' as the larger category, meaning any deviant or individualized form of speech. A 'trope' (etymologically 'turn') is basically a figure in which the meaning of an individual word, or short phrase, is altered or 'turned' from its conventional sense. Thus alliteration, for instance, is a figure - a special usage of language - but not a trope: in the sentence 'Around the rugged rock the ragged rascal ran' the words continue to bear their conventional literal meaning. The non-tropical figure with which we need to be concerned in this study is *simile*, in which one thing is likened to another - for example, Hosea 6:4: 'Your love is like the morning cloud'. Again, we note that the *individual words* here are to be taken literally.

The other important distinctions to be made, for our purposes, are those between different tropes. Although for some purposes it is possible simply to subsume them all within metaphor,[49] I want to show the importance, in the study of the parables, of keeping them distinct. I will list and define in their simplest form the six tropes regarded as central by the distinguished American literary critic Harold Bloom,[50] and offer examples from Scripture.

Irony is using a word to stand for something *opposed* to its literal referent. When Job in frustration bursts out to his friends 'How you have helped him who has no power' (Job 26:2), what he means is 'how you have *not* helped him who has no power'.

Synecdoche is using a word to stand for the *whole* of which the literal referent is only a part, or a *part* of which the literal referent is the whole. When Jesus says that the Son of man came 'to give his life a ransom for many' (Mk. 10:45), he is using a part-for-whole synecdoche, meaning 'to give his life a ransom for *all*'.[51] Conversely, 'the Jews' in John is regularly a whole-for-part synecdoche, meaning not *all* the Jews, but a particular group that was vocally opposed to Jesus (e.g. Jn. 8:48,52,57); the narrative makes it quite clear that not all were in fact so opposed (8:31).

Metonymy is using a word to stand for something *associated* with the literal referent, e.g. as cause for effect, attribute for thing itself, or vice versa. When the Lord promises to David 'I will . . . build your *throne* for all generations' (Ps. 89:4), he means 'I will give you an everlasting *kingdom*'.[52]

Hyperbole is using a word to stand for something *less* than the literal referent - such that the literal referent appears as an exaggeration. The speaker seems to have 'thrown beyond' the mark in her use of language. When the author of John 21:25 writes 'I suppose that the world itself could not contain the books that would be written' were all Jesus' deeds to be recorded, he is using a standard kind of hyperbole (not whole-for-part synecdoche, for no specific part of the world is in view).

Metaphor is using a word to stand for something *different* from the literal referent, but connected to it through some similarity. When Jesus says 'Go and tell that fox' (Lk. 13:32) he means 'Go and tell *Herod*', and implies that Herod possesses the traditional fox-like qualities of deceitfulness and / or destructiveness.[53]

Metalepsis is using a word to stand *for another tropical expression*. When Jesus says 'I am the true vine' (Jn. 15:1), 'vine' is not only an illuminating metaphor from nature for what he is, but an evocation of the old trope of Israel as the Lord's vine or vineyard (Ps. 80; Is. 5:1-7).[54]

It is important to note several things about the usage, recognition and interpretation of figures and particularly of tropes. First, they are usually not just stylistic devices,[55] but *powerful vehicles of cognition and tone*. Hosea's 'Your love is like the morning cloud' plaintively pictures Israel's fickleness and expresses God's (and the prophet's) sorrow. Job uses irony as an expression of bitter sarcasm. Jesus' 'many' means 'all', but the use of the synecdoche is not idle; it emphasises, in accordance with Hebrew thinking, the magnitude of God's purposes rather than their totality. John's 'the Jews' does not mean literally 'all the Jews', but the use of the general expression does imply a characterization or stereotyping of the race as a whole as opponents of Jesus. 'Throne' stands for 'kingdom' as a vivid and concrete emblem. The hyperbole of John 21:25 expresses awe, not only at the numerousness of Jesus' deeds, but perhaps also at their weight of significance, at how much there would be to say about them. To call Herod a 'fox' was to pass a value-judgement upon him. To evoke an old tradition by the use of a word like 'vine' was in its context no mere superficial toying with an image, but to make a powerful claim. This recognition that tropes are more than ornaments, that indeed there can be an 'exchange of meaning' between their two terms ('the vine' illumines Jesus, but Jesus also illumines 'the vine') marks much recent study of metaphor and parable.[56]

Secondly, tropes *need a context* if they are to be recognized and understood, and especially so in written language.[57] In the most obvious sense, they need the context of the basic unit of meaning, the sentence.[58] The tropical words considered above, 'helped', 'many', 'the Jews', 'throne', 'world', 'fox', 'vine', owe their tropicality first of all to their presence in the particular sentence; on their own (as in a list of dictionary entries) they would be taken as literal. Yet a still wider context is often needed. In Job's exclamation, we would not recognize the irony if the sense of deep frustration with his friends had not been building up through the book; the sentence on its own could be taken quite literally, as an outpouring of gratitude that his friends had helped him. In an oral context, tone of voice and the mood of conversation enable us to distinguish between sarcasm and praise. With reference to our examples of synecdoche, a Semitic audience / readership, we may imagine, would instinctively have recognized that in Mark 10:45 'many' stood for 'all', because this was a widespread usage. A Calvinist theologian, however (though recognizing that this synecdoche sometimes occurs) took 'many' here in its literal sense, in the context of other passages of the NT similarly interpreted, as supporting the theory of 'limited atonement' (which says that Christ died for many, but *not* for all).[59] And we need to read John's gospel as a whole if we are to see the synecdochic force of 'the Jews' (whole for part) in particular instances (i.e. that he did not mean literally all, but he did mean to categorize the race). In the case of the metaleptic 'I am the vine', a knowledge of the OT as context is a prerequisite for grasping the full purport of the saying.

Thirdly, it is generally recognized that though 'trope' refers primarily to the non-literal use of individual words or short expressions, it can operate on both a broader and a deeper level. A trope can be extended in linear fashion, for instance into a story: Madeleine Boucher calls *allegory* 'an extended metaphor in narratory form'.[60] Or it can be seen as operating in the deeper structures of language, patterns of social interchange, human self-understanding and development, scientific inquiry or trends in history.[61] This breadth and depth in the perception of tropes is especially significant for a study of parables.[62]

Fourthly, any figures may be more or less striking and strange depending on how established they have become in the language. The existence of 'dead metaphors',[63] expressions whose original strangeness had been ironed out completely, led Ferdinand de Saussure to his statement of the 'arbitrary nature of the sign' and of the generally *conventional* nature of linguistic expression.[64] The scale between the new and striking at one end, and the stale and conventional at the other, is usefully expounded by Mogens Stiller Kjärgaard, through a distinction between 'present', 'imperfect' and 'perfect' metaphors.[65] The 'present' are living and fresh; the 'imperfect' are becoming familiar, but not yet established; the 'perfect' are so established as to be almost indistinguishable from 'literal' language.

We may illustrate Kjärgaard's distinction with reference to the example of Herod as fox. This was probably an 'imperfect' metaphor at the time of Jesus: quite well-used, but not having lost its spice. It is likely that others before and besides Jesus gave Herod this label. It may have been on its way to becoming a mere cliché, but had probably not arrived there yet. Further, the 'tense-status' of a figure may be different for different people, even within the same society. In a single interchange the speaker may intend to shock, while the hearer remains bored; or the hearer may be shocked by something the speaker thought quite conventional. For some, to call Herod a fox would have been more consciously daring than it would have been for others; for some, to *hear* Herod called a fox would have been more surprising than it would have been for others. An example of a (probably) near-'perfect' trope, one which has become purely conventional, might be the synecdoche of Mark 10:45 ('many' for 'all').

All of this strengthens the claim that the comprehending of figurative language involves a creative response by the receiver, a response that takes place on an instinctive as well as a conscious level. It is the hearer or reader who detects that a figure is in play, in a word or longer unit of discourse, and asks what that token of individuality is saying - not just what its words mean, but what it is saying about its maker. She asks what sensation, tradition, or mood is being evoked. Especially if the figure is a trope, the receiver needs to recognize the tone conveyed by or associated with its turning of language. She needs a context within which to grasp its purport, and will respond differently to it depending on the degree of familiarity in the figure.

What, then, *are* the parables of Jesus? This is the question that their interpreters have always had to ask. The next four chapters trace some significant stages in the history of interpretation, identifying the figures which best characterize the interpreters' creative construal of the parables at each stage.

First, in chapter 2 we look at Luke the interpreter, in whose gospel the six parables I have chosen for detailed consideration are to be found. As he weaves them into his interpretation of the story of Jesus, they become encapsulations in miniature of the gospel message, metonymies representing the good news through the portrayal of its concrete outworking.

Next, we turn to the period of 'premodern' parable commentary, represented in the work of commentators from the fourth century to the sixteenth. 'Allegory' is the term often used to characterize the figure by which interpreters of this period construed the parables.[66] But this is a rather general term (loaded with pejorative overtones by opponents of the interpretative tactics of this period).[67] Angus Fletcher notes that 'allegory' as an extended figurative discourse may encompass a variety of tropes,[68] and it can be more illuminating to ask what these are and how they are being employed to understand the parables than to use the umbrella term 'allegory'. We shall note in Chapter 3 that a number of different tropes are used as keys to unlock the parables in this period.

In Chapter 4, I consider the work of Jülicher. Jülicher believed that the parables had been obscured through the kind of 'allegorical' treatment they had received through the centuries, the seeds of which (he thought) were seen in the gospels themselves. He proposed instead that on the lips of Jesus they were *similes* - i.e. not tropical and non-literal, but plain comparisons between some 'religious truth' and a recognizable, human situation.

Chapter 5 brings the story up (nearly) to the present, and concentrates on the commentary of Scott. This represents the move, popular in recent times, to construing the parables once again as tropes, and in particular as *metaphors*: therefore as more mysterious and less explicit than Jülicher believed.

My own suggestion with respect to these parables is found in Chapters 6 and 7. It seems to me that if we imagine Jesus in the socio-religious context which historians are now able to present to us in some depth (albeit with many disputed details), these parables could have functioned as *synecdoches*, presenting a 'part' of a new order of things and suggesting the 'whole'. This is the 'synchronic' dimension of his voice. And if we consider his larger context in the history and culture of Israel (the 'diachronic' dimension), the whole range of tropes may be used to describe different aspects of his stance in these parables in relation to that of various voices heard in the Hebrew Scriptures.

It is a commonplace to say that the earlier interpreters (including, sometimes, the Evangelists), were 'allegorizing' - that is, imposing a framework of meaning on the parables which was not original to the stories themselves. My argument is that such an 'imposition' is a natural and inevitable response to figurative language, and is evident in *all* periods of interpretation.

4. Intention, Influence and Insight

Since the interpretation of the parables, as figures, involves a creative response to them, it is inadequate to treat previous interpreters as if they were simply presenting arguments which can subsequently be tested in accordance with historical or logical criteria. Parable interpreters need and deserve appreciation as creative writers. I therefore try to deal with them

with the same literary sensitivity as with the texts themselves; only so, I
believe, will the true value of their contributions become apparent.

Three terms structure my discussion of parable interpreters and inform
my own readings. At the outset I examine the *intention* of the interpreters.[69]
This is not a matter of pretending to penetrate their psyches, but of
elucidating their texts,[70] and especially of protecting them against the
reductive misreadings which the earlier ones have sometimes suffered.
Having described their parable interpretations, I consider how the
influences upon them - both 'horizontal' (from their contemporary milieu)
and 'vertical' (from the tradition) - may intersect with their intention in
such a way as to yield *insight* into the 'voice' of Jesus in the six parables.
'Insight' then leads us backwards and upwards, in a kind of spiral, to
intention and influence once again - this time in relation to Jesus himself.
For the 'insight' sought by the interpreter of figurative language is above all
insight into an *intention* (on the part of a writer / speaker) and into the
influences which, when discerned, give us a larger perspective on the
peculiar 'figurativeness' of the figure than was available to the writer /
speaker himself.[71] Each of the three terms now needs further clarification.

Intention

I do not hold any naïve view of the accessibility of an author's intention.[72]
Nor do I propose to enter the debate about the general usefulness of the
concept of intention in literary theory.[73] If texts are human products, to
attend to the intention behind them is important,[74] as long as we are also
alert to disclosures they make which may not have been intended in any
straightforward sense by the author. Here again historical and literary
interests meet. Historians, including historians of Jesus, still want to know
about human motivation.[75]

I believe, then, that it is important to try to discern and respect the
intention of the interpreters whose work we discuss. But when we consider
the question of their insight into the parables, a further reason for a concern
with intention appears: it is required by the nature of figures. Boucher
writes: 'Apprehending the meaning of any trope requires perceiving what
the speaker intends'.[76] We need to go beyond Boucher and say that to
apprehend the 'meaning' of any figure, whether or not it is a trope, involves
more than this: we must not only have insight into the intention of the
speaker *but perceive the figure as a figure*; the speaker may have intended
no figure, but the hearer may see one, for she is aware of a context in which
the speaker's use of language stands out as unusual. But it is important to
stress that understanding a trope involves perceiving intention, because
some recent parable scholarship has highlighted the need for a creative
response but not the object of that response. For instance, John Dominic

Crossan writes of the endless renewability of metaphor:[77] one person's metaphor inspires another's. But he does not mention the fact that the 'meaning' of a metaphor as a trope involves, in Boucher's terms, 'a crossing of the objective and the subjective',[78] in which the objective is the conventional meaning of the word(s) and the subjective is *not only what the hearer / reader makes of them, but what the speaker / writer intended by them.*[79] To focus only on the response-side is to miss *what the receiver is responding to.*

The existence and nature of tropes is indeed one of the strongest arguments for retaining the importance of intentionality in discussion of language generally: as Boucher shows, irony above all depends on the existence of this distinction between intentional and conventional meaning.[80] Without conceiving that Job's intentional meaning might be different from the conventional meaning of 'How you have helped him who has no power', how will we understand the force of the exclamation? Mary Ann Tolbert, like Crossan, has stressed that the parables demand a creative interpretation (as against the emphasis of the 'new hermeneutic' movement on the parables interpreting *us*),[81] but her understanding of a good interpretation is simply one that corresponds to the 'entire configuration' of the story, [82] without any necessary reference to the intention of the parable's speaker. Again, this misses the dynamic interplay in a trope between intentional and conventional.

Such a concern for the discernment of intonation beyond inscription, the maintenance of some sense of an encounter with the author behind a text, is not as eccentric as some of the louder voices in secular and biblical criticism would suggest. It continues to be central to the business of literary studies. Bloom's statement of intent is noteworthy:

> What concerns me in a strong poem is . . . the utterance, within a tradition
> of uttering, of the image or lie of voice, where 'voice' is neither self nor
> language, but rather spark or *pneuma* as opposed to self, and act made one
> with word . . . rather than word referring only to another word . . .[83]

This voice is not 'self', for it is notoriously difficult to substantiate any claim to direct encounter with a 'self' through a text. But nor is it merely 'language'.[84] Bloom is not alone in standing against dehumanizing tendencies in literary criticism. Critics such as de Man, Roland Barthes, Michel Foucault and Jacques Derrida have tried to set aside the necessity for a personal response to the personal in the reading of texts, but this has been shown up as the hyperbolic outworking of particular philosophical predilections. Seán Burke demonstrates how the importance of the author is inescapably implied in the very text of Barthes which proclaimed the author's death, as well as in similarly anti-authorial texts of Derrida and Foucault.[85] Burke shows that the irrelevance of 'author' as a category in literary criticism has not been argued for, but simply asserted by those who proclaimed the death of the divine Author himself. Barthes, seeming to exalt aesthetic response, proclaimed that 'the birth of the reader must be at the cost of the death of the Author',[86] but Burke shows the deceptive rhetoric at work here, concluding that in fact 'the birth of the reader is not achieved at the cost of the death of the author, but rather at that of showing how the critic *too* becomes an author'.[87] Barthes' outlook implies readerly irresponsibility, but Burke's response implies that the reader only defines and attains her true dignity when she approaches a text as (at least potentially) a personal rather than an impersonal creation. The critic must indeed acknowledge the aspects of 'authorship' (e.g. creativity) in her *own* working; but that entails a responsible construal of the written signals of another mind, not a pretence that such a mind does not exist. Barthes' negative philosophy of literature buys literature's autonomy at the price of its humanity.[88] I hope, then, to communicate some sense of encounter with the human beings who have interpreted the parables, and with the one who spoke them.

Influence

My concept of 'influence' owes much to the work of Bloom.[89] We have seen above that for Bloom, the 'voice' of a poem is *utterance within a tradition of uttering*. 'Voice' is thus not only tone, but also 'stance', a metaphor which presupposes the question: stance in relation to what or whom?[90] The deflation of an idealism which exaggerates the individuality of creative writing is of crucial significance for parable studies, in an era which has exalted not only the authorial skill of the NT writers but also the *originality* of Jesus' words, sometimes at the cost of properly locating him in history.[91] Bloom's theory that the 'anxiety of influence' is the central subject of poetry through the centuries[92] may be (consciously) hyperbolic, and has not been without its critics,[93] but is compelling enough to be used to illuminate the dynamics of creativity. His aim is 'to de-idealize our accepted accounts of how one poet helps to form another'.[94] This concept of poetic 'influence' seeks to block not only assumptions of a poem's self-sufficiency, characteristic of the mid-twentieth century literary movement known as the 'New Criticism', but also a return to an older approach to inter-poetic relationships limited to a study of the way that a poet has 'used' (by implication consciously) various 'sources'.[95] Bloom shows how both of these approaches ignore the subtle workings of 'influence'.

In Bloom's usage 'influence' evokes its ancient connotation of a power that works upon the human world from a source in the planets or stars.[96] A writer may not know, often does not know, the way in which he is being 'influenced'. Indeed, Bloom writes, *he may even be 'influenced' by poems he has never read.*[97] 'Influence' is thus itself a trope which describes the relationship between texts in such a way as to draw attention to the impulse (whether conscious or unconscious) simultaneously to draw on the wealth of one's precursors' inspiration, and to mark out one's own creative territory in distinction from theirs. Poetic parents may reassert themselves, unasked and uninvited, in the poet's work.

Bloom recognizes that the processes of influence are not always marked by 'anxiety'. He finds, for example, a sense in Dante of *loving,* not anxious, emulation of his precursor Virgil, though Dante's work remains a great 'sublimation' of Virgil's.[98] Further, the reality of 'influence' and the drive for creative newness are not limited to what in modern times we call 'literature'. It may take a 'religious' shape, as when the prophets called people back to Torah using fresh language and imagery which itself became incorporated into the 'canon'.[99] A tension similar to that which Bloom discerns in the history of poetry may be seen in this process, as loyalty to the old, the source of inspiration, struggles with the desire to give it fresh linguistic expression. Bloom's achievement is to demonstrate the naïveté of ignoring this agonistic dynamic of creativity, the striving of 'strong' poets 'to clear imaginative space for themselves'[100] and not be submerged in the influence of their precursors.[101]

An illuminating aural metaphor associated with the process of 'influence' is *echo.* Though a voice may not have been recorded for us, it may still echo on in the voices of others, in the adoption by speakers and writers of stances or tones reminiscent or imitative of it. 'Echo' is a suggestive word. If we speak of hearing in a text the 'echoes' of a previous text we are sensitive to the fact that the writer may not be *deliberately* quoting or alluding. The later writer may in fact be saying something *in opposition* to the earlier one, but using a telltale turn of phrase that crops up, as it were, unasked - a clue to influence. There may be no verbal correspondence at all; it may be purely an echo of tone or attitude that is heard in the text. The metaphor of 'echo' implies that it is the *earlier* author who has started the process, and that what we hear in the later one may be the product neither of the later author's settled intention, nor merely of impersonal chance or linguistic convention, but of the ambiguous relationship in which she stands to her precursor. To hear in a later writer an echo of an earlier one is to be alerted to the mysterious process of 'influence', by which thinkers and writers are formed by their predecessors even as they try to find their own voice.[102]

For Bloom, the process of influence is deeply bound up with the process of figuration. 'To originate anything in language we must resort to a trope, and that trope must defend us against a prior trope.'[103] To find and comprehend a figure is to find and comprehend a sign of individuality, but how can individuality be measured? We may think we have found such a sign, but if we set it in a large enough context, we frequently find that the figure is a product of earlier influence. The mark of true originality, according to Bloom, is not 'new' formulations, but the ability so to twist, turn, 'trope' the old ones that a personal vision and meaning emerges. Figurative language is slippery: words once shaped into a figure are the more readily reshaped into another. Dibelius recognized the ease with which Jesus' own use of such language could be a spur to his followers not only to use it themselves, but to turn (i.e. trope) what he had said to their own purposes.[104] To be attentive to the presence of influence in the reading of figures is thus to be sensitive to the true dimensions and limitations of their originality.

Bloom's quest to recapture the power of texts by linking them in diachronic chains through history has certain similarities with the 'new hermeneutic' approach to NT and especially parable studies, popular in the 1960s. Eta Linnemann emphasised the character of the parables as 'language events' and also the fact that language 'is subject to historical change'.[105] The uniqueness of the event means that it 'cannot be transmitted', but 'it can be made intelligible'[106] (i.e. by historical study). Bloom offers to supply a missing link in the argument here. The 'new hermeneutic' privileged Scripture, and especially the parables, as *unique* language events. But it idealized and in fact *dehistoricized* the Scriptural texts by obscuring their membership of the class of human writings.[107] Honestly to admit this involves no denial of the peculiar authority or uniqueness of Scripture. Bloom is a literary critic who unashamedly prizes the aesthetic:[108] but he demonstrates that an aesthetic response (such as I am arguing to be necessarily involved in understanding the parables), far from leading us away from history, naturally leads us deep *into* history as the hidden story of human wills. Frank Lentricchia has even written of Bloom's argument 'on behalf of the historicity of literature'.[109]

To read newer texts beside older ones under the sign of 'influence' is therefore *a mode of interpretation which takes seriously the presence of both genuine originality and unconscious dependence.* Bloom stands in the lineage of Schleiermacher, who wrote: 'We must try to become aware of many things of which . . . [the author] may have been unconscious . . . So formulated, the task is infinite.'[110] But Bloom's post-Freudian awareness of the infinity of the task leads to a still more ironic estimation of the capabilities of the interpreter. In the study of Scripture Bloom is thus a useful guide in this post-Romantic era which rightly doubts its ability to 'divine' textual origins, for indeed the Bible, as a text that is 'self-effacing with respect to its origins . . . has proved . . . a stumbling block to . . .

Romantic hermeneutics'.[111] He preserves a keen awareness of the dynamics of creativity without fostering the illusion that we can scientifically establish the true origins of a text.

Bloom's thinking, then, lies behind much of my discussion of the history of parable interpretation and of the 'diachronic' influences upon Jesus himself (Bloom has not been so interested in 'synchronic' influences). Not least, it has led me to spend considerable time and space with the works of my predecessors in the interpretative tradition; for Bloom teaches us that insight is frequently won not by trying to escape the influence of one's precursors, but by immersing oneself in it.

Insight

By the word *insight* I allude particularly to the image which the Venerable Bede borrowed from Bishop Acca, who encouraged him to write his commentary on Luke. Bede mentions in his Prologue to the commentary that in addition to that which he has drawn from his predecessors, there are things which the 'author of light' has opened up to him personally.[112] Jülicher belaboured the Fathers with this concept (*Scharfsinn*, 'keen perception'): in his view personal insight, compromised by its attendant claim to particular divine revelation, was deeply suspect.[113] In fact, however, Jülicher's careful historical work discloses the necessity of insight - Schleiermacher's 'divination'[114] - as well as historical comparison, if the individuality of Jesus is to be characterized.[115] Scott is one of those who has rehabilitated a concept of 'insight' in parable studies. He writes that insight 'results from inquiry and is cumulative'; it is 'an intuitive grasp of a whole, and as such is preconceptual'.[116] 'Insight', in short, implies the immediate apprehension that is aesthetic response, a seeing or a hearing;[117] in relation to a text it implies that what is written discloses some reality to us.

The claim to insight implies that what is 'seen' or 'heard' behind an outward exterior is *really seen or heard;* it is not a chimaera, a mere illusion.[118] But equally, it implies the *personal engagement of the one seeing or hearing.*[119] This is not to say that the claim (though strictly unverifiable) is beyond the bounds of being tested; testing can take place on both a comparative historical level (is this supposed 'insight' plausible in view of what may be known from other sources about the subject of the insight?) and an aesthetic level (do others 'see' it too?).

With respect to tropes, Boucher points to the necessity of insight when she states the importance of 'perceiving, or interpreting, the natural as well as the conventional meaning of the words'[120] (by 'natural meaning' she means associations or connotations which allow a word to be used tropically - the deceitfulness of the fox, etc.). Indeed, insight is even more necessary than she suggests, for the trope as figure may possess not only 'natural' connotations, but new and personal ones: the word or phrase may have connotations for the user which it does not have for the receiver, or *vice versa*. This is why historical investigation of the meanings of words in their ancient contexts will only take us a certain distance in grasping the original impact of a figure of speech.[121] If an aesthetic response was necessary in the original reception of a figure, how much more is it necessary when that figure is an ancient one, and much that was taken for granted in the original situation is lost to us. Over the centuries, *insight*, as well as historical scholarship, has become *increasingly* necessary for interpreters of the parables. My discussion will indicate that it may equally be necessary for our interpretation of the interpreters.

5. Texts

There is an inevitable tension between a general concern with the hearing of the voice of Jesus through the reading of his parables as figures, and the fact that specific and detailed examples will be able to tell the story and make the case most plainly. I hope it will be clear that I do not wish to over-generalize from my specific examples, but also that there would be benefit from pursuing the line of inquiry with reference to other parables (and interpreters) too.

The six parables chosen for detailed consideration are these:

The Good Samaritan (Luke 10:25-37)
The Prodigal Son (Luke 15:11-32)
The Shrewd Steward (Luke 16:1-9)
The Rich Man and Lazarus (Luke 16:19-31)
The Judge and the Widow (Luke 18:1-8)
The Pharisee and the Customs Officer (Luke 18:9-14)[122]

This group, I believe, hangs together in an interesting way internally. All these stories are found in the central section of Luke's gospel, the so-called 'Travel Narrative'. None has a parallel in any other gospel, either canonical or apocryphal. All are full-length narratives; other, shorter parables in this section of the gospel with an opening formula like 'what man of you'[123] have been excluded. There are many links in thrust, tone, theme and structure between the six. And, although it is a distinction which I want eventually to dismantle, it is interesting to note that the group contains two kinds of parable frequently perceived as distinct from one another. Of the six, three (the first, fourth and sixth) have been described since Jülicher as 'example-stories', *Beispielerzählungen*, in which the situation pictured offers an actual example of conduct to be imitated or avoided. The other three have been seen as 'parables proper', *Gleichniserzählungen* or *Fabeln*, in which the situation pictured relates more indirectly to the reality (e.g. that of the kingdom of God) about which Jesus wished to speak.

To begin to attempt to interact with all the literature with some bearing on the subject at hand - works concerned with the history of biblical interpretation, with the gospel of Luke, with study of the parables, with the historical Jesus, not to mention literary theory - would be to risk not just a brush with the anxiety of influence, but a drowning in the despair of influence. I hope that I have interacted with enough to make my contribution profitable to those working in any or all of these areas.[124]

NOTES

1. Friedrich D.E. Schleiermacher, *Hermeneutics: The Handwritten Manuscripts* (Missoula: Scholars Press, 1977), 64, cited in Anthony C. Thiselton, *New Horizons in Hermeneutics: The Theory and Practice of Transforming Biblical Reading* (London and New York: Harper Collins, 1992), 224.

2. Harold Bloom, *Poetics of Influence* (New Haven: Henry R. Schwab, Inc., 1988), 415.

3. 'Ohne besonnene Prüfung kann man nirgends die Stimme Jesu mit den Stimmen der Evangelisten identifizieren': Adolf Jülicher, *Die Gleichnisreden Jesu*, 2 vols. [1886/1898], 2nd ed. (Freiburg I.B., Leipzig & Tübingen: J.C.B. Mohr [Paul Siebeck], 1899) I, 11.

4. Joachim Jeremias, *The Parables of Jesus* [*Die Gleichnisse Jesu*, 1947], revised ed. (London: SCM Press, 1963), 114. Cf. his discussion of parables as a mark of the *ipsissima vox* of Jesus in idem, *New Testament Theology* [*Neutestamentliche Theologie I. Teil: Die Verkündigung Jesu*, 1971] (London: SCM Press, 1971), 29f.

5. Ibid., 25f. Cf. Brad H. Young, *Jesus and his Jewish Parables: Rediscovering the Roots of Jesus' Teaching* (Mahwah, NJ: Paulist Press, 1989), arguing for Hebrew rather than Aramaic originals for the parables.

6. Jeremias, *Parables*, 25-114. M.F. Wiles saw Jeremias's 'principles of transformation' as continuing to operate beyond the period of the gospels' formation, in the parable-exegesis of the Fathers: 'Early Exegesis of the Parables', *Scottish Journal of Theology* 11 (1958), 287-301. On the limitations of form criticism and of Jeremias's work in particular, see John Drury, *The Parables in the Gospels: History and Allegory* (London: SPCK, 1985), 40.

7. For a study attentive to different 'voices' in the text of a gospel see James Dawsey, *The Lukan Voice: Confusion and Irony in the Gospel of Luke* (Macon: Mercer University Press, 1986).

8. 'We are in quest of [Jesus'] voice, insofar as it can be distinguished from many other voices also preserved in the tradition': 'The Issue of Jesus', *Forum* 1, no.1 (1985), 7, quoted in Marcus J. Borg, *Jesus in Contemporary Scholarship* (Valley Forge, PA: Trinity Press International, 1994), 161.

9. Bernard Brandon Scott, *Hear then the Parable: A Commentary on the Parables of Jesus* (Minneapolis: Fortress Press, 1989), 65.

10. Ibid., 66.

11. Ibid., 65-8.

12. Ibid., 64.

13. Charles W. Hedrick, *Parables as Poetic Fictions: The Creative Voice of Jesus* (Peabody, MA: Hendrickson, 1994).

14. In support of this, see e.g. M. D. Hooker, 'On Using the Wrong Tool', *Theology* 75 (1972), 570-81; E. P. Sanders, *Jesus and Judaism* (London: SCM Press, 1985), 16f.; Stephen Fowl, 'Reconstructing and Deconstructing the Quest of the Historical Jesus', *Scottish Journal of Theology* 42, no. 3 (1989), 319-33. Particularly trenchant are the comments of Sanders on the so-called 'criterion of dissimilarity', by which 'authentic' Jesus-material is identified as that which stands out both from his Jewish background and his ecclesiastical following: 'The test rules out too much . . . The material which remains after the test is applied is biased towards uniqueness' (*Jesus*, 16). Scott himself recognizes that 'by excluding common wisdom we risk presenting an eccentric portrait of the Jesus material': *Hear*, 65.

15. Contra Drury, who on account of the pitfalls of trying to get 'back to Jesus' prefers to keep discussion of the parables to the Evangelists' usage (*Parables*).

16. For a sustained and powerful critique of the historical-critical method see Andrew Louth, *Discerning the Mystery: An Essay on the Nature of Theology* (Oxford: Clarendon Press, 1983), *passim* but clearly focused on 13-16.

17. Again, contra Drury's pessimism: 'Parable', in R. J. Coggins and J. L. Houlden (eds.), *A Dictionary of Biblical Interpretation* (London: SCM Press, 1990), 509-11.

18. Jülicher wrote that he would have liked to be able to do this, though he recognized the goal as too ambitious: *Gleichnisreden* I, 203. Cf. p. 140 below. The 'postmodern' epistemological climate in which we now work entails, at its most fundamental, a recognition of the overblown nature of such ambitions.

19. Louth, *Discerning*, 95, and see the entire chapter 'Tradition and the Tacit' (73-95).

20. This theme is approached in various ways in Craig Bartholomew, Colin J.D. Greene and Karl Möller (eds.), *Renewing Biblical Interpretation* (Carlisle / Grand Rapids: Paternoster / Zondervan, forthcoming).

21. These are of course closely related to questions about how *God* may be understood as speaking through written texts, on which see Nicholas Wolterstorff, *Divine discourse: Philosophical reflections on the claim that God speaks* (Cambridge: CUP, 1995).

22. For a brief but fascinating literary-theological study of the parables see Ruth Etchells, *A Reading of the Parables of Jesus* (London: Darton, Longman & Todd, 1998). For further discussion of some larger literary-theological issues in handling Scripture see my chapter 'An Experiment in Biblical Criticism: Aesthetic Encounter in Reading and Preaching Scripture', in Bartholomew et al. (eds.), *Renewing*.

23. Note the metaphorical character of these words themselves, notably the substitution of the aural for the spatial in the replacement of 'stance' by 'voice'.

24. Pierre Fontanier, *Les figures du discours* (1830) (Paris: Flammarion, 1968), 64, 179, cited in Paul Ricoeur, *The Rule of Metaphor: Multi-disciplinary Studies of the Creation*

of Meaning in Language [La métaphore vive, 1975] (Toronto: University of Toronto Press, 1977), 52.

25. Fontanier believed that any 'deviation' that was 'forced', imposed by the language, rather than 'free', no longer deserved the name of figure: Ricoeur, *Rule*, 53.

26. Roland Barthes exposes the problems with the notion of 'figures of speech'. 'Every structure of "figures" is based on the notion that there exist two languages, one proper and one feigned, and that consequently Rhetoric, in its elocutionary part, is a table of deviations of language': *The Semiotic Challenge [L'aventure sémiologique*, 1985] (New York: Hill and Wang, 1988), 88. This fact bequeaths its oddities: '[T]here is a relation of strangeness between the "commonplace words" each of us uses (but who is this "we"?), and the "unaccustomed words" alien to everyday use: "barbarisms" (words of foreign peoples), neologisms, metaphors, etc. . . . From national / foreign and normal / strange, the opposition has gradually shifted to proper / figured. What is the proper meaning? "It is the first signification of the word" (Dumarsais): "When the word signifies that for which it was originally established." Yet the proper meaning cannot be the earliest meaning (archaism is alienating), but the meaning immediately anterior to the creation of the figured: the proper, the true is, once again, the foregoing (the Father). In classical Rhetoric, the foregoing has been naturalized. Whence the paradox: how can the proper meaning be the "natural" meaning and the figured meaning be the "original" meaning?': ibid., 88f. In this last sentence Barthes is saying that figuration implies, precisely, 'originality', yet it is also understood as deviation from an 'original'. 'Proper' has associations of ownership, yet the 'proper' meaning is understood precisely as that which is not owned by an individual, but is natural, common or conventional.

27. Hedrick's *Parables* represents a recent attempt to dissociate the parables altogether from figurative language, preferring the term 'poetic fiction'. However, 'fiction' and 'figure' are both derived from the Latin fingere, 'shape' or 'mould', and the notion of 'poetic fiction', in particular, is closely similar to the concept of 'figure'. Both suggest the agency of a shaping hand or mind. Hedrick wishes to escape as far as possible from allegorical readings of the parables, but neither 'figure' nor 'poetic fiction' prejudges the questions of whether or how the parables may or should be read in an allegorical way.

28. See Chapter 3 below. On the figurative nature of scripture as a whole cf. Louth, *Discerning*, 109f., citing John Henry Newman's celebration of it.

29. See Chapter 4 below. Jülicher designated the parables as different types of *Redefigur* (figure of speech): *Gleichnisreden* I, 80, 98.

30. Cf. Robert H. Stein, 'Parables', in Bruce M. Metzger and Michael D. Coogan (eds.), *The Oxford Companion to the Bible* (New York and Oxford: OUP, 1993), 568, for a recent reassertion that the parables are the 'bedrock of authentic Jesus tradition'.

31. Drury, *Parables*; 'Parable'; *Tradition and Design in Luke's Gospel* (London: Darton, Longman & Todd, 1976); 'Luke', in Robert Alter and Frank Kermode (eds.), *The Literary Guide to the Bible* (London: Collins, 1987), 625-48.

32. Paul de Man, *Blindness and Insight* [1971], 2nd ed. (Minneapolis: University of Minnesota Press, 1983), 285.

33. Ibid., 276.

34. '[A]t the heart of the historical quest for Jesus is a literary task . . . Understanding Jesus' teaching requires . . . the skills to make sense of his metaphors and symbols':

Robert Morgan and John Barton, *Biblical Interpretation* (Oxford: OUP, 1988), 240. See Louth's helpful discussion of ways of knowing appropriate to the humanities, in *Discerning*, 17-44. Cf. Robert P. Armstrong, *The Affecting Presence: An Essay in Humanistic Anthropology* (Urbana: University of Illinois Press, 1971), 75: 'The only nonreductivistic [sic] way of coping with the affecting presence is in wholly affecting terms.'

35. See Martin Dibelius, *From Tradition to Gospel* [*Die Formgeschichte des Evangeliums*, 1919], revised ed. (London: Ivor Nicholson and Watson, 1934), 7.

36. Ibid., 1.

37. Ibid., 7.

38. The word 'aesthetic' comes from the Greek αἰσθετικός meaning 'capable of perception' or 'perceptive'. Recollection of this derivation may help to save the word from the burden of its complex modern history, on which see Michael Bell, 'The Metaphysics of Modernism: Aesthetic Myth and the Myth of the Aesthetic', in David Fuller and Patricia Waugh (eds.), *The Arts and Sciences of Criticism* (Oxford: OUP, 1999), 238-56. When I write about an 'aesthetic' response or judgement I am not concerned with a decision about 'good taste', nor am I implying at all that the original purpose of the literature in question was simply to give pleasure.

39. Stephen Neill and Tom Wright, *The Interpretation of the New Testament 1861-1986* (Oxford: OUP, 1988), 258. On contemporary attention to so-called 'literary qualities' in the Bible as a whole see Wolterstorff, *Divine Discourse*, 16f.

40. E.g., on Luke, Drury, *Tradition*; Luke T. Johnson, *The Literary Function of Possessions in Luke-Acts* (Missoula: Scholars Press, 1977); Dawsey, *Voice*.

41. See e.g. Kenneth E. Bailey, *Poet and Peasant* (Grand Rapids: Eerdmans, 1976), 158, citing C. W. F. Smith, *The Jesus of the Parables* (Philadelphia: Westminster, 1948), 19, on the parables as 'the mark of Jesus' supreme genius', providing material 'that neither the philosopher nor the theologian can exhaust'; cf. Amos N. Wilder, *Early Christian Rhetoric: The Language of the Gospel* (London: SCM Press, 1964), 89; Hedrick, *Parables*.

42. Robert Alter describes the problem we face in recognizing the signs of 'authorship' in Scripture: 'Biblical tradition . . . went to great lengths to hide the tracks of the individual author . . . the writer disappears into the tradition, makes its voice his, or vice versa': *The World of Biblical Literature* (London: SPCK, 1992), 2f.

43. Cf. Louth, *Discerning*, especially 27-35 (discussing the work of Hans-Georg Gadamer); Theodore A. Harman, *New Testament and Modern Parables: Their Relationship and Literary Character: A Reader's Response* (M.A. Thesis, University of Durham, 1990), 76-9.

44. Thiselton, *New Horizons*, 222, citing Schleiermacher, *Hermeneutics*, 205.

45. I have drawn on a variety of works in which illuminating descriptions and examples of figures are given, particularly William Little, H.W. Fowler, Jessie Coulson, and C.T. Onions (eds.), *The Shorter Oxford English Dictionary*, 3rd ed. (Oxford: Clarendon Press, 1973); Terence Hawkes, *Metaphor*, (London: Methuen & Co Ltd., 1972); Hayden. White, *Metahistory: The Historical Imagination in Nineteenth-Century Europe* (Baltimore and London: John Hopkins University Press, 1973), 31-9; Mogens Stiller Kjärgaard, *Metaphor and Parable: A Systematic Analysis of the Specific Structure and*

Cognitive Function of the Synoptic Similes and Parables qua Metaphors (Leiden: E.J. Brill, 1986); G. B. Caird, *The Language and Imagery of the Bible* (London: Duckworth, 1980), 131-71; Ricoeur, *Rule*, 44-64; E. W. Bullinger, *Figures of Speech Used in the Bible Explained and Illustrated* [1898] (Grand Rapids, Michigan: Baker, 1968); Angus Fletcher, *Allegory: The Theory of a Symbolic Mode* (Ithaca and London: Cornell University Press, 1964); Madeleine Boucher, *The Mysterious Parable: A Literary Study* (Washington, D. C.: The Catholic Biblical Association of America, 1977), 11-40; and many places in Harold Bloom's writings.

46. Barthes, *Semiotic Challenge*, 11-94. Figures of speech were studied by Aristotle under the umbrellas of both rhetoric and poetry: Hawkes, *Metaphor*, 7. In ancient times the subject was conceived in practical terms: one learned about figures in order to be able to use them to good effect in speeches or literary works, whereas in the modern era the emphasis has been on the critical task of discerning figures in works of literature and exploring their effects: ibid., 4.

47. *Contra* Ben Witherington III, who assumes that to use a modern understanding of metaphor in appraising the parables entails anachronism: *Jesus the Sage: The Pilgrimage of Wisdom* (Edinburgh: T. & T. Clark, 1994), 149. By contrast, we may cite the insight of Coleridge, following Goethe, into the nature of symbol: the general truth it represents may be *unconsciously* in the writer's mind - whereas in allegory, according to this nineteenth-century view, all is conscious and contrived: A. Fletcher, *Allegory*, 15-18. So too we may discuss the tropical structure of sayings in Luke's writings or Jesus' speech without implying that they were conscious of using the figures we ascribe to them.

48. The credit for reviving this distinction in modern times goes to Fontanier: Ricoeur, *Rule*, 52. A. Fletcher describes the distinction purely in terms of length: a trope is a play 'on single words', a figure 'on whole groups of words, sentences and even paragraphs': *Allegory*, 84, citing Quintilian, *Institutes* VIII.ii.44-47, IX.i.1-28.

49. As preferred by Hawkes for general literary-critical purposes: *Metaphor*, 4. Ricoeur also concentrates on metaphor: see *Rule*. Cf. Bernhard Heininger, *Metaphorik, Erzählstruktur und szenisch-dramatische Gestaltung in den Sondergutgleichnissen bei Lukas* (Münster: Aschendorff, 1991), 16, where even simile (*Vergleich*) is subsumed within metaphor: 'die Metapher ein semantisches Basisphänomen darstellt und als Oberbegriff alle sprachlichen Formen des Bildes wie Metonymie, Synekdoche oder Vergleich umschließt.'

50. *A Map of Misreading* (New York: OUP, 1975), 94f. For the significance of the order in which Bloom gives them, see below, p. 236. The conventional number of tropes from the Renaissance onwards was four (omitting hyperbole and metalepsis from the list below): White, *Metahistory*, 32.

51. According to Semitic idiom: Max Zerwick and Mary Grosvenor, *A Grammatical Analysis of the Greek New Testament*, 2 vols. (Rome: Biblical Institute Press, 1974,1979), 143.

52. Metonymy and synecdoche are sometimes conflated into one category, or their definitions even reversed, as in Etchells, *Reading*, 8.

53. E. Earle Ellis lists these as possible connotations of 'fox': *The Gospel of Luke*, revised ed. (London: Marshall, Morgan & Scott, 1974), 190. Another is 'inconsequential

person' (it is not clear to me how this last could have arisen). This is an example with a long pedigree: Gottfried Wilhelm Leibniz referred to 'certain English fanatics who believed that when Jesus called Herod a fox he was actually turned into one': *New Essays on Human Understanding* [*Nouveaux Essais sur l'entendement humain*, 1705] (Cambridge: CUP, 1981), cited in Wolterstorff, *Divine Discourse*, 238. The fanatics' error was a failure to understand the use of metaphor!

54. Metalepsis can be seen also in the other 'I am' sayings of Jesus in John.

55. Hawkes traces the historical developments which led to metaphor and other tropes being regarded in the eighteenth century purely as ornaments: *Metaphor*, 22-33.

56. See e.g. Claus Westermann, *The Parables of Jesus in the Light of the Old Testament* [*Vergleiche und Gleichnisse im Alten und Neuen Testament*, 1984] (Edinburgh: T. & T. Clark, 1990), and literature cited there; Kjärgaard, *Metaphor*. Janet Martin thinks that '[m]etonymy and synecdoche function as oblique reference and as such are primarily ornamental ways of naming', whereas metaphor goes beyond ornament to give new vision: 'Metaphor amongst Tropes', *Religious Studies* 17 (1981), 55-66, here 58. Cf. Anthony C. Thiselton, 'Semantics and New Testament Interpretation' in I. Howard Marshall (ed.), *New Testament Interpretation* (Exeter: Paternoster, 1979), 75-104, here 95. But this is a questionable distinction, especially when the tropes are discerned in the larger structures of discourse, not just in individual words.

57. Cf. Westermann, *Parables*, 173; Wolterstorff, *Divine Discourse*, 172f.; Richard Swinburne, 'Meaning in the Bible' in S. R. Sutherland and T. A. Roberts (eds.), *Religion, Reason and the Self: Essays in honour of H.D. Lewis* (Cardiff: University of Wales Press, 1989), 1-33, cited in Thiselton, *New Horizons*, 36.

58. The most persuasive modern statement of this view has been that of Ricoeur: cf. *Rule*, 44-64.

59. John Owen, *The Death of Death in the Death of Christ* [1650] (Edinburgh: The Banner of Truth Trust, 1959), 102.

60. *Mysterious Parable*, 20.

61. On Friedrich Schlegel's Romantic concept of irony as a sense of the superiority of the infinite to any finite concrete expression of it, see Paul Tillich, *Perspectives on 19th and 20th Century Protestant Theology*, ed. Carl E. Braaten (London: SCM Press, 1967), 89f. The inability of language to escape from trope led to Friedrich Nietzsche's statement that truth is a 'mobile army of metaphors, metonymies, anthropomorphisms': 'On Truth and Falsity in their Ultramoral Sense' in Oscar Levy (ed.), *Collected Works*, vol. II (London and Edinburgh: T.N. Foulis, 1977), 180, cited in Janet Martin Soskice, *Metaphor and Religious Language* (Oxford: Clarendon Press, 1985), 78. The deep linguistic distinction between metonymy as the power to combine and metaphor as the power to substitute was expressed classically in Roman Jakobson, 'Aphasia as a linguistic problem' [1956] in *Fundamentals of Language* (The Hague: Mouton, 1980), 69-96, cited e.g. in Scott, *Hear*, 29. Etchells' *Reading* is built around this distinction. See also Soskice, *Metaphor*, 74f. on conclusions drawn from the ubiquity of metaphor concerning the nature of thought and consciousness; Kenneth Burke, *Permanence and Change* (Los Altos: Hermes Publications, 1954), 95f., Sallie McFague TeSelle, *Speaking in Parables: A Study in Metaphor and Theology* (Philadelphia: Fortress Press, 1975), 59, and David E. Cooper, 'Science, Interpretation and Criticism', in Fuller and

Waugh (eds.), *Arts and Sciences*, 60-70, here 62f., on metaphor in science; Hayden White, *Metahistory* and *Tropics of Discourse: Essays in Cultural Criticism* (Baltimore and London: John Hopkins University Press, 1978) on the functioning of tropes within the discourses of historiography and the other human sciences; Armstrong, *Affecting Presence*, 55-79, James W. Fernandez, *Persuasions and Performances: The Play of Tropes in Culture* (Bloomington: Indiana University Press, 1986) and idem (ed.), *Beyond Metaphor: The Theory of Tropes in Anthropology* (Stanford: Stanford University Press, 1991) on tropes in anthropology.

62. One of the most influential explorations of what it means to treat narratives such as the parables as metaphors has been Paul Ricoeur, 'Biblical Hermeneutics', *Semeia*, no. 4 (1975), 29-145.

63. Cf. Paul Ricoeur, *Interpretation Theory: Discourse and the Surplus of Meaning* (Fort Worth: Texas Christian University Press, 1976), 52.

64. Ferdinand de Saussure, *Course in General Linguistics* [*Cours de linguistique générale*, 1916] (London: Peter Owen, 1974), 68, cited in Soskice, *Metaphor*, 71f.

65. Kjärgaard, *Metaphor*, 101-5.

66. This is the way that exegesis of that period in general tends to be categorized - even by those who appreciate it, like Louth (*Discerning*, 96-131).

67. Klyne R. Snodgrass tells the story of parable interpretation with a sadness I cannot really share: 'From Allegorizing to Allegorizing: A History of the Interpretation of the Parables of Jesus', in R.N. Longenecker (ed.), *The Challenge of Jesus' Parables* (Grand Rapids: Eerdmans, 2000), 3-29.

68. Fletcher, *Allegory*, 75-88.

69. On the importance of the intention of interpretative acts, see E. D. Hirsch, *Validity in Interpretation* (New Haven: Yale University Press, 1967), 24.

70. Louth's discussion of Gadamer is helpful here: against the Romantic aspiration to understand authors better than they understood themselves, Gadamer 'sees in our understanding of an author an engagement with what he has said': *Discerning*, 31.

71. I agree with Louth (ibid., 32, following Gadamer) that this does not imply that our understanding is *superior* to that of the original author, simply that it is different.

72. Cf. the classic essay on the subject: W. K. Wimsatt and Monroe C. Beardsley, 'The Intentional Fallacy' [1946], in David Lodge (ed.), *20th Century Literary Criticism: A Reader* (London: Longman, 1972), 334-45.

73. The leading proponent of the usefulness of 'intention' as a concept in literary studies has been Hirsch (see note 69 above). Both sides of the argument are represented in W. J. T. Mitchell (ed.), *Against Theory: Literary Studies and the New Pragmatism* (Chicago and London: The University of Chicago Press, 1985). Cf. Seán Burke, ed., *Authorship: From Plato to the Postmodern* (Edinburgh: Edinburgh University Press, 1995).

74. Cf. Amos N. Wilder, *The Bible and the Literary Critic* (Minneapolis: Fortress Press, 1991), 25.

75. See the opening sentence of E.P. Sanders, *Jesus*, 1: 'It is the purpose of the present work to take up two related questions with regard to Jesus: his intention and his relationship to his contemporaries in Judaism.' Such questions are the driving force behind many studies of the historical Jesus during the last two decades.

76. Boucher, *Mysterious Parable*, 26. Bernard Brandon Scott writes that '[t]his is the intentionality of the speaker - to allow the hearer to participate in the original insight': *Jesus, Symbol-Maker for the Kingdom* (Philadelphia: Fortress Press, 1981), 96. In *Hear*, Scott retreats from the idea of intentionality: see below, Chapter 5.

77. John Dominic Crossan, *In Parables: The Challenge of the Historical Jesus* (San Francisco: Harper & Row, 1973), 14.

78. Boucher, *Mysterious Parable*, 27.

79. Ibid., 26.

80. Ibid. Essentially the same point is made by Wolterstorff when he writes that 'literality and metaphoricity are a matter of use rather than meaning': *Divine Discourse*, 193.

81. Mary Ann Tolbert, *Perspectives on the Parables: An Approach to Multiple Interpretation* (Philadelphia: Fortress Press, 1979), 42, arguing against TeSelle, *Speaking*, 71f.

82. Tolbert, *Perspectives*, 71.

83. Harold Bloom, *The Breaking of the Vessels* (Chicago and London: University of Chicago Press, 1982), 4. Cf. Bloom's proposal to replace Jacques Derrida's 'scene of writing' with a 'primal scene of instruction', thus asserting the primacy of the spoken word (with all its associations of life, flexibility, intentionality and ambiguity) over against the written (associated with conventionality, arbitrariness and fixity): *Map*, 29-62.

84. Note how Bloom mixes oral and visual or spatial metaphors ('the image or lie of voice'); this captures the paradox of a voice being heard in a *text*. Bloom thus challenges the subjection of humanity to language implicit in the philosophy of Martin Heidegger and adopted in biblical studies, with particular modulations, by the 'new hermeneutic': cf. Eta Linnemann's approval of Heidegger's statement 'Man speaks in so far as he conforms to language': *Parables of Jesus: Introduction and Exposition* [*Gleichnisse Jesu: Einführung und Auslegung*, 1961] (London: SPCK, 1966), 32, citing Martin Heidegger, *Unterwegs zur Sprache*, 2nd ed. (Pfüllingen, 1960), 33.

85. Seán Burke, *The Death and Return of the Author: Criticism and Subjectivity in Barthes, Foucault and Derrida* (Edinburgh: Edinburgh University Press, 1992).

86. Ibid., 130.

87. Ibid., 61.

88. Cf. Alter, *World*, 2. Wolterstorff points out that in contemporary philosophical hermeneutics a 'pervasive theme . . . is that there is something deeply misguided about reading texts to find out what someone might have been saying thereby': *Divine Discourse*, 15. He counters the arguments against 'authorial-discourse interpretation' mounted by Ricoeur (133-52), Derrida (153-70) and Hans Frei (229-36).

89. I draw on what I regard as helpful in Bloom's thought without dealing with its more problematic aspects from a Christian perspective, on which see David Lyle Jeffrey, *People of the Book: Christian Identity and Literary Culture* (Grand Rapids: Eerdmans / Institute for Advanced Christian Studies, 1996), xvii, 1-10.

90. I owe this observation to Professor James D.G. Dunn.

91. Jülicher wrote of Jesus' *hohen Originalität*: *Gleichnisreden* I, 68. Cf. note 41 above; and the emphasis of the 'new hermeneutic' on the power of Jesus' words as themselves

bringing in the kingdom of God: e.g. Eberhard Jüngel, *Paulus und Jesus: Eine Untersuchung zur Präzisierung der Frage nach dem Ursprung der Christologie* (Tübingen: J.C.B. Mohr [Paul Siebeck], 1962), 135.

92. First formulated, with reference to poetry since Milton and especially the Romantics, in Harold Bloom, *The Anxiety of Influence: A Theory of Poetry* (New York: OUP, 1973); recently restated on a broader scale in idem, *The Western Canon* (London: Papermac, 1995), 4-12.

93. See the account of Bloom and responses to him in Frank Lentricchia, *After the New Criticism* (Chicago: University of Chicago Press, 1980), 318-46; also Michael O'Neill, 'Poetry as Literary Criticism', in Fuller and Waugh (eds.), *Arts and Sciences*, 117-36, here 122f. For a sympathetic attempt to build on Bloom's project see Peter de Bolla, *Harold Bloom: Towards Historical Rhetorics* (London and New York: Routledge, 1988).

94. Bloom, *Anxiety*, 5.

95. 'Poetic influence, in the sense I give to it, has almost nothing to do with the verbal resemblances between one poet and another': Bloom, *Map*, 19.

96. Bloom, *Anxiety*, 95.

97. Ibid.

98. Ibid., 123.

99. See Bloom, *Poetics*, 414-20, especially this passage on 420: 'The paradoxical evidence for the voice's authority, for the word being sent from Yahweh, is that the figuration be wholly personal and magnificently individual. A writing prophet is received only because of his rhetorical power, and this power of troping always must make its anxious way against the facticity of Moses, which means against the facticity of J [the putative 'source' for much of the Pentateuch].' On the issue of prophecy and 'canonicity' see John Barton, *Oracles of God: Perceptions of Ancient Prophecy in Israel after the Exile* (London: Darton, Longman and Todd, 1986).

100. Bloom, *Anxiety*, 5.

101. A fellow-critic evaluates Bloom thus: 'Bloom has put forth bold and important ideas which threaten to make the moribund subject of influence the pivot of the most satisfying historicism to appear in modem criticism . . . No theorist writing in the United States today has succeeded, as Bloom has, in returning poetry to history': Lentricchia, *After the New Criticism*, 325, 342.

102. See the sensitive exploration of echo in Richard B. Hays, *Echoes of Scripture in the Letters of Paul* (New Haven and London: Yale University Press, 1989). Hays himself draws on John Hollander, *The Figure of Echo: A Mode of Allusion in Milton and After* (Berkeley: University of California Press, 1981). Bloom's emphasis on the *origins* of influence in precursor texts is however, distinct from that of Hays on echo as something *heard* by Paul's readers, or *intended* by Paul.

103. Bloom, *Map*, 69.

104. Dibelius, *Tradition*, 249, where he comments on 'the possibilities given to preaching by the use of metaphor'.

105. Linnemann, *Parables*, 32.

106. Ibid., 33.

107. This is the case notwithstanding Linnemann's emphasis on the humanity of Jesus and his words (ibid., 34f.), since her model, in which historical discovery of their original context and meaning leads on straightaway to theological appropriation, leaves no space for an aesthetic response which seeks to grasp their place in the larger story of literature.

108. Found e.g. in Bloom, *Canon*, 10f.

109. In his 'Introduction' to Bloom, *Vessels*, ix.

110. Schleiermacher, *Hermeneutics*, 112, cited in Thiselton, *New Horizons*, 227. On the restatement of the principle by Gadamer, and the connection of this position with Dan Otto Via's desire to move beyond the search for intentional meaning in the study of the parables, cf. Anthony C. Thiselton, *The Two Horizons: New Testament Hermeneutics and Philosophical Description with Special Reference to Heidegger, Bultmann, Gadamer and Wittgenstein* (Exeter: Paternoster, 1980), 301. (On Via see below, p. 152). On the special demands of interpreting a 'manifestation' (i.e. a revelation through an event or text, as distinct from a proposition purporting to bear a revelation) cf. Wolterstorff, *Divine Discourse*, 29.

111. Gerald L. Bruns, 'Midrash and Allegory: The Beginnings of Scriptural Interpretation', in Robert Alter and Frank Kermode (eds.), *The Literary Guide to the Bible* (London: Collins, 1987), 625-48, here 627.

112. Beda Venerabilis, *In Lucae Evangelium Expositio*, Corpus Christianorum (Series Latina), CXX (Turnhout: Typographi Brepols Editores Pontificii, 1960), Prol., 116, 120.

113. E.g. Jülicher, *Gleichnisreden* I, 48: see below, p. 132.

114. On Schleiermacher see Thiselton, *New Horizons*, 221-7; Paul Ricoeur, 'Schleiermacher's Hermeneutics,' *Monist* 60, no. 2 (1977), 181-97, here 185-8; Louth, *Discerning*, 24, 31, 102.

115. See below, Chapter 4.

116. Scott, *Symbol-Maker*, 17.

117. The Greek root beneath the word 'aesthetic' is ἀίειν, which can mean to hear or to see, or indeed to know. It is a pity that English has no word related to the aural faculty corresponding to insight - inhearing, for instance. In the thought of Clement of Alexandria, 'perception' of 'perceptible things' (αἴσθησις αἰσθητῶν) was one aspect of the insight indispensable to interpretation: Thomas F. Torrance, *Divine Meaning: Studies in Patristic Hermeneutics* (Edinburgh: T. & T. Clark, 1995), 174f. Cf. Harman, *Parables*, 76f.: 'The intuitive perceptions of the heart vital to the artist are also necessary for those who would enjoy and respond to the artist's work.' As colours are invisible without light, so 'the text surrenders its meaning by the light of thought we bring to it' (ibid.). On interpretation as art cf. Tolbert, *Perspectives*, 68ff.

118. Cf. Paul Ricoeur, *The Conflict of Interpretations: Essays in Hermeneutics* (Evanston: Northwestern University Press, 1974), 17: 'An encounter with texts occurs when the reader both "conquer[s] a remoteness" and meets with the other' (cited in Thiselton, *New Horizons*, 36).

119. For the purposes of my argument this does not mean the engagement of Christian faith, but that 'productive encounter between the text and the reader' enabling a disclosure or an illumination which is possible not only in the case of 'sacred' but also

of 'secular' texts: Frank Kermode, *The Genesis of Secrecy: On the Interpretation of Narrative* (Cambridge, MA: Harvard University Press, 1979), 40.

120. *Mysterious Parable*, 27. For Scott, 'insight' into the 'symbol' of the kingdom of God is grasped through the parables as metaphors: *Symbol-Maker*, 17.

121. On Clement of Alexandria's recognition of the need for insight into the tropical language of Scripture see Torrance, *Divine Meaning*, 169f.; on Athanasius's rejection of tropical exegesis and the aim for careful precision in discerning Scriptural meanings, see ibid., 272-84. If I seem to be in danger of regressing from a more enlightened Athanasian position to a problematic Clementine one, which as Torrance says 'obstructs straightforward investigation or scientific interpretation' (170), I would plead (a) that my argument is not based on the 'divine meaning' of Scripture, but on the nature of literature, and especially of figurative language, and (b) that I am not setting up insight in opposition to historical investigation, but as a necessary complement to it. Torrance's tell-tale use of the word 'scientific' here is characteristic: see Louth's critique of the use of the discourse of science in theology, referring to Torrance, in *Discerning*, 48-72.

122. Henceforth I will try to avoid repetition by referring to the parable by only its title *or* its chapter and verse reference. When I am referring to the parable, I use capitalization of major words, as above, and without speech marks: The Good Samaritan is the story, the good Samaritan is the man.

123. That is, those in the category labelled by Jülicher 'similitude': *Gleichnisreden* I, 58-80.

124. Works particularly pertinent to my own of which I am aware, but which I have been unable, on account of inaccessibility or recent appearance, to consult directly, include K. Dorn, *Die Gleichnisse des lukanischen Reiseberichts aus Sondergut und Logienquelle* (Diss. theol. Thesis, Marburg, 1988); David A. Holgate, *Prodigality, Liberality and Meanness: The Prodigal Son in Graeco-Roman Perspective* (Sheffield: Sheffield Academic Press, 1999); Kyoung-Jin Kim, *Stewardship and Almsgiving in Luke's Theology* (Sheffield: Sheffield Academic Press, 1998); Bertram Pittner, *Studien zum lukanischen Sondergut: Sprachliche, theologische und formkritische Untersuchungen zu Sonderguttexten in Lk 5-19* (Leipzig: St Benno Verlag, 1991); Jeffrey T. Tucker, *Example Stories: Perspectives on Four Parables in the Gospel of Luke* (Sheffield: Sheffield Academic Press, 1998); Stephen L. Wailes, *Medieval Allegories of Jesus' Parables* (Berkeley and London: University of California Press, 1987); Brad H. Young, *The Parables: Jewish Tradition and Christian Interpretation* (Peabody, MA: Hendrickson, 1998).

CHAPTER 2

Parables and Proclamation: Luke's Interpretation of the Parables

---

Far from being objective conduits of received tradition, the tradents, authors, and redactors of the New Testament effected a massive construal of the material . . . At the heart of the process lay a dialectical move in which the tradents of the developing New Testament were themselves being shaped by the content of the material which they in turn were transmitting, selecting, and forming into a scriptural norm.[1]

Despite all the careful hedges that we plant around texts, meaning has a way of leaping over, like sparks. Texts are not inert; they burn and throw fragments of flame on their rising heat.[2]

1. Luke: The Intention to Interpret

In this chapter we consider Luke as the first known interpreter of the parables in question. We do not have access to the parables unmediated, as they fell from the lips of Jesus. We find them in a larger narrative, and that narrative not only records, but also interprets them.[3]

We should note carefully the stated intention of Luke in the prologue to his gospel (1:1-4). Many, he writes, have undertaken to draw up a narrative of 'the things fulfilled among us'; his own particular purpose is to give an 'orderly' account so that Theophilus might 'know the truth' concerning what he has heard. As Joel B. Green points out, this does not mean that Luke is simply repeating to Theophilus what he already knows so as to verify it.[4] Rather, Luke's 'ordering' of the narrative is designed as an authoritative *interpretation* of events of which Theophilus is already aware, but whose full implications may not yet have dawned.[5] 'The truth' means not merely 'the facts', but 'the meaning'.

This sets our expectations of Luke's work in proper perspective. On the one hand, his narrative is intended, like others which have preceded it, to record actual events. On the other, it is a narrative which has been arranged in such a way as to interpret those events, to bring out their true significance as the climax of Israel's history and the gateway to the new age of God's worldwide kingdom.

Another useful perspective on these verses is given by Frank Thielman.[6] He writes of the tension that is evident between Luke's apologetic purpose, of demonstrating to Rome the essentially peaceable and conservative nature of early Christianity, and his adherence to the canons of ancient historiography, which encouraged the historian to present the facts - however unpalatable they were to oneself or one's intended readership. An awareness of this tension warns us against trying to trace a single intention through every section of the gospel and Acts. As Luke tells the story of Jesus and the earliest church, there will be points where faithfulness as a historian compels him to record (for instance) moments of painful conflict between the emerging movement and the authorities, Jewish and Roman, despite the fact that elsewhere he takes pains to stress Christian continuity with tradition.

What does this imply for the parables? That we can expect them to be woven into the narrative, a part of Luke's interpretation of events, but also to be presented in their broadly historical context, as parables of Jesus, not only of Luke.[7] This is indeed what we find. The six parables on which we are focusing (and many others besides) appear in Luke's text as 'figures' because they are striking units within the narrative. 'Figures are to discourse what contours, characteristics, and exterior form are to the body.'[8] These parables illustrate well the statement of Dawsey: 'There is a sense in which the author backed off from what he told and allowed his characters to speak . . . and so to come alive in the story.'[9] Luke certainly lets Jesus the parabolist, as well as the characters in the parables, come alive for us; the device of interior monologue (used in 15:17ff.; 16:3f; 18:4f.) is an important tactic, for it enables Luke 'to characterize his hero with specially sharp and penetrating insight, as glimpsed in his masterful storytelling'.[10]

Luke, then, intends to give an accurate representation of the words and deeds of Jesus, and also to interpret their significance. How particularly does he interpret the parables which he records? What figure of speech best describes his creative response to them, his construal of the intention of Jesus?

2. Luke's Interpretative Key: Metonymy

It has long been recognized, as the next two chapters will make clear, that powerful interpretative currents run to and fro between the parables and the narrative which surrounds them - in each of the gospels. Modern commentators (as will be exemplified in Chapter 5) have often been too ready to attribute a definite and reductive purpose to the Evangelists in this embedding of the parables in the gospel story. In fact, the occasions on which they spell out in detail an interpretation for a parable are very rare. The introductions and conclusions Luke gives to four of the six parables dealt with here are brief indeed, allowing the parable itself (in conjunction with the wider context) to say much more than this small framing implies.[11] I suggest that rather than pinning down the meaning of the parables in a simplistic fashion Luke has set up a powerful interpretative field in which each miniature story (told by Jesus) and the larger story (about Jesus) shed light upon each other.[12]

More precisely, this means that each parable is not only a striking figure, but also a trope which can be read as substituting for the larger story - and for the gospel message itself. This is not a novel assertion. Indeed I take as foundational the statement of John R. Donahue:

> Jesus proclaimed the parables in the context of the kingdom: God's entry into history with an offer of forgiveness to the 'sick' and the marginal. And the church proclaimed the parables in the context of 'gospel': the narrative of Jesus' life as a testimony to this gift and a sign of its power.[13]

But what *kind* of trope is operating when the parables are thus read as encapsulating the proclamation of Jesus? I suggest that Luke treats these vivid tableaux in his narrative as *metonymies,* presenting aspects of what God was doing in the ministry of Jesus and in that presentation proclaiming the gospel itself. 'By Metonymy . . . one can simultaneously distinguish between two phenomena and reduce one to the status of a manifestation of the other.'[14] When in the Psalms 'throne' stands for 'kingdom', the writer, singer, reader or listener knows that 'throne' and 'kingdom' are not simply synonymous; the phenomena are distinguished. But at the same time 'throne' is 'reduced' to the status of a manifestation of 'kingdom': it is not the size, shape or material composition of the throne upon which the image fastens our interest. Similarly, by focusing on one aspect of the operation of the gospel, each parable manifests the gospel itself. Thus Luke does in a sense *reduce* the parables, withdrawing them to one remove from the details of their setting in the ministry of Jesus, and making them focus and manifest the overall gospel narrative. But in another sense this move *enlarges* them, for he opens the parables on to a wider interpretative context than would have been available to Jesus' hearers.

The parables are not offered by Luke as isolated stories without explanation, in the expectation either that they will be transparent in themselves or that a group 'in the know' will be able to decode them. They are offered within a larger narrative within which they make sense, not as allegories to be deciphered but as suggestive, tropical stories. As with all the tropes, a mutual enlightenment takes place between the substituting and substituted entities.[15] The parables illuminate the workings of the gospel in specific situations,[16] while the gospel story illuminates the working of the parable stories; further, the gospel story *causes* the parables, while the parables bring the gospel to expression.[17]

3. Luke's Parable Interpretations

We will now trace in more detail how this happens: first with a brief overview of the six parables individually, then through a more detailed examination of the thematic and linguistic connections which bind the parables with the surrounding narrative.

The Six Parables

Luke interprets these parables of Jesus as proclaiming the gracious invitation and commands of the gospel. This proclamation as heard in the six parables and in the whole story can be well summarized with reference to a programmatic passage, the song of Mary in Luke 1:46-55, and especially the section vv. 51-53.[18] This gospel announcement is of God acting in strength to save his people - scattering the proud, dethroning the mighty, dismissing the rich, exalting the humble, filling the hungry: but the gospel story emphasises also the requirement of obedient co-operation with what God is doing, of righteousness as the way to life, epitomized in Mary's trusting response to God in Luke 1:38. The parables both dramatize these great reversals and enjoin this obedient response.[19]

The Good Samaritan is set by Luke in the context of a lawyer's question to Jesus: 'what shall I do to inherit eternal life?' (10:25) and the supplementary query 'who is my neighbour?' (10:29). However one understands the apparent disjointedness between this query and Jesus' final question 'which of these three . . . proved neighbour?' (10:36), it is clear that Luke understands the Samaritan's action as exemplifying the kind of obedience required by the law.[20] Moreover, he does not present Jesus as challenging the lawyer's basic premise that obedience to the law will lead to life.[21] But this is (quite literally) only half the story. When we hear the descant of the Magnificat over the melody of the parable, we see a half-dead victim uplifted, a half-caste made the hero of the story, and comfortable, establishment figures passing on their way, heedless of the needy and humiliated by the narrative. This is a gospel story; the great reversal is seen in action.

In The Prodigal Son hunger is fed and humility rewarded, while self-satisfaction cannot see anything to be gained from the outpouring of generosity: never could there be a better illustration of the rich being sent empty away than the picture of the older brother - nor a better demonstration that if the rich do depart empty, they have only themselves to blame. Luke places the story where its moral challenge can be shown up most sharply. The father functions as an example of co-operation with the activity of God in welcoming the penitent - by analogy with Jesus and by contrast with his detractors in 15:1f. Again, here is both good news and moral demand.

Gracious reversals and challenges to action go together also in The Shrewd Steward, as we shall see further. This parable shows us the poor being cared for, a rich master discovering generosity and a worldly-wise, tainted employee being held up as an example. 'Righteousness' is being redefined, but not dispensed with; Luke's appending of various sayings in 16:10-13 about the need (and reward) for *true* faithfulness are (contrary to frequent supposition) quite consistent with the parable. It is the surprising *location* of faithfulness in the parable that exemplifies the Magnificat reversal.

In The Rich Man and Lazarus a wealthy man who has 'sent the poor away empty' throughout his life is ultimately sent away empty himself.[22] The mercy and judgement of God, with the call both to imitate his generosity and trust in his love, are very apparent.

The Judge and the Widow finds a poor woman getting redress and a man of the world held up as a surprising model for the pious. Whatever their motivations, both characters show an exemplary response to the good news. The widow in her trusting persistence, the judge in his eventual right action, both breathe the atmosphere of a world invaded by the gospel in which there is nothing to lose and everything to gain by trust and obedience. For Luke the parable offered hope to a suffering church, an encouragement to go on praying (18:1) because God's new order had already irrupted into the world (18:7,8); as Mary proclaimed, 'he *has* helped his servant Israel' (1:54).

In The Pharisee and the Customs Officer the great reversal is at its starkest: the story dethrones the powerful, the one who thinks he is righteous, and lifts up the meek, the one who knows he has not been. The implicit call to imitate the one and not the other is also clear. When God acts, it makes sense for human beings to co-operate and not to oppose.

We turn now to allow the smaller and larger stories, parables and gospel, to interpret each other in more depth by examining thematic connections built around key words.[23] This will disclose a rich play of intersignification not only between the parables and Luke-Acts, but among the parables themselves.[24]

Characters

The presence of certain designated persons in the parables and the wider story serves to link the parables firmly to Luke's narrative world, and warns us against crude stereotyping of parable characters.

The priest (ἱερεύς, 10:31) passes by the wounded man. But in the larger story, priests are presented in a positive as well as negative light. Though Luke, like the other Evangelists, places great emphasis on the part played by the *high* priests in the downfall of Jesus, and though priests arrested Peter and John (Acts 4:1[25]), a 'crowd' of them were later 'obedient to the faith' (Acts 6:7), and the first character to be introduced in the gospel is a good priest, Zacharias (1:5f.). So although a parable told by Luke's Jesus presents a priest as a heartless character, Luke's overall portrayal of priests means that this is not part of a stereotypical presentation by Luke.

Something similar can be said about the Samaritan (Σαμαρίτης, 10:33).[26] Outside the parable, we find that the one leper out of ten who turned back to give thanks to Jesus for his cure was a Samaritan (17:16), and that Samaritans are among those who receive the gospel (Acts 8:12-25). But there are negative portrayals of Samaritans too: a Samaritan village is unwilling to receive Jesus (Lk. 9:52f.), and Samaria is the scene of enthusiastic response to the activity of Simon the magician (Acts 8:9-11). So for a Samaritan to appear as a hero does not simply fit with a neat Lukan schema, as is implied by Scott when he writes that only from a Gentile perspective (i.e. a perspective of sympathy with Samaritans) can the story be read as an example.[27] Luke has not created a new stereotype, the 'compassionate Samaritan'. Within his wider story a distinctive voice seems to be preserved in the parable.

Widows, such as the one in Luke 18:3 (χήρα), are seen in the overall story as the victims of oppression (Lk. 20:47), in need of special help from the community of believers (Acts 6:1). Two individual widows are held up as examples: prayerful Anna in Luke 2:36ff., and the generous donor in Luke 21:2f. But another slant is given to Luke's presentation of widows in 4:25f., where Jesus reminds the Nazarenes that Elijah was sent not to one of the many widows of Israel, but to a foreigner. This story adumbrates Jesus' own ministry to the poor, and thus casts the parable of 18:1-8 (in which a widow receives justice) in the light of an announcement of the gospel. But it also disallows a simple stereotyping of widows, by the distinction made between the widows of Israel and the widow of Sidon. No person from any sector of society can, according to Luke, rest complacent in the knowledge of favour. The widow in the parable must, indeed, persist in her asking.

The Pharisee (Φαρισαῖος) in 18:10f. is a negative character, but it is wrong of Scott to say that in Luke's hands this has become an 'anti-Pharisaic' story, as if Luke simply used it to harden an already hostile impression of Pharisees.[28] In fact Luke's introduction in 18:9 generalizes the application of the parable so that it applies to a whole class defined *morally*, not according to some social grouping ('some who trusted in themselves that they were righteous and despised others'). Elsewhere hospitality is extended to Jesus by Pharisees (7:36; 11:37; 14:1). This implies the readiness of Jesus to appeal to them[29] and strengthens the sense that certain parables, especially 18:9-14 and 15:11-32, far from condemning the Pharisees in some way, are aimed at winning them over. 7:30 states that God had a purpose for the Pharisees and lawyers, but that they rejected it.

The appearance in a parable of a customs officer (τελώνης, 18:10,11,13) connects with the charge made against Jesus that he is a 'friend of customs officers and sinners' (7:34), the call of one such to follow him (5:27), and his conviviality with a large number of them (5:29). They draw near to hear Jesus (15:1). The justification of the customs officer in the parable is therefore of a piece with the affirmation his kind receive from Jesus in the gospel. But Luke does not suggest that they are a class so favoured that repentance is not required of them. In 3:12f. customs officers come to be baptized by John and ask, and are told, how they should show their repentance. Zacchaeus, a 'chief customs officer' (ἀρχιτελώνης, 19:2), shows active repentance. The lack of a specific mention of practical repentance on the part of the customs officer in the parable is seen by some as indicating that it was originally a parable of free grace that has become overlaid with moralism.[30] But in the terse vividness of the story, the posture and prayer of the customs officer is more than adequate to evoke the sense of a change of heart. Luke should not be made out as presenting, through the mouth of Jesus in the parable, a different message from that which he gives in the larger narrative; it is reasonable, rather, to assume that he expects that larger narrative to interpret the parables, whose vivid realism has no need for pedantic spelling-out of lessons. Further, Zacchaeus illustrates that the Pharisee / customs officer contrast in the parable cuts right across the rich / poor contrast which is found in Luke-Acts. Customs officers and Pharisees are both shown as failing in their attitude to money (as are *both* brothers in The Prodigal Son).

This survey of the presentation of five parable characters within the overarching story shows that they do not form a part of any simple stereotyping of favoured or unfavoured groups by Luke, just as there is no exclusion of any from the demand of repentance. It is appropriate to deal here with two further designations, which will crystallize this point for us.

Abraham (Ἀβραάμ), an important figure in The Rich Man and Lazarus (16:22f, 25, 29f.), has a special prominence in Luke's writings. Israel is seen as heir to the promises made to Abraham, now being fulfilled (Lk. 1:55,73; Acts 3:13,25; 13:26). John the Baptist warned against presumption upon descent from Abraham, and told his hearers that God was well able to raise up new 'children' for the patriarch even from stones (Lk. 3:8, cf. Mt. 3:9). Abraham, along with the other patriarchs and prophets, are in the kingdom, but Jesus warns his fellow-Israelites of the danger of being excluded themselves (Lk. 13:28, cf. Mt. 8:11). Jesus calls a woman with a spirit of infirmity, whom he heals, a 'daughter of Abraham' (Lk. 13:16), and Zacchaeus a 'son of Abraham' (19:9). This last reference especially, together with the warning in 13:28, suggests that Jesus wishes to remind those with a narrower outlook, such as the Pharisees, that Jews of all classes are children and heirs of Abraham, and that therefore no 'sinner' among them is beyond redemption; but equally that they should all be careful lest they reject the promised gift of the kingdom when it comes to them. In this light Abraham's position in the parable in ch. 16 is especially poignant. The rich man calls him 'Father' (vv. 24,27,30) and Abraham uses the familiar term τέκνον, 'child' (v. 25). The rich man is still presuming upon his ancestry, and Abraham is not repudiating him, but the gulf forbids the child's return to the father's bosom.[31]

The word meaning 'sinner' (the dative ἀμαρτωλῷ appears in 18:13) is more frequent in Luke than in the other gospels. 'Sinners' are closely associated with 'customs officers' (5:30; 7:34; 15:1f.; 19:2,7). But in interpreting the parable in 18:9-14 it is especially interesting to note what other textual company the customs officer keeps as a 'sinner'. Simon Peter described himself thus (5:8). A woman, probably a prostitute, is called a 'sinner' in both Luke's narrating and Simon the Pharisee's speech (7:37,39). The angel reminded the women at the empty tomb how Jesus had said that the Son of man must be delivered into the hands of sinful people (24:7). So in Luke's context the customs officer, in confessing that he is a sinner, is not acknowledging membership of a particular narrow class, but putting himself alongside weak and powerful, men and women, murderers and prostitutes, one whose name would be famous through history and many whose names would never be recorded at all. For Luke, the offer and demand of the gospel upset all the conventional divisions, and impinge on all sorts and conditions of people.

Wealth and Poverty

Riches, possessions, and poverty form a major theme in the six parables, as they do in Luke-Acts as a whole. Luke T. Johnson has argued that in Luke, 'possessions' have a symbolic function in addition to their literal signification. That is, 'the poor' seem to represent not only the economically poor but the outcast in general, portrayed as accepting Jesus, the new Prophet; 'the rich' represent not only the well-off but the powerful, portrayed as rejecting Jesus.[32] Johnson rightly stresses, however, that the significance of possessions for Luke is not 'exhausted by their symbolic function': Luke 'takes with great seriousness both the literal problem and opportunity presented by men's actual use of and attitude towards possessions. He grasps the literal power possessions exert in centering and dominating men's lives.'[33] Without denying the symbolic dimension, it is the literal force of wealth language that I wish to highlight as we consider the connection of the six parables with the wider story. As we shall see, it is this literal ring of the language *within* the parables which make the parables metonymic, not metaphorical, within the gospel story. This in turn makes the frequent 'spiritualization' of the parables a misreading of Luke's rendering.

We begin with the designations 'rich' and 'poor'. The unquestionably literal force of these designations in Luke-Acts as a whole gives a powerful resonance to their occurrence in the parables. Our two parables in ch. 16 both involve a 'rich man' (πλούσιος, 16:1,19,21,22). A survey of other uses of the word in Luke is instructive. Jesus pronounces a woe upon the rich in 6:24. A rich man appears in a parable in 12:16, and is portrayed in a similarly unflattering way to the rich man of 16:19-31. In 14:12 a host is told not to invite his rich neighbours who would be able to repay him. In 18:23,25 Jesus states the difficulty, though not impossibility, of the rich entering the kingdom of God, as illustrated by the departure of a rich ruler from him. The story of Zacchaeus, showing that it *is* possible, follows soon after, in 19:2-8. In 21:1-4 the rich are implicitly accused of hypocrisy, for they 'give' much, yet sacrifice little. A related verb (πλουτεῖν) is used in 1:53, where Mary proclaims that God has 'sent the rich away empty', and 12:21, where a warning is drawn from the parable The Rich Fool for those who are not 'rich towards God'.

The rich man of 16:19-31 obviously fits into the pattern of Luke's negative portrayal of the rich, though Zacchaeus stands as a sign that the rich are not *beyond* repentance: the man in the parable simply leaves it too late. These other texts also shed light on the master in 16:1. His opening designation as 'rich', in the context of the gospel, makes him a negative character, but his commendation of his steward's action in remitting a part of the debts owed to him shows that he is one of those who awake to a right and just use of wealth.[34] He is like Zacchaeus and the prodigal, but unlike the rich ruler of 18:18-23, the rich fool of 12:16-20 and the rich man of 16:19-31. In the Lukan context, therefore, *his* 'repentance' is an important element of the parable.

Lazarus is poor (πτωχός, 16:20,22). In the Nazareth synagogue Jesus announces that the prophetic word which declared 'The Spirit of the Lord is upon me, because he has anointed me to preach good news to the poor' has been fulfilled (4:18,21), and later he assures John in prison that this proclamation is happening (7:22). The first beatitude is pronounced on 'you poor' (6:20). Jesus tells one of his hosts that he should invite the poor to his feasts (14:12-14) and in the parable The Great Banquet the host tells his servants, when the originally invited guests have declined, to go and bring in the poor (14:21). The rich ruler is told to give the proceeds of the sale of his goods to the poor (18:22), and the reformed Zacchaeus gives away half his goods to the poor (19:8). A poor widow's offering is said to be 'more' than the gifts of the rich (21:3). These verses leave us in no doubt that Luke is reporting a concern of Jesus with literal poverty; in whatever other senses 'poor' might be understood, it cannot mean *less* than this in the gospel. The story of Lazarus's destiny thus becomes a proclamation of the good news for the literal poor.[35]

We turn to other words pertaining to the theme of wealth. βίον (15: 12,30), meaning 'life' or 'living', has an economic connotation. In The Prodigal Son the narrator relates the dividing of the father's 'living' or 'estate', v. 12, and the elder brother complains that the younger has devoured the 'living' with harlots, v. 30. In 8:43 (a passage with a number of textual variants, including omission) a woman with a flow of blood is said to have spent all her 'living' on doctors; and in 21:4 a widow is said by Jesus to have put her 'whole living' into the treasury. In 8:14, in Luke's version of the interpretation of The Sower, the word occurs in the phrase 'the cares and riches and pleasures *of life* (τοῦ βίου)'; its occurrence here in Luke, and its absence in the parallels, suggest that here too it has the special connotation of 'material things'. We are thus alerted to the importance of wealth in The Prodigal Son.[36] It is not simply 'sin' in a general sense, but *abuse of the family fortune*, which is depicted in the behaviour of the younger son.[37]

The rich man in 16:19-31, like his equivalent in 12:18f., received in life 'good things' (ἀγαθά, 16:25). Mary has sung in 1:53 that God has filled the hungry with 'good things'. The Rich Man and Lazarus, therefore (as we have already seen), announces the same truth as the Magnificat. The hungry are to be filled, and the rich sent empty away. The parable suggests that even if it does not happen in this life, it will happen with awesome finality beyond death.

When Abraham tells the rich man 'you received (ἀπέλαβες) your good things' (16:25), he uses a verb with two suggestive parallels in Luke. In 6:34 Jesus asks what good it will be if people lend only to those from whom they hope to 'receive'. This fits with the emphasis on gracious generosity in The Prodigal Son, and accentuates the rich man's selfishness: he has received much, but given little. In 18:30[38] Jesus promises his hearers that no one who has left property or family for his sake will not 'receive manifold more in this time, and in the age to come eternal life'. Retrospectively this heightens the rich man's folly; generosity would have led not to deprivation, but to blessing.

The prodigal son recalls that his father's hired servants 'have more than enough' (περισσεύονται, 15:17). This verb is found also in 12:15, where Jesus teaches that a person's life does not consist in the 'abundance' of possessions. The two instances are mutually interpretative. The occurrence in The Prodigal Son ensures that we do not see 'abundance' as a bad thing in itself. It is precisely the thought of the plenty enjoyed even by his father's hired servants that motivates the son, and his return to this haven of ample sufficiency is seen in the parable as a wise move. It is not *possession* of wealth but its *use* which comes under Jesus' searing critique in Luke. In 21:4 (cf. Mk. 12:44) the rich give to the treasury out of their 'abundance', but it is the meanness of their giving when compared to that of the widow which Jesus points up.

The older son says that his brother has 'devoured' the father's living (καταφαγῶν, 15:30). In Luke 20:47 the disciples are warned to beware of the scribes 'who devour widows' houses'. In his older brother's eyes, the younger had 'devoured' his father's estate. Although Jesus (and Luke) may be presenting the older brother here as exaggerating the younger's crimes, there is nevertheless a link suggested between the younger son's behaviour and that of the scribes and Pharisees, who are portrayed as greedy and oppressive (cf. Lk. 16:14). This is an interesting reversal of identification from that suggested by the *immediate* context of the parable in ch. 15, where it is the *older* brother's behaviour that seems to reflect the Pharisees', and reminds us of the folly of trying to tie down figurative reference in an absolute way. The link between prodigal and Pharisees is not so much a statement as a teasing question appearing in the text. We would be rash to be too precise about the intention of Luke, his sources or Jesus himself here. Is Jesus being portrayed as making a real appeal to the greedy and oppressive?[39] If *they* are willing to see themselves in the guise of a wayward son, they may also see the possibility of a return.

Luke is especially fond of the word for 'possessions' or 'goods' used in Luke 16:1, ὑπάρχοντα. He recounts Jesus' warning that a person's life does not consist in the abundance of their possessions (12:21) and his exhortation to the disciples to sell their possessions (12:33). In another parable about stewardship, to be set over all the master's possessions is the reward for faithfulness (12:44); 12:42-44 can then be read in the Lukan context not just as an allegory about 'spiritual' responsibility, but as an appeal, on the basis of a situation in the everyday world, for the right use of money in that world.[40] This verse (12:44), taken as a reflection of a situation that might actually arise in master-steward relationships, sheds light on the boldness of the steward in 16:4-7: there the steward had *already* been given a high degree of responsibility over all his master's goods,[41] and was therefore acting within his rights in reducing the debts. Further references are 14:33, where renunciation of all one's goods is given as a condition of discipleship; 19:8, where Zacchaeus declares that he is giving half his goods to the poor; and Acts 4:32, where the early Christians renounce ownership of goods. In the light of these references the charge that the steward was wasting his master's goods sets that parable on a serious practical track, and permits us to expect a lesson about use of possessions as its outcome.

A noun meaning 'debtors' (χρεοφειλετῶν, 16:5), and its root verb meaning 'owe' (ὀφείλεις, 16:5,7) are found in The Shrewd Steward. A glance at parallel occurrences suggests an interplay in Luke between literal debt and debt as a metaphor for what is owed to God. In 7:41 both words occur: Jesus tells a short parable about a creditor with two debtors, to teach his host a lesson about forgiveness and love. The verb also appears in 11:4 and 17:10. In the former, in the Lord's Prayer, we find a particularly significant parallel. The first two clauses of the verse read 'And forgive us our sins, for we also forgive everyone *who is indebted* (ὀφείλοντι) to us'. In the equivalent Matthaean verse (Mt. 6:12), nouns related to ὀφείλειν, ὀφειλήματα (debts) and ὀφειλέταις (debtors), are used in both clauses: 'And forgive us our debts, as we also have forgiven our debtors'.[42] In Matthew 'debts' seems to be used as a familiar figuration for what we owe to God,[43] and that a desire for literary neatness has led to the use of the same word to denote both what we owe to God and what others owe to us. Luke, however, has preserved the distinction between literal indebtedness and the greater sense in which we fall short of God's requirements, for which 'debt' will inevitably be an inadequate metaphor.[44] Set beside the Lord's Prayer, the usage of debt-language in The Shrewd Steward, unquestionably literal in the realism of the story, should not be dismissed as insignificant colouring beyond which we must move to get to the 'point'. According to Luke, Jesus seems to have encouraged the literal forgiveness of debts.[45]

Celebration and Friendship

The verb meaning 'make merry', εὐφραίνεσθαι, is a key word in The Prodigal Son. The father says 'let us make merry' (15:23) on his son's return, and they begin to do so (v.24). The elder brother complains that his father has never given him a kid that he might 'make merry' with his friends (v.29), and his father seeks to persuade him that it was fitting 'to make merry' when his brother came back (v.32). The rich man of 16:19 also 'makes merry' daily. This occurrence, together with the only other one in the gospel, 12:19, where the rich fool in Jesus' story determines to tell his soul 'eat, drink, be merry', point to the fact that sometimes it is *not* fitting to make merry. In 12:19 and 16:19, merrymaking is a hallmark of carelessness about the future and, implicitly, callousness towards others. These instances imply a reason why the father in The Prodigal Son had never given his older son the kind of merrymaking opportunity that he laid on for the younger. The older son suggests that he might have wanted to make merry with his *friends*, though we may well detect in his reaction the dynamic of jealousy - perhaps he had never thought of the possibility until he saw what his father was doing for his brother. Be that as it may, the reason he now gives is essentially selfish. He has no cause for celebrating, but only thinks of having a good time with his cronies. Like the case of the rich men of 12:19 and 16:19, such would have been an unfitting merrymaking. The father's throwing of a party for the younger son, by contrast, is an act of complete *unselfishness*. It is *fitting* precisely in proportion to the *selfishness* of the lad in squandering the family fortune, for it symbolizes not cliquish self-indulgence but the reaching-out of love in gratuitous forgiveness and generosity. These two contrasting kinds of merrymaking are reflected in the two usages of the verb in Acts: 2:26, where Peter cites Ps.16:9 [LXX 15:9] as fulfilled in Jesus ('my heart *was glad*'), and 7:41, where Stephen recalls the Israelites' idolatrous 'merrymaking' before the golden calf.

The prodigal's father says that it was fitting 'to rejoice' (χαρῆναι, 15:32) at his return. This verb, along with the related noun χαρά, is found frequently throughout the gospels and Acts. We may especially remark on some other instances in Luke. Joy is said to have accompanied the births of John and Jesus (1:14, 2:10), the shepherd's discovery of the lost sheep (15:5), Zacchaeus's welcome of Jesus (19:6), the disciples' meeting with the risen Jesus (24:41) and their return to Jerusalem after his ascension (24:52). Joy is said to have characterized the crowd's reaction to Jesus (13:17, 19:37), and to mark the heavenly reaction to the penitence of a sinner (15:7,10). Jesus encourages his disciples to rejoice when opposition comes (6:23),[46] not merely when they experience great triumph (10:20), for the true cause of joy is that their names are written in heaven (10:20). They are warned against receiving the word with joy, but then falling away (8:13). The rejoicing in The Prodigal Son, tinged with incompleteness still by the self-exclusion of the older brother, is thus an echo of the rejoicing that is recorded as marking Jesus' appearance on the scene and its divine meaning for human beings: that rejoicing, too, is incomplete insofar as some remain 'outside', 'lost', or superficial and unpersevering.

φίλος, 'friend', is found frequently in Luke's writings.[47] We may draw out the significance of its occurrence in 15:29, already hinted at in the above discussion of 'merrymaking', by contrasting 15:29 with 16:9. The older brother complains that he was never given the wherewithal to make merry with his 'friends'. In 16:9 hearers / readers are encouraged to make 'friends' by means of the 'mammon of unrighteousness'; making friends was the aim of the steward in the story. A contrast with the older brother puts the steward's activity in a good light. Unlike the older brother, who simply wanted a party with his existing friends, the steward wanted to make new friends. This involved a mutually beneficial transaction. A contrast between the steward and the older brother implies a *comparison* between the steward and the younger: the steward may have had his hands dirtied in the use of money, like the prodigal, but both respond to their point of crisis by taking up a new attitude to money. The younger son comes home prepared to forego the privileges of sonship and work for his living. The steward discovers care for the poor when dismissed from his post.

Other Lukan usages of φίλος are most instructive. Jesus is said to have been accused of being a 'friend of customs officers and sinners' (7:34), and to have addressed the crowds as 'friends' (12:4). The steward, and those who follow his example as enjoined in 16:9, are seen in this light as friend-makers *after the pattern of Jesus.*[48] Jesus tells one of his hosts that he should not invite his *friends* when giving a banquet (14:12), lest they invite him in return, but rather to invite the poor, i.e. make new friends. The shepherd of 15:6 and the woman of 15:9 who call their friends together have *a reason to celebrate.* A lost coin, it is true, is not as valuable as a lost son, but still the woman's festivities are in the same category as those laid on by the forgiving father, not the aimless partying the older brother wanted. Just as merrymaking can be either fitting or selfish, so can friendship.

Friendship's limitations or negative possibilities are suggested elsewhere too. In the parable of 11:5-8 friendship is tested severely by a 'friend' who knocks at midnight. In 21:16 'friends' are among those identified as future betrayers of the disciples, and in 23:12 Herod and Pilate become 'friends' through their co-operation in Jesus' downfall. Friendship as a socially-established bond of camaraderie or cliquishness is not enough in Luke's perspective. Friends must be made and kept through sometimes costly generosity.

The steward hopes that his master's debtors will 'receive' him into their homes (δέξωνται, 16:4), and the same verb is used in 16:9: 'make friends . . . so that . . . they may receive you'. The interest of this verb is its regular use, in the synoptic gospels and Acts, of the welcome accorded (or not) to Jesus and his disciples. From Luke we may note 9:5, 10:8,10 (what to do when 'received', or not); 9:48 (receiving a child in Jesus' name, and thereby also Jesus and the one who sent him); 9:53 (a Samaritan village not receiving Jesus). The word is also used for receiving the λόγος, in the interpretation of The Sower (8:13; a different word is used in the parallels) and three times in Acts: 8:14, 11:1 and 17:11. The significance of the occurrences in The Shrewd Steward seems to be that the steward's hope to be 'welcomed' into people's homes is a reflection of the disciples' hope to be 'received' as they went out on the mission of Jesus. The steward's action may therefore hint at the practical aspect of the disciples' mission (forgiveness of debts),[49] while their mission in Jesus' name enables us to interpret the parable (the steward's action towards the debtors is not roguish, as frequently assumed, but compassionate and just). Mission is seen as the earnest outworking of true repentance: the wasting of goods is transformed into their use for the poor. Further, since the steward acted in his own interest, mission is seen also as an activity that will benefit the disciples themselves: as in Luke 18:29f., they may leave much for the sake of the kingdom of God, but they will gain far more.[50] The application in 16:9 simply draws out this lesson present in the parable. The disciples are to make friends by means of the disposal of goods, the forgiveness of debts; the 'tabernacles of the age to come' into which they should aim to be received are not other-worldly dwellings but the welcoming homes of the recipients of the gospel.[51]

The steward hoped to be received into the debtors' 'houses' (οἴκους, 16:4). The rich man wanted Abraham to send Lazarus to his father's 'house' (16:24), and the customs officer, not the Pharisee, went to his 'house' justified (18:14). All the Synoptic Evangelists, but especially Luke, write of 'houses' in a literal or a figurative sense. Houses are a significant setting for the gospel mission. 'Peace to this house' is to be the greeting of the disciples (10:5). Jesus invited himself into Zacchaeus's house and declared that salvation had come to it (19:5,9). Jesus dines at the house of a Pharisee (14:1). The man who gave the banquet in the parable wanted his house to be filled (14:23).[52] But 'house', like merrymaking and friendship, has two sides in Luke-Acts. Jesus says that Jerusalem's 'house' (the city as household, or the temple specifically?) is forsaken (13:35). He foresees a time when in one house five will be divided, three against two (12:52). The house the rich man has left behind (16:27) is, by implication, a house under condemnation. In this light one aspect of The Shrewd Steward's message in the context of Luke is that true security will not be found in the household of unrepentant Israel, but only through the generous and practical sharing of the gospel. But it is a hopeful parable; the assumption is that there are many friends waiting to be made, many houses waiting to open their doors.

Compassion and Mercy

The Samaritan *had compassion* (ἐσπλαγχνίσθη, Lk. 10:33) on the wounded man. Exactly the same word is used of the father's compassion towards his returning son in Luke 15:20. The lawyer refers to the Samaritan as the one who showed 'mercy' (ἔλεος, Lk. 10:37). The rich man in Hades cries 'have mercy' (ἐλέησόν, Lk. 16:24). Both these roots for 'compassion' and 'mercy' have resonances in the wider story.

Jesus' own compassion is designated by the same verb as the Samaritan's and the father's, in the story of his encounter with the widow of Nain (Lk. 7:13). The related noun σπλάγχνα is found at Luke 1:78, in the song of Zacharias, followed by ἔλεους to make a phrase indicating the 'tender mercy' of God (RSV). A string of verses in ch. 1 (50,54,58,72,78) proclaim God's 'mercy' to Mary and to Israel. Lepers and a blind man cry to Jesus for mercy in 17:13 and 18:38f. The compassion and mercy which the Samaritan and the prodigal's father bestowed, and the rich man craved too late, are thus suggestive of the love which God himself has demonstrated in Jesus.[53]

Righteousness and Unrighteousness

Luke's introduction to The Pharisee and the Customs Officer implicitly puts the Pharisee among those who trust in themselves that they are 'righteous' (δίκαιοι, 18:9).[54] The outcome of the story suggests that the Pharisee's trust is misplaced. Luke attests the genuine righteousness of a number of individuals in both the gospel and Acts: Zacharias and Elisabeth (Lk. 1:6), Simeon (Lk. 2:25), Joseph of Arimathaea (Lk. 23:50), Cornelius (Acts 10:22). When Jesus says his mission is not to the righteous (Lk. 5:32), and that heaven rejoices more over a penitent sinner than the righteous, who need no repentance (Lk. 15:7), it does not mean in the Lukan context that he has no time for the 'self-righteous' (many of his appeals appear particularly directed to them, e.g. Lk. 15:11-32, 18:9-14), still less that righteousness itself is suspect; simply that if a person is already righteous they do not need his attention in the way that 'sinners' do.[55] His words reflect a belief that there will be a resurrection of the righteous, when they will be rewarded (Lk. 14:14). The problem is not with righteousness but with the *pretence* of righteousness. In a passage about the plot against Jesus, Luke describes the spies sent to Jesus as 'pretending to be righteous' (Lk. 20:20). The Pharisee in the parable is presented in a worse light still, for he deceives not only others, but even *himself* that he is righteous. He is contrasted with Jesus, who to the world's eyes is condemned as a criminal, but is recognized as righteous by a Roman centurion (Lk.23:47) and proclaimed the Righteous One by the early Christians (Acts 3:14; 7:52; 22:14). Luke, then, sets up self-attested righteousness as something readers ought to be suspicious of, while readily naming as righteous those (above all Jesus) for whom the description is appropriate.

This becomes still clearer when we examine the Pharisee's self-description. Each of the terms he uses is found elsewhere in the gospel, in such a way as to reveal the parading of his virtues as flawed.

First, he thanks God that he is not like others who are 'extortioners' (ἅρπαγες, 18:11). But in the one other place where a similar word is used in Luke (a part of the noun ἁρπαγή, 'extortion', in 11:39), Jesus accuses the Pharisees of precisely this - however upright they seem outwardly.

The nature of the Pharisee's self-deception becomes a little clearer when we consider his next claim, that he is not 'unrighteous' (ἄδικοι, 18:11) like others, a claim which again Luke throws into question. For in 16:10 Jesus has said 'he who is unrighteous [RSV 'dishonest'] in a very little is unrighteous also in much', and in 16:11 he encourages faithfulness even in 'the unrighteous mammon'. In 16:14 the Pharisees are described as 'lovers of money',[56] and are said to have scoffed at Jesus' words. Jesus responds in 16:15 that they are those who 'justify [δικαιοῦντες] themselves before people'. The clear implication is that the Pharisees were brushing aside words which had all too pertinent an application to their own hearts. Maybe the reference to the 'unrighteous mammon' in 16:11 reflects a Pharisaic attitude to money: they thought of it as unclean and overcame this by dealing with it in what they considered upright ways (e.g. tithing) but this had become a substitute for, rather than an aid towards, true faithfulness in its usage.[57] This would fit also with the reference in 16:9 to using the 'mammon of unrighteousness [ἀδικίας]'. That verse would then be understood as an exhortation to put the 'unclean money' to use in more thoroughgoing, radical, creative and practical ways than the Pharisaic customs permitted.[58] The 'steward of unrighteousness' (16:8), someone caught up in monetary affairs in a way that to Pharisaic eyes dirtied his hands,[59] is put forward as an example of such a *right* use of money.[60] The 'judge of unrighteousness' (18:6) is also a surprising and challenging example: he may indeed have been someone beyond the bounds of Pharisaic piety,[61] but he did the right thing. 'Unrighteousness' is seen by Luke as a quality of the *Pharisees*, but *they* are pictured as projecting it on to characters like the steward[62] and the judge, and it is the Pharisees' use of the word which Luke's Jesus ironically adopts when communicating with them (cf. Lk. 5:32).

The third cause for the Pharisee's thanksgiving is that he is not among the adulterers (μοιχοί, 18:11). This claim too is made dubious by the gospel context. The related verb μοιχεύειν occurs in Luke 16:18; 18:20. The saying in 16:18, in which Jesus declares remarriage after divorce to be adultery, though linked to vv. 16f. which concern the law, looks at first sight oddly out of context, coming after sayings about money and before the parable The Rich Man and Lazarus. But in fact it highlights another Pharisaic failing, another self-deception. They considered themselves innocent of adultery, but they could only do this because of their acceptance of divorce and remarriage, which Jesus challenged.[63] The reference in 18:20 is instructively contrasting. The rich ruler claims to have kept the commandments mentioned by Jesus, including 'Do not commit adultery'. Jesus does not try to expose this as a sham, but simply tells him what he still lacks (v.22). Again the gospel artlessly warns us against too easy a stereotyping of different classes. Not all the wealthy and influential are adulterers! But one's genuine obedience to certain commandments must not be allowed to obscure one's failure in other respects.

When the Pharisee turns to his positive acts of piety, he mentions first that he fasts ($\nu\eta\sigma\tau\epsilon\acute{\nu}\omega$, 18:12). The only other use of this verb in Luke is at 5:33ff. There the fasting practised by the disciples of John and of the Pharisees is contrasted with the apparently indulgent lifestyle of Jesus' disciples. Jesus' answer to this - that there is a time to feast, and a time to fast - illuminates the prayer of the Pharisee in the parable, for it shows up fasting as a means not an end, an activity that may or may not be appropriate depending on circumstances. The observance of the practice by no means guarantees that one is 'righteous'. The impression Luke gives is not that fasting is wrong - godly Anna worshipped with fastings (2:37), and sometimes the early church felt it fitting to fast (Acts 13:2f., 14:23) - but that it is not *necessarily* right, and that one's practice of it can lead to self-delusion.

The other practice for which the Pharisee is thankful is his tithing ($\alpha\pi\sigma\delta\epsilon\kappa\alpha\tau\hat{\omega}$, 18:12). We may link this with the only other occurrence of the word in the gospel at 11:42, where Jesus says that the Pharisees do tithe, and rightly, but neglect justice and the love of God. Again the true condition of the Pharisee in the parable appears more sharply. His active piety is not wrong, but it conceals massive sins of omission.[64]

Correspondingly, the parable shows not that '[t]he justice of God accepts the unjust and the ungodly and judges the virtuous',[65] or that 'justification depends on the mercy of God to the penitent rather than upon works which might be thought to earn God's favour'[66] but that God vindicates the *righteous*. The *shock* of the parable is not the Pauline shock of Romans 4:5 (God justifies the ungodly) but the reversal of social stereotype: the righteous man (as attested by his penitence) turns out to be the customs officer and not the Pharisee.

The theme of righteousness and unrighteousness in our parables and in Luke-Acts can be focused in the use of the verb 'justify', 'declare to be right'. The customs officer went home justified ($\delta\epsilon\delta\iota\kappa\alpha\iota\omega\mu\acute{\epsilon}\nu\circ\varsigma$, 18:14): by God, though implicitly also by Jesus, the teller of the small story, and Luke, the teller of the larger one. Why? The clue is in Luke 7:29. There, customs officers were among those who 'justified God' as they received

Jesus' affirmation of John's ministry; that affirmation deepened, as it were, their assurance that God was righteous. They were therefore 'wisdom's children', for 'wisdom [here nearly a periphrasis for God?] is *justified* [declared righteous] by all her children' (7:35). Though John and Jesus had different modes of ministry (7:32ff.), the customs officers and others recognized God's wisdom at work in each, and declared that wisdom to be a *righteous* wisdom. The reason for the justification of the customs officer in the story, the nature of his righteousness, is thus suggested: he justified God, not himself, and therefore God justified him. For Luke he is also an exemplary forerunner of those who accept the good news after Pentecost - the message proclaimed by Paul that in Jesus *everyone* may be justified, despite much that would stand in the way of such justification under the law of Moses (Acts 13:38f.). In contrast, a lawyer wishes to justify *himself* (Lk. 10:29) and Pharisees justify *themselves* (16:15) - but Jesus, the gospel narrator and the reader all know the heart, as does God (16:15).

We may also remark on the widow's cry 'vindicate me' (ἐκδίκησόν με, 18:3), and the 'vindication' (ἐκδίκησιν, 18:7) which, Jesus says, God will bring about for his elect. There is no suggestion that she is asking to be vindicated *despite guilt*; her hope is based on the fact that her suit is just. For Luke, The Judge and the Widow speaks to the just cause of the suffering church. The issue for Luke generally, then, is not *whether* 'righteousness' is to be pursued in the hope of 'vindication' by God (clearly it is), but the fact that all kinds of people may do so. The 'elect' God pledges to help are any and all who 'cry to him day and night' to vindicate their just cause (Lk. 18:7).

Life and Death

The lawyer asks how he may inherit eternal 'life' (ζωήν, 10:25); Abraham tells the rich man that in his 'lifetime' (ζωῇ, 16:25) he has received many good things. There is a bridge between these two usages in the warning of Luke 12:15 that a person's 'life' does not consist in the abundance of their possessions. (We may compare, as E. Earle Ellis does,[67] the usage of the equivalent verb in 4:4, where Jesus tells the devil that 'man shall not live by bread alone'). 'Life', then, is not an otherworldly reality in Luke, but nor ought it to be seen in purely material terms. The breadth of usage is reflected in Acts. In 17:25 God is said to have given 'life' to all people, but elsewhere 'life' is seen as the possession of the believer. The gospel is described as 'the words of this life' (5:20), God is said to have granted the Gentiles 'repentance to life' (11:18), Paul is reported as telling the Jews of Pisidian Antioch that they were judging themselves 'unworthy of eternal life' (13:46) whereas those 'ordained to eternal life' believed (13:48). Jesus is called 'the author of life' (3:15). Luke thus presents the object of the lawyer's quest as the object of the Christians' discovery. It is noteworthy also in these cases in Acts that what is sometimes described as 'eternal life' is sometimes simply designated 'life'. Something similar is seen in Jesus' dialogue with the lawyer: the lawyer asks about 'eternal life', but Jesus in Lk. 10:28 says simply 'do this and you will live'. The idea of the 'life of the age to come' is here blended with the idea of 'life' itself as the consequence of obedience (Dt. 30:15-20, etc.).

We note also the verb meaning 'inherit' used by the lawyer in his question to Jesus (κληρονομήσω, 10:25). At 18:18 the same question ('what must I do to inherit eternal life?') is repeated by the rich ruler.[68] The significance of this parallel is seen in the answer Jesus gives to the ruler: the severely practical measure of selling up, giving to the poor and following Jesus is the one thing he lacks if he would have eternal life (18:22). This suggests that for Luke the lawyer, too, is being shown in Jesus' story that definite practical action of a certain kind is the way to life - *contra* those commentators who see The Good Samaritan as a means of exposing human failure and therefore teaching (in a roundabout way, it has to be said) justification by faith.[69] With Donahue I find in Jesus' acceptance of the lawyer's question 'Luke's . . . positive estimation of Judaism and its institutions and his understanding that the law was to bring the fullness of life'.[70]

When the servant in The Prodigal Son reports that the father has received his younger son back 'safe and sound' (15:27), he uses the participle ὑγαίνοντα. This is also found, referring to those who do not need a doctor, in the proverbial saying of Luke 5:31, and referring to the slave healed by Jesus in Luke 7:10. The related adjective ὑγιής is used in Acts 4:10 of the cripple healed at the Beautiful Gate. The use of ὑγαίνοντα to describe the younger son in the parable after his return thus stresses physical as well as spiritual well-being, and links this fictional character with those who are the objects of Jesus' attention in his ministry (those who need to be made whole, Lk. 5:31) and of actual healing carried out by Jesus and in his name (Lk. 7:10, Acts 4:10).

The younger son declares that he is 'perishing' with hunger (ἀπόλλυμαι, 15:17), and the father later rejoices that though his son was 'lost' (ἀπολωλώς, 15:24,32), he is now found. Apart from two occurrences in the closely-related parable The Lost Sheep (Lk. 15:4,6), significant parallel usages of this verb are found in 13:3,5, where Jesus draws a warning lesson from disasters ('unless you repent you will all likewise perish'), and 19:10, concluding the story of Zacchaeus ('the Son of man came to seek and to save the lost'). The prodigal's fate (or near-fate) is thus connected with that of the impenitent of Jesus' day more widely, which injects an extra urgency into the parable: it is not merely a hypothetical or extreme case, but a representation of the kind of situation that was occurring at the period, a situation to which people must respond (and to which many *were* responding). The fictional young man also mirrors the wealthy real-life customs chief, who was 'lost' but then 'found'.

Humiliation and Exaltation

The parables and the larger narrative reveal intertwining patterns of humiliation and exaltation. These are evident in the movement of the stories as wholes, but may be focused in the study of a few words.

The saying about exalting oneself and humbling oneself (ὑψῶν . . . ταπεινωθήσεται . . . ταπεινῶν . . . ὑψωθήσεται), which concludes Luke's rendering of The Pharisee and the Customs-Officer (18:14), also appears in Luke 14:11. The instruction of Jesus about choosing the lowest place at feasts in 14:7-10, and the parable in 18:9-14a, may thus be mutually interpretative. An ultimate sanction is added to the warning to social climbers (they may not only be asked to take a lower seat by their hosts, but fail to be justified by God). Conversely, the concern of the Pharisee in the parable with social standing and public appearance is heightened. Moreover, it is not only Pharisees who dangerously exalt themselves: the whole city of Capernaum is charged with this, and warned of its consequent downfall (Lk. 10:15). As justifying *oneself* is not the way to be justified, so exalting *oneself* is not the way to be exalted. The gospel proclamation is of *God's* exaltation of the humble and meek (Lk. 1:52);[71] conversely, what is high is brought low (Lk. 3:5). God 'exalted' Israel in Egypt (Acts 13:17), but the supreme example of one exalted by God is Jesus himself (Acts 2:33; 5:31).

At 18:9 Luke uses the word ἐξουθενοῦντας, 'those who despise or treat with contempt', to characterize those to whom The Pharisee and the Customs Officer is directed. It also occurs in Luke 23:11 to describe the contempt of Herod and his soldiers for Jesus, and in Acts 4:11 for the 'rejection' of the stone by the builders, in Peter's application of Psalm 118:22 to Jesus.[72] Thus the word in 18:9, taken in the whole Lukan context, implies the identification of Jesus with those like the customs officer, as one despised by those like the Pharisee. Conversely, the customs officer is like Jesus in his being held in contempt and in his being raised up.

The parables seem to be connected by Luke not only with the situation of Jesus, but with that of his followers after the ascension. This is suggested first by a parallel between The Good Samaritan and the story of Paul and Silas in Philippi. The robbers on the Jerusalem-Jericho road left their victim half-dead, 'having inflicted blows' on him (πληγὰς ἐπιθέντες, 10:30). Exactly the same expression is found in Acts 16:23 of the treatment meted out to Paul and Silas by the magistrates. Their wounds (πληγὰς, 16:33) are tended by the gaoler. Just as an outsider, a Samaritan, was the means of the victim's healing in the parable, so a pagan Roman ministers to the missionaries' injuries; as a Samaritan was revealed in the parable as one who might truly keep the law, so the Roman gaoler is revealed in his actions towards God's servants as one who has truly responded to the word of the Lord (cf. Acts 16:32).

There is also a connection between The Prodigal Son and the story of Peter and Cornelius. The prodigal was humiliated when he joined himself (ἐκολλήθη, Lk. 15:15) to one of the citizens of the far country where he had gone. The same word appears in Acts 10:28, where Peter reminds those gathered in Cornelius's house that a Jew could not lawfully 'associate' with someone of another nation. Through resonance with this verse the defilement of the prodigal by contact with a foreigner is further emphasised. In the parable Jesus 'exalts' the younger son, not the stay-at-home elder brother. Luke 'exalts' Peter in a similar way in the narrative of Acts, for table-fellowship with Gentiles becomes accepted (15:7-31).[73]

This theme of the exaltation of the 'unclean' and the humiliation of the 'clean' links all six parables. In The Good Samaritan, the priest and Levite seem reluctant to help the victim for fear of defilement,[74] but the 'unclean' outsider ends up as the hero. In The Prodigal Son, the action expected of the older brother is that he should humble himself to accept his defiled brother - now 'exalted' by his father. The steward's hands are tainted with 'unrighteous mammon', but he becomes exemplary, as even his master recognizes. The rich man kept his distance from the unclean Lazarus, but defilement by contact with him would have been better than the torments of Hades where he suffers the ultimate humiliation. The judge, like the steward, is 'unrighteous', unclean by Pharisaic estimation, but the story shows that he can nevertheless execute justice. The widow is not abashed, on account of 'purity' scruples about his impiety or her gender, about regular contact with him,[75] and both characters are 'exalted' by Luke (18:1: the disciples are to follow the widow's example; 18:6: 'Hear what the unrighteous judge says'). The Pharisee keeps his distance from the customs officer, implicitly because of his impurity,[76] but it is the 'unclean' person, not the 'clean', who is lifted up.

4. From Influence to Insight: The Voice of Jesus in Luke

The six parables thus appear in Luke-Acts as metonymies, representations in miniature of the gospel story, expressing and epitomizing the great reversal initiated by the grace of God and the call to repentance which accompanied it. Moreover the exemplary characters[77] are linked to Jesus himself, the embodiment of the gospel within Luke's story - the compassionate one, the righteous one, the friend of the poor and sinners, the one humbled and exalted - and to the disciples who are taught to go his way. What kind of 'voice', then, does Jesus have in Luke?

With respect to Jesus' stance in relation to his contemporary society (the 'horizontal' dimension), Luke presents Jesus speaking with prophetic concern for this world, the world in which Luke's history is set, the material world of life and death. Characters from Luke's larger story feature in Jesus' smaller ones. The same issues of riches and poverty, celebration and friendship, life and death, appear in the story *about* Jesus and his followers as appear in the stories told *by* Jesus. Both levels of story upset the stereotyped expectations of who can share in the bountiful gifts of God, of who is able to obey him and be acceptable to him, and of what that obedience consists in.

This is why metonymy, in which something is represented by one of its own attributes or aspects, is to be preferred to 'metaphor' as a way of describing the parables' function in Luke. Metaphor implies a transference between two different spheres, for example the earthly and the heavenly. The parables have frequently been taken as teaching about 'spiritual' or other-worldly matters, as if the kingdom of God were entirely future or ethereal. But we have seen that Luke's overall story and these examples in parable of how the good news works in practice are alike concerned *both* with what our modern era divides into the 'material' and the 'spiritual'.[78] In the larger story, for instance, use of possessions is symbolic as well as literal, but in the smaller stories, it is literal as well as symbolic. Luke's Jesus tells his contemporaries that the great reversal of God is happening in the circumstances of here and now, and that they can and must be part of it.

With respect to Jesus' stance in relation to the tradition from which he comes (the 'vertical' dimension of voice), Luke presents in these parables a conservative Jesus, one who affirms Jewish ideals of righteousness and obedience to Torah. He does not contradict the law, but in his stories he exemplifies how it is truly practised, and who may practise it.[79] Though he challenges those who mistakenly think they are righteous, the form of his stories is also an invitation to them to awaken, not a condemnation which simply writes off one group (e.g. the Pharisees) in favour of another (e.g. the customs officers).

The tone of this voice, as horizontal and vertical dimensions cross, is a *suggestive* one that does not deal in codified language and one-to-one correspondences, but in connotation and allusion. The linguistic links to which I have drawn attention suggest interplays of meaning too subtle and varied to be brought under the rubric of 'allegory'. We have noted that the presentation of different parable characters in the context of the whole work is not controlled by some Lukan stereotype. We have also seen that a character in a parable can have resonances with different individuals or groups who elsewhere may be contrasted with each other. From one angle the prodigal is aligned with the customs officer who humbled himself; from another angle he is aligned with the Pharisees who loved and misused money. Yet Pharisee and customs officer are *contrasted* in another parable. Tolbert's view that 'the gospel contexts, far from providing one normative view of the parables, as often as not confuse and obscure any attempt to understand them'[80] is misguided. Luke in fact offers to us a Jesus who speaks the very type of suggestive and polyvalent parable that she seems to value.[81] And perhaps surprisingly, this multiplicity of possible meanings does not dull the sense of the sharp prophetic edge that Jesus' words could have had in their original context. A Pharisee truly attending to the story of The Prodigal Son may have heard all kinds of resonances, but simultaneously felt the application to himself as singly and sharply as any parable-teller could wish.

If such are the insights Luke's writing offers into the voice of Jesus, how may we assess their credibility? As indicated in Chapter 1, my intention is not to reach firm historical conclusions, but rather to seek to appreciate the dynamics of an interpreter's text. His insights may be the product of a creative tension between conscious intention and conscious or unconscious influence. These insights may themselves go beyond what he intended to discover and disclose; we may 'see' that Luke 'sees' more than he knows.

Although it seems clear that Luke *intended* this interpretative, tropical exchange between the larger story and the smaller ones, and that he *intended* to portray the parables as stories actually told by Jesus, this does not imply that he intended with equal deliberateness all the interconnections that I have mentioned. Still less, of course, does it imply that he intended us to see all these interconnections as deliberate on the part of Jesus himself. Ancient authors were not ignorant of the power of individual words to trigger memories and associations within a text,[82] but equally, a reader aware that an ancient text is pregnant with meaning may well be inclined to see in it more than its authors wished to put there. But if we consider the influences upon Luke, both 'horizontal' and 'vertical', we may gain a clearer picture of the credibility of Luke's insight into the voice of Jesus in the parables.

One aspect of 'horizontal' influence seems especially pertinent. This is the culture of orality inhabited by Luke. If, as seems plausible, the gospel was meant for reading aloud,[83] attentiveness to the figurative qualities of its language, the echoes going back and forth between one text and another, is especially appropriate. Before our modern era, in which literacy has taken precedence over orality, communication was 'richly sonorous rather than merely "clear" for it was the echo of a cognitive world experienced as if filled with sound and voices and speaking persons'.[84] Beyond the deliberate craftsmanship of the literary artist - undoubtedly evident in Luke - we may hear the tones of an oral tradition alive with reverberations of meaning, an atmosphere in which figures *of speech* will flourish. This atmosphere would surely have been a 'carrier' for the voice of Jesus; equally, it would have provided a congenial ambience for creative construals of meaning by Luke and his sources.

Of 'vertical' influences, one looms large: the Hebrew Scriptures, known to Luke in the Greek Septuagint version.[85] As is frequently noted, Luke roots his story in the traditions and tales of Israel, from the appearance of godly Zechariah and Elisabeth in Luke 1 to the disciples' worship in the temple in Luke 24, and on into Acts. Above and beyond Luke's desire to tell the story of Jesus and of the early church as the continuation and climax of the story of Israel, there are many linguistic echoes of the Scriptures in which that story is found, which may be conscious or unconscious. The point of interest for us here is the way in which the realistic tales told by Jesus may be fashioned after the pattern of the realistic narrative of the Old Testament. In a manner parallel to the parables' metonymic reflection of the gospel, OT stories in different ways suggestively focus the grand narrative in which they are set: we may think of the way that many themes of that grand narrative can be concentrated in a short book like Ruth or Jonah. Drury deals well with the similarity of the parables in Luke with the Scriptural tradition;[86] for him it appears that Luke has himself fashioned these stories found only in his gospel out of the raw material of the Septuagint. But granted that, in any case, the *linguistic* echoes of the Septuagint - Greek turns of phrase - will belong to Luke rather than to Jesus, Drury's solution is too simple, as we shall see in Chapter 7. For we need to deal with the influence of Scripture not just as that of a written text on another writer (Luke) but that of a living tradition on a speaker (Jesus). And we need not only to trace continuities, but to measure difference.

The main question, of course, as we think of influences on Luke, is the extent to which he was *influenced by Jesus*. Aside from his *intention* to give an accurate and interpreted record of Jesus' life and words, did he - even if unintentionally - preserve echoes of his tone? *Prima facie*, it is likely that any writer in the first-century Christian communities would have done so to some extent. In the case of Luke, what is especially telling is the absence of a universalizing or spiritualizing gloss upon the parables. His desire to weave his material into an orderly narrative unfolding the universal implications of the gospel might well have led to a loosening of the moorings of the stories in the social context of Jesus. The fact that this does not happen may be taken as strong testimony to the presence of Jesus' own powerful and continuing influence in the church to which Luke belongs. This dovetails with what we have noted about the suggestive tone of Jesus in Luke's narrative. Jesus does not come through as the dispenser of clearly-explained, neatly-packaged nuggets of wisdom, but as the teller of evocative stories which have the power, amidst their multiple resonances, to hit their target. This does not sound like the synthesising of general instruction one might expect from the editor of a great teacher's words a generation on, but the preservation of the teacher's accents themselves.

Further perspective on Luke's insights must wait until we make the imaginative leap into Jesus' ministry and background in Chapters 6 and 7. For now we keep in our minds the impression given by Luke's gospel of Jesus' voice. In this text, the parables of Jesus are about the real world invaded by the gospel; and the corollary of this is that the real world of Jesus' ministry, depicted in the gospel story, becomes parabolic.[87]

NOTES

1. Brevard S. Childs, *The New Testament as Canon: An Introduction* (Philadelphia: Fortress Press, 1984).

2. Hays, *Echoes*, 33.

3. On the parables in their Lukan context I have found particularly useful Bailey (*Poet*, 79-85), Drury (*Parables*, 112-54), Johnson (*Function*, 127-71) and John R. Donahue, *The Gospel in Parable: Metaphor, Narrative and Theology in the Synoptic Gospels* (Philadelphia: Fortress Press, 1988), especially 126-93.

4. Joel B. Green, *The Gospel of Luke* (Grand Rapids: Eerdmans, 1997), 36, 45f.

5. 'For Luke, "narrative" is proclamation. Luke has in mind the use of history to preach, to set forth a persuasive interpretation of God's work in Jesus and the early church, and the medium of that proclamation is the narrative account whose "order" is crucial for our understanding of that interpretation': ibid., 38.

6. Frank Thielman, *The Law in the New Testament: The Question of Continuity* (New York: Herder & Herder, 1999), 136-40.

7. This is one of the flaws in the argument of Drury, who avoids questions about the historical Jesus by stressing (in keeping with his treatment of the other Evangelists) the Lukan character of the parables' language (*Parables*, 112-54). The language is certainly Lukan, but that does not mean that Luke was unconcerned with the meaning and tone of Jesus.

8. Ricoeur, *Rule*, 53, alluding to Fontanier, *Figures*, 63.

9. Dawsey, *Lukan Voice*, 3.

10. P. Sellew, 'Interior Monologue as a Narrative Device in the Parables of Luke', *Journal of Biblical Literature* 111, no. 2 (1992), 239-53, here 253.

11. See Lk. 10:25-29; 16:10-13; 18:1; 18:9.

12. As implied by Drury: the parables 'refer to the greater story unfolding around them': 'Luke', 434.

13. Donahue, *Gospel*, 17.

14. White, *Metahistory*, 35.

15. See above, p. 8.

16. In a wider sense, too, the 'microcosm' of the stories may be seen as reflecting the 'macrocosm' of Luke's view of history: Drury, 'Luke', 426f.

17. Metonymic substitution can be seen in terms of the interplay of cause and effect: cf. A. Fletcher, *Allegory*, 86.

18. Cf. Johnson's discussion of this passage with reference to the theme of rich and poor in Luke: *Function*, 136ff.

19. Contra the view that 'if the evangelists regard the narrative meshalim [i.e. parables] as the primary and dominating element in Jesus' preaching . . . then we must notice that they present him as a legalistic wisdom teacher rather than as one who proclaims a gracious and generous gospel': Birger Gerhardsson, 'If we do not cut the parables out of their frames', *New Testament Studies* 37, no. 3 (1991), 321-35, here 329. Luke surely means us to interpret Jesus' voice in the parables in the light of other parts of his gospel. Gerhardsson is right to point to the moral force of the parables, but seems strangely deaf to their ground bass of grace. It is precisely passages like 1:46-55 which help to attune us to this ground-bass, and to ensure that the impression Luke gives of Jesus' teaching in the parables is *not* simply that of a 'legalistic wisdom teacher'.

20. Cf. J. Ian H. McDonald, 'Alien Grace (Luke 10:30-36): The Parable of the Good Samaritan', in V. George Shillington (ed.), *Jesus and His Parables: Interpreting the Parables of Jesus Today* (Edinburgh: T. & T. Clark, 1997), 35-51, here 40.

21. Contra Kenneth E. Bailey, who ridicules the lawyer's question: *Through Peasant Eyes* (Grand Rapids: Eerdmans, 1980), 55.

22. Cf. Johnson, *Function*, 142.

23. I omit treatment of some words and phrases whose place in Luke-Acts is well dealt with elsewhere. On Moses and the prophets (Lk. 16:29,31) cf. Johnson, *Function*, especially 70-126; on repentance (Lk. 16:30) cf. Donahue, *Gospel*, 207; on prayer (Lk. 18:1,10f.), cf. ibid., 180-93. Particularly useful in drawing attention to the importance of resonances between one part of the text and another is Robert C. Tannehill, *The Narrative Unity of Luke-Acts: A Literary Interpretation*, vol. I (Philadelphia: Fortress Press, 1986): see 3f. on interconnections in the narrative generally, 109f. on connections between the parables and the wider story. Cf. too Green, *Luke*.

24. On the importance of the parables' intersignifications cf. Ricoeur, 'Biblical Hermeneutics', 101. See further Chapter 6 below.

25. A few manuscripts, including B, have 'high priests'.

26. Cf. McDonald, 'Alien Grace', 40f.

27. Scott, *Hear*, 200.

28. Ibid., 93.

29. He was willing to go to their 'houses', just as he went to that of the tax-collector Zacchaeus (19:1-10); so in principle, presumably, he could have said in any one of them 'salvation has come to this house today' (19:9). On the favourable presentation of Pharisees by Luke, as compared with the other Evangelists, cf. Donahue, *Gospel*, 172, citing also Lk. 13:31, Acts 5:34; 23:6, and J. Ziesler, 'Luke and the Pharisees', *New Testament Studies* 25 (1978-1979), 146-57.

30. E.g. Scott, *Hear*, 97; Hedrick, *Parables*, 226f.

31. He is like those who 'rejected the purpose of God for themselves' (Lk. 7:30).

32. Johnson, *Function*, 132-40.

33. Ibid., 159.

34. Cf. Tannehill, *Narrative Unity*, 131, on the exemplary nature of the steward's action. On the interpretation of this difficult parable see further below, Chapter 6, and my 'Parables on Poverty and Riches' in Longenecker (ed.), *Challenge*, 217-39.

35. Notwithstanding the possible Marxist objection that such a story merely diverts the attention of the poor from seeking fulfilment in this life (cf. Tillich, *Perspectives*, 186). In fact, of course, the parable offers no encouragement to oppressors, and the sharpest incentive to them to live in this world in compassion and justice. It is of interest that the word πτωχός used by Luke for 'poor' referred classically to those living in absolute, rather than merely relative poverty, those whose very survival is constantly under threat: Ekkehard W. Stegemann and Wolfgang Stegemann, *The Jesus Movement: A Social History of Its First Century* [*Urchristliche Sozialgeschichte: Die Anfänge im Judentum die Christusgemeinden in der mediterranen Welt*, 1995] (Edinburgh: T. & T. Clark, 1999), 88f.

36. Cf. Johnson, *Function*, 159-61.

37. Cf. the description of him as 'squandering' his inheritance (διεσκόρπισεν, 15:13), the same word as is used of the steward accused of 'wasting' his master's possessions (16:1). On this juxtaposition see Donahue, *Gospel*, 167.

38. B and D have λάβη, as in Mk. 10:30, instead of ἀπολάβη.

39. Contra those who portray Luke as crudely anti-Pharisaic, e.g. Scott, *Hear*, 93f., 103ff.

40. It is interesting that in the putative chiastic parable-source postulated by Craig L. Blomberg as discernible in Luke's central section, 12:42-44 and 16:1-8 balance each other, and should therefore perhaps interpret each other: 'Midrash, Chiasmus, and the Outline of Luke's Central Section', in R. T. France and D. Wenham (ed.), *Studies in Midrash and Historiography* (Sheffield: JSOT Press, 1983), 217-61, here 241f.

41. Cf. William R. Herzog II, *Parables as Subversive Speech : Jesus as Pedagogue of the Oppressed* (Louisville, Kentucky: Westminster / John Knox Press, 1994), 243; David Daube, 'Neglected Nuances of Exposition in Luke-Acts', *Aufstieg und Niedergang der römischen Welt* II.25.3 (1984), 2329-56, citing papyrus evidence and Mt. 25:14ff. / Lk. 19:12ff.

42. I am grateful to Dr John Squires of Sydney for pointing out to me the curiosity of the difference between Matthew and Luke here. One might have expected Luke, with his interest in money matters, to have used the 'debt' language in both halves of the clause. David Hill writes that ὀφείλημα means a literal 'debt' in the LXX and NT, except at Mt. 6:12: *The Gospel of Matthew* (Grand Rapids / London: Eerdmans / Marshall, Morgan and Scott, 1972), 138. No doubt, therefore, even in this verse 'what is owed' would have economic as well as spiritual overtones, and this perhaps strengthens the case for seeing ὀφείλοντι in Luke as having literal significance, distinguished as it is from the general word for 'sins' (Lk. 11:4a). On the material-economic dimension of Lk. 16:1-8 and of the Lord's Prayer see Douglas E. Oakman, *Jesus and the Economic Questions of His Day* (Lewiston, New York / Queenston, Ontario: Edwin Mellen Press, 1986), 153-6.

43. Hill notes that this figuration is already present in the Aramaic of the Targums: *Matthew*, 138.

44. In Lk. 13:4 the noun ὀφειλέτης, 'debtor', is used in the more general sense of 'sinner'; nevertheless, the distinction between 'debt' and 'sin' in 11:4 still seems to me significant.

45. On the theme of remission of debts and jubilee release in Luke, see James A. Sanders, 'Sin, Debts, and Jubilee Release', in Craig A. Evans and James A. Sanders (eds.), *Luke and Scripture: The Function of Sacred Tradition in Luke-Acts* (Minneapolis: Fortress, 1993), 84-92. Sanders writes, with reference to Lk.11:4 / Mt.6:12, that Luke 're-signifies debts to God as "sins" ' (91), but I am suggesting that it is at least equally significant that Luke *preserves* debts to others as 'debts'.

46. Another link between this verse and The Prodigal Son is noted by Jeremias. Persecuted disciples are to 'skip' (σκιρτήσατε, 6:23) and the father's feast included 'dancing' (χορῶν, 15:25): *Parables*, 130 note 82.

47. See Johnson's discussion of friendship as a Hellenistic *topos* used in Acts (*Function*, 2ff.). On Lk. 16:9 in the light of this *topos* see Tannehill, *Narrative Unity*, 134.

48. In the Lukan context, therefore, Jesus' words in 16:9 about making friends 'by means of the mammon of unrighteousness' do not sound absurd and ironic, as claimed by (among others) Elton Trueblood, *The Humour of Christ* (San Francisco: Harper and Row, 1964), 102 (cited in Dawsey, *Lukan Voice*, 153) and Stanley E. Porter, 'The Parable of the Unjust Steward (Luke 16:1-8): Irony *is* the Key', in David J. A. Clines, Stephen E. Fowl, and Stanley E. Porter (eds.), *The Bible in Three Dimensions* (Sheffield: JSOT Press, 1990), 127-53, here 149.

49. William Loader has made the suggestion that Jesus portrays in the parable his own programme of the cancellation of debt: 'Jesus and the Rogue in Luke 16,1-8a: The Parable of the Unjust Steward', *Revue Biblique* 96 (1989), 518-32 (cited in Herzog, *Parables*, 236).

50. Green takes a slightly different view, *contrasting* the 'friend-making' of 16:9 with Jesus' teaching that disciples should give without expectation of return (Lk. 6:32-35; 14:12-14): *Luke*, 594. As I will explain further in Chapter 6, I believe that an appeal to wisdom, involving an element of self-interest, is preserved by Luke in these parables, and does not contradict Jesus' ethic of extravagant generosity: see pp. 207ff.

51. σκηνή, the word for 'tabernacle' used in this verse, is also the word used for the 'booths' which Peter proposed making for Jesus, Moses and Elijah at the Transfiguration scene (Lk. 9:33 and parallels). In the background of both this scene and the parable seems to be the Feast of Tabernacles with its theme of celebrating God's act of liberation (Lev. 23:39-43). Cf. Willard M. Swartley, *Israel's Scripture Traditions and the Synoptic Gospels: Story Shaping Story* (Peabody, MA: Hendrickson Publishers, 1994), 127f. The idea that 16:9 is holding out an *other-worldly* hope has been tenacious in the history of interpretation: recently cf. John Nolland, *Luke 9:21-18:34* (Dallas: Word Books, 1993), 806, 808, but I believe that both Luke and Jesus had in mind something more down to earth. Thielman rightly sees the connection between this verse and the 'eternal dwellings' of Abraham's bosom in 16:22f.: *Law*, 150. But lest this give the 'eternal dwellings' of 16:9 too exclusively otherworldly a feel, we should reflect that

the thrust and focus of the later parable is precisely that mutual hospitality, welcome and reconciliation *should* happen *in this life*, before it is too late.

52. Donahue notes that the younger son in 15:11-32 also hopes for acceptance into a household: *Gospel*, 167.

53. Donahue notes a further link: in 7:13, 10:33 and 15:20, 'seeing' precedes compassion: ibid., 132. He also comments that the rich man in 16:19-31 'is blinded by his wealth: he does not see Lazarus': ibid., 176.

54. Cf. Tannehill, *Narrative Unity*, 186.

55. There is irony of the 'dramatic' kind in Jesus' words in Lk. 5:32 and 15:7: those addressed by Jesus who think they are righteous are revealed to the reader by the gospel narrative as unrighteous.

56. Halvor Moxnes argues that this is a literary formulation of Luke, in which a money-loving attitude is taken as a symbol of being a false teacher: *The Economy of the Kingdom: Social Conflict and Economic Relations in Luke's Gospel* (Philadelphia: Fortress Press, 1988), 8, cited in Andreas Lindemann, 'Literatur zu den Synoptischen Evangelien 1984-91', *Theologische Rundschau* 59 (1994), 252-84, here 262. The Lukan emphasis on wealth suggests to me that the Pharisees' attitude to money was as important to him as the question of their teaching, although, as Johnson shows, their attitude to Jesus was more important to him than either: *Function*, 103-61.

57. Cf. Herzog, *Parables*, 178-84, on the oppressive economic dominance of the Temple of which the Pharisee stands as an ideological representative.

58. Cf. Donahue, *Gospel*, 168: 'the children of light can be as shrewd as the children of this world; they are not to flee engagement with "unrighteous mammon" but to remain faithful in its midst.'

59. Jeremias reads 'mammon of unrighteousness', with reference to an Aramaic equivalent, as 'money gained by unjust means, tainted money': *Parables*, 46.

60. The connection between 16:1-9 and the following verses of exhortation to right use of money may thus be closer than normally assumed, and Linnemann's verdict that the 'six different applications - all of them attempts to overcome by interpretation the difficulties this parable gave rise to when its original meaning was no longer understood' (*Parables*, 18) is reversible: it is *modern scholars* who attempt to overcome, by theories about gospel composition, the difficulties the parable gave rise to when its practical force, remembered by Luke (and - to anticipate my next chapter - the Fathers, medievals and Reformers), was forgotten through the spiritualizing of Jülicher and Jeremias.

61. Cf. Hedrick, *Parables*, 195.

62. This seems to me the real locus of irony in Lk. 16:1-9, *contra* Donald R. Fletcher, 'The Riddle of the Unjust Steward: Is Irony the Key?', *Journal of Biblical Literature* 82 (1963), 15-30. Fletcher sees irony in the entire exhortation to imitate the steward, implicit in v. 8 and explicit in v. 9; he rightly believes that Luke presents 16:1-13 as a unity rather than a lame appending of 'clear' sayings to a 'difficult' parable, but he reconciles vv. 1-9 and vv. 10-13 by arguing that the point of the parable is that the steward is *not* to be imitated. But Luke, I believe, means the steward to be a genuine example; the phrase τῆς ἀδικίας is used of him because that was how the Pharisees

would view such a person, inextricably caught up in dubious dealings. The true irony lies in the incommensurability of the Pharisees' view and that of Luke.

63. A further link between 16:18 and its context is noted by Donahue: divorce was an economic issue, 'and often the woman suffered deprivation': *Gospel*, 174. The polemic against Pharisaic greed is thus closely connected with the implication of their lax attitude to marriage.

64. Herzog (*Parables*, 191) writes that: the Pharisee's prayer 'masks the fact that he and the toll-collector belong to parallel streams of tributary exaction' (i.e. the oppressiveness of the Temple and of Rome respectively). Cf. Michael Farris, 'A Tale of Two Taxations (Luke 18:10-14b): The Parable of the Pharisee and the Toll-Collector' in Shillington (ed.), *Jesus*, 23-33.

65. Donahue, *Gospel*, 190.

66. I. Howard Marshall, *The Gospel of Luke: A Commentary on the Greek Text* (Exeter: Paternoster, 1978), 681.

67. Ellis, *Luke*, 178.

68. On the link between the two passages cf. Tannehill, *Narrative Unity*, 171.

69. E.g. Linnemann, *Parables,* 56: 'As soon as we let ourselves be called out of the shell we have made of the world into the unprotected life of real encounter, we shall unquestionably make the discovery that we are exposed to the possibility of failing in life, in fact are always doing so already. Then the question about our life makes us realize that we can no longer ourselves provide the answer to it. It is no longer this or that fault for which we need forgiveness; our whole life needs justification.' A similar stance is adopted by Bailey: *Peasant Eyes*, 55. The tradition of finding justification by faith in the parables was prominent, predictably, in Luther: see Robert H. Stein, *An Introduction to the Parables of Jesus* (Philadelphia: Westminster Press, 1981), 49. But much earlier than this the Priest and Levite were seen as epitomizing the impotent law, in contrast to the Saviour. In Origen they signified the law and the prophets: see A. M. Hunter, *Interpreting the Parables* (London: SCM Press, 1960), 25f. Theophylact wrote that '[t]he law came and stood over him where he lay, but then, overcome by the greatness of his wounds, and unable to heal them, departed': Richard Chenevix Trench, *Notes on the Parables of our Lord* [1840], 5th ed. (London: John W. Parker and Son, 1853), 316.

70. Donahue, *Gospel*, 129.

71. Cf. Johnson, *Function*, 137f.

72. Luke's use of this word for 'rejected' here should be noted, for the LXX of Ps. 118[117]:22 uses a different one, ἀπεδοκίμασαν.

73. On further connections between Lk. 15 and Acts 15 see N. T. Wright, *Jesus and the Victory of God* (London: SPCK, 1996), 128.

74. Cf. Bailey, *Peasant Eyes*, 44ff. But contrast the view of Green (*Luke*, 430).

75. On Jewish evidence for women's appearance in court being a sign of immodesty, cf. Bailey, *Peasant Eyes*, 134.

76. Ibid., 148.

77. Donahue notes the importance of teaching by *example* in Hellenistic education, and that Luke's parables reflect this: *Gospel*, 206f.

78. Cf. Donahue, *Gospel*, 193.

79. Cf. Thielman, *Law*, 147-51. Thielman shows how, in Luke, themes such as mercy, forgiveness, care for the stranger and almsgiving, not absent from Torah, are made by Jesus its controlling centre.

80. Tolbert, *Perspectives,* 61. She adduces each of the six parables that I am discussing among her examples.

81. Ibid., 62-6.

82. 'Ancient literary art . . . rejoices in integration of narrative by very minute historical particulars': Drury, *Parables*, 51, alluding to Robert Alter, *The Art of Biblical Narrative* (London: George Allen & Unwin, 1981).

83. See F. Gerald Downing, 'Theophilus's First Reading of Luke-Acts', in C.M. Tuckett (ed.), *Luke's Literary Achievement: Collected Essays* (Sheffield: Sheffield Academic Press, 1995), 91-109; Witherington, *Sage*, 153f.

84. Walter J. Ong, *Ramus, Method and the Decay of Dialogue* (Harvard: Harvard University Press, 1958), 212, cited in Hawkes, *Metaphor*, 27.

85. On the influence of the Septuagint on Luke see especially Drury, *Tradition*. Cf. Evans and Sanders (eds.), *Luke and Scripture*.

86. Drury, *Parables*, 114-54.

87. Cf. Donahue, *Gospel*, 134-8, 159.

The Age of Divine Meaning: Parable Interpretation from the Fathers to the Reformers

---

Any normative concept in interpretation implies a choice that is required not by the nature of written texts but rather by the goal that the interpreter sets himself. It is a weakness in many descriptions of the interpretive process that this act of choice is disregarded and the process described as though the object of interpretation were somehow determined by the ontological status of texts themselves.[1]

A great age . . . when influence was generous.[2]

1. A Heritage Misconstrued

We begin now to accompany the parables on their long journey through the Christian centuries, and the theme of this chapter is the tradition of parable interpretation from the Fathers to the Reformation. The reaction against this tradition, a reaction largely initiated by Jülicher, has continued to influence parable scholarship to this day. Since reaction can lead to amnesia with respect to what has been reacted against, I wish to bring to the fore again some central features of the period.[3] The aim is that in this way suppressed memories may be reawakened, the terms of contemporary discussion clarified, and a more positive expectation re-established concerning what we might learn from this era of the voice of Jesus.

My point of entry into this long tradition is the account of it which begins C.H. Dodd's *The Parables of the Kingdom*,[4] the work through which the great reaction begun by Jülicher established itself in the English-speaking world. Dodd's account well illustrates how a broad statement of what one is reacting against can conceal as much as it reveals. Here is his summary of the older position, from the second paragraph of the book:

In the traditional teaching of the Church for centuries [the parables] were treated as allegories, in which each term stood as a cryptogram for an idea, so that the whole had to be de-coded term by term.[5]

There follows his rendering of Augustine's interpretation of The Good Samaritan, and then this concise dismissal:

This interpretation of the parable in question prevailed down to the time of Archbishop Trench, who follows its main lines with even more ingenious elaboration; and it is still to be heard in sermons. To the ordinary person of intelligence who approaches the Gospels with some sense for literature this mystification must appear quite perverse.[6]

We may note what Dodd's remarks imply concerning the intention of these early interpreters, the influences upon them, and their insight into the parables.

Dodd's main claim is that according to the Fathers and their successors, the parables were repositories of secret knowledge, left by Jesus for succeeding generations of disciples to unlock; further, that those who read the parables in such a way were guilty of 'mystifying' what was 'really' plain; and that it was the synoptic Evangelists themselves who set this unfortunate tradition of misinterpretation in train, as seen in the passage about the purpose of parables, followed by the interpretation they give of The Sower (Mk. 4:11-20 and parallels).[7] I will argue that this fundamentally misreads the parable interpretation of this premodern period. It implies that the *intention* of the interpreters was to uncover the voice and intention of the historical Jesus, that they found a mystifying voice and intention, and ascribed this mistakenly to Jesus. In fact, however, they were treating the text as a sacred document through which *God* had revealed himself. They were interpreting it for the *divine meaning*.[8] To state the point sharply: the Jülicher-Dodd-Jeremias tradition thinks that the earlier commentators, and to some extent the Evangelists themselves, misunderstood Jesus' parables; I think that the Jülicher-Dodd-Jeremias tradition misunderstands the earlier commentators and the Evangelists.

Central to the Jülicher-Dodd-Jeremias tradition is the claim that Mark misunderstood the early logion which he incorporated in his gospel at 4:11f.:

11 And he said to them, 'To you has been given the secret of the kingdom of God, but for those outside everything is in parables; 12 so that they may indeed see but not perceive, and may indeed hear but not understand; lest they should turn again, and be forgiven.

Mark, so the argument runs, mistakenly linked the saying of v. 11 to Jesus' teaching in parables, whereas παραβολαῖς in the saying's putative original context would have connoted 'riddles'.[9] In other words, the saying should not have been made to imply (as, according to this view, it does in its Markan context) that Jesus intended to mystify people with his parables; it simply meant that for many, his teaching in general remained puzzling because their eyes had not been opened by the grace of God. As for v. 12, Jeremias recognized that the ἵνα ('so that'), which has proved a stumbling block to interpreters, referred, through the allusion to Isaiah 6:9f., to the mysterious purpose of *God* in the hardening of people when confronted with a prophetic message - not to the purpose of *the historical Jesus* in telling the parables.[10] Jeremias's implication, though, is that *Mark* did not appreciate this.

It is, indeed, very probable that the saying in v. 11 referred to the whole range of Jesus' teaching, and has an eye to the variety of actual responses to it, as much as to the effects intended by him. It seems unlikely that Jesus intended to befuddle people with his parables, though it is equally implausible that he was always 'painfully clear';[11] a colleague describes the parables as time-bombs, designed for devastating but not necessarily immediate effect.[12] But why should we assume that though Jesus was originally referring to God's purpose in the saying in v. 12, Mark or the other Evangelists misunderstood this, and took the ἵνα-clause to refer to the purpose of Jesus himself? This assumption seems to be a tell-tale sign of that particular form-critical mentality of the earlier twentieth century which underrated the Evangelists' own grasp of the material they were dealing with. It is, rather, highly probable not only that Mark knew very well what the allusion to Isaiah 6 implied, but that with the benefit of hindsight he would have wished himself to underscore the conviction that in the teaching of Jesus and the varied responses to it, *God* had been working his purpose out.[13]

If this is the case with Mark himself, that he is knowingly repeating a saying purportedly indicating Jesus' awareness of the divine purpose at work in his ministry, it is not surprising if the early interpreters were more concerned with the *divine meaning* of Jesus' sayings than with his human intention. Whatever specific grounds they may have thought they had in the gospels for treating the parables as they did, the driving force in the Fathers' parable interpretations was surely this sense that God was purposefully at work in what Jesus was saying and doing: a sense which seems to go back to Jesus himself, but which at the very least must have been felt by Mark.

Dodd's portrayal of the work of these parable interpreters is therefore seriously misleading. They could not have been misrepresenting Jesus so greatly if it was not in fact the meaning of Jesus that they were writing about.[14] We fail to appreciate the richness, and profit from the insight, offered by earlier Scriptural interpreters when we misread their work as if they were modern historical-critical scholars *manqués*. Their alertness to allegorical significations in the texts is not to be regarded simply as a 'method' which we in the twenty-first century see to be mistaken and can therefore replace with another 'method'. As Louth says of the Fathers' allegorical approach: 'We are not concerned with a technique for solving problems but with an art for discerning mystery.'[15] Nor is it sufficient to dismiss their 'allegorizing' as the imposition of their own meanings, while allowing that in some cases the parables may have a 'genuinely' allegorical character.[16] We need to recognize, rather, that their way of interpreting was a direct function of their view of Scripture, a matter of 'the order and connection of things inherent in the Scriptures themselves'.[17]

Moreover, the parables were not set apart from the rest of Scripture. Thus Irenaeus:

> The parables will agree with what is given in direct, explicit speech, and what is plainly stated will serve to explain the parables, and so through a great variety of expressions one harmonious theme will be heard in praise of the God who created all things.[18]

Irenaeus, in fact, believed that the parables were basically clear; the reason for his (moderate) 'allegorization' of them in practice may therefore not be mere inconsistency, as implied by Warren S. Kissinger, but the fact that he was interpreting their divine significance, not their historical intention.[19] A similar view continued to obtain in medieval times. The 'unity' and 'harmony' of Scripture

> were often affirmed through a metaphor derived from the Psalter. When a cithar is played, strings and wood function together to produce a unified sound by means of its diverse parts.[20]

The Bible was seen as a whole in which God's truth was revealed in a consistent way. The part could be seen in the whole and the whole in the part.[21]

It might be asked why, if all this is the case, an investigation into 'the voice of Jesus' should not pass over immediately to the modern period - like all major commentaries on the parables since Jülicher and Dodd:[22] not, as in the thinking of these commentators, because the early interpreters are 'wrong', but simply because their concern is different from mine. If the premodern commentators were not aiming to find the historically-situated voice of the human Jesus, what place need they have in an inquiry concerning that voice? This, however, would be to ignore the workings of influence: writers may reveal, artlessly and even unconsciously, aspects of the tradition in which they stand. If the parables about which they write go back to Jesus, we might plausibly look at least for some trace of his meaning, some echo of his tone, in these commentaries, even though it was the 'divine meaning' of the texts which they were intent upon expounding.

What, then, does Dodd say about the influences under which the premodern exegetes worked? In a throwaway remark, he says that the 'allegorical' interpretation 'is still to be heard in sermons'. The remark hints at a truth Dodd does not mention: that the sermon is precisely the setting where this kind of interpretation first arose. Far from being 'mystifiers' as in the standard caricature, the Fathers' impetus was a very practical, expository one. They wished to commend the gospel to congregations,[23] and to do so involved the demonstration of the coherence of the meanings of Scripture. Their sources of influence therefore were the Christian tradition in which they stood, consisting of Scripture and its great expositors, and their contemporary situation to which they sought to relate the sacred text. The didactic setting seems to have been one of the chief motivating forces behind the 'allegorical' approach: the aim was to show how the parables illuminated Christian doctrine and contemporary life. Not only do we need to remind ourselves that insights gained through such practical and highly-motivated use of Scripture may well be as valid as those gained in the detached setting of the academy; we need at least to raise the question whether the tradition they knew preserved memories of Jesus' tone which were subsequently forgotten.

What of the impression Dodd leaves us of the insight of earlier interpreters into the parables and the voice behind them? His understanding of their tactics was that they read them under the rubric of the figure of *allegory,* with the parables' different terms as 'cryptograms'. He focuses on the early interpreters' concentration upon the individual elements of the parable - of which Augustine on The Good Samaritan is indeed an excellent example (thieves as the devil and his angels, the Samaritan as Christ, the innkeeper as the Apostle Paul, and so on). His conclusion is that anyone 'with some sense for literature' must regard this approach as 'quite perverse': in other words, according to Dodd, these interpreters yield no insight into the true nature of the parables or into the voice of Jesus; what they 'see' is, perhaps, just a figment of their imagination, or a mirror of their own concerns. Thus it is on *literary* as well as historical grounds that the 'allegorical method' is rejected. But I suggest that if we were respectfully to treat the *great texts of interpretation* as 'literature' themselves (Dodd, now, included!), to be appreciated in their own right, and pay attention to what their authors claim and do not claim for their work, we may find in them an insight into the parables that we had not suspected, even perhaps an insight into the voice of Jesus of which the early interpreters were hardly aware, concentrating as they were upon the voice of God. This seems preferable to treating the older commentaries merely as texts that are parasitic upon the great Text being expounded, and are therefore dispensable when they can be 'shown' to have 'got it wrong'. The response of these early commentators to the texts was an unashamedly aesthetic response, of the kind that continues to be necessary, even though the last century has underplayed the need for it. As we shall see, there are many affinities between their work and the literary-critical sensitivities (in biblical and secular disciplines) of our present era - most fundamentally in their exploitation of the possibilities inherent *in the text itself.*[24]

We shall now examine four commentaries on Luke representative of different periods, illustrating the continuity and development within the tradition, to demonstrate the interpreters' intention, their interpretation of the parables using a range of tropes as keys, the influences at work on them and the insight they disclose. We shall then be in a position to assess the nature of the contribution they may still make to an inquiry into the voice of Jesus.

Alfred Plummer listed extant commentaries on Luke.[25] The earliest complete Latin one, that of Ambrose of Milan,[26] is my first example. This was completed by 389 but began life as sermons delivered in 377-378.[27] Ambrose is especially important for his influence upon Augustine.[28] My second is the commentary of Bede,[29] written at Jarrow between 709 and 715, and described by Plummer as 'an oasis in a desert'.[30] Bede will also give us a taste of Augustine and Gregory the Great, from whom he quotes extensively. My third commentary is not listed by Plummer: it is that of the Franciscan Bonaventure,[31] written between 1254 and 1257,[32] perhaps when he was lecturing at Paris, or after he had had to cease when the Mendicant orders had their privileges removed.[33] It is noteworthy especially for its preface, characteristic of the Aristotelian revival at the time,[34] and is more individually stamped than Thomas Aquinas' *Catena aurea in Evangelica*, a collection of quotations from the patristic age which is Plummer's only listed work on Luke from that significant period.[35] My final example is a Reformation commentary, that of John Calvin written in Geneva in 1553.[36]

2. The Intention of the Premodern Commentators

Clues to the commentators' intentions are found both in explicit form in the prologues to their work and more implicitly in the text of the commentaries themselves.

Ambrose and Bede

Commentators in this period were intent on searching out God's meaning. This does not imply that they were seeking his intention in any very precise fashion. In the parable expositions of Ambrose and Bede one will not find many explicit turns of phrase indicating a search for the divine meaning, addressing openly such questions as 'what was / is God saying through this verse?' That search is rather the basic premise which alone makes adequate sense of what they are doing. The belief that Scripture was God's written Word, bearing testimony to his living Word, Jesus Christ, was rather a charter of *freedom* in interpreting the texts.[37] This was a freedom to bring texts from different parts of Scripture alongside each other in mutual illumination, to draw out meanings from the text within the broad boundaries of the rule of faith. Certainly this sometimes had the unfortunate consequence that even minor words and expressions were given a weight disproportionate to their natural place in the text, as it were to squeeze out every last drop of meaning;[38] this is sometimes evident in Ambrose.

But this does not mean that there was no interest in the human qualities of the texts. Ambrose states the necessity of attention to the *style* of Luke's gospel. The prologue to his commentary stresses the importance of treating Luke as a historical work:

> We have said that this book of the gospel has been arranged in historical mode. In short, we see that in comparison with the others [i.e. the other Evangelists] more fruitful study has been spent [i.e. by Luke] in describing things than in expressing precepts.[39]

This warns us, for Ambrose, against treating Luke's historical sense too lightly. But he then turns to the traditional link between the four creatures in Revelation and the four Evangelists, saying that the bull or calf is a fitting symbolic designation of the book:

> And this book of the gospel concords well with a calf, because it began with priests [i.e. in Lk. 1:5] and reached its climax in the calf, who, bearing the sins of all, was sacrificed for the life of the world.[40]

But Ambrose does not say here that Luke *intended* to present Christ as a sacrificial offering; he says that Luke's book *reveals* it to us.[41] He thus asserts the importance of recognizing Luke's historical style but does not couch the exposition of the rich significance of his work in terms of a search for his intention. This is a fair statement of what is to be his actual practice in the commentaries on the parables. Not only is there none of the modern concern with an Evangelist's provenance, community, theological tendency and so on; there are scarcely any phrases such as 'he says' or 'he writes' to introduce words or passages to be interpreted. Occasionally we find a word such as 'inducit' ('he brings in') where the subject could be Luke or Jesus or possibly God, but is clearly not the important factor.[42] When writing about words attributed by Luke to Jesus, he displays no doubt about Luke's historical concern, but does not feel himself limited by any supposed 'original' meaning for those words (whether a meaning of Luke or a meaning of Jesus).

Bede, on the other hand, does refer in his prologue specifically to the 'intention' of Luke, drawing on Augustine's *De consensu euangelistarum*. The bull, he writes, is connected with Luke, 'whose intention / purpose was concerning the priesthood of Christ'.[43] This intention is further spelled out a little later. Luke's interest in the priesthood of Christ is clearly seen, Bede says, in his selection of stories with a priestly theme:

> For there the tale of the narrator begins with the priest Zacharias . . . there the sacraments of the first priesthood, fulfilled in the infant Christ, are narrated, and whatever other things may be carefully noted by which it appears that Luke had an intention [sc. of writing] about the person of a priest.[44]

However, in the commentary itself, as in Ambrose's, concern with Luke's intention is not much in evidence.

With reference to the question of interest in *the meaning of Jesus* we need to draw a distinction between Ambrose and Bede. In Ambrose, it hardly seems to be a concern at all. His emphasis on Luke's historical style shows his belief that what were put forward as words of Jesus truly were such. But the meaning extracted from the texts is in no way a meaning conditioned or limited by what Jesus may have intended to say in the historical setting of his ministry. The power of the words themselves as *divine* words, that can be directly applied in teaching and exhortation of a congregation, carries his exposition along without any need to pause and reflect that these are words of the human Jesus, even a human Jesus who is also Son of God - let alone make any distinction between what he may have said and meant originally and what the Evangelist meant when he included the words in his gospel.

A good example of this directness of style is found in Ambrose's exposition of Luke 10:34a, '[He] came to him and bound up his wounds, pouring on oil and wine.' After citing the text he immediately begins to interpret the Samaritan's medicaments as the word of Christ, with power variously to bind, soothe and sting.[45] He also uses apostrophic addresses to the reader. He extols the blessedness of an 'innkeeper':

Blessed is that innkeeper, who is able to tend the wounds of another, blessed is he to whom Jesus says 'whatever you spend over and above I will repay to you on my return'. Good is the steward, who thus spends over and above. Good is Paul the steward, whose sayings and letters overflow as if with the doctrine of his which he had received. Good, therefore, is that keeper of an inn . . . in which the flocks of lambs are shut, lest there be an easy assault upon the little sheep by roaring, rapacious wolves [coming] to the pens.[46]

We note the lively, rhetorical manner in which the exposition is proceeding (it is not simply an expansion on what has already been said; the end of v.35 - 'whatever you spend over and above' - has not been previously mentioned). Here is no slavish system of one-to-one correspondences. The innkeeper is not only Paul: he is the other apostles, he is any contemporary guardian of Christ's fold. Ambrose is exploring the suggestiveness of the text, not treating it as a code to be mechanically cracked. It is the language of preaching, which then turns into the language of personal devotion[47] as he goes on to address the departed but returning Christ - seen in the guise of the Samaritan - directly:

When will you return, Lord, if not on the day of judgement? . . . You will repay what you owe. Blessed are those to whom you are indebted. Would that we were worthy debtors, would that we could discharge that which we have received, and that the office of priesthood or of ministry would not puff us up![48]

This is a heartfelt personal appeal by Ambrose that he and his fellow-stewards be found worthy in the humble discharge of *their* duties so that Christ would repay them at the last day; the thought of debts leads to reflection on the sense in which the servants also are debtors. Such is the tone of the writing as a whole: not theoretical or abstract, but rather engaging directly with the text and allowing it to suggest its 'meanings' in the light of faith.[49]

Bede seems slightly more sensitive to the fact that the parables purport to be words *of Jesus*. In introducing The Good Samaritan he specifically says that *the Lord* not only taught that everyone who showed mercy was a neighbour, but designated himself as son of God.[50] This is the kind of assertion of a 'Christological' claim in the mouth of Jesus that modern scholarship finds deeply suspect. But we should not read a passage such as this as if Bede were a Romantic seeking to penetrate a human mind. There is no emphasis here on the thought or communicative impulse of Jesus in the parable. 'The Lord' is merely a textual signal; Jesus is the one who says these things in Luke's narrative, but their significance is divine.

Bonaventure

For Bonaventure, 'behind the great diversity and range of the styles found in the Bible, lies the singleness and security of divine authority'.[51] The Prologue to his commentary[52] beautifully exemplifies the new sophistication introduced to biblical exegesis by the revival of Aristotelian learning. The different 'causes' behind the gospel text are carefully laid out so that the reader may approach it with the proper expectation and understanding. The very structure of this layout indicates a significant shift from the patristic period. For the main division is between the 'extrinsic' cause, which is Luke, and the 'intrinsic', which is Christ. The idea of the overarching 'divine meaning' - already in Ambrose and Bede more of an unquestioned assumption than a stated principle of interpretation - has receded further into the shadows, while the part of Christ in the causing of the gospel has come into view.

These two main causes are further subdivided. The 'extrinsic cause', the Evangelist, is viewed from two angles.[53] On the one hand there is the 'efficient cause' of the gospel, which is the Holy Spirit coming upon Luke. This 'efficient cause' is itself divided into three: the 'supreme efficient cause', the Spirit himself; the 'intermediate efficient cause', the anointing of Luke by the Spirit; and the 'lowest efficient cause', Luke himself as an especially Spirit-filled person. On the other hand there is the 'final cause' of the gospel, which is Luke's *purpose* in writing it. This also is threefold: the manifestation of truth, the healing of infirmity, and the reference of eternity.[54] Here Bonaventure writes specifically of Luke's *intention*. The healing purpose of the gospel is not only, he says, in accordance with the tradition that Luke was a doctor, but is 'according to what was intended by blessed Luke: that thus through the knowledge of the truth we should come to the remedy of infirmity'.[55]

The 'intrinsic cause' of the gospel is Christ himself.[56] This cause has two dimensions, 'material' and 'formal'. Christ is the 'material' cause because the gospel revolves around him as mediator, preacher, redeemer and victor. This in turn leads to his being the fourfold 'formal' cause, both in the necessity that the one gospel should come to us in four gospels (each focusing on one of these aspects of Christ's work), and in the necessity that Luke's gospel should fall into four parts according to these same aspects. The issue of the precise intention of Jesus in *speaking the words* attributed to him by Luke does not arise here. But it is most interesting that Christ is seen as the 'intrinsic cause' of the gospel. Here we have a harbinger of modern historical inquiries concerning the period between Jesus' life and the writing of the gospels. But Bonaventure is not quite speaking of *historical* causality: it is more a matter of the *divine necessity* worked out in the coming of Jesus and the writing of the gospels.[57] The gospel arises not just from the plan of a human author, albeit a Spirit-inspired one; not just from the impact of an astonishing man, albeit the Son of God. There is a greater intention determining its nature and shape. In the purpose of God himself, it *had* to be so.

Bonaventure's expositions of the parables are distinguished from those of his predecessors mainly by the careful categorizations which typically mark medieval exegesis. In many cases there are elaborate subdivisions of the material; in the exposition of The Prodigal Son we reach four levels of sub-headings.[58] But he does not follow through in a pedantic manner the points raised in his prologue: that is, he does not examine with each text or passage how it illustrates the purpose of Luke as the 'final cause', or the roles of Christ as the 'material cause'. In fact he states his main points concisely, and much of the commentary on individual parables is devoted to the assembling of allegedly supportive and illuminating OT texts, as well as citations from the Fathers. The presence of the Scriptural quotations gives a strong sense that the meaning of the texts to hand is to be construed as part of a far wider web of meaning - God's revelation as a whole.

Meaning thus still has its locus in the text, seen as part of the great Text, and interpreters of the past act as a check on the exegesis. Bonaventure does not show any intention of detailed inquiry into the intention of the human author(s). Nevertheless, such a concern may at least be emerging in the distinction he draws between a 'literal' and a 'spiritual' reading of The Good Samaritan.[59] In describing the thirteenth-century shift towards the acknowledgement of the human role in producing Scripture, A.J. Minnis states that by this period '[t]he literal sense was believed to express the intention of the human *auctor*'.[60] Confusingly for our use of language today, this meant that the 'literal' sense could even be 'figurative', if the human author had intended to speak in a parable or some other figure, according to Thomas Aquinas.[61] A 'spiritual' reading was one that looked beyond the human intention behind the text. But the two-level nature of the human authorship of the parables - Jesus' speaking and Luke's writing - is not explored. Perhaps this is simply because Jesus' divinity was so taken for granted that his 'intention' on earth was assumed to be identical with the overarching divine meaning.[62] Certainly, when the commentary refers to a human producer of the text, it is to Luke - not only in linking sections where Luke's arrangement of stories and sayings is described,[63] but sometimes in actual expositions of parables, where we would expect Jesus (in modern critical parlance it would be 'Luke's Jesus') to be the subject.

The introduction to the exposition of The Prodigal Son reads: 'In this parable the Evangelist describes four things'.[64]

Fundamentally, then, the aim of interpretation remains the discovery of *divine* meaning. This is surely the assumption behind the repetitive formula of this commentator, 'because . . . therefore there follows' ('quia . . . ideo subdit'). A reason from the (divine) ordering of the world is given, as a way of *introducing* the segment of text in question. Here for instance is the introduction to Luke 15:16b: 'And because a human being cannot be satisfied with such things: therefore there follows, "And no one gave to him." '[65] The 'pods' with which the prodigal son desired, but failed, to fill himself have just been interpreted as 'the delights of vices', and the fact that no one gave to him is regarded as divinely-ordained confirmation of the folly of seeking satisfaction in such things. The formula 'ideo subdit' seems in the majority of cases, as here, to have an impersonal subject understood (i.e. 'there follows'), rather than a personal one (i.e. 'he puts next'); if it is personal, no emphasis is placed on the personality. Thus the focus is above all the meaning of the text itself, rather than that of Luke or Jesus; but behind that impersonal 'there follows' lurks the figure of a supreme Author.

Calvin

Calvin's commentary marks a further break with the past. Though absolutely at one with his predecessors in reverence for Scripture as the word of God,[66] he presents the fruit of greater reflection upon the role of the human authors.[67] The arrangement of the commentary as a 'harmonized' version of the synoptic gospels leads him, for example, into discussion about the relationship between the different versions of the dialogue between Jesus and the lawyer (Mt. 22:34-40; Mk. 12:28-34; Lk. 10:25-37). Luke's omission of this from the Passover week narrative, where the other gospels place it, 'seems intentional, because he had related it elsewhere'.[68] He goes on:

> It may be that Luke told the incident out of place, or it may be that he omits the second time of asking (considering that the first narrative covered the doctrine well enough). It seemed to me that the lesson was so much the same that I ought to bring the three Evangelists together.[69]

There is here an awareness of the significance of Luke's intention. The bringing-together of the three Evangelists, however, sets severe limits on inquiry into Luke's particular motives and strategy.

Attention to the human writer does, though, lead Calvin to the issue of the setting and purpose of Jesus' words within his own ministry. The matter of whether the different accounts reflect different occasions is raised. So is the matter of what Jesus intended in his parable. Calvin contemptuously dismisses the old allegorical interpretation, which saw rich doctrinal significance in The Good Samaritan, as the device of 'proponents of free-will':

> As if Christ would have intended to speak here about the corruption of human nature, and discuss whether the wound Satan struck on Adam was fatal or curable: as if He had not plainly declared, without any figurative talk, that all are dead unless He quickens them with His voice (John 5.25).[70]

Three things are noticeable here. First, Calvin artlessly yet pregnantly raises the issue of *what the human Jesus* (called 'Christ', to be sure) *might have intended*. Second, he objects to the 'allegorical' interpretation because he suspects it is being used to further erroneous doctrine, but the allusion to John 5:25 shows that the framework of divine meaning, discerned in the unity of Scripture, is still in control. Third, here is an early sign of that obfuscation of the nature of earlier approaches to the meaning of the parables which Jülicher and Dodd were to reinforce so influentially. Calvin objects strongly to the attribution of particular intended meanings to Jesus; but the earlier commentators we have considered were not in the habit of making such attributions.

3. The Premodern Commentators' Interpretative Keys: The Range of Tropes

As we might expect over such a long period, there is a considerable variety of ways in which the parables appear as 'figures of speech' in these interpretative texts. The term 'allegory' is much too broad and inaccurate to summarize even the earlier commentators' perception of them.

As hinted in Chapter 1, there is a sense (paradoxically, given the general view about this period) in which the parables are less 'figurative' for these commentators either than for Luke or for modern scholars. As part of the unique outpouring of divine speech that was Scripture itself, the parables did not to the same degree stand apart as discrete units. Indeed, for Clement of Alexandria it was the plainer sayings in the gospels which required particular attention, lest one be beguiled by their simplicity into missing their deeper import. Thomas F. Torrance writes:

[Clement] remarks that in spite of their apparent simplicity the words of Jesus have a measureless range of intention behind them which calls forth from us more concentration than his obviously enigmatic utterances.[71]

The parables blend into the surrounding Scripture, seen as equally, if not always so obviously, rich in meaning; and their tropical character for these interpreters is therefore often found in individual elements within them, stretching their tentacles out beyond the parable, rather than in the parable itself as a whole. Modern scholarship has objected to this concentration on individual elements, but has often caricatured it unfairly, and missed the reason for it in the conception of Scripture as a unified tapestry of meaning.

Two tropes may be seen as dominating the parable reading of the early and medieval periods, while a third runs through both of these and continues into the Reformation. For the Fathers, the parables were richly *metaphorical*. They involved the substitution of language proper to one sphere for that which was proper to another. The earthly stood for the heavenly, the human was a window on to the divine. This did not mean only that an individual figure (like the father in The Prodigal Son) stood for God. An entire narrative, like The Good Samaritan, could be taken as a metaphor for the narrative of salvation. In the medieval period, *metonymy* becomes prominent. Figures in the parables are seen as epitomizing certain moral characteristics. The metonymy works in a broader context than that which we have seen in Luke's gospel itself, where the parables in their overall shape and thrust epitomize the evangel. Here it is characteristics drawn from all parts of Scripture which the parable characters typify.

The trope which runs like a thread through the whole period is *synecdoche*. As with the other tropes, it is seldom named as such. But this surely is the trope at work in what were called 'literal' readings of the parables (never absent even in Ambrose[72]). When, for instance, the challenge of The Good Samaritan to neighbour-love is stressed, this does not (strictly speaking) mean that the story is being read in 'literal' fashion, but that the challenge at the end ('Go and do likewise') reflects back upon the story and invites us to see the Samaritan as an exemplary figure, one who stands as a trope for the class of people to which the lawyer (and by implication others) are summoned to belong. More clearly still, this is the trope at work, sinisterly, when a parable-character such as a priest or Pharisee is seen as representative of the whole Jewish race. In Calvin, as we shall see, though metaphor and metonymy have taken a back seat, synecdoche is still to the fore.

4. The Premodern Commentators' Parable Interpretations

One thing will soon become clear: there is no slavish adherence in these commentators to a particular method of interpretation. Though there are, along the way, signs of the influence of the famous tradition of 'four senses of Scripture'[73] in one form or another, these commentators are as far as could be imagined from being hidebound or pedantic in their readings.

The Good Samaritan

Ambrose does not explicitly use any term like 'allegory' as a key to The Good Samaritan, but his exposition is 'spiritual' and Christological: he treats the story as a metaphor of the saving activity of God. The victim's descent from Jerusalem to Jericho is understood as the fall of Adam,[74] and the robbers as deceptive angels of night.[75] Hardly anything is made of the significance of the priest and Levite.[76] The weight of the story for Ambrose falls upon the Samaritan,[77] who is one both 'outwardly and inwardly': outwardly, not that he is a foreigner, but that 'Samaritan' can be etymologically understood as 'guardian'; inwardly, that his actions display the character of a guardian.[78] He also 'came down', and his coming alongside the wounded man signifies Christ's becoming our neighbour.[79] Subsequent parts of the reading have been mentioned in section 2 above. This is quintessential 'allegorizing' of a parable as readers since Jülicher and Dodd have learned to know it. The charge of 'allegorizing' implies in this context the mistreatment of a text, the imposition of unwarranted tropical meaning upon it by the interpreter. I suggest that we may more sympathetically describe the approach as the attunement of a reader (or hearer) to metaphorical reverberations within the mysterious overarching purpose of God.

However, it is vital to note that Ambrose does not leave the parable simply as the story of salvation through Christ. He draws out its moral implications, though remaining tightly within the Christological framework and the context of the dialogue with the lawyer. The upshot of the story, Ambrose says, is that we should love Christ as lord and neighbour, and also those who imitate him in showing compassion beyond the bounds of kinship.[80] The exemplary force of the story has not been lost in the allegory.

A significant shift is noticeable when we turn to Bede's treatment of this parable, for already the danger that an allegorical reading might undermine the practical challenge is recognized. At the outset Bede says that the Lord was teaching in the parable that whoever showed mercy to someone was a neighbour, and also that he himself was God's son who in his humanity became our neighbour.[81] But he warns that 'we ought not to interpret the neighbour (whom we are commanded to love as ourselves) as Christ in such a way that we weaken and divert the moral principles of mutual brotherhood under the rules of allegory'.[82] In his concluding comments, on Luke 10:36f., Bede allows for two distinct ways of reading the parable: 'by the letter' ('iuxta litteram') and 'with a more sacred understanding' ('[s]acratiore . . . intellectu').[83] In his section on the 'literal' meaning, he summarizes the point by saying that the foreign Samaritan became more of a neighbour to the wounded man, on account of his pity, than those born and brought up in the same city had been.[84] Under the rubric of the 'more sacred' or figurative meaning, he follows Ambrose's opinion that Christ is the supreme neighbour, so we ought to love him and those who imitate him.[85] But his conclusion reflects his earlier emphasis on the danger of attenuating the moral force of the parable through an allegorical understanding. For in his remarks on v. 37b, 'And Jesus said to him, "Go and do likewise" ', though Bede does not specifically say that one's neighbour is *anyone* in need, it is undoubtedly the neighbour in general - not simply Christ and his imitators - and the practical challenge of serving him which is in view: 'that you may show that you are indeed loving your neighbour as yourself, work devotedly according to your power in relieving his necessity, whether bodily or spiritual.'[86] The victim on the road is seen as a synecdoche for all those that we should regard as 'neighbours', and by the same token the Samaritan is a synecdoche for the ideal Christian.

Coming to Bonaventure's commentary on the parable, one sees immediately that this trend has gone much further. The 'spiritual' reading has been relegated to a definite second place subsequent to the 'literal' interpretation.[87] What for Ambrose had been central has become a supplementary option ('Other doctrine *can* be drawn out according to the spiritual sense . . .'[88]). The main emphasis is upon reading the story as a 'documentum' or 'teaching aid' to help the lawyer understand the precept he has been given.[89] The characters are by no means seen as allegorical figures, but are related to a wider context by much reference to Scripture and by allusion to Bonaventure's own world. They are 'personae' in a drama, and as such reflect certain fates and traits known or conceivable in reality;[90] we could describe them in Bonaventure's treatment as *metonymies*, single terms standing for related entities from a single sphere (here the sphere of the human) and bringing them into connection.[91] Thus the 'person in need through wretchedness' is related, through consideration of the good he has lost, to Job in his state of loneliness (Job 19:13-19), and, through consideration of the evil he has suffered, to proverbial awareness of the plight of the innocent at the hands of robbers (seen in Prov. 1:11ff.).[92] The 'person who despises out of harshness' (i.e. the two passers-by viewed as one 'character') is related to the OT via various uncomplimentary texts concerning priests and Levites, and via the command not to turn aside one's face from a poor man in Tobit 4:7.[93] The 'person who comes to help out of mercy' is an example of obedience to OT precepts concerning the support of the weak and the relief of the poor from the need to beg. His love is *not* 'like a morning cloud, like the dew that goes early away' (Hos. 6:4).[94] Bonaventure summarizes the parable's teaching thus: 'the name of neighbour extends not only to kinsmen, but also to foreigners.'[95]

It should be noted that this climactic point of the exposition is reached *before* Bonaventure proffers, like a loyal afterthought, the 'spiritual' sense.[96] The 'point' of the parable, for him, derives not from a metaphorical or allegorical understanding but from a realistic reading of its characters as known types and moral examples, in the context of the gospel setting, the OT and his own time.[97]

Calvin goes one stage further. He not only relegates, but rejects the old allegorical treatment completely. The moral point is clear enough for him:

> Therefore the Lord declares all men to be neighbours, that the affinity itself may bring them closer together. For anyone to be a neighbour, then, it is enough that he be a man; it is not in our power to deny the common ties of nature . . . It turns out that our neighbour is the man most foreign to us, for God has bound all men together for mutual aid.[98]

But he sees a secondary aim in the parable too:

> It fits in with His purpose to include some criticism of the Jews and priests in particular, for although they boasted that they were the children of the same Father and separated by the privilege of adoption from other races to be the holy heritage of God, nevertheless they held each other in savage, vile contempt, as if there were nothing of importance between them. No doubt Christ is describing their cruel neglect of love, and they knew they were guilty.[99]

Thus the priest and Levite are treated (with gross overstatement) as synecdoches, representative 'parts' of their whole race, but this is subsidiary to the chief lesson of neighbourliness beyond the bounds of kinship - which depends on the Samaritan being a synecdoche for all disciples.

Calvin appreciates the realism of Jesus' language, using the image of the mirror to describe the parable's disclosure of ideal human nature:

> As in a mirror we can see the brotherhood of man which the scribes with their sophistry had tried to efface.[100]

His rejection of the traditional reading, as well as having a doctrinal impetus, is grounded in caution about treatment of the text:

[W]e should have more reverence for Scripture than to allow ourselves to transfigure its sense so freely. Anyone may see that these speculations have been cooked up by meddlers, quite divorced from the mind of Christ.[101]

The word 'transfigure' pinpoints what has always been the fundamental fear about allegorical parable readings, that their 'figures' are the creation of the hearer or reader and not substantiated either by the text itself or the intention of its author. But Calvin himself, while safeguarding (like his predecessors) the general moral thrust of the story, exemplifies a kind of tropical reading that is far from benign: that which sees the negative characters, baldly and stereotypically, as representative of a whole race.

The Prodigal Son

Unlike the interpretations of The Good Samaritan, in which a historical progression can be traced from readings dominated by the sense of the story as a metaphor of salvation to an outright rejection of this approach in Calvin, we find in the treatments of The Prodigal Son a consistently metaphorical tendency differing from one interpreter to the other only in the extent and details of the meaning thus drawn out. The basic identification of the father with God was irresistible even to Calvin.

The delight of pre-Reformation interpreters in the fullness of significance they found in this parable was exuberant. Colourful touches inevitably bring a smile to a modern reader's lips. The pigs of Luke 15:15f. are brought into connection with those of Matthew 8:32 and seen either as demons,[102] or people into whom the devil enters to their destruction.[103] Ambrose contrasts the goat which the jealous elder brother complains of never having had (15:29) with the lamb of God desired by the innocent for their pardon,[104] and adds for good measure a comment about the goat's bad smell.[105] But the fanciful (to us) nature of such interpretations should not be allowed to blind us to the attunement of these commentators to a world of rich signification, to the poetic quality of the text, and to profound and suggestive correspondences between the parable and the contours of salvation.

For example, there is some sensitive playing upon the imagery of departure and return so central to the parable. Ambrose sees the youth as going away from the church, from himself, and from Christ.[106] It is then appropriate that he should 'come to himself'; and this moment of self-knowledge and his physical return to his father are read as figures of the same reality:

> Well does he return to himself, who departed from himself. For indeed the one who returns to the Lord returns to himself and the one who departs from Christ disowns himself.[107]

Bede also sees the son's departure in inward terms, substituting the idea of the 'mind / soul' ('animus') for that of the 'self' (the reflexive pronoun 'se') to give a perhaps less striking but more psychologically sophisticated picture:

> He journeyed far by changing not place, but mind. For indeed the more anyone offends in perverse action, the further he recedes from the grace of God.[108]

Bonaventure is characteristically more expansive, reading the distance travelled as that between goodness and iniquity, light and darkness, eternity and nothingness.[109]

Calvin's discussion is of interest because though his reading is unashamedly tropical, he is sensitive to the dangers of too detailed an allegorical understanding. He does not hesitate to see God in the father, or the penitent sinner '[u]nder the person of a prodigal young man'.[110] But having suggested that the younger son might more precisely represent one blessed with great riches, yet desiring freedom from God, he withdraws from this with the caveat that

> this allusion may be too subtle, and therefore I will be content with the literal sense - not that I do not think that under such a figure there is reproved the madness of those who imagine that they will live happily if they have something of their own and are rich apart from their heavenly Father, but because I now keep within the proper limits of an interpreter.[111]

The 'literal sense' that Calvin says he is content with must be the *tropical* sense of the son as representing (by synecdoche) any sinner who repents. He calls it 'literal' because the *sensus literalis* had become equated with the author's intentional meaning. But it is intriguing that it is the meaning which adheres more precisely to the son as described in the story - that he represents not merely any sinner, but particularly a person with possessions who wants his freedom - of which Calvin is cautious, as perhaps too 'subtle' an 'allusion'. There is a tussle here between two instincts: that the meaning of Jesus 'ought' to be as universally-embracing as possible (an instinct which came to fullest expression in Jülicher), and that his parables do contain individual elements which have a more specific suggestiveness. The more general reference to 'all sinners who become disgusted at their own madness and return to the grace of God' is not, in our sense, 'literal', nor - very likely - 'intentional' in the sense that that is how Jesus would have thought of it; it is a later doctrinal reading of the younger son as a synecdoche for the great 'whole' of fallen humankind. Conversely, the more specific allusion to 'anyone who is blessed by God with an abundance of possessions . . .', far from being unintended as Calvin implies, may well have been designed deliberately to resonate with the social realities of Jesus' context.[112] Perhaps we see here Calvin desiring to withdraw from too much allegory, but withdrawing instead from too specific an application. If so he would be a herald of more recent developments.[113]

Of special importance in the interpretation of this parable is the construction put upon the two sons and their relationship to the father. It has always seemed a tempting proposition to Christian readers to see them as synecdochic figures representing in some way Gentiles and Jews. It is noteworthy that our four interpreters, though playing with the idea, generally eschew stereotyping them in this way. They offer sensitive meditations on the suggestiveness of the parable without attempting to tie it down to a single 'meaning'.

For Ambrose, the younger son's separation from the father is a moral one;[114] his race is not an issue. He is contrasted with the Christian as he is now. The prodigal became an exile from his homeland: we, says Ambrose in an allusion to Ephesians 2:19, are not foreigners and aliens.[115] But this is to be no cause for complacency. The younger brother reminds 'us' of our own past.[116] On Luke 15:24 ('this my son was dead . . .') Ambrose offers several options for interpreting the son: as the live Christian, in contrast with the dead 'peoples' (*gentes,* here understood, like ἔθνη sometimes in the NT,[117] as 'non-Christians', rather than 'non-Jews' or 'nations' in general); as humanity, dead in Adam, alive in Christ; as the Gentiles, who 'were not' but now 'are', who were chosen by God 'that he might destroy the people of the Jews';[118] or as *anybody* doing penance.[119] The plurality of options offered is a mark of humility in the commentator and mollifies the unfortunate anti-Jewish streak.[120]

In discussing the elder brother, Ambrose likens his complaining to that of the Jews when Christ feasted with the 'peoples' - a tropical equation of the 'sinners' of Luke 15:1 with Gentiles.[121] Crucially, he stresses that the father wanted to 'save' this son too.[122] 'You were always with me' is read as a reference to the Jew having the law, or more generally to any just man who participates spiritually in this possession.[123] But he must stop his envy.[124] 'And all that I have is yours' is taken to point either to the Jew possessing the sacraments of the OT, or the baptized person possessing those of the New.[125] Thus the harshness of the identification of the elder brother with the Jewish race is softened by mention of the father's continuing favour towards him, and by the suggestion that a Christian also should heed the warning that he represents; the moral challenge of the parable thus also emerges.[126]

Bede says that 'the elder son signifies those who have remained in the worship of the one God, the younger those who have deserted God to the extent of worshipping idols'.[127] Although the classic distinction between the Israelites as worshippers of the Lord and the Gentiles as idolaters is clearly present, the fact that the division is delineated in terms of actual worshipping behaviour immediately lifts the reading on to a moral rather than a racial plane, and awakens many-toned resonances in the parable. For (as Jesus and his hearers, Luke and his readers, and Bede and *his* readers would all have been aware) Israel had had its own share of idolaters; sensitive listeners to speaker, Evangelist and commentator will thus be warned at the outset against too comfortable an identification of Israel with the son who remained with the father. Jews may be found under the guise of the runaway, too. But this opening move of Bede has a wider suggestiveness. If the possibility is kept open that Israel herself can sometimes be idolatrous, then the prodigal's action indicates that, nevertheless, penitence is open to Israel as well as to the typically-idolatrous Gentiles. Conversely, perhaps a Gentile can be a true Godfearer: but in that case he or she also will have to heed the warning to faithful Jews contained in the portrait of the elder brother. Bede's statement implies the content of that warning: shunning idolatry is not enough. In the parable, one who (on this reading) has remained in faithful monotheistic observance is nonetheless found wanting.

In his comments on Luke 15:25ff., Bede identifies the elder son (more narrowly than in his opening statement) with Israel, and takes his position in the field as indicating Israel's ambiguous stance towards God.[128] This son's (Israel's) problem is diagnosed as a fixation upon external things to the detriment of keeping the heart of the law. But the note on which the exposition, like the parable itself, ends, is the loving appeal of the father. In an allusion to Romans 11:25f., Bede sees the father's coming-out as pointing to the time when, once the 'fullness of the Gentiles' have come in, all Israel will be saved.[129] In the final sentence Bede rediscovers the breadth implied in his opening gambit - that one need not limit the reference of the sons to two peoples (viz. Jews and Gentiles) - asserting that what matters is the challenge to adopt a certain attitude.[130]

Bonaventure moves away still further from a rigid identification of the two sons with the Jews and Gentiles. He distances himself from the standard medieval commentary, the *Glossa Ordinaria*:

> By the two sons we understand the entirety of the human race, not only as referring to Gentiles and Jews as the Gloss expounds them, but also and generally to the innocent and the penitent, as must be understood from the very application of the parable.[131]

This reading of the parable as the story of *humanity* is pursued throughout Bonaventure's discussion. He finds in it, we might say, an encapsulation of the biblical narrative from Adam onwards, not just from Abraham. The younger son illustrates not Gentile idolatry but general human presumption.[132] His youth is accorded a significance that is moral rather than metaphorical: 'that man is called younger, who is vainer, and more intent on the good things of the senses.'[133] The elder brother is seen as archetypically more mature in behaviour, more conforming and obedient towards the father.[134] His action in the story reflects that of any righteous man presuming upon his own merits and thus not accepting the justice of God.[135] The celebration from which he excludes himself is the joyful concord of the church.[136] In particular, 'he . . . who does not receive the overflowing mercy of God, but the sufficiency of his own justice, cannot come in to the love of [i.e. that belongs to] the church's unity.'[137] It is interesting that at this point Bonaventure brings in a reference to the Jews, but they serve as a particular example of how the general truth seen in the elder brother may be applied, rather than the basic reference which might then be widened.[138] He then returns to the plane of universality:

> The one who presumes upon justice, and is indignant at mercy held out to a brother, does not walk according to justice, but according to injustice.[139]

Consistent with this reading, the father's going out to the older son is interpreted not as God's ultimate salvation of the Jews, but his manifestation in the flesh - for all people.[140] Like his predecessors, Bonaventure reads the parable as teaching of a God who is gracious to all humankind. The father's approach to the elder son is seen as the perfect exemplar of Proverbs 15:1: a soft answer turns away wrath.[141]

I have discussed above[142] Calvin's comments on the younger brother, as illustrating a paradox in his sensitivities about metaphorical-allegorical interpretation. It remains to note what he writes about the elder:

Those who think that by 'first-born son' is meant a type of the Jewish people, although there is some reason in it, do not seem to me to be attending sufficiently to the context as a whole. For what gave rise to this parable was the grumbling of the scribes, who could not bear Christ's humanity towards the wretched and men of doubtful lives. He therefore compares the scribes, swollen with their arrogance, to thrifty and canny men who by their honest and careful life have always taken good care of the household.[143]

The grounds of Calvin's caution here are interesting. He sees the importance of context to the interpretation of the parable. When read in the light of 15:1f., 15:11-32 naturally suggests to a reader a correspondence between the elder brother and those who grumbled at Jesus' consorting with 'sinners'. For Calvin it is not a question of *whether,* in some sense, the elder brother stands for some person or group in the real world, but of who that person or group is. Here again Calvin's more advanced historical sensibility, as compared to his precursors, is evident. His reference to the gospel context implies a concern also about the intention of Jesus, and it is assumed that it would be more natural to read Jesus as referring in the parable to specific interlocutors than to see an allusion to the entire Jewish race. But this historical sense blends easily, indeed imperceptibly, into the awareness that there is nevertheless a far broader application of this figure of the elder brother. He is not only the Scribes and Pharisees, but 'we':

The sum of it therefore is: if we want to be reckoned the children of God, we must in a brotherly way forgive our brethren their faults which He pardons in a fatherly way.[144]

This survey of the older commentators' interpretations of the two brothers shows that all escape the pitfalls of crude stereotyping which is a danger inherent in rigidly allegorical reading (whether it be metaphorical, metonymic or synecdochic). There is a gradual movement away from the view of the brothers as types of Jew and Gentile, though already in Ambrose a possible more universal significance is acknowledged. Most importantly, none evade, indeed all emphasise, the challenge to *Christian* people which the parable represents. 'Allegorical' reading is not used merely in the cause of self-justification or the pillorying of enemies. It serves the end of bringing out the parable's universal yet pointed moral thrust.

The Shrewd Steward

Since Ambrose's comments on The Shrewd Steward are confined to a few lines, we begin our sketch of early approaches to this parable with Bede, who follows Augustine's *Quaestiones euangeliorum* quite extensively. For Bede the parable's moral purport is clear. He does not read it as a repository of abstrusely-expressed Christian doctrine. In it the Saviour 'shows that those who have shared their earthly goods and given to the poor are fit to be received by them into the eternal tabernacles'.[145] The problem for interpreters of the parable is that if this truly summarizes its message (in accordance with the conclusion given it in Lk. 16:9) we have to reckon with the fact that though the steward is put forward as an example, his actual behaviour does not seem wholly exemplary. Commentators have therefore often been cautious to stress that he is not to be imitated *in everything*. So Bede, citing Augustine, and assuming an identification of the master with God, says that God is not to be defrauded;[146] and he hedges the praise of the steward in v. 8 around with the qualification that those who do *good* works will be praised all the more.[147] The argument of the parable The Judge and the Widow is adduced in support of such a 'how much more' interpretation.[148]

A moral or exemplary reading of a parable does, however, as we have already seen, depend upon the drawing of certain figurative correspondences. The most basic is that between the hearer / reader and the character(s) to be imitated, but seeing that correspondence naturally leads to seeing others. So there is in Augustine's and Bede's reading a simple, unstressed assumption that the master stands for God. There is also speculation about who more precisely the remitter of debts and the debtors themselves might stand for, and what the act of remission and its consequences might mean. In linking ch. 16 with the theme of penitence in ch. 15, Bede suggests that the monastic calling (which involved giving away one's worldly goods) is an appropriate expression of the penitent's obedience to Jesus' words.[149] Augustine had not wanted to read the absolved debtors too crudely as 'debtors of God'. Rather, they were to be seen as the holy and just who have been ministered to in their earthly necessities.[150] After quoting this passage Bede goes on to indicate that he understands the removal of the man's stewardship as the solemn watershed of death, and offers this interpretation of his reluctance to dig:

To be sure, once the stewardship is taken away we have no strength to dig; because once this life is finished, in which we are permitted to be so active, we are by no means permitted any further to seek out the reward of good conduct with the mattock of devoted compassion.[151]

The implication is that when death is imminent, and there is no time left for good works, to remit others' debts is all one can do to secure one's future.[152]

Finally, having quoted Augustine's contrast between the steward's generous remissions and the scribes' and Pharisees' tithing, and his comparison of the steward with the reformed and open-handed Zacchaeus,[153] Bede offers respectfully a simpler reading of the steward's action and its intended consequence:

> Unless, perchance, anyone should think that it is simply to be accepted [sc. from Lk. 16:5ff.] that everyone who alleviates the lack of any poor person among the saints, whether to the extent of a half or at least of a fifth part - as much as twenty or fifty percent - is fit to be presented with a sure reward of his mercy.[154]

This is 'simple' by comparison with Augustine's interpretation because the reference is made broader: no allusion is found to the scribes and Pharisees and their comparative meanness. The steward simply stands for any generous person. However, it is interesting to note the precision of Bede's application. He does not read the remission of debts as a metaphor for the forgiveness of sins, or any other 'spiritual' reality. The steward's action is seen as an example on a literal, practical, financial level. Bede is not even content with discerning that example in general terms; he spells out in two different ways the proportion of a person's need that Jesus encourages us to alleviate. If in our own day we react against such a reading, we should note carefully why we do so. Is it not that Bede is being too *literal* for our liking - taking the text too much at its plain, face value - rather than that he is being too *allegorical,* wantonly imposing mystification where there is none (the usual allegation against the Fathers)? The respect in which he *could* be accused of importing some alien signification into the text is the assumption that it is the poor *of the saints* to whom we are here commanded to be generous; but there the question is not literal vs. figurative, but how broad the figurative interpretation of the debtors should be. Is the 'whole' of which they are a part the entirety of the poor, or the entirety of the poor saints?

Bede's interpretation is instructive. It is anchored in the fact that this is a story about what someone does with money. In its application to his own monastic situation Bede implies that the central characters of steward and debtors, and the relationship between them, may be seen from two angles. On the one hand, the steward figures the penitent who - anxious to express his penitence in tangible means - gives to the poor, perhaps to the extent of giving up all and joining a monastic order. These recipients of his generosity are not any poor, but the deserving - good Christian folk. On the other hand, the one who has given up all becomes *himself* poor and in need; and it is hard not to see in the reference to the 'holy and just' an allusion to the impoverished monks themselves, not only to the recipients of their largesse when they entered orders. The steward is then interpreted as anyone who wins great hope of reward by alleviating that particular, monastic poverty.

Bonaventure's treatment is typically more wide-ranging and systematic. His didactic concern is shown in the structuring of his commentary on the parable as a seven-point sermon. In a splendid sequence of gerundives (demonstrating, incidentally, the particular suitability of Latin for scholastic purposes) he shows how the parable offers us in turn things to be thought over, repelled, dreaded, tolerated, provided for, imitated, and commanded.[155] (One misses from Bonaventure's 'sermon' - unlike, for instance, Ambrose's reading of The Good Samaritan - a sense of the logic of the story *as a whole*.) Sensitive to the problems The Shrewd Steward presents, Bonaventure asserts that it is to be understood in part as 'example', in part as 'parable':

> [F]or if it had not been expressed as an example, it would not be added at the end of the parable that the master praised the steward of iniquity, because he had done foolishly . . . but again if it had not been spoken in parabolic fashion, a deed of such deception and so much to be detested should by no means have been put forward by the master as an example.[156]

He summarizes the lesson of the steward thus:

> Thus that steward is to be deprecated, because he committed fraud: for which reason he is called a steward of iniquity, and he is to be praised, because he found for himself a remedy against danger.[157]

The point behind the distinction between the 'exemplary' and 'parabolic' senses must be this: what can be taken *prima facie* in accordance with Christian teaching should be taken thus: the steward is commended, and therefore we should inquire in what *sense* he is exemplary. What, on the other hand, seems contrary to such teaching if taken 'literally' should be understood 'parabolically'. Parable is the face-saving category into which the literally unacceptable should fall.[158]

We note three things here. First, this is a moral or doctrinal unacceptability, not a linguistic one: it would make perfectly good *sense* to read the parable as exhorting us to follow the steward in his shadiness as well as his shrewdness. Second, there is in consequence a tacit assumption about the stance of the author here - not probably so much that of Jesus, as that of the Evangelist as the one who has penned divine words. Something unworthy - and contradictory, when brought alongside other passages of Scripture - is not to be predicated of him.[159] But third, Bonaventure might just as well have dispensed with the language of 'parable' altogether, and simply spoken of the puzzling steward in exemplary terms: that he is in one sense a good example, in another a bad. 'Parabolic' speech, at any rate, is seen here not as the cloak of great mysteries but rather as that terseness of style which enables different messages to be sent out from a single short text.

A moral intention is brought out clearly by Bonaventure. The steward stands for anyone who has worldly power or wealth to dispense. Such a one is thereby reminded that he holds it in stewardship rather than possession.[160] The steward's wasting of his master's goods is taken as a negative example. Bonaventure's instinctive realism imagines what this squandering would have meant in practice: that the poor were somehow being deprived. Thus the accusers are in the position of the poor of James 5:4 whose cry ascends to the Lord.[161] He says that Luke 16:2 ought to resonate with the conscience of any person: '[f]or this voice ought to ring in the ear of anyone at all, because without a doubt divine justice will exact a reckoning.'[162] The figurative net, so to speak, is here being cast as wide as possible. The steward's plan, says Bonaventure, shows a right instinct - that his stewardship will be properly discharged 'by the acquiring of friends rather than by the amassing of riches'.[163] What modern readers tend to see as a cynical ploy, Bonaventure (like Lk. 16:9) takes as exemplary, for the steward was acting out of love in order to avoid danger (in the spirit of Rev. 2:5, where the church at Ephesus is commanded to repent of its lack of love, lest its lampstand be removed). His action is contrasted not with some ideal of selflessness, but with the materialism which puts money above people. Bonaventure remembers that the steward has been implicitly characterized as one who was feathering his own nest at the expense of the poor, and it thus appears as a genuine act of contrition that at this point he is thinking about turning those same poor into friends, rather than trying to exploit them further. Despite some dabbling in the typological significance of the numbers of Luke 16:6f., it is the literal, exemplary force of the steward's 'munificence and mercy' which is emphasised.[164]

Calvin understands the parable similarly:

> The sum of this parable is that we must treat our neighbours humanely and kindly, so that when we come before God's judgement seat, we may receive the fruit of our liberality.[165]

Morally his comments are even sharper than those of Bede and Bonaventure, for he broadens the application, sweeping away the restriction of the objects of charity to the 'saints'.[166] The old interpretation was that the departed righteous welcomed those who had been generous to them, or those like them, into the heavenly mansions, and this was linked to the view that the dead might help the living by their prayers; but:

> in this way whatever was bestowed on the unworthy would be lost. But man's depravity does not prevent God from recording in His account book whatever we give to the poor . . . so that our benefits, even if made to the ungrateful, will be accounted (*respondeat*) to us before God.[167]

On the difficulty the parable presents, Calvin's main direction of argument is against over-attention to details:

> Hence we perceive that those who investigate minutely every single part of a parable are poor theologians. For Christ does not here bid us to redeem by gifts the frauds, extortions, squandering and other faults of bad administration; but since God has appointed us stewards of all the good things He bestows on us, a method is prescribed which one day, when the time of rendering account shall come, will lighten us from the extremest strictness.[168]

Calvin's own comments themselves adhere very closely, however, to several details of the story: the calling of the steward, the time of rendering account, the remission of debts as a means of mollifying strict justice.[169] The presence of aesthetic, intuitive judgements about the significance of different elements is thus exposed.

The most striking thing is Calvin's readiness to acknowledge that Jesus is speaking about something that human beings can do to alleviate the rigours of God's judgement. This is remarkable from the pen of this great Reformation exponent of humanity's moral bankruptcy and need to depend upon the grace of God alone.[170] It is true that he will not countenance interpreting the steward's actions as a way of freeing oneself from guilt. But they do betoken a method which 'will lighten us from the extremest strictness'; 'our humanity to our brethren may stir up God's mercy to us'.[171] In response to the possible misunderstanding that 'eternal life is a recompense for our merits', Calvin replies

> that the context makes it clear that this is spoken in a human sort of way. Just as a flourishing and rich man who makes friends during his prosperity will have them to help him when misfortune strikes, so our

kindness will be like a timely refuge in that the Lord acknowledges as bestowed on Himself whatever we give liberally to our neighbour.[172]

The 'human sort of way' in which the story is told - Calvin's equivalent of Bonaventure's awareness of its 'parabolic sense' - means that it is not a serious challenge to Calvin's doctrine, but he will not back down on its moral force. Our kindness is not merely a response to God's grace, but a 'timely refuge'. Like his patristic and medieval forbears, Calvin finds here not rarefied mysteries, but practical exhortation.

The Rich Man and Lazarus

Given our discussion of the three preceding parables, it will be no surprise that premodern interpreters were all concerned that the *practical* message of The Rich Man and Lazarus concerning poverty and wealth should be communicated.

Ambrose, after some reflection on the five brothers of Luke 16:28 as the five senses of the body,[173] succinctly captures the exhortatory force of the parable as a whole:

> He placed Lazarus in the bosom of Abraham, as if in a certain enclosure of quiet and recess of holiness, lest enticed by the pleasure of present things we should remain in vices, or overcome with the weariness of labours we should flee from hardships.[174]

He reads it as a moral tale to arouse the sinful and encourage the fainthearted. The question then naturally arises: whom may one see figured in the person of Lazarus - that is, who is the object of encouragement? Ambrose offers a choice. He can be one who is 'poor in the world, but rich towards God'; or the 'apostolic pauper in word, who is rich in faith'; or the contemporary refuter of heresies, who is likewise an 'apostolic person who holds the true faith, and does not require ornaments of words'.[175] At the end of his exposition he writes of the parable as an 'incentive for showing mercy' ('incentiuum misericordiae') - towards the poor in general, whereas Luke 16:1-9 seemed to envisage specifically the saints as the object of compassion.[176] Lazarus's figurative reference, then, is not to be tightly limited; but to be avoided is the crudity which would see in the parable a sanctifying of all poverty or a vilifying of all wealth:

> for neither is all poverty holy nor riches blameworthy, but as extravagance brings riches into disrepute, so holiness is a recommendation for poverty.[177]

Here Ambrose shows sensitivity to the story's precise figurative tone. The rich man and poor man do not stand in a wooden way for whole classes of people ('the rich go to hell and the poor to heaven'), but simply suggest a warning and an encouragement respectively to members of those classes about the possible danger of riches and the possible compensation of poverty. They are synecdoches, but not stereotypes.

It is only *after* this laying of the basic moral groundwork of the parable that Ambrose launches into a baroque and bewildering passage[178] playing with the meaning of the crumbs, the dogs, the sores, and alluding rather obscurely to various passages of Scripture, such as the story of the Canaanite woman in Matthew 15:22-28 (linked to the crumbs and dogs of Lk. 16:21), and the gaoler washing Paul's wounds in Acts 16:33 (linked to the washing of Lazarus' sores by the dogs in the same verse). Despite its arcane tone, this passage nevertheless centres upon the mystery of Christ and the self-understanding of the early church, the 'newness that allegory grasps as it seeks to interpret the Scriptures'.[179] The story is heard resonating with divine meaning.

Bede borrows almost his entire interpretation from Gregory's *Homeliae in euangelia*. This reading is clearly divided into two parts, a 'literal' (though that word is not used) and an 'allegorical' (it is Bede who explicitly marks the division, adding the words 'uero iuxta allegoriam'[180]). In the first part the parable's moral force is brought home. Gregory sees in it an instance of the greater strictness of the NT's precepts as compared with those of the OT:

> There [sc. in the O.T.] a thing unjustly taken away brings the punishment of fourfold restitution, but here this rich man is reproved not for having taken away another's goods but for not having given his own, and it is not said because he oppressed someone but because he exalted himself in the things which he had received.[181]

The story's contours are highlighted in this comment on the sharp reversal it pictures: 'The one who did not wish to give even the smallest amount from his table, when placed in hell reached the point of asking for the smallest amounts.'[182]

Gregory seems anxious to explain in realistic, credible terms certain points which might present difficulties for a 'literal' reading. This contrasts with what we find in a later period, for instance in interpretations of The Shrewd Steward by Bonaventure and Calvin, where difficulties in the story were precisely what pointed the reader away from too realistic a reading to a 'parabolic' understanding (Bonaventure) or a commonsense recognition of the story's 'humanness' (Calvin). For instance, Gregory finds it necessary to explain that the rich man's reception of 'good things' in this life showed that there had been *some* (moral) good in him, and conversely that Lazarus' reception of 'bad things' showed that there had been *some* (moral) bad in him.[183] Divine justice, for Gregory, clearly did not allow a *total* disparity between one's behaviour and one's lot on earth.

The final section, in which Gregory treats the parable 'iuxta allegoriam', draws a correspondence between the rich man and the Jews, Lazarus and the Gentiles.[184] A connection is also made between the licking dogs and preachers administering the curative Word, a traditional point.[185] But of chief interest to us in this allegorical section[186] is its clarity of style. The 'meanings' are set out straightforwardly and sequentially. This contrasts with the suggestive, much more complex, and meditative ethos of Ambrose's commentary where 'moral' and 'spiritual', 'literal' and 'allegorical' are intertwined. The 'allegorical' readings, as they became more fixed in tradition, seem to have lost this vigorous exuberance. The tropical meanings perceived and passed on so vividly by earlier interpreters have become, if not dead, at least established metaphors, synecdoches and so on. Arguably it was that process of ossification which made this tradition appear so unpalatable to Jülicher and his successors.[187] It seems that as commentators became increasingly aware of the possible dangers and eccentricities of allegorical readings, those readings tended to be given in more summary form, as here in Gregory and Bede (out of faithfulness to tradition), to supplement a more realistic one; and summaries can sound like mechanical listings.[188]

Bonaventure's exposition of The Rich Man and Lazarus need not detain us; in it, characteristically, the moral takes precedence over the allegorical. The description of the rich man first in his luxury and then in his torment makes it, he says, more an example than a parable.[189]

The parable is discussed by Calvin with real depth of literary insight. As painters in the early Renaissance discovered the art of perspective, so it seems that commentators of the Reformation had won a new feel for the contours of a text. Calvin is in continuity with the tradition in emphasising the moral thrust of the story. He is concerned with 'the substance of what is taught':

> For Christ interrelated these two things - that the rich man was given up to drunkenness and display, an insatiable whirlpool devouring heaps of food, and yet untouched by Lazarus' poverty and wretchedness but knowingly and willingly letting him waste away of hunger, cold and stinking ulcers.[190]

Again like his predecessors, he is alert to the ironies in the story. The height of the rich man's ungodliness, he says, was 'that he did not learn mercy from the dogs . . . He would not give even a crumb to this starving man; but the dogs lent him their tongues to heal him.'[191] Calvin is as careful as Ambrose to stress that the story is neither a bald condemnation of the rich nor a simple commendation of the poor. He quotes Augustine: 'the pauper Lazarus is carried into the bosom of wealthy Abraham to teach us that the gate of the Kingdom of heaven is shut against no rich man but lies open for all in common who either have used their riches well or have been patient in poverty.'[192] The true message of the story, he says, should be clear, and again he uses the image of the mirror: 'the rich man is like a bright mirror in which we can see that temporal felicity is not to be sought for if it ends in eternal destruction.'[193]

It is in Calvin's sensitivity about too much concentration on detail that the advance marked by his comments is chiefly seen. He is anxious to guard against misunderstandings that might arise from Jesus' language about an after-life.

Significantly, he identifies at least four different figures of speech as used here by Jesus. He wants to emphasise that it was the *soul* of Lazarus which was carried into Abraham's bosom (since according to Christian teaching the resurrection of the body must await the last day), and so he says that 'Lazarus was carried' is a 'synecdoche' in which 'the name of the whole man' is given to his soul, 'his more excellent part'.[194] He finds in 'Abraham's bosom' a double *metaphor*. 'It is a metaphor taken from children returning, as it were, to the bosom of their father when they meet at home in the evening after their day's work.'[195] But he especially wants to emphasise that the *Christian* can picture this peaceful scene in a sharper, more up-to-date way; and so, in a lovely glimpse into the forward-looking, provisional nature of even Jesus' language, he adds this:

> So far as the name goes, that quiet haven which opens for believers after the voyage of this present life can be called either Abraham's or Christ's bosom. But because we have gone higher than did the fathers under the law, the distinction becomes clearer if we say that Christ's members are gathered to their Head. And so the metaphor of Abraham's bosom comes to an end, as if the brightness of the risen sun obscured all the stars.[196]

Further, sensing the need to remain reticent about the details of the after-life, he comments on Luke 16:23f.:

> Although Christ is telling a story, yet He describes spiritual things under figures which He knew were on the level of our understanding. For souls have not been endowed with fingers and eyes, nor are they tormented with thirst, nor do they hold conversation with one another in the way

here described of Abraham and the glutton. The Lord is painting a picture
which represents the condition of the future life in a way that we can
understand.[197]

The reader is not to be confused about Abraham's addressing of the rich
man as 'Son' (v. 25). This word 'seems to have been used *ironically*, so that
the sharp reproof might pierce the rich man to the heart, for in his life-time
he had falsely boasted of being one of the sons of Abraham.'[198] Finally,
when the rich man responds to Abraham in v. 30 that one returning from
the dead would secure his brothers' repentance, Calvin calls it 'a
prosopopoeia (personification) . . . in which is uttered rather the thought of
the living than the anxiety of the dead'.[199] In other words, the deceased rich
man is made to stand for *living* humanity's desire for a 'sign'. This is a
recognition that the sentiments of a dead person may only be imagined by a
projection of familiar sentiments from this life, but also that the true focus
of the parable is on this life rather than the next. It shows Calvin's
imaginative attunement to the human Jesus, who is for him a
communicator, not of arcane mysteries, but of profound truth, in a simple
way that people can understand. The fact that these tropes are named is
itself significant; the parable is now being treated self-consciously as a
literary form, deriving from a purposeful human author, and not only as a
part of the divine tapestry of Scripture.

Thus for Calvin the story gives us a warning example, but it is also
parabolic in the sense that it cloaks in accessible language truth which is
beyond the powers of human comprehension or expression. In a tradition
stretching at least as far back as Origen, he seeks to protect untrained minds
against crude literalism by sensitizing them to figurative language. From a
modern perspective, we might well deem him to have not gone far enough.
In fact he stands roughly midway between his predecessors and his more
recent successors. Bonaventure had commented that Christian teachers used
the parable as evidence of the status of the damned.[200] Calvin goes to some
lengths to hedge around its *evidential* nature with qualifications. In the
twentieth century Jeremias would write plainly that here 'Jesus does not
intend to give teaching about the after-life':[201] that is, Jesus was simply
using an accepted mythological picture. The movement from premodern to
modern conceptions of the parables' language is often described as a
movement from the metaphorical language of allegory to the literal
language of simile. This example illustrates that it is sometimes the other
way round: the picture of Hades was taken much more literally in medieval
times than in the twentieth century. The key progression, rather, is in the
increasing attunement to the original working of the story in the encounter
between Jesus and his hearers.

We may summarize Calvin's stance here by citing three throwaway lines - two about story, one about authorship. On account of the fact that 'Lazarus' has a name, Calvin believes that Jesus

> is telling a true story. Nevertheless, this is not very important, so long as readers hold the substance of what is taught.[202]

He holds together here an awareness of the realism of the story (or at least of its opening earthly scene) and an instinctive sense that it is *teaching* something beyond itself. Then he seems, in a passage already quoted, to *contrast* story and figurative speech:

> Although Christ is telling a story, yet He describes spiritual things under figures which He knew were on the level of our understanding.[203]

The 'although . . . yet' signals the tension that later debates were to bring to full expression, between story as realistic description and story as meaningful mode of teaching. Modern writers have driven a wedge between the two;[204] Calvin held them together. Perhaps this was precisely because although he did not depart from inherited belief in the divine authorship and therefore divine meaning of Scripture, he also gave due weight to Christ the human teller of the parable, as this interesting juxtaposition, where he comments on the dogs' attentiveness to Lazarus, demonstrates:

> There is no doubt that those dogs were directed by the secret counsel of God to condemn [the rich man] by their example. Christ brings them here as if to bear witness and reprove the man's accursed hardness.[205]

Here parable and world are interwoven. The human author of the parable introduces the dogs, but they are also directed by divine sovereignty. The parable (in its first part, at any rate) is read as a story reflecting the real world, but also a story pregnant with didactic power, for the Author of both story and world is seen as one.

The Judge and the Widow

The essential features of the parable interpretations of this long period have now been delineated, and our treatment of the commentators' readings of the final two short parables may be briefer. The Lukan introduction to The Judge and the Widow, designating it a lesson in prayer (Lk. 18:1), is assumed to provide the key to the parable. Its central thrust is regarded as exhortatory, not allegorical. Bede and Bonaventure (and the tradition generally, as the latter cites it) see a reference to the canonical hours of prayer in the 'always' of v. 1, though also to the idea that one's whole life can be regarded as prayer.[206]

Bede and Bonaventure make it clear that it is to be taken as a parable of dissimilarity: God is not at all like the reluctant judge.[207] This foreshadows later interpretations of the parable as ironic in tone.[208] Bonaventure points out that Jesus 'is not comparing a person to a person, but a thing to a thing'[209] - and thus adumbrates an emphasis of Jülicher.[210] Even these 'things', however, appear in a relationship of contrast; on v. 7a, Bonaventure says that 'if persistence in prayer softened the hardest judge and inclined the most unjust to do justice, how much the more surely will it incline [the ear of] the holy and just God.'[211] Calvin agrees with the tenor of the 'how much more' reading, though he wants also to press the *likeness* between the widow's petitioning and the Christian's praying in a literal way:

> He uses a parable which is difficult at first sight, but is especially apt for His purpose in teaching them to wait importunately on God the Father until at last they wring from Him what it seemed He was not willing to give. Not that God is overcome by our prayers and at last unwillingly moved to mercy, but because the actual event does not at once bear witness to the fact that he is favourable to our wishes.[212]

Here again, then, throughout the period, is serious wrestling with the figurative working of the parable, the attempt to do justice to its rhetorical technique, within the assumed framework of a divine meaning.

The Pharisee and the Customs Officer

Though the early commentators tend to stereotype the Jews as being like the Pharisee in Luke 18:9-14, there is another aspect to their perception. Bede, for instance, says that 'the Pharisee as a type . . . is the people of the Jews who extol their merits, whereas the publican is the Gentile who, positioned far from God, confesses his sins.'[213] But in the next paragraph he sees v.14 as pertinent to any proud or humble person, and specifically warns that 'we' should be humbled.[214] For him this is not simply a parable for the 'others'. Bonaventure even refers to Romans 11:18ff. to warn that though the proud Jewish people are reproved in the parable, the Gentiles should not fall into the same trap of pride.[215]

Calvin makes no reference to the tradition of seeing the Pharisee as a type of the Jews; perhaps this character's similarity to 'papist monks' who 'proclaim works of supererogation, as if they could easily fulfil God's

Law'[216] had made too strong an impression for him to think of mentioning the earlier identification. It is of interest, though, that his description of the Pharisee is sophisticated and not crudely blackening:

> [H]is thanksgiving . . . is not at all a glorying in his own power, as if he had made himself righteous or merited anything by his own industry; rather he ascribes it to the grace of God that he is righteous . . . Therefore let us realize that although a man may ascribe the praise for good works to God, yet if he imagines that the righteousness of those works is the cause of his salvation, or trusts in it, he is condemned for perverted pride.[217]

Sometimes Calvin, like others before him, hangs a polemical point on what we would regard as the rather flimsy peg of parabolic language. But here is a case where a perceptive grasp of the character as Jesus draws him leads quite naturally to an elucidation of a doctrine. To those who might object that he is nevertheless being too literal-minded and too anachronistic with the parable, one must pose the alternative: is it better to leave the Pharisee as a cardboard cut-out, a villain the precise nature of whose villainy can remain largely irrelevant? As the commentators take seriously the synecdochic force of parable characters, so inevitably they run the risk of making stereotyped identifications, but the alternative may be to reduce the parables to blandness.

5. From Influence to Insight: The Voice of Jesus in the Premodern Commentators

We must now survey the terrain we have crossed in this chapter.

We have described the intention of the commentators of this period as the intention, above all, to discern and communicate the divine meaning of the parables. This is the all-encompassing framework of their thought - whether they are in 'literal' or 'allegorical' mode, or (to use my more precise terminology) whatever tropes describe their treatment of different elements of the parables. It is beyond the scope of this work to evaluate whether they were successful in discovering 'divine meaning' - even to begin to consider criteria by which such an ambitious enterprise might be assessed.

Has this, then, been an amiable but pointless excursus? If 'the voice of Jesus' was not the primary voice they were trying to hear, why should we pay them any attention? As I indicated in section 1 above, I believe it would be foolish to write off this period as telling us nothing of Jesus' voice. This is because we may hear in a text voices other than an author's own, voices from the stream of influence in which the author stands.

Although their focus is on divine meaning, the voice of the human parable-teller is not obscured altogether in these writers. They were clearly aware that the parables, so rich in suprahistorical significance, had been represented in the gospels as coming from the historical figure of Jesus. Sensitivity to historical context is especially evident in Calvin but is present as early as Ambrose's prologue. Despite the flights of fancy, a reasonably clear picture of Jesus the parabolist emerges.

In the synchronic dimension, this is a Jesus whose voice is sharp and practical. The tone implied is a moral, exhortatory one. There is a sense of direct applicability to humans and the choices they must make in this world: the neighbour is to be loved, the poor helped and so on. Of the 'four senses' traditionally assigned to Scripture, the moral one was called 'tropological'; the text was 'turned' or 'bent' to make it instructive about human behaviour.[218] The Fathers and medievals would readily have acknowledged that the *specific* application they found to situations of their own time did not belong to the 'original' sense. It is the more impressive that the moral *power* they found in these parables does not seem wrung forcibly out of them, but inherent in the texts themselves.

In the diachronic dimension, the voice of Jesus as it may be heard here is one in which the whole truth of God disclosed in Scripture has found expression. On one level, this means that the parables are loaded down with significance imported from all over the Bible - and to make Jesus the mouthpiece of so much truth from the OT or the Epistles naturally strikes us as implausible. But on another level, the parables are seen as pointedly illuminating the precise historical juncture at which Jesus stood, the inauguration of the new era in which Gentiles were included in the people of God, the moment when the Scriptures became the 'Old' Testament.[219] Sadly, this perspective sometimes entailed a malign anti-Jewish reading of the stories.[220]

What, then, of the influences which may have contributed to these insights, and which may help us to assess the extent of their validity? Synchronically, there was of course the influence of powerful intellectual currents in the various periods. Upon the earlier commentators there was the influence of the allegorical strategies of Philo in reading the OT and of Hellenistic writers in reading ancient classical authors.[221] Fearghus O. Fearghail, for example, remarks how Philo's legacy inspired Ambrose 'to plunder the "profound secrets" of the biblical text, that rich paradise where God walks, that sea full of profound senses and prophetic enigmas where every word is a potential gold-mine'.[222] The Neo-Platonic emphasis on the radical disjunction between God and creation[223] created an atmosphere in which early biblical interpreters such as Ambrose would be acutely aware of faith's need for the language of metaphor, and it was therefore natural to read the parables through this lens. Aristotelian scholasticism and Renaissance humanism played an equivalent role for the commentators of the late medieval and Reformation periods respectively, with their developing realism and literary sophistication. We are right when we read these commentaries to remember what they owe to these various currents.

And there were much more specific contemporary situations which influenced interpreters' thinking and became vehicles of insight. It was second nature to these commentators that the parables spoke directly to their own time; there was no modern split between 'exegesis' and 'application'. So we find Ambrose comparing the rich man of Luke 16:19-31 with the Arians 'who strive after an alliance with kingly power',[224] have made 'many gospels' and 'several philosophies',[225] and the poor man with the (true) church, with its 'sole gospel' and 'one God'.[226] It is clear that this is proposed not as 'the' intentional, or absolute, meaning of the parable, but as a contemporary application thought to be persuasive: 'Do not [the Arians] seem to you as those lying in a kind of purple and linen, on raised couches?'[227] Bede is defending the monastic calling, which depended heavily upon the charity of others, when he assures readers that the begging of which the steward would have been ashamed (Lk. 16:3) was the 'worst kind of begging' ('pessimo genere mendicandi'), i.e. that which was necessitated by being unprepared, as in the case of the foolish virgins of Matthew 25:8.[228] Bonaventure gives this a different twist. He says that though the steward's words in v.3b make him like one who flees from a monastic order, nevertheless he did not say that he *despised* begging,[229] which would not have been a feature to be tolerated.[230] Both Bede and Bonaventure defend monasticism against the charge that begging was intrinsically shameful, as well as defending the steward from being a totally negative example. Readiness to apply a parable against one's enemies is seen in Calvin's comparison of the rich man's fine linen (Lk. 16:19) with the 'so-called surplices' of 'the sacrificing papists'.[231] These influences from their own time, though leading to 'anachronistic' interpretations, surely show not only the parables' innate versatility in speaking to different situations, but preserve something of their original sharpness of focus, which gets lost when we try to generalize their message.

Diachronically, the main source of influence on these early interpreters was of course the tradition of the church. Significantly, it was an influence against which they felt no need to defend themselves. They did not aim for innovation for its own sake. There were clear boundaries for the drawing of meanings out of the texts: Scripture as a whole, the rule of faith, the tradition handed down from the earliest days of the gospel.[232] They were certainly aware of the mystery involved in their belief about the nature of

Scripture, and the corollary that mistakes could arise.[233] They knew that the insights of the great doctors and of the church as a whole needed to be brought and held together if they were not to fall into serious error. Many of Ambrose's interpretations had probably been current in the church for generations.[234] Certainly Bede expressed to Bishop Acca considerable reluctance to undertake a commentary,[235] being overawed by the shadow of his great predecessor Ambrose. He was afraid of being told, in the words of an old proverb, that there was no point in putting fish in the sea or water into rivers - that he should indeed pour out 'generous gifts', but 'in needy places'.[236] In the event he acknowledged his great debt to Ambrose, Augustine, Gregory, Jerome and the other Fathers,[237] quoted extensively from them throughout his work and marked the quotations as such,[238] and beseeched anyone who had a mind to copy his commentary to copy these acknowledgements also.[239] Numerous patristic references lend authority to the interpretations of Bonaventure also, and protect him from any charge of wanton innovation or departure from Catholic tradition. The continuing influence of the tradition on Calvin is seen in his many references to earlier interpreters; it was, as we have seen, in controversy with them that the new focus on what Jesus originally meant came to the fore.

The fundamental question is the same as the one we posed about Luke. Is there, behind all the influences from their own eras and from the tradition of the church, at least the trace of an inherited memory, a clue to the way the words had always been understood? The earlier interpreters did not intend with any precision to reveal anything about the voice of the historical Jesus; they intended to show the divine meaning of Scripture for their day. Nevertheless they may *unintentionally* reveal something about it. Not, perhaps, in their meditations which belong more obviously to 'divine' significance, but in the earthy practicality of their moral readings, and the sharpness of their location of the parables at the turning-point of history, their response to the texts may betoken a hearing of the voice. Influence may have come not only from a tradition, but a person, whose tones still echo in the interpreters of his words. Quite without intending it, those interpreters may yield insight into the voice of Jesus.

NOTES

1. Hirsch, *Validity*, 24.
2. Bloom, *Anxiety*, 123.
3. For a helpful positive reappraisal of the biblical interpretation of this period generally, see Louth's chapter 'Return to Allegory' (*Discerning*, 96-131).
4. C.H. Dodd, *The Parables of the Kingdom* (London: Nisbet & Co., 1936).

5. Ibid., 11.

6. Ibid., 12f.

7. Ibid., 13ff. Jeremias, after Dodd, was to call 'allegorical interpretation' the means of 'the distortion and ill-usage which the parables have suffered' over the centuries: *Parables*, 18. More recently Hedrick, though mentioning the moral dimension of premodern parable interpretation, writes that these interpreters read the parables also 'as figures representing some unearthly reality, and as allegorical riddles of the resurrected "Lord of the Church" whose words spoke specifically, if differently, to the early Christian communities of faith': *Parables*, ix. Like Dodd, neither Jeremias nor Hedrick considers the *aim* of the Fathers' interpretative acts.

8. Cf. Torrance, *Divine Meaning*. Carl R. Holladay writes of the 'divine oracle paradigm' which has controlled biblical exegesis for most of Christian history: 'Contemporary Methods of Reading the Bible', in Leander E. Keck et al. (eds.), *The New Interpreter's Bible* (Nashville: Abingdon, 1994), 125-49. Wolterstorff distinguishes the activity of reading Scripture in order to discern God's discourse from reading it to apply it to a contemporary situation, or to discern allegorical or typological patterns (*Divine Discourse*, 202f.), but I suggest in this chapter that the intention to discover the 'divine meaning' itself carried with it both the concern for contemporary application, and the allegorical or typological strategies. Wolterstorff recognizes this when he comments that when Jews and Christians have read the Song of Songs allegorically, they have been ascribing an allegorizing discourse not to a human author, but to the divine one (ibid., 214).

9. Jeremias, *Parables*, 16-18.

10. Ibid., 17. Cf. C.E.B. Cranfield, *The Gospel According to St Mark* (Cambridge: Cambridge University Press, 1959), 156ff. Luke preserves the ἵνα in 8:10; Matthew softens it to ὅτι in 13:13.

11. Cf. the sensitive discussion of this passage and of the purpose of the parables in Madeleine Boucher, *The Parables* (Wilmington, Del.: Michael Glazier, 1981), 41-50. Contrast Andrew Parker, *Painfully Clear: The Parables of Jesus* (Sheffield: Sheffield Academic Press, 1996).

12. I am grateful to Mr Arthur Rowe for this illuminating metaphor.

13. This is clearly expressed by Drury, who sees Mk. 4:11f. as aptly placed in the surrounding chapter of parables and in the gospel as a whole, imbued as they are with a stark sense of divine purpose: *Parables*, 41, 50, 53.

14. As we shall see, the meaning of *Jesus* becomes a serious consideration at the Reformation, but mainly as a check upon excessively fanciful interpretations, not yet as a goal to be aimed at with historically rigorous investigation.

15. Louth, *Discerning*, 113.

16. This is the position argued for by Hans-Josef Klauck, *Allegorie und Allegorisierung in synoptischen Gleichnistexten* (Münster: Aschendorff, 1978).

17. Torrance, *Divine Meaning*, 33, describing how Irenaeus saw this order threatened by allegorizing of a Gnostic kind. On Augustine's view of the 'inexhaustible meanings' of Scripture see Thomas Finan, 'St Augustine on the "mira profunditas" of Scripture: Texts and Contexts', in Thomas Finan and Vincent Twomey (eds.), *Scriptural Interpretation in the Fathers* (Dublin: Four Courts Press, 1995), 163-99, here 170. Cf. Frank Kermode,

The Genesis of Secrecy: On the Interpretation of Narrative (Cambridge, MA: Harvard University Press, 1979), 36f.

18. Irenaeus, *Adv. haer.* 2.28.3, quoted in Torrance, *Divine Meaning*, 113. The jaundiced modern view of this is expressed by A.M. Hunter: 'all down the centuries the interpretation of the parables by the Church's scholars has been coloured, and often vitiated, not only by their doctrine of the Holy Scripture but also by their theology': *Interpreting*, 21.

19. Warren S. Kissinger, *The Parables of Jesus: A History of Intepretation and Bibliography* (Metuchen, NJ and London: Scarecrow Press, 1979), 1-4.

20. A. J. Minnis, *Medieval Theory of Authorship: Scholastic literary attitudes in the later Middle Ages* (London: Scolar Press, 1984), 46.

21. Cf. Minnis's comment on Gilbert of Poitiers' prologue and commentary on the Psalter: ibid., 52.

22. The last book on the parables to make the voice of the early commentators heard in a serious and sympathetic way is probably that mentioned cursorily by Dodd, Richard Chenevix Trench's *Notes on the Parables of our Lord*. Trench, incidentally, took the rather modern position, not indeed completely dissimilar to Jülicher's, that parable differs from allegory 'in form rather than in essence', being aligned with simile, whereas allegory is aligned with metaphor (ibid., 8f.); though he also wrote that 'the expositor must proceed on the presumption that there is import in every single point, and only desist from seeking it, when either it does not result without forcing, or when we can clearly show that this or that circumstance was merely added for the sake of giving intuitiveness to the narrative' (ibid., 36).

23. Ambrose's commentary on Luke, for instance, started life as sermons: see p. 67. On Ambrose's high view of biblical preaching see Hans von Campenhausen, *The Fathers of the Latin Church* [*Lateinische Kirchenväter*, 1960] (London: A. & C. Black, 1964), 93ff. On the pastoral concern of Origen (the archetypal 'allegorizer') see Thiselton, *New Horizons*, 168. On the friars (such as Bonaventure) as preachers, see Minnis, *Theory*, 136ff. 'Tropological' interpretation meant contemporary, moral application: Wolterstorff, *Divine Discourse*, 202f.

24. Cf. Wolterstorff, *Divine Discourse*, 16ff., and Chapter 5 below.

25. Alfred Plummer, *A Critical and Exegetical Commentary on the Gospel According to St Luke* (Edinburgh: T. & T. Clark, 1910), lxxx-lxxxiii.

26. Ambrosius Mediolanensis, *Expositio Evangelii Secundum Lucam*, Corpus Christianorum (Series Latina), XIV (Turnhout: Typographi Brepols Editores Pontificii, 1957). References will be given by 'book' number in Roman numerals followed by line number in Arabic.

27. Ibid., Praefatio, vii.

28. The influence on Augustine of Ambrose's commentary can be seen by a glance at the references in the 'Index Fontium et Imitationum': ibid., 436.

29. Beda, *Expositio*. References will be given by section number in Roman numerals followed by line number in Arabic.

30. Plummer, *Commentary*, lxxxii.

31. Bonaventura, *In sacrosanctum Jesu Christi Evangelium secundum Lucam Elaborata Enarratio* (Venice: Apud Petrum de Francisci et nepotis, 1574).

32. Minnis, *Theory*, 80.

33. F. L. Cross (ed.), *The Oxford Dictionary of the Christian Church* (London / New York / Toronto: Oxford University Press, 1957), 184.

34. Minnis, *Theory*, 80.

35. Beryl Smalley comments on Bonaventure's 'originality and his refusal to be obstructed by current classroom methods' in his works on Ecclesiastes, Luke and John: *The Gospels in the Schools, c.1100 - c.1280* (London: Hambledon Press, 1985), 203.

36. Jean Calvin, *A Harmony of the Gospels Matthew, Mark and Luke*, 3 vols. (Edinburgh: The Saint Andrew Press, 1972). References will be given by volume number in Roman numerals and page number in Arabic. Plummer also lists commentaries on Luke by Erasmus, Bucer and Beza.

37. Cf. James McEvoy, 'The Patristic Hermeneutic of Spiritual Freedom and Its Biblical Origins', in Finan and Twomey (eds.), *Interpretation*, 1-25.

38. Cf. this comment on the hermeneutics of the influential Origen: 'The fact that each word in the Bible was chosen by the Holy Spirit meant, as Origen saw it, that we must often look further than the obvious meanings of the word, extensive as the range of these meanings might already be': Gerard Watson, 'Origen and the Literal Interpretation of Scripture', in ibid., 75-84, here 81.

39. 'Historico stilo diximus hunc euangelii librum esse digestum. Denique describendis magis rebus quam exprimendis praeceptis studium uberius conparatione aliorum uidemus inpensum': Ambrosius, *Expositio*, Prol., 110-12.

40. 'Et bene congruit uitulo hic euangelii liber, quia a sacerdotibus inchoauit et consummauit in uitulo, qui omnium peccata suscipiens pro totius mundi uita est inmolatus . . . ': ibid., Prol., 119-21.

41. The subject of the verbs 'inchoauit' and 'consummauit' in the above quotation is the book, not the author.

42. See ibid., VII, 2554f. on Lk. 15:23: 'Bene autem . . . epulantem patrem inducit . . .' ('And with good reason . . . he brings in the celebrating father . . .').

43. '[C]uius circa sacerdotium Christi erat intentio': Beda, *Expositio*, Prol., 167f.

44. 'Ibi enim a sacerdote Zacharia incipit sermo narrantis . . . ibi sacramenta primi sacerdotii in infante Christi impleta narrantur, et quaecumque alia possunt diligenter adverti quibus appareat Lucas intentionem circa personam sacerdotis habuisse': ibid., Prol., 198-203. Note the modern-sounding reference to a 'narrator' ('narrantis'), balanced by a healthy concern with Luke himself!

45. Ambrosius, *Expositio*, VII, 767-72.

46. 'Beatus ille stabularius, qui alterius curare uulnera potest, beatus ille cui dicit Iesus: *quodcumque supererogaueris reuertens reddam tibi.* Bonus dispensator, qui etiam supererogat. Bonus dispensator Paulus, cuius sermones et epistulae ueluti ei ratione quam acceperat superfluunt . . . Bonus ergo stabularius stabuli eius . . . in quo greges clauduntur agnorum, ne frementibus ad caulas rapacibus lupis facilis in ouilia sit incursus': ibid., VII, 801-05, 808-11.

47. Cf. Thiselton's comment on the style of Rupert of Deutz (1070-c.1129): he 'allows gentle contemplation to move amidst a kaleidoscope of ever-changing biblical imagery in a way which almost anticipates the post-modernist notion of textual play': *New Horizons*, 142.

48. 'Quando reuerteris, domine, nisi iudicii die? . . . Reddes ergo quod debes. Beati quibus es debitor. Utinam nos simus idonei debitores, utinam quod accepimus possimus exsoluere nec nos aut sacerdotii aut ministerii munus extollat!': *Expositio*, VII, 812, 815-18.
49. '[Ambrose's] speech is always aimed at the essential and decisive for practice': von Campenhausen, *Fathers*, 90.
50. '[D]ominus ita responsum temperauit suum ut et omnem qui misericordiam faceret cuilibet proximum doceret et tamen haec eadem parabola specialiter ipsum Dei filium designaret': *Expositio*, III, 2202-06.
51. Minnis, *Theory*, 127.
52. Bonaventura, *Enarratio*, 1b-5a.
53. Ibid., 3.
54. '[M]anifestatio ueritatis . . . curatio infirmitatis . . . referatio aeternitatis': ibid. The last is the so-called 'anagogical' reference of the text, whereby it pointed to future glory.
55. 'Et hoc est secundum intentum a beato Luca: Ut sic per ueritatis cognitionem ueniremus ad infirmitatis medicamentum': Ibid., 3b.
56. Ibid., 4.
57. Cf. the 'it is necessary' (δεῖ) attributed to Jesus in the gospels (Mk. 8:31 etc.).
58. *Enarratio*, 335a-37a.
59. 'Sic igitur patet secundum sensum literalem doctrina elicita ex parabola. Alia et potest elici secundum sensum spiritualem . . .': ibid., 231b.
60. *Theory*, 73. See Thomas Aquinas, *Summa Theologiae*, 60 vols., vol. I, ed. Thomas Gilby O.P. (London: Eyre & Spottiswoode, 1964), 1a. 1,10.
61. Aquinas, *Summa* 1a. 1,10.
62. In his comments on The Good Samaritan Bonaventure draws attention to the wisdom of Jesus' *tactics* in dealing with the lawyer ('Ideo dominus sagacissime ex ore ipsius veritatem extorsit . . .': *Enarratio*, 231b); but this is not the same as probing behind the Evangelist's words for the meaning of Jesus, or even assuming that Jesus' meaning is to be identified with Luke's. Those matters are not addressed.
63. E.g. on the transition between Lk. 15 and 16: 'Post expressionem impietatis Iudaicae, et notificationem pietatis divinae, subintroducit hic *euangelista* commendationem, et persuasionem pietatis humanae': ibid., 341b (my emphasis).
64. '[I]n hac parabola quatuor [sic] describit euangelista': ibid., 331a.
65. 'Et quia talibus non potest homo satiari: ideo subdit, et nemo illi dabat': ibid., 333a.
66. '[A]bove human judgement we affirm with utter certainty (just as if we were gazing upon the majesty of God himself) that [Scripture] has flowed to us from the very from the very mouth of God by the ministry of men': Jean Calvin, *Institutes of the Christian Religion*, Library of Christian Classics, XX, 2 vols. (Philadelphia: Westminster Press, 1960), 1.vii.5.
67. On Calvin's concern to understand and expound the *mens auctoris* cf. Thiselton, *New Horizons*, 191f.
68. Calvin, *Harmony* III, 34.
69. Ibid.
70. Ibid., 39.
71. Torrance, *Divine Meaning*, 162, citing Clement, *Quis div. salv.* 5.2-4.

72. The comment of von Campenhausen about Ambrose's 'credulous and unsuspecting neglect of any literal meaning' in favour of allegorical intepretation (*Fathers*, 94) is, as we shall see, exaggerated.

73. The four senses were the literal, allegorical (referring to the work of Christ), moral and anagogical (pointing to future heavenly realities). This tradition itself existed in more than one form: see the discussion by Aquinas in *Summa* 1a. 1,10. On the four senses cf. Louth, *Discerning*, 115-18.

74. Ambrose illustrates the flexibility of patristic reading by interpreting this descent elsewhere as a Christian's shrinking back from a martyr's conflict: *De Poenitentia* I.vii.28, I.xi.51f., cited in Stein, *Parables*, 46.

75. *Expositio*, VII, 735-48.

76. Unlike other readings of this period: see above, p. 60 note 69.

77. 'Non mediocris iste Samaritanus, qui eum quem sacerdos, quem leuita despexerat, non etiam ipse despexit': ibid., VII, 752-54. This is Ambrose's only explicit reference to the first two passers-by.

78. Ibid., VII, 755-59.

79. Ibid., VII, 759-66.

80. Ibid., VII, 822-27.

81. *Expositio*, III, 2202-06.

82. 'Neque enim ita proximum quem sicut nos diligere iubemur super Christo interpretari debemus ut moralia mutuae fraternitatis institute sub allegoriae regulis extenuare et auferre conemur': ibid., III, 2206-09.

83. Ibid., III, 2297, 2301.

84. Ibid., III, 2297-301.

85. Ibid., III, 2301-05.

86. '[U]t uere te proximum sicut te ipsum diligere manifestes quicquid uales in eius uel corporali uel spiritali necessitate subleuanda deuotus operare': ibid., III, 2307-10.

87. The 'spiritual', i.e. the traditional 'allegorical' reading, in which Bonaventure follows the Fathers, occupies only about an eighth of his commentary on the passage Lk. 10:25-37 (*Ennaratio*, 231b). J. Huizinga comments that medieval literature had taken allegory in 'as a waif of decadent Antiquity': *The Waning of the Middle Ages: A Study of the Forms of Life, Thought, and Art in France and the Netherlands in the Fourteenth and Fifteenth Centuries* [1924], (Harmondsworth: Penguin, 1955), 197. Peter Stuhlmacher writes that 'allegory finally came to rest and ossified in the commentaries of scholastic tradition': *Historical Criticism and Theological Interpretation of Scripture* ['Historische Kritik und theologische Schriftauslegung', 1975] (Philadelphia: Fortress Press, 1977), 31. Despite the undoubted process of gradual formalization of allegories such as that of The Good Samaritan, this should not be allowed to dull the memory of the genuine excitement in the perception of the parallel seen in earlier writers such as Ambrose.

88. My italics. 'Alia et potest elici secundum sensum spiritualem . . .': Bonaventura, *Enarratio*, 231b.

89. Ibid., 227b.

90. Bonaventure's use of the word 'persona' is interesting. Originally meaning 'mask', this word came to be used metonymically of the actor who wore it. Although a meaning

closer to modern English 'person' is attested from classical times, it appears that it is used here with the sense of 'character' in a drama (cf. *dramatis personae*). See Sir William Smith, *A Smaller Latin-English Dictionary* [1855], 3rd ed. (London: John Murray, 1933), 534. The story is being examined with a literary-critical eye for realistic fiction; but see note 97 below.

91. Cf. White, *Metahistory*, 35.
92. '[P]ersona indigens ex miseria': Bonaventura, *Enarratio*, 230a.
93. '[P]ersona despiciens ex duritia': ibid., 230a,b.
94. 'P]ersona subueniens ex clementia': ibid., 230b, 231a.
95. '[P]roximi nomen non solum se extendit ad propinquos, uerumetiam ad extraneos': ibid., 231a,b.
96. The powerful image of Christ as the Samaritan was tenacious. Evelyne Proust describes a French twelfth-century carved stone capital which makes the identification, though this stands out as rare in the architecture of the period: 'Vigeois (Corrèze): un ensemble de chapiteaux historiés en Bas-Limousin', *Cahiers De Civilisation Médiévale* 35, no. 1 (1992), 49-63, here 53.
97. This is not yet 'realism' in a modern sense, though it is an advance towards it as compared with the Fathers. It is realism in the medieval sense, which, as Huizinga notes, we call nowadays *idealism*. 'People feel an imperious need of always and especially seeing the general sense, the connexion with the absolute, the moral ideality, the ultimate significance of a thing. What is important is the impersonal. The mind is not in search of individual realities, but of models, examples, norms': *Waning*, 207.
98. Calvin, *Harmony* II, 38.
99. Ibid.
100. Ibid.
101. Ibid., 39.
102. Bonaventura, *Enarratio*, 333a.
103. Ambrosius, *Expositio*, VII, 2393ff.
104. 'Inuidus haedum quaerit, innocens agnum pro se desiderat': ibid., VI1, 2589f.
105. Ibid., VII, 2612.
106. Ibid., VII, 2359, 2361, 2364.
107. 'Bene in se reuertitur qui a se recessit. Etenim qui ad dominum regreditur se sibi reddit et qui recedit a Christo se sibi abdicat': ibid., VII, 2411-13.
108. 'Longe profectus est non locum mutando sed animum. Quanto etenim quisque plus in prauo opere delinquit tanto a Dei gratia longius recedit': Beda, *Expositio*, IV, 2301ff.
109. Bonaventura, *Enarratio*, 331b, 332a.
110. Calvin, *Harmony* II, 221. Note again the use of the word 'person'.
111. Ibid.
112. See further Chapter 6 below.
113. See further Chapters 4 and 5 below.
114. 'Sed moribus separari . . .': Ambrosius, *Expositio*, VII, 2362.
115. Ibid., VII, 2364-66.
116. Ibid., VII, 2368f.
117. Already perhaps in Eph. 4:17; more clearly in 1 Pet. 2:12. In Rev. 11:2 the 'Gentiles', to whom the outer court of the temple is given over, presumably stand for the

opponents of Christ, just as the 'twelve tribes of Israel' in Rev. 7:4-8 presumably stand for his adherents. The Vulgate translates as 'gentes' in all three instances; no doubt this was the standard equivalent of ἔθνη with which Ambrose would have been familiar.

118. '[U]t destrueret populum Iudaeorum': Ambrosius, *Expositio*, VII, 2572f.

119. Ibid., VII, 2563-78.

120. The reference to God destroying the people of the Jews is a tendentious interpretation of 1 Cor. 1:28: 'God chose . . . things that are not, to bring to nothing things that are.'

121. 'Quod faciebant Iudaei, cum quererentur quia Christus cum gentibus epularetur': *Expositio*, VII, 2610f.

122. Ibid., VII, 2632f.

123. '[V]el quasi Iudaeus in lege uel quasi iustus in conmunione': ibid., VII, 2633f. I read the compacted expression 'in conmunione' as expressing the spirit of Rom. 2:12-16: there are those outside the domain of the law who nevertheless possess it inwardly.

124. Ibid., VII, 2634f.

125. Ibid., VII, 2635-37.

126. In his treatise *De Poenitentia* against the Novatian heresy, Ambrose uses the example of the forgiving father to teach that no true penitent should be denied reconciliation: Manfred Siebald and Leland Ryken, 'Prodigal Son', in David Lyle Jeffrey (ed.), *A Dictionary of Biblical Tradition in English Literature* (Grand Rapids: Eerdmans, 1992), 640-44, here 640.

127. '[M]aior enim filius eos qui in unius Dei permansere cultura, minor eos qui usque ad colenda idola Deum deseruere significat': Beda, *Expositio*, IV, 2288-90.

128. Ibid., IV, 2479-85.

129. Ibid., IV, 2509-13.

130. Ibid., IV, 2579-83.

131. 'Per duos autem filios intelligimus humani generis uniuersitatem, non solum quo ad Gentiles et Iudaeos sicut Glossa exponit, sed et generaliter quo ad innocentes et poenitentes, sicut oportet intelligi ex ipsa applicatione parabolae': Bonaventura, *Enarratio*, 331a. The medievals understood the *applicatio* of a text as its 'interpretation', in the sense of its use as a guide for the present: Wolterstorff, *Divine Discourse*, 311. By 'applicatio' here, therefore, Bonaventure presumably means a traditional interpretation.

132. Bonaventura, *Enarratio*, 331a.

133. 'Iste adolescentior dicitur ille, qui uanior est et ad sensibilia bona magis intentus': ibid., 331a,b.

134. '[M]oribus maturior est, patri conformior et obedientior': ibid., 338b.

135. Ibid., 339b.

136. Ibid., 338b.

137. 'Qui . . . non acceptat affluentiam misericordiae Dei, sed sufficientiam iustitiae suae, non potest introire ad unitatis ecciesiasticae charitatem': ibid., 339b.

138. Ibid.

139. 'Iste praesumens de iustitia, et indignans de misericordia fratri impensa, non ambulat secundum iustitiam, sed secundum iniustitiam': ibid., 340a.

140. 'Egressus scilicet iste non est aliud nisi manifestare se exterius in carne': ibid. Bonaventure had seen the father's running to meet the younger son as an example of

prevenient and concomitant grace (335b); his interpretation thus does not, from one angle, place great weight on the difference between the two sons. Both are objects of the father's love and purposeful activity.

141. Ibid., 341a.

142. See p. 80.

143. Calvin, *Harmony* II, 225.

144. Ibid., 224f.

145. '. . . manifestat eos qui bona terrena disperserint dederintque pauperibus ab his in aeterna tabernacula recipiendos . . .': Beda, *Expositio* V, 7ff.

146. 'Non enim . . . domino nostro facienda est in aliquo fraus ut de ipsa frauda elemosinas faciamus': ibid., V, 38ff.

147. '[S]i laudari potuit ille a domino cui fraudem faciebat quanto amplius placeant domino Deo qui secundum eius praeceptum illa opera faciunt': ibid., V, 47ff.

148. Ibid., V, 49-52.

149. Ibid., V, 12-16.

150. Ibid., V, 38, 40-46.

151. 'Ablata quippe uilicatione fodere non ualemus quia finita has uita in qua tantum licet operari nequaquam ultra bonae conversationis fructum ligone deuotae compunctionis licet inquirere': ibid., V, 60-63.

152. Such a reading was no doubt influenced by (but perhaps originally also an influence upon) the reading of the Vulgate in Lk. 16:9b, 'cum defeceritis' - i.e. 'when you die', not 'when the mammon fails'. The verse was clearly a problem from early times. Other Latin variants were 'defecerint' (subject: the forgiven debtors) and 'defecerit' (subject: mammon): Adolf Jülicher, *Itala: Das Neue Testament in Altlateinischer Überlieferung*, 2nd ed., vol. III (Lucas-Evangelium) (New York: Walter de Gruyter, 1976), 186. Barbara Aland et al., eds., *The Greek New Testament*, 4th revised ed. (Stuttgart: Deutsche Bibelgesellschaft / United Bible Societies, 1994), and Kurt Aland, *Synopsis of the Four Gospels*, 6th revised ed. (Stuttgart: United Bible Societies, 1983) give no variant readings for this expression ('when it fails'). John Nolland, *Luke 9:21-18:34*, 804, reports the reading ὅταν ἐκλ(ε)ίπητε ('when you die') found in ℵ W and elsewhere, and says it glosses the sense correctly (my own reading of the parable in Chapters 2 and 6 favours ὅταν ἐκλίπη). 'When you die' is also found in Irenaeus, Clement of Alexandria, Basil and Chrysostom: Joseph Fitzmyer, *The Gospel According to Luke*, 2 vols. (Garden City, New York: Doubleday & Co., 1985), 1110.

153. Beda, *Expositio*, V, 78-84.

154. 'Nisi forte quis simpliciter accipiendum putet quod ominis qui indigentiam cuiuslibet pauperis sanctorum uel ex dimidia uel certe ex quinta parte quantum uiginti uel quinquaginta ad centum sunt adleuiauerit certa suae misericordiae sit mercede donandus': ibid., V, 84-88.

155. '. . . recogitandum . . . refutandum . . . formidandum . . . tolerandum . . . providendum . . . imitandum . . . commendandum': Bonaventura, *Enarratio*, 342a.

156. '[N]isi enim esset exemplum expressum, non subderetur in fine parabolae, quod laudauit dominus uillicum iniquitatis, quia prudenter fecisset . . . sed rursus nisi esset

parabolice dictum, factum tantae fraudis adeo detestandum, in exemplum nullatenus a domino proponi deberet': ibid.

157. 'Sic uillicus iste detestandus est quia fraudem commisit: ratione cuius uillicus iniquitatis dicitur, et laudandus est, quia prudenter sibi contra periculum, remedium adinuenit': ibid., 345b.

158. Cf. the view of Hugh of St Victor, in the century before Bonaventure, that '[w]hen the obvious or literal sense . . . is inadequate, seems absurd, or has no obviously clear meaning, then the deeper meaning is to be searched for': Philip Rollinson, *Classical Theories of Allegory and Christian Culture* (Pittsburgh / London: Duquesne University Press / Harvester Press, 1981), 80. Such was, indeed, the motivation behind much early Christian allegorization of 'difficult' parts of Scripture, especially in the Old Testament. But Louth rightly warns against seeing the allegorical mode of interpretation as merely motivated by the desire to 'paper over the cracks' of Scripture: it was bound up with the desire to communicate the richness of Scriptural meaning (*Discerning*, 113).

159. This is the point made by Wolterstorff when he argues that a conviction about *the intention of the speaker*, not merely a defectiveness in the utterance *per se*, invites us to take a statement metaphorically: *Divine Discourse*, 195.

160. *Enarratio*, 342b.

161. Ibid., 342b, 343a.

162. 'Haec namque uox in aure cuiuslibet debet resonare, quia absque diuina aequitatis rationem exiget': ibid., 343b.

163. '[M]agis de acquirendis amicis, quam de congregandis diuitiis': ibid.

164. '[A]d literam ostenditur liberalitas munificientiae et misericordiae': ibid., 344b.

165. Calvin, *Harmony* II, 111.

166. Seen in Bede (*Expositio*, V, 84-88) as well as Bonaventure (*Enarratio*, 346b, 347a).

167. Calvin, *Harmony* II, 112f.

168. Ibid., 111.

169. Ibid., 111ff.

170. Cf. *Institutes* III.xi.16: 'God deigns to embrace the sinner with his pure and freely given goodness, finding nothing in him except his miserable condition to prompt Him to mercy, since he sees man utterly void and bare of good works; and so he seeks in himself the reason to benefit man.'

171. *Harmony* II, 111.

172. Ibid., 113.

173. Ambrosius, *Expositio*, VIII, 130ff. Cf. Beda, *Expositio*, V, 448f. (following Gregory); Bonaventura, *Enarratio*, 359b.

174. 'Lazarum . . . in Abrahae gremio quasi in quodam sinu quietis et sanctitatis recessu locauit, ne inlecti praesentium uoluptate maneamus in uitiis uel taedio uicti laborum dura fugiamus': Ambrosius, *Expositio*, VIII, 132-35.

175. '[P]auper in saeculo, sed deo diues . . . apostolicus . . . pauper in uerbo, locuples fide . . . apostolicus qui ueram teneat fidem, uerborum infulas . . . non requirat': ibid., VIII, 135-41. Ambrose is echoing Jas. 2:5, as well as Paul's language about apostolic poverty and lack of dependence on fine rhetoric in 1 Cor. 1 - 4, 2 Cor. 10 - 12.

176. Ibid., VIII, 214-18.

177. '[N]eque enim omnis sancta paupertas aut diuitiae criminosae, sed ut luxuria infamat diuitias, ita paupertatem conmendat sanctitas': ibid., VIII, 137ff.

178. Ibid., VIII, 159-85.

179. Louth, *Discerning*, 120.

180. Beda, *Expositio*, V, 393.

181. '[I]bi res iniuste sublata restitutione quadrupli punitur, hic autem diues iste non abstulisse aliena reprehenditur sed propria non dedisse nec dicitur quia unum quempiam oppressit sed quia in acceptis rebus se extulit': ibid., V, 257ff.

182. 'Qui . . . mensae suae uel minima dare noluit in inferno positus usque ad minima quaerenda peruenit': ibid., V, 324f.

183. Ibid., V, 337-41.

184. Ibid., V, 393-99.

185. Ibid., V, 409-14.

186. Ibid., V, 393-461.

187. Cf. note 87 above.

188. Cf. Bonaventure's allegorical appendix to his exposition of Lk. 10:29-37: *Enarratio*, 231b.

189. Ibid., 353a.

190. Calvin, *Harmony* II, 116.

191. Ibid., 117.

192. Ibid., 119.

193. Ibid., 117.

194. Ibid.

195. Ibid., 118.

196. Ibid.

197. Ibid., 118f.

198. Ibid., 119 (my italics).

199. Ibid., 122.

200. Bonaventura, *Enarratio*, 353a.

201. Jeremias, *Parables*, 186.

202. Calvin, *Harmony* II, 116.

203. Ibid., 118f.

204. E.g. Hedrick, *Parables*, 35: 'To assume that the stories were designed to take the reader away to a specific point of reference outside the story, treats the story as an allegory and ultimately reduces the narrative to a discardable husk.'

205. *Harmony* II, 117.

206. Beda, *Expositio*, V, 1051-60; Bonaventura, *Enarratio*, 380b.

207. Beda, *Expositio*, V, 1076f.; Bonaventura, *Enarratio*, 380b.

208. E.g. Wolfgang Harnisch, 'Die Ironie als Stilmittel in Gleichnissen Jesu', *Evangelische Theologie* 32 (1972), 421-36.

209. '[N]on comparat personam personae, sed negotium negotio': Bonaventura, *Enarratio*, 380b.

210. Jülicher, following Aristotle's *Rhetoric*, stresses that in an extended simile (*Gleichnis*) it is not two individual things or people that are compared, but the *relationship* (*Verhältnis*) between two elements of a pair that is compared to the

relationship between two elements of another pair (*Gleichnisreden* I, 75). When Bonaventure says that Jesus is comparing 'negotium negotio' he presumably means the same: God is not being likened to a harsh judge nor the disciples to a widow, but the *entreaty* of a widow to a judge is being likened to the *entreaty* of the disciples to God. Such instances show Jülicher's continuity with a tradition from which he is usually held to have made a radical departure. A comparison of medieval commentators' use of Aristotle with that of Jülicher would make a fascinating study but is beyond the scope of this book.

211. '[S]i instantia precis emolluit iudicem durissimum, et inclinauit iniustissimum ad faciendum iudicium, quo multo fortius inclinabit Deum pium et iustum': *Enarratio*, 382b, 383a.

212. Calvin, *Harmony* II, 125.

213. 'Typice . . . Pharisaeus Iudaeorum est populus qui ex iustificationibus legis extollit merita sua, publicanus uero gentilis est qui longe a Deo positus confitetur peccata sua': Beda, *Expositio*, V, 1171-74.

214. Ibid., 1177-92.

215. Bonaventura, *Enarratio*, 387b.

216. Calvin, *Harmony* II, 128f.

217. Ibid., 128.

218. G. R. Evans, *The Language and Logic of the Bible: The Earlier Middle Ages* (Cambridge: CUP, 1984), 109.

219. Cf. Louth, *Discerning*, 121f.

220. On anti-Judaism in parable interpretation see especially Aaron A. Milavec, 'A Fresh Analysis of the Parable of the Wicked Husbandmen in the Light of Jewish-Catholic Dialogue', in Clemens Thoma and Michael Wyschogrod (eds.), *Parable and Story in Judaism and Christianity* (New York and Mahwah, NJ: Paulist Press, 1989), 81-117, especially 81-4.

221. Cf. Hunter, *Interpreting*, 23.

222. Fearghus O. Fearghail, 'Philo and the Fathers: The Letter and the Spirit', in Finan and Twomey (eds.), *Interpretation*, 39-59, here 59.

223. Cf. von Campenhausen, *Fathers*, 99.

224. '[Q]ui societatem potentiae regalis adfectant': *Expositio*, VIII, 187.

225. '[E]uangelia multa . . . philosophia plures': ibid., VIII, 197ff.

226. '[S]olum euangelium . . . unum deum': ibid., VIII, 198f

227. '[N]onne tibi uidentur in quadam purpura et bysso exstructis iacentes toris . . .': ibid., VIII, 188f.

228. Beda, *Expositio*, V, 63-9.

229. Smalley depicts the background of Bonaventure's teaching in the conflict between the friars and the secular doctors: *Gospels*, 201. Therefore '[p]overty is stressed wherever the text gives occasion for it; the commentaries [on Lk. and Jn.] might be called "treatises on gospel poverty in a lecture framework" ' (212).

230. '[N]on ait mendicare contemno, quia hoc non esset infirmitatis tolerandae, sed impietatis detestandae': Bonaventura, *Enarratio*, 344a,b.

231. Calvin, *Harmony* II, 116.

232. Cf. Torrance, *Divine Meaning*, 115-29 (on the 'hermeneutical principles' of Irenaeus), 172f. (on Clement of Alexandria); Louth, *Discerning*, 73-95, 121-31, on tradition in interpretation.

233. See for instance Augustine's discussion, used by Bede, of the disputed meaning of the goat in Lk. 15:29: the sinner or the antichrist? (Beda, *Expositio*, IV, 2531-50). The fact that both meanings sound far-fetched to us does not affect the point I am making. On the tentativeness of the Fathers in their allegorical interpretations, cf. Louth, *Discerning*, 121.

234. Irenaeus had seen the Samaritan as Jesus (*Adv. Haer.* III.xvii.3; IV.xxxvi.7), as had the heretic Marcion. This interpretation had reached the West and Ambrose (followed by Augustine), via Jerome's translation of Origen's *Homily 34* on Luke. It may well go back to apostolic times. See Raymond St-Jacques, 'Good Samaritan', in Jeffrey (ed.), *Dictionary*, 315f.; Stein, *Parables*, 43f. Cf. McDonald, 'Alien Grace', 38f., on the affinity of the 'allegorical' interpretation with the basic tenor and logic of the parable.

235. Beda, *Expositio*, Prol., 5-18.

236. 'In mare quid pisces quid aquas in flumina mittas? / Larga sed indiguis munera funde locis': ibid., Prol., 17f.

237. Ibid., Prol., 98-102.

238. He explains his system in ibid., Prol., 105-11.

239. Ibid., Prol., 111-115.

CHAPTER 4

The Age of Historical Quest: the Parable Interpretation of Adolf Jülicher

*A considerable percentage of the questions which appear insoluble today
derives from our being burdened with the failures and oversimplifications
of earlier generations.[1]*

*The strong poets have followed [Oedipus] by transforming their
blindness towards their precursors into the revisionary insights of their own
work.[2]*

1. Jülicher and Historical Criticism

Space forbids consideration of the three centuries after Calvin, and so we
turn directly to the work of Adolf Jülicher, Professor of Theology at
Marburg from 1888 to 1923. In 1886 the first volume of his great work on
the 'parable-speech of Jesus', *Die Gleichnisreden Jesu,* was published. In
1898 the second volume, giving his detailed parable expositions, appeared,
followed by a second edition of volume I in the following year.[3]

Jülicher's name is associated with the beginnings of modern parable
scholarship because it was his work that was to prove pivotal in bringing
the rigour of historical criticism to bear on the course of parable
interpretation.[4] But the lively, sometimes heated interaction with
contemporaries and nineteenth-century predecessors in his book shows him
as a man very much caught up in central debates of his time. This was the
era in which biblical scholarship had sought to throw off the straitjacket of
orthodoxy and escape from submission to ecclesiastical authority. No
longer did belief in the divine origin of Scripture act as a check upon
serious critical inquiry into its sources and background.[5] The words of Jesus
himself could not evade this 'scientific' scrutiny: indeed, insofar as scholars
continued to want to give a place of high esteem to Jesus, such 'higher
criticism' was perhaps considered more important with respect to the
gospels than to any other part of the Bible. The stakes were high. Could

such criticism 'save' Jesus for modern humanity from the 'mythological' trappings with which he was seen to be beset in the gospels?[6] Or should it not even be seeking to do so - should it seek to free itself from subordination not only to a revered text, but also to a revered man? In such an atmosphere it is not surprising to find a left and a right wing, a radical avant-garde as well as reactionary voices of protest.

We shall begin, again, by examining the intention of Jülicher. We shall then go on to discuss the figurative construction he places upon the parables as words of Jesus and the outworking of this in their interpretation. We will then be in a position to assess his insight into the voice of Jesus with reference not only to his intention but his response to the influences upon him.

2. The Intention of Jülicher

In his opening chapter, 'Die Echtheit ['authenticity'] der Gleichnisreden Jesu',[7] Jülicher stakes out his position between the reactionaries and the radicals. He launches straight into an attack on the reactionary position represented by S. Göbel, who had abjured the new criticism of the synoptic gospels because it had not yet shown that it could succeed in distilling an 'original gospel' (*Urevangelium*) from them.[8] Of special interest is the fact that Jülicher turns against Göbel a quotation used by him from Calvin: 'nihil amplius quaerendum est quam quod tradere Christi consilium fuit' ('nothing more is to be sought than what it was the purpose of Christ to hand on').[9] The purpose or intention (*consilium*) of Christ was for Jülicher the all-important object of the search in gospel study. Göbel is criticised because although he believed this too, he did not follow up his belief with historical source-criticism. Thus Jülicher finds the seeds of his own work in a principle enunciated at the Reformation. Jülicher was opposed in principle to the Romantic hermeneutics of penetrating an author's mind,[10] later criticizing Karl Barth for what he saw as his 'pneumatic' reading of Romans, going beyond what could be established by historical scholarship.[11] However, Jülicher's own work makes it plain - as we shall see - that some such act of penetration is inevitably involved once the issue of intentionality has been raised.

To seek the intention of Jesus in the words attributed to him in the gospels must mean also to take seriously the intention of those who handed them on and wrote them down. Against the reactionaries, Jülicher spells out this necessity and draws attention to the evidence in the gospels themselves that the words of Jesus were not passed on in perfectly preserved fashion.[12] So, he says, we must attempt to understand Jesus better than did those who preserved his words.[13]

When Jülicher turns his fire on the radical position, he is able to call to his aid both David Friedrich Strauss and Ferdinand Christian Baur.[14] Both had recognized that among the traditions of Jesus' words and deeds preserved in the gospels the parables, or some of them, had a high claim to have originated with Jesus. The synoptic writers, Jülicher says, betray through their 'strange mixture of dependency and freedom' ('seltsame Mischung von Abhängigkeit und Freiheit') a basic sense that they were indeed writing *history* of a kind, not pure creative literature.[15] Recognition of the literary worth of the parables should not lead one to conclude that they are 'late' compared to other less striking examples that have come down to us from the period.[16]

There are for Jülicher wider points to be made against the radical position too. 'Tendenzkritik', the study of the bent of the individual evangelists, is inclined to propagate itself, unhelpfully in Jülicher's view; for it needs to consider the 'tendency' or theological stance of sources as well as gospels, the choice, arrangement and framing of material as well as the basic impulse to write.[17] Jülicher suspects that the 'results' of such criticism are as much a product of the search as the conclusion of it: 'Wer sucht, der findet'.[18] He points out that picture-stories are by nature easier to pass on than abstract theses;[19] that we have no evidence (e.g. in Paul) that anybody imitated Jesus' parable-style;[20] and finally, that the parables that are presented to us as coming from Jesus bear the marks of originality and genius, and are far superior to anything of a comparable genre from the period, for instance in Paul or Hermas.[21]

So Jülicher ends his first chapter on an optimistic note: we have good grounds for asserting the basic authenticity of Jesus' parables. The stated determination to discover the 'consilium Christi', the intention of Christ in speaking them, seems capable of fulfilment through source-criticism and a newly methodical treatment.

3. Jülicher's Interpretative Key: Simile

The second chapter of Jülicher's book[22] constitutes his main proposal. Through clear definitions, eloquent illustrations and forceful repetitions he seeks to establish beyond a doubt that when Jesus spoke in parables, it was a teaching device designed to clarify a point by means of a simile, *not* a veiling of the truth under a cloak of allegory. The chapter's title, 'Das Wesen der Gleichnisreden Jesu', encapsulates the spirit of this powerful argument. Jülicher is in pursuit of the *essential nature* of the parables. His great protest against the tradition is that it has not faced up to what the parables *are*. Even the Evangelists' handling of the parables is contrasted with what they are 'in reality', 'in Wirklichkeit'.[23] Throughout, it is clear that he links 'what the parables are' with 'what Jesus intended by them'. For him, they are not free-standing texts or works of art which can 'be' different things for different individuals or generations. They sufficiently reveal a clear purpose, and that intention is to be determinative for our understanding. What, then, *are* the parables for Jülicher, and how does he think he knows?

The general category under which Jülicher brings the first two of his three main divisions of parable-speech, the *Gleichnis* (short similitude) and *Fabel* (story-parable), is that of *Redefigur* (figure of speech).[24] He does not use this expression with regard to the third division, *Beispielerzählung* (example story), but he would probably not have disputed that these could be placed in the same broad category.[25] Jülicher's discussion of *how* the nature of the parables is to be determined is a model of balanced handling of the peculiarities of an individual's speech within a historical context, and points up the basic challenge which figures of speech peculiarly present:[26] how does one recognize and affirm uniqueness, that which is *sui generis*, within a historical method that depends on the principle of analogy, that is 'the assumption of an intrinsic similarity in all historical occurrence'?[27]

Jülicher operates between two poles. On the one hand he stresses that the Evangelists did not divide Jesus' sayings into rhetorical categories,[28] nor did Jesus give training in rhetoric to enable people to understand him.[29] Neither speaker nor transmitters were interested in conceiving or executing precisely defined forms of communication. The use of the word παραβολή in the gospels seems fluid and somewhat arbitrary.[30] We must, then, pay attention to the texts themselves and not be over-controlled by categories which we bring to them. On the other hand he sets the parables, as rhetorical devices, in two broad historical contexts. They are descendants of OT *meshalim*, forms of speech which express a comparison; they can also profitably be understood in the light of Aristotle's *Rhetoric*.[31]

Between these poles (the texts themselves, and their broad contexts in rhetorical history) Jülicher stakes out this position: that the parables were originally, in the mouth of Jesus, plain, readily comprehensible *meshalim*, of the same rhetorical nature as the great *meshalim* of the OT;[32] they speak of *one* general truth drawn from ordinary life and applied to the sphere of the Kingdom; the Evangelists, however, portrayed them as *meshalim* in the narrower sense of which the term had become capable in the intertestamental period, i.e. as riddles or enigmas.[33] (Aristotelian terminology about simile then provides Jülicher with useful clarificatory tools: he is not claiming that Jesus or his Jewish contemporaries would have been familiar with it, only, by implication, that it is better for us to use ancient categories than modern ones.[34])

Jesus' intention, then, for Jülicher, is to be discovered through holding together a historical awareness of rhetorical forms available to him, and attention to the texts themselves in their particularity, recognizing that they do not suggest *conscious* use of carefully defined rhetorical devices. At the heart of Jülicher's position is much that subsequent generations, down to the present, will almost instinctively affirm. Many recognize, with him, natural, realistic and didactic qualities in Jesus' parables.[35] Many feel the persuasiveness of Jülicher's insistence that they be taken as similitudes in the sense that Aristotle had expounded. That is, the comparisons are not simply between two elements (e.g. 'God is like a shepherd'), but between the *relationship* of two elements from one sphere and that of two elements from another (e.g. 'As a shepherd searches for a lost sheep, so God goes in search of lost people'), on the basis of a point of comparison or *tertium comparationis* (e.g. the care of the searcher).[36] This figure of simile seems to fit certain parables, such as Luke 15:3-7, very well. Jülicher thus protects the parables from over-crude identifications, especially between God and various human figures. Further, many would agree with Jülicher that where a plain sense emerges from this approach, it is somewhat unnatural to assume that Jesus' meaning will be on a deeper level.[37] It is easy to assent to the intrinsic improbability of Jesus' propounding elaborately wrought allegories in the midst of profoundly serious debate and controversy.[38]

The century of parable scholarship since the publication of *Die Gleichnisreden Jesu* has taken shape largely in response, both developmental and critical, to Jülicher's work; and it would be superfluous to my purpose to describe the twists and turns of a debate which have been chronicled by others.[39] Three major shifts are now well known. First, Jülicher regarded 'the kingdom' as the theme of the parables, but his rather vague understanding of it as 'die unsichtbare Welt' ('the unseen world')[40] has been replaced by a sharper awareness of its first-century Jewish meaning - a final, decisive and dramatic act of God in history.[41] Second, Jülicher's insistence (following Bernhard Weiss, father of Johannes) that 'the interpretation of the parable can only lie in a general truth, which results from the carrying-over of the rule set forth to the sphere of the explicitly religious life, to the arrangements of the kingdom of God'[42] has been challenged not only with respect to the generality, but the singularity of the truth concerned.[43] Third, Jülicher's opposition between simile and metaphor / allegory has been fundamentally questioned over the last thirty-odd years.[44] It is widely recognized that metaphorical qualities in the parables may plausibly have belonged to Jesus' intention - though how to construe that metaphorical operation both in general and in specific cases remains a matter of discussion. Even apart from the fact that the 'simile' form of a parable would often have to be reconstructed, since that is not how it appears in the gospels, it is recognized that the parables do not simply ground the realities of the kingdom in normal, universally-accepted features of life; they have a mysterious character,[45] and the situations they present are often surprising and unusual.[46]

To understand and profit from Jülicher's contribution, however, we need to dig deeper than this. We have already seen evidence in Chapter 3 that the reaction by Jülicher, Dodd and their successors against the earlier interpreters has been a reaction partly against a figment of the imagination, viz. the idea that the older interpreters *claimed that Jesus spoke in allegories.* What is the significance of this? I do not believe this confusion on the part of Jülicher was due simply to a lack of thought or study, or that it can be explained and answered wholly in similar terms - e.g. 'we now know how to differentiate what he ignorantly confounded'. We will need to address, in section 5, oppositions that lie (perhaps) at a deeper level in his work than the consciously intentional. First, however, we shall illustrate quite briefly how Jülicher's use of simile as an interpretative key shapes his interpretation of specific parables.

4. Jülicher's Parable Interpretations

As we read his comments, it should become clear that (like the Fathers) Jülicher himself has suffered a degree of misrepresentation; he by no means always makes the parables as trite and bland as his critics have made out.[47] Indeed, he follows their contours and imagines their impact very carefully.

The Good Samaritan

Like the other parables named by Jülicher 'example stories' in Luke (12:16-21; 16:19-31; 18:9-14), The Good Samaritan does not easily fit into the 'simile' shape. Jülicher recognizes that rather than comparing the everyday with the sphere of the 'kingdom' or the 'religious life', such a story is (as it were) in the 'kingdom' all along. (It is also, of course, in the everyday; we shall pursue the significance of this in Chapter 6). This, therefore, is how he encapsulates its 'point' ('Pointe'):

> The gladly-offered exercise of love earns the highest worth in the eyes of God and men, no advantage of office or birth can replace it. The compassionate person, even if he be a Samaritan, deserves blessing more than the Jewish temple-officer who indulges in self-seeking.[48]

We note the careful nuancing. The 'point' is by no means reduced to a simple lesson in neighbour-love. The contrast between the Samaritan and the priest and Levite is carefully brought out, not so as to make it into a crudely anti-Jewish statement, but so as to highlight the subversive quality of the story. Jülicher remarks that it would have sounded pretty 'dull' ('matt') and 'tasteless' ('geschmacklos') if 'priest' and 'Levite' had been replaced by 'one Jew' and 'another Jew'.[49] Against a tendency to read too heavy an intentionality behind priest and Levite - and thus ascribe that intentionality, as some of his contemporaries did, to someone later than Jesus - Jülicher imagines for us Jesus' lightness of touch, the natural colouring of the story, yet without losing the significance of the identity of the two passers-by altogether.

Jülicher's exposition displays not only literary, but also, naturally, historical sensibility. In keeping with his quest for the 'consilium Christi', he is very restrained about 'translating' the story into contemporary terms. He does not try to 'update' the Samaritan and the Jewish dignitaries. The universal principle is allowed to emerge, unforced. But we may ask whether the biblical exegete's work is quite completed, as Jülicher gives the impression that he has finished his, when he writes of the direct, unmediated ('unmittelbar') way that the thoughts of the parable 'fall into our lap' ('fallen uns in den Schoss').[50] For the way in which the parable made its full *original* impact surely depended upon the way that hearers or readers placed themselves in the story and related it to their own world. For those hearers who were not actually Samaritans, priests or Levites, there would have been already a task of translation to perform, perhaps indeed an instinctive one, in order to place themselves in the parable's world. It might seem at first sight as if Jülicher were offering, already in the late nineteenth century, what Paul Ricoeur called a 'second naïveté' which 'bears the stigmata of a post-critical age',[51] through his stressing of the obviousness and accessibility of the parables. But this would be an inaccurate understanding of Jülicher. In fact, in his reaction against the 'mystifying' approach, he has paradoxically continued the patristic and medieval tradition of bringing the parables immediately into his own time: not now with their blatant and unashamed transposition into (for instance) encouragements for the monastic calling, but by the more sophisticated move of claiming that in their pristine naturalness their meaning is as plain for us (once proper historical investigation has been carried out) as it would have been for the first hearers. We see also how Jülicher privileges one aspect of 'voice' over the other: he stresses the deliberateness of Jesus' intention, but not the issue of how he was *heard*. As we shall see in the next chapter, this will be reversed in more recent studies.

The Prodigal Son

Jülicher wants to get behind the Lukan setting of The Prodigal Son. This is how he reads the interpretation Luke offers:

> In the example of a father, who greets with warm love the guilt-laden son who comes home in penitence, and justifies his joy over against the wrath of the elder son who always stayed faithful, Jesus, who welcomes the customs officers and sinners, although the Pharisees and Scribes grumble about it, is supposed to be justified.[52]

For Jülicher, though, the thought of Jesus' original parable is to be conceived as a simile expressing a general but profound truth:

> As a father of two sons, from whom the one goes away, in order to squander property and honour, nearly also life, greets this one as soon as he returns in contrition, with warmth, indeed with an ardour of love that is almost on fire after smouldering for so long, without injustice being done in the process to the other son, who always did his duty, and without him feeling that he was less blessed with the love of his father, so the way to the father-heart of God stands always open, even to the most rotten sinner, if he will only enter in, and re-adoption to the status of child is certain for him, without this ever meaning a neglect of justice, or that it would somehow cut it [i.e. justice] off from the love of God.[53]

The story is thus lifted beyond the setting of controversy in which Luke places it and turned into an expression of a lofty, universal reality. It is interesting also to note Jülicher's assumption that the appeal of the father to the elder son was successful. This contrasts with more recent readings which have stressed the openness of the ending.[54] The attractiveness of this exposition is Jülicher's sense (before the days of reader-response theory) of the way that the story involves the emotions of the hearer / reader, who *wants* the elder brother to join the party, as the natural though unspoken conclusion to the story.

There are four features of this interpretation to which we should pay attention. First, the parable as Luke records it does not use the simile form that Jülicher gives it ('as a father, so God . . .'). From the start, therefore, Jülicher is twisting or troping the text as he imagines the parable's form on the lips of Jesus. This is not to say that it was not, or could not have been, an original simile in the mouth of Jesus. It is simply to underline the fact that the strategies of historical-critical method entail putting a figurative construction on the texts, no less than the strategies of pre-critical commentators.

Secondly, the attractiveness of the 'general truth' theory for Jülicher seems to have been that it allowed him to say (in essence) that it did not *matter* that the *original context* of Jesus' words had been lost, for his parables were addressing questions that transcended all contexts. This seems like a convenient escape from the potential black hole of our historical ignorance. Of course, as soon as one admits that Jesus' parables may have arisen in very specific situations, and been addressed to particular needs of the moment, one begins to allow the possibility that individual elements of the parable would correspond to individual elements in the situation, and this Jülicher cannot countenance. Thus the parable

> is not so much a defence of Jesus as a friend of sinners against attacks from conceited super-pious folk, as - and this heightens its value - an exalted revelation about a fundamental question of religion, namely this: can the God of righteousness receive sinners in mercy?[55]

This is ironic, for Jülicher seems to be admitting by the back door what he has dismissed from the front, namely a doctrinal thrust in the parable.[56] Jülicher's justification for this, though, is that it is consistent with the Scriptural view (expressed in Jn. 10:30, 'I and the Father are one') of Jesus' relationship to his Father; with this surprising dependence on the Fourth gospel, a trace thus remains of the ancient adherence to the framework of Scriptural meaning.

Thirdly, we find here a good illustration of Jülicher's attempt to penetrate into the mind of Jesus, even to hazard at the process of creation behind the parable:

> In the consciousness of recognizing aright the Father's heart in his own heart, he paints for humans the Father's picture: because he, Jesus, without having to accuse himself of any lack in esteem for righteousness, nevertheless feels himself drawn so much more towards - has joy in - those who need him, for whom he can be of some help, who without him would belong to hell, his Father must also feel thus, and so he boldly *proclaims God as the real father of sinners.*[57]

Jülicher writes that it was a natural story to tell among hearers whom Jesus had already taught to feel in respect to God as children with respect to a father ('sich gegenüber Gott wie Kinder gegenüber dem Vater zu fühlen'). Jesus, despite his own piety, felt drawn to sinners; conscious of his own deep affinity with God as Father, he felt that God must feel likewise drawn; so he teaches sinners to regard God as a loving, welcoming Father. Jülicher has not imagined an alternative *social* or *historical* setting for the parable to the one put forward by Luke. He has instead imagined (in Romantic fashion) an *internal train of thought* or *feeling* in Jesus.

Fourthly, Jülicher writes that Jesus' originality did not consist in his being divorced from his Jewish heritage, or in a message with a new content:

In Jesus' terms, God has thus already forgiven, welcomed back, rejoiced, even before Jesus; he would have done it thus gladly for each depraved person since the beginning of the world: the new era of the gospel arises with Jesus not because his atoning death first made an act of mercy towards sinners possible for God, but because for the first time he, through his life and preaching, unveiled this God for people, brought him near, created for them confidence, that is faith, in God's mercy, and made them courageous to hope in God.[58]

What Jesus is said to *reveal* with fresh clarity is already existing, indeed eternal, truth. Here is insight into the human Jesus interestingly different from the 'radical' picture given by some more recent scholars;[59] Jesus' perception is fresh, but its object is eternal. What Jülicher sees, in fact, is *Jesus the man of insight*, the passionate communicator of unchanging truth about the forgiving love of God.

The Shrewd Steward

The message of The Shrewd Steward in the text up to Lk. 16:8 - and as crystallized in v. 8, in which the master praises the steward - is expressed by Jülicher as follows:

> In that way [i.e. according to v. 8] the steward would be presented as a model of wisdom for the believers, and the parable would continue current in the tradition as a recommendation of wisdom.[60]

V. 9 ('make friends for yourselves by means of unrighteous mammon') is then read as the beginning of later 'allegorical' interpretation, in which not merely 'wisdom' in a general sense, but specific *actions* are commanded on the basis of the parable's details. But though he rejects interpretations that take their starting point from v. 9, Jülicher is not satisfied with seeing the parable as a mere injunction to wisdom, as v. 8 on its own might imply; Jesus would hardly have needed to tell such a story for that simple purpose.[61] This is how he understands the story:

> I see it made clear in the parable, much rather, how someone seizes in time the appropriate means in order to reach his goal, how he still rescues himself from an apparently hopeless plight, because he considers and acts, so long as both can still be of use to him, so long as he still has means in his hands.[62]

Not the right employment of wealth, but the decisive use of the present as a precondition for a joyful future should be imprinted on the story of the steward, which depending on the occasion which called it forth, could have a more seriously warning character: be on guard against being too late, since if once the new age has broken in, one cannot do anything more for it . . . so long as it is still 'today', there is a means to make tomorrow favourable for you.[63]

The question of the morality of the steward's actions should not, says Jülicher, be an issue; it is enough that we should go along with Jesus' judgement on the story in v. 8, highlighting the steward's shrewdness, and apply it 'in our religious life' ('in unserm religiösen Leben').

Again, Jülicher is careful not to offer too reductive an interpretation. The contours of the parable are to be respected; it is not just an exhortation to wisdom, any more than The Good Samaritan is just an injunction to love. Yet the principle of seeking the 'general truth' dominates. No specific reference concerning the use of money is allowed; we must remain on the widest plane, covering the greatest number of possible situations.

Interpreters had always recognized the moral difficulty of this parable, and Jülicher's diagnosis is not essentially different from those of Bonaventure or Calvin, who had dealt with the problem by seeking to draw out, respectively, the distinction between that which was 'parabolic' and that which was 'exemplary', or that between the basic thrust and the mere colouring of the story.[64] Jülicher, however, celebrates what the earlier writers appeared to find embarrassing. In response to pietistic qualms about the story, he points to the earthy realism of the simile ('like an unscrupulous steward, so you'):

Jesus relates what has, first, occurred to him, and what occurs to him is what he experiences; he spoke in order to have a direct effect on his fellow-countryfolk, not concerned about the taste of modern Bible readers.[65]

This sentence illustrates both Jülicher's strength and his vulnerability: he wants to lead us into the situation of Jesus, and take us out of the prejudices of our own, away from the desire to be comfortable with the text; yet he cannot, of course, escape his own sense of religious and literary taste.

His final remarks on the parable are an instance of his decisive tendency to move away from the specific moral reference and challenge, that we found to be a hallmark of earlier interpretations, towards an apparently more lofty or 'spiritual' reading. It is a tendency full of irony, given his desire to move away from so-called 'spiritual' readings: as we have seen, 'spiritualization' is a misleading description of the strategy of the older commentators, who were acutely aware of the parables' practical moral challenge. Here Jülicher says that given the verbal link between Luke 16:3 and Mark 10:17 (τί ποιήσω, 'what am I to do'), it is not surprising that someone has added to the parable, in Luke 16:9, an 'answer' ('make yourselves friends of the mammon of unrighteousness') which corresponds to the answer Jesus gives to the rich man in Mark 10:21 ('sell your possessions . . . and you will have treasure in heaven'). But, he says, *Jesus* in both passages 'thought of something more than almsgiving'.[66] In fact, Jülicher has already stated that in the parable Jesus was not intending to teach about almsgiving at all. It sounds as if, though he cannot deny that the story of the rich man has *something* to do with giving wealth away, he wants to lift it above the level of mere practicality to a higher plane, the injunction to commitment of heart or soul. The danger (one might suppose) of thus generalizing or spiritualizing the injunction of Mark 10:21 is twofold: it removes Jesus from his concrete historical context, and while making his words applicable to a broader range of situations it weakens their stinging specific force. We see here that it is not only via the parables that Jülicher presents Jesus as the purveyor of elevated general truths, and we need to ask whether in fact this is closer to Jesus than the down-to-earth picture suggested by the commentators of the premodern period.

The Rich Man and Lazarus

'The worst misjudgement', Jülicher says, which The Rich Man and Lazarus could suffer, 'was the illusion that it was composed in order to proclaim new revelations about the conditions in the other world.'[67] That 'illusion' was a standard medieval position, mentioned by Bonaventure, and from which Calvin, as we saw, had already moved some distance.[68] Most contemporary commentators would agree with Jülicher on this negative point about the purpose of the parable. But Jülicher overreacts to this position by drawing a wedge between the two halves of the parable. He believes that though Luke 16:19-26 could have come from the mouth of any Israelite, it could well go back to Jesus, but that vv. 27-31 (where the rich man asks Abraham to send Lazarus to warn his brothers, and is told this would be fruitless if they did not attend to Moses and the prophets) are an addition by a later hand.[69] These latter verses, if authentic, would have implied (he thinks) an identification of the rich man with unbelieving Jews, and of Lazarus with Jewish Christians or Gentiles; the story of vv. 19-26 would appear quite overdrawn for the simple message that unbelievers will go to hell, and indeed would caricature the Jews unworthily, a road from which one could only escape by 'determined allegorizing' ('entschlossene Allegorese')[70] - i.e. by treating the story as a mere husk which did not have anything to do with the people of 'Moses and the prophets' (v. 29). The authentic example-story is simply meant to induce 'joy in a life of suffering, fear of a life of indulgence'.[71]

Jülicher here falls short of the literary sensitivity that was shown by the earlier interpreters and especially by Calvin. They managed very well to read the story as a whole without degenerating into crass codebreaking (e.g. they never saw the rich man's fate as indicating the fate of the rich - or the Jews - *en masse*). They knew that the story could be a warning to the rich (and to the Jews) without implying their blanket condemnation. They saw no great incongruity between the beginning of a story speaking of a rich man and a poor man, and the end of the same story associating the rich with the inheritors of the Law and the Prophets. They found no crass equations; simply allusion, breathing the atmosphere of a mutual knowingness and play of associations between Jesus and his hearers. It is of course precisely that mutual knowingness that Jülicher wants strenuously to deny.[72] We note the stark either / or of Jülicher's argumentation. In fact we do not need to choose between a plain, simple 'picture from life' and an 'allegory' in which the mere words are curiously empty. We can have *resonant* realism, *suggestive* communication.

The Judge and the Widow

Jülicher believes that Luke 18:2-5 is a lesson concerning prayer - the homely picture, again, illustrating the 'general truth'. He thinks that 18:6-8, speaking of God avenging his elect, is an interpretative addition 'which originally was not intended' ('die ursprünglich nicht intendiert war').[73] He thinks that Luke's source saw in the widow a picture of the church crying for vindication, and that the words καὶ μακροθυμεῖ ἐπ᾽ αὐτοῖς (v. 7) have been added in reminiscence of Sirach 35:18.[74] He ridicules the readings of Hippolytus (the judge as the antichrist, the adversary as the son of God, the widow as [unbelieving] Jerusalem, bereft of her heavenly bridegroom) and Cyril (the judge as God, the widow as a soul let loose by the devil, the adversary as the devil).[75] He also distances himself from the interpreters of his own time who believed that in the parable Jesus is comparing the disciples' situation after his departure to that of a bereft widow.[76]

Jülicher's repudiation of the idea that Jesus might have intended an allegorical correspondence between the widow and the disciples, the judge and God, is too easily bolstered by ridicule of patristic readings which naturally sound quaint to a historical age intent on discovering the intention of Jesus. 'The elect', after all, was a Jewish notion before it was a Christian one.[77] And if Luke's source could have introduced an allusion to Sirach, could not Jesus himself have made such an allusion with equal probability? Indeed, does not the whole tradition of Israel's 'humble poor' crying out to God stand behind Jesus' parable? Such considerations do not, of course, prove that Luke 18:6-8 go back to Jesus, and 'proof' in any case is not my concern. We simply note Jülicher's assumption that the presence of something like 'allegory' implies lateness or inauthenticity.[78] In fact, 'allegory' is the wrong word to describe the way that the first and second halves of the passage are related. There is, rather, a true 'parabling', a laying of one situation 'alongside' another, setting up a suggestive interpretative field. And if the widow in the story was suggestive of the people of God - whether the suggestiveness was present to Jesus himself, or only to the early church - it does not preclude the story from giving a practical lesson. Again, Jülicher's desire to find general truths in the mouth of Jesus tends, paradoxically when we consider Jülicher's historical intentions, to divorce Jesus from his historical setting in Judaism.

The Pharisee and the Customs Officer

In the example-story The Pharisee and the Customs Officer, writes Jülicher, 'Jesus wanted to teach that in all circumstances humility is more pleasing to God than self-righteousness'.[79] He regards continuing fondness for allegorical readings such as Pharisee / Judaism, customs officer / Gentile world, or Pharisee / empirical Israel, customs officer / ideal Israel, as erroneous though harmless.[80] But despite protestations against the interpretation of individual elements, Jülicher's interpretation assumes that the Pharisee stands synecdochically for the proud, and the customs officer synecdochically for the humble sinner.[81] This becomes clearer when we see the link which Jülicher makes between this parable and The Good Samaritan:

> As a Samaritan, who exercises love, is more worthy of the highest honour in the eyes of God and human beings than pitiless Priests and Levites, so the customs officer, who in penitent humility pleads for mercy, is nearer the kingdom than a puffed-up Pharisee: God looks on the heart alone . . .[82]

Jülicher sees the importance of the contrasted characters in both parables: they are not merely examples of love or indifference, humility or pride respectively. It is the characters' social identity which gives the tales their particular pointedness. But if we are to capture that pointedness we need to ask whom, more precisely, Jesus *intended to* sting by them, and who would have in fact been stung by them, with offence or challenge, encouragement or joy. To convert these parables into statements of universal truth entails blunting their edge of sharp suggestiveness.

5. From Influence to Insight: The Voice of Jesus in Jülicher

We may now summarize the insights into Jesus revealed in Jülicher's parable interpretations, and ask what the influences are which have contributed to them.

Synchronically, the voice of Jesus in Jülicher is one which rises above its surroundings; which speaks beyond the situation of his contemporaries in its utterances of lofty, universal truth. It is a voice which speaks clearly, for immediate understanding.

Diachronically, the voice of Jesus in Jülicher is rooted in eternal verities. It speaks them out, but does not bring them into being. It is not essentially innovative, but revelatory.

We need to spend longer discussing the influences on Jülicher. First we will consider three oppositions which lie deep in the structure of his text. We will then be in a position to appreciate more clearly two strands of synchronic influence and the ambiguous relationship in which Jülicher stands to the great diachronic influence of the tradition of parable interpretation.

Underlying the polarity which Jülicher sets up between simile and allegory / metaphor there are three more fundamental polarities, pairs of opposites whose members he seeks to keep as far as possible from each other. Recognition of these will, I suggest, not only serve the historical aim of a better understanding of a great interpreter, but the exegetical aim of a better understanding of the nature of our task in dealing with the parables today.

The first is a polarity between *speaker and transmitters*. Jesus is contrasted with those who passed on his words. Jesus, writes Jülicher, *possessed* wisdom, and therefore 'did not need to seek wisdom in unclarity';[83] so he probably preferred the classic sense of *mashal* - plain wisdom saying - to the sense of 'riddle'. He did not use symbolic speech (or action): 'Jesus had too much Logos in him, to put the clear λόγος behind such obscure gesticulation.'[84] He needed to speak clearly to answer his critics: 'a riddling answer from his side would of necessity have been taken as escape.'[85] He is unlikely to have used allegory, for allegory is an artistic speech-form. '[This] speech-form is simply too difficult to bear the weight of his holy eagerness, of any high pathos at all. Passion, pure as much as impure, makes its expression spontaneously; the thought-out, considered nature of an allegory is no match for its onslaught.'[86] And one should not entertain the possibility that an 'enthusiastic' ('begeitsterte') speaker like Jesus could have used allegories that were muddled or badly formed.[87] Further, 'it would have been highly astonishing to him, if in his teaching he had provided the dominant influence upon an art-form [i.e. allegory] which is indeed aesthetic, but not didactically effective.'[88] Finally, Jülicher is in no doubt that 'each word of Jesus was effective in training for the kingdom of heaven':[89] therefore, he asserts, we can cope with the disappointment that the explanatory half (*Sachhälfte*) of the parables is in many cases lost, for at least we know what the subject was. The individuality of the parables and the possible variety within Jesus' message from one parable to the next is less important for Jülicher than the single main subject assumed for them all - the kingdom of God.

The Evangelists and their sources, however, 'confused the "parable" of Hellenistic scribalism, as we know it from Sirach - the twin sister of "riddle" - with the mashal of the Scripture in all its breadth and naturalness, which will have been at the same time the mashal of Jesus'.[90] The synoptic Evangelists ascribed a 'secretiveness' ('Heimlichkeit') to the parables, regarding them as the 'profound disguising of strangely higher thoughts',[91] and in this respect their view of Jesus' speech was similar to that of John.[92] All four gospel-writers agree that the parables 'required an interpretation even for the most initiated'.[93] It was the hand of 'over-eager over-workers'[94] which turned the parables from plain into obscure speech. Those who handed on Jesus' sayings frequently failed to record their context, and it is this, not any intrinsic obscurity in the sayings themselves, which sometimes causes us difficulty in understanding them.[95] In any case, a written form could not reproduce the freshness of his oral delivery: 'Jesus' parables were calculated to work instantly, children of the moment, deeply immersed in the particularity of the present; the magic of immediacy could not be reproduced in any [written] letters.'[96]

This polarity is neatly focused in a single sentence: 'it is very possible', says Jülicher, 'that these writers [the Evangelists] have brought from their sphere of learning certain preconceptions to the parables, from which Jesus in his high originality was completely free.'[97]

A second polarity in Jülicher's work is between *text and interpretation*. Jülicher, of course, was no fundamentalist. He did not take the gospels as infallible records of Jesus' words. That is implied in his embrace of source-criticism and his attempt to understand Jesus better than the Evangelists.[98] But there remains an anxious polarity between the text as a perspicacious document, and the idea - anathema to Jülicher - that it needs an 'interpretation'. The reader, for him, has nothing to do but read off the text's plain, literal sense.

With regard to the text, Jülicher is submissive to the Reformation tenet of the perspicuity of Scripture:

Allegories without an accompanying interpretation, according to their nature, can never possess the degree of perspicuity which dogma demands for Holy Scripture.[99]

The text, so the argument runs - this particular text - *must* be clear: therefore to read allegorical meanings into parables where no hint of such an intention has been left to us in the text is erroneous. There is a particular reason for this emphasis. To surrender the perspicuity of Scripture would be to open the door to subjectivist claims to personal illumination. In the following passage Jülicher appears as a staunch defender of Lutheran orthodoxy against a pietism which he sees as foreshadowed in the patristic period:

> Whoever does without an understanding, whoever adheres without a murmur to the thesis that such a grasp of the parables comes, to this very day, to no one but the one to whom the Lord grants it from on high through revelation, that therefore this part of Scriptural exegesis is accessible not to science and methodically taught research, but only to faith and inspiration - for him, indeed, this dilemma [of the subjectivity and therefore variety of parable interpretations] entails nothing which might suggest to him another construction of the nature of the parables [i.e. other than an 'allegorical' reading].[100]

For 'to this day nothing is hard and fast for allegorizing parable interpretation . . . nothing is impossible.'[101] 'One could indeed object . . . that each generation and each church party has read in [the parables] what just lay in their [own] heart.'[102] The reader, then, has a straightforward task. She is not to interpret at all.

Jülicher's repeated insistence that Jesus' parables, as similes, require no *Deutung* (interpretation) may be illustrated from his correction of Bernhard Weiss, whose basic opinion - that the point of the parables is to be sought in a 'general truth' - he is going to adopt, for this sole fault: that he used the word *Deutung*.[103] It is not only that Scripture *must* be clear. Modern readers do understand it, it *is in fact* clear to them. Even the 'most ignorant' ('Unkundigste') can understand parables such as The Good Samaritan and The Pharisee and the Customs Officer 'without an interpretative word'.[104] Jülicher allows that there are some stories where the sense is not so clear, but insists that this is the fault of the tradition, not the speaker.[105] The straightforward way in which ordinary, uneducated people can feel the power and grasp the message of the *clear* stories is seen as testimony to the *original* plainness of the others. Thus for Jülicher the necessity of careful historical investigation does not entail the impossibility of the parables' speaking directly across the centuries; on the contrary, it helps *recover* a directness which had been overlaid, or lost completely.

The third polarity is the most deeply rooted: it is the opposition between Jülicher himself and those who had interpreted the texts in earlier generations. Jülicher was a part of the emergent stream of modern biblical criticism, and that meant, above all, a part of the overthrow of ecclesiastical authority as a check upon research and exegesis. But what was to replace this authority? The light of reason: and that meant, in practice, the reasoning of the individual scholarly mind. Despite the existence of a community of scholarship, study of the Scriptures in this modern period was to become a much lonelier, more individualistic enterprise than it had been.[106] One who chose to take on the giants of the past and the tradition of the church universal might well feel both defensive and aggressive in his quest, and we should not be surprised to find expressions of these stances in Jülicher's work. This polarity cannot be described in the same neat fashion as the two preceding ones, for Jülicher, in the great tradition of modern 'objective' scholarship, does not talk *about* himself. But he *reveals* himself in the mighty assault he launches on the 'allegorical' tradition.

We might have expected this assault to be at its most powerful in the weighty account of the history of parable interpretation which forms Chapter VI of the first volume of *Die Gleichnisreden Jesu*, but in fact it is not so. Here Jülicher's carefulness to distinguish between different movements and strands is notable. He is ready to acknowledge real insight and exegetical skill where he finds it. From the early centuries his hero is Tertullian, who wrote a passage (whose terseness makes translation difficult) that he finds strongly supportive of his own stance:

> Although a figure is in the image of truth, its very image is in truth. It is necessary that it should exist first for itself, whereby it may be configured to another thing. From emptiness a similitude does not work, from nothing a parable does not succeed.[107]

(Despite this apparent support for the realistic and didactic rather than mystical nature of the parables, however, Tertullian is later found by Jülicher again 'in the false parable-concept of his contemporaries'.[108]) Jülicher also remarks on the positive direction in which the rhetorically trained Cappadocian Fathers led parable interpretation, treating the parables as a particular class and appreciating their clarificatory purpose.[109] He appreciates Cyril of Alexandria's emphasis on seeking the thought (νόησιν) which Christ brings to perfection (ἐξυφαίνει) in a parable.[110] He recognizes the fresh wind of change which blew at the Reformation[111] with the humane sensibility of Erasmus[112] and the spurning of scholastic complexity and playfulness by Luther, Bucer and Calvin.[113]

Similarly, the identity of Jülicher's main antagonists is clear in this chapter; and the reason for his antagonism is interesting. It was the Alexandrians, Clement and, especially, Origen who *par excellence,* as part of their emphasis on the different senses of Scripture, treated the parables as

enigmas to be deciphered.[114] Jülicher summarizes what he sees as the nadir
of the early period as it finds expression in Origen:

> Every thought of the unity of the parable is given up; word for word their
> terms are turned into figures, without any consideration of the context.[115]

The really baneful consequence of this, for Jülicher, is the *uncertainty* and
subjectivity thrown into the process of interpretation. He seems un-
appreciative of Origen's modesty in leaving open the possibility of different
interpretations, in averring 'that he does not trust himself to have fathomed
all the depths of the parable-sense, but a little is better than nothing'.[116] He
finds nothing to commend this stance:

> The uncertainty of all parable-exegesis is principally established by this;
> only the one whom Jesus wishes to enlighten with the light of insight may
> speak about them - who is to tell whether the so-called inner
> enlightenment is not an illusion?[117]

'All' parable-exegesis means here, in context, all exegesis of the parables
that has been coloured by this idea of their 'mysterious' character - which,
in Jülicher's view, has been the dominant model throughout the Christian
centuries. As I have shown in my previous chapter, the predominance of
such a model as an interpretative key in the earlier period seems largely an
illusion. It is the aim of Jülicher's own work to replace constant uncertainty
with at least the possibility of certainty. The untenability of the Origenist
view is clearly seen, for him, in the logical consequence drawn from it by
Jerome, that authoritative doctrine could never be based on the uncertain
understanding which was all a parable could offer.[118] But he does not raise
the possibility that Jesus may never have intended to utter stories which
could be clearly reduced to a certifiable 'meaning' - still less the possibility
that Jerome might be accepted happily on his own terms, and that we need
not be anxious if one part of Scripture *does* turn out to be unsuitable for
grounding doctrine.

Missing, however, from this great chapter is a sense of the all-
encompassing divine meaning within which the earlier Scriptural exegetes
lived and breathed. Correspondingly, the real nature of the break with
tradition which Jülicher is making is also largely concealed.
Notwithstanding comments along the way about those who have made an
effort to discover the intention of Jesus, the fact that this is indeed the main
fault-line is not made clear. Probably it was *not* clear to Jülicher himself;
we have the advantage of a historical perspective on his work. We can see,
for instance, the contrast with Trench half a century earlier - classed since

Jülicher's time, of course, among the pre-critical 'allegorizers' - who wrote that 'the possibility of a real teaching by parables' rests on the fact 'that the world around us is a *divine* world, that it is God's world, the world of the same God who is teaching and leading us into spiritual truth'.[119] The modern era of parable interpretation, of which Jülicher stands as the greatest representative, has cast off the entire framework of divine meaning, as silently as shedding a soft garment on the ground. There were no rites of passing.[120] The new era which Jülicher decisively - if not totally without precursors - ushers in is the era of seeking the intention of the man Jesus in the parables. But this is largely hidden under the powerful rhetoric of Jülicher's opposition between plain simile and obscure allegory.[121] The debate is seen as being between two different constructions of figurative speech. It is in passages from his crucial second chapter that the *agon* between Jülicher and his precursors comes most clearly to expression, and that we discover the full extent of his misreading of the heritage I sketched in Chapter 3.

Here is his first main summary of the old interpretative strategy:

> The pre-reformation church . . . almost unanimously held fast to the Evangelists' concept and struggled to fathom with ever new keen perception the real, full meaning of all these multisignificant riddle-sayings, always with greatest success in the cases where [the meaning] was inconsistent enough to allow itself to be determined in the exegesis by a healthy sense of tact, instead of by the parable-concept.[122]

Jülicher's opposition to the idea that 'insight' might be needed to interpret the parables is seen in his reference here to 'keen perception', *Scharfsinn*. His sentence as a whole seems to mean that the older interpreters retreated into a plainer style of exegesis when 'allegorizing' gave rise to gross inconsistencies, but this is the opposite of what we have found in Chapter 3. Each interpreter whom I considered there had a basic feel for the natural, moral impetus of the text; allegorical readings were supplementary to that, and where they were given greatest weight, in Ambrose, there is no embarrassment about 'inconsistencies'. To us, Ambrose may seem to tie himself in knots when he expounds the sores of Lazarus, the dogs who licked them, and the crumbs which fell from the rich man's table;[123] to himself, no doubt, he seemed simply to be exploring the wealth of interconnected significances which Scripture suggests. In fact, we noticed that there is movement in the opposite direction from that which Jülicher suggests. It was when a more *straightforward* sense seemed to be problematic that interpreters espoused a sense that was *parabolic*. The shrewd steward could not (it was thought) simply be taken as an exemplary character: therefore the parable as a whole was indeed a 'parable', i.e. the words betokened a sense beyond the literal. Jülicher goes on to say that since the Reformation no great improvement in parable studies has been seen, despite attempts at classifying the parables.

Later Jülicher has a detailed discussion of the nature of allegory. He writes that an allegory must hang together as a comprehensible piece of discourse before the transition is made to its deeper meaning.[124] He pictures it as a plane ('Ebene') from which the reader is to draw equidistant lines to discover another plane above. Or rather, when just one line has been drawn, the whole of the upper plane ought to come into view:

> Of course each point of the given plane must be set at the same distance from the one sought. The ideal of allegory is to report something which corresponds in such an excellent way with what is truly meant, that whoever has recognized what is meant at one point of the report, could also immediately carry out the transposition of the whole into the higher situation.[125]

The unspoken corollary of this description of allegory would be that the Fathers read Jesus' parables not only as allegories, but often as *bad* allegories: Ambrose on The Rich Man and Lazarus would again be an excellent example. Jülicher's omitting to make this point may be significant. He wants so to identify the older hermeneutic with 'reading the texts as allegories' that any admission that often this seemed to be 'reading the texts as poor allegories' would undermine his case, and weaken his fierce polarization between metaphor-allegory and simile-similitude.

Jülicher then makes an admission which is indeed his Achilles' heel:

> Neither Mark nor Matthew nor Luke himself carried through consistently their principle of parable-interpretation in the case of all the examples of parables of Jesus which they set down.[126]

The simple reason for this, of course, is that they probably never had a 'principle of parable-interpretation'. It is Jülicher and his successors who have assumed that the Evangelists treated the parables as mysteries that need decoding like allegories, despite the fact that there are hardly any such full-blown allegorical interpretations recorded in the gospels (Jülicher's assertion here is a considerable understatement). But our particular concern is with the point which Jülicher links to this. The Fathers are set against the Evangelists:

> With their naïve arbitrariness [the Evangelists], anyhow, treated the parables in this respect far better than the church Fathers, who, filled with

enthusiasm for allegorizing, did not now tolerate any single literal jot in these sayings.[127]

The hyperbole of the last part of this statement hardly needs further comment after our survey in the previous chapter. But Jülicher's struggle must continue. He proceeds to cast a slur upon the way that the Fathers treated their own predecessors in the church:

> Insofar as they . . . assert, by the ridiculing of their predecessors, that these things mean that and that and not something else, so may we, with a glance at Mk. 4:34, ask: who then has explained all this to you κατ' ἰδίαν [in private]?[128]

It is true that the Fathers were not above using strong words about each other on occasion. Jerome, in the prologue to his Latin translation of Origen's homilies on Luke, said that the recent commentator Ambrose 'plays in words, is drowsy in meanings'.[129] But the impression given by Jülicher that they were always ridiculing each other's interpretations of specific texts is grossly unfair. We have already seen the reverence of Bede for his precursors, indeed his reluctance to undertake a commentary of his own.[130] We have seen the strong sense of a *tradition of interpretation* which pervades the early commentators' writings. There was frequent quotation of, and allusion to, earlier works. There was preservation of ancient readings (e.g. the allegorical reading of The Good Samaritan summarized in Bonaventure) even when they seem to have appeared somewhat archaic beside the main interpretation being offered;[131] there was no embarrassment about conflicting interpretations, 'the inexhaustibility of the text being greater than the authority even of Augustine'.[132] The closest thing to ridicule (*Bespöttelung*) of predecessors that we discovered in Chapter 3 was Calvin's comments about the Fathers' allegorical readings. But that was a scorning not of individual interpretations, but of a particular interpretative style - a forerunner, indeed, of the scorning of the same style by Jülicher himself, and a faint foreshadowing of Jülicher's own vehement ridiculing of his precursors. Of the interpreters we surveyed, Calvin came closest in stance to Jülicher himself. Calvin, like Jülicher, had his own conscious and perhaps unconscious reasons for standing out at times so strongly against the tradition. One is tempted, then, to venture that in this passage Jülicher is projecting his own acerbic tendency towards earlier interpreters on to the Fathers.

It seems as if in his characterizing - or caricaturing - of the Fathers Jülicher had one particular target in mind, to whom he assimilated a full fifteen centuries-worth of interpreters. He argues against some contemporaries thus:

One who allows himself to indicate the ὅμοιον ['like thing', i.e. the point of comparison] of some simile from quite foreign writers, or anyway from quite a different context, has sunk back to the standpoint of Origen.[133]

Jülicher wants to affirm that the meaning of a simile should be determined by its own immediate context alone, without seeking (as Origen did) a kind of comprehensive biblical tropology whereby all words in Scripture should be interpreted with reference to other occurrences of the word elsewhere within it.[134] But when he writes

> What a gross error it is then, to ascribe at all costs to individual ideas within a parable the metaphorical meaning which they have in other places in holy Scripture[135]

he is countering an excess the danger of which the majority of the old interpreters seem to have sufficiently recognized. In the history of interpretation Origen looks somewhat eccentric. Certainly, the early commentators we have studied - Ambrose, Augustine, Gregory, Bede - did not venture far down this path. It was indeed as a part of the developing sense of realism which Aristotelian learning brought to the study of Scripture that Bonaventure so carefully distinguished the *different* senses which the same word may bear in different parts of Scripture: he is quite clear that we are *not* to interpret a word in one place blindly according to the sense it bears elsewhere.[136]

A little later comes another misrepresentation of the tenor of ancient parable interpretation:

> The parable-author [according to the older view] would often himself announce his gold as small change; he would let his story fall immediately like shells of no worth, so that he could reach the kernel, the application; it would be indeed much, if in the case of a parable one did not notice right at the beginning where it was heading, if the cold soaking of the application came upon us completely unforeseen and unexpected.[137]

Note the eloquence of this rhetoric: the gold of the story despised as worthless; the shells shed to reach the kernel; the punch line designed to hit us like a torrential shower-bath ('Sturzbad'). It is powerful, but as a generalization it does not well fit the view of the Fathers or the medievals concerning Jesus. Even if one were to take Ambrose's highly 'allegorical' reading of The Good Samaritan as an instance of the kind of understanding of the parables Jülicher is attacking, it would not fit. The story is not despised as a mere outer husk (and still less is Jesus, the parable-author, portrayed as despising it thus!). Without the story and its entire pattern, there could be no glimpse for Ambrose of Christ coming to the rescue of the fallen human race; that was not a mere interpretation of the individual elements ('einzelnen Züge'[138]) but precisely a construal of the whole movement of the tale, from start to finish. Yet the climax of the interpretation, as we saw, beyond this suggestive portrayal of salvation-history, was the plain injunction to love. That was not a 'kernel' that required much shell cracking, nor a particularly rude awakening for the hearers after the telling of the story. It is not in fact very different, in its moral thrust, from Jülicher's own reading of the parable.[139] We do not need to overstate the case. No doubt from time to time there have been eccentric interpretations which have given the impression of a parable-teller simply conjuring with words. But Jülicher seems deaf to the subtle modulations, and insensitive to the aim and spirit, of the mainstream discussions of significant parables we considered in Chapter 3.

When he discusses the category 'example-story' (*Beispielerzählung*) Jülicher seizes a further opportunity to pillory the 'allegorical' tradition. In the case of these parables, he says, the futility of their method was truly shown up:

> On these rocks the method of allegorical parable-interpretation always pitifully founders; it had no success in making out the foolish rich man [of Lk. 12:16-21] to be something other than a foolish rich man and the customs officer more than a poor sinner; here indeed is 'interpretation' [the bogey-word *Deuten*] too difficult an undertaking. Also, a comparison of the individual elements has no sense at all; since if one describes the Pharisee as a picture of all the haughty, can one seriously compare all the haughty with one haughty person, and thus the category with the individual belonging to it?[140]

The older interpreters did show restraint in allegorical readings of the example-stories (Ambrose on The Good Samaritan[141] and The Rich Man and Lazarus[142] being exceptional among the commentaries we considered). But why? Not, surely (in Jülicher's metaphor) because the brave ship of allegorization finally meets its doom in the treacherous waters of example-story. But simply in that the stories offered a more straightforward meaning. There never was any universal agenda of unremitting allegorization.

There is not the slightest sense of embarrassment among the early interpreters that a story like The Pharisee and the Customs Officer does not admit of easy 'spiritualization'. That does not mean, however, that figures or tropes are absent. Jülicher himself, perhaps without realizing it, acknowledges this when he makes the customs officer 'a poor sinner' - that is a synecdoche, representative of a class. Indeed, the embarrassment seems more the other way round, that Jülicher cannot impose *his* unremitting agenda of 'similization' (to coin a word) upon the example-stories. It is this agenda which makes it difficult for him to admit the *tropical* character of an individual element. In encouraging us to take the story whole, and yield a single point, he repudiates the idea that a single element (the Pharisee) can be 'compared' to the category of which it is a part. It would be much simpler to drop the idea of comparison altogether and admit the presence of the trope synecdoche in individual elements. Speaker, hearer and reader do instinctively make a link between (for instance) the portrayal, in story, of an individual haughty person, and the haughty in general. This is not the mysterious allegorical encoding which Jülicher and Dodd loved to hate. But, as should be more than apparent by now, that kind of encoding is largely a straw man.

Our final example must be the magnificent purple passage with which the chapter ends:

No means did [Jesus] leave untried, no medium of language, in order to bring the word of his God to and into the hearts of his hearers - only allegory, which does not proclaim, but conceals, which does not reveal, but shuts up, which does not join, but divides, which does not persuade, but repels: this speech-form the clearest, the most powerful, the plainest of all speakers could not use for his purposes.[143]

This is an absolutist view of the nature of allegory which many would now regard as tinged by the particular literary-cultural prejudices of Jülicher's age:[144] but our main point is that it is doubtful if many ever said that Jesus did use such a form.

What, then, are the influences that may have contributed to these powerful oppositions underlying the surface opposition between simile and allegory?

In addition to the trends of biblical criticism in which Jülicher was caught up, it is of interest to note two aspects of Romanticism which form part of the general *Zeitgeist*, the 'horizontal' stream of influence. The first is the Romantic idea of the poet. Claude Welch writes of the Romantics' 'near worship at times of originality and genius', quoting Friedrich Schlegel:

It is precisely individuality that is the original and eternal thing in men . . . The cultivation and development of this individuality, as one's highest vocation, would be a divine egoism.[145]

It is hard not to see this exaltation of originality in Jülicher's presentation of Jesus. For him, Jesus is indeed the truly original individual, the one who drew his sparkling figures of speech direct from nature, not from some code that would remain a closed book to many. As such he is contrasted with all his interpreters. Welch then writes that following Jean-Jacques Rousseau, Romanticism 'exalted the immediacy of feeling - in the self, for humanity and for the world', and that in Novalis's formulation even philosophy 'is originally feeling, dreaming'.[146] German Romanticism owed much to the *Sturm und Drang* movement[147] upon which Johann Gottfried Herder had been influential.[148] Herder's emphasis on poetry as 'the expression of the indwelling 'Kraft' (energy, power) of the poet'[149] and 'as the product of . . . intense emotion'[150] has distinct affinities with Jülicher's portrayal of the speech of Jesus. Jülicher refers to Jesus' 'holy eagerness' ('heiligen Eifer'), and to the 'high pathos' ('hohes Pathos') whose weight allegory was not fitted to bear.[151] However, he would not have wanted to give the impression that Jesus was a 'poet' in the basically aesthetic mode in which his own century had understood 'poetry'. Jesus, for him, had another aim entirely from that of giving pleasure.[152]

The other aspect of Romanticism worth noting in this context is its attitude to figures of speech. Terence Hawkes describes how Romantic poetry reacted against the strong tendency in the seventeenth and eighteenth centuries to separate content from form, to drive a wedge between plain logic and ornamental figures, to privilege the supposed fixity of written words with their dictionary definitions over the ambiguities of living speech.[153] This tendency had given figures of speech a bad name in some quarters: eighteenth-century literary metaphors 'are at their worst prepackaged, predigested, finished products, unloaded strategically in the poem when triggered by taste'.[154] For the Romantic, metaphor in its ideal form is fresh, alive, the opposite of merely conventional; a means of communication, but not instantly transparent; it demands imaginative work of its hearer. Johann Wolfgang Goethe's *Maximen und Reflexionen*[155] (contrasting symbol and allegory) and William Wordsworth's *Preface to Lyrical Ballads*[156] are *loci classici* repudiating mere ornamentation in favour of more natural expression. A significant influence upon the Romantics was Giovanni Battista Vico, who held that metaphor was 'not fanciful "embroidery" of the facts' but 'a way of *experiencing* the facts'.[157]

Craig L. Blomberg rightly links the Romantic view that 'the highest aim of all art ought to be the representation of the general by the specific (rather than the substitution of one specific for another as in allegory)'[158] with Jülicher's approach to the parables. Yet, as with the Romantic view of the poet, Jülicher retains a certain independence with respect to Romantic influence. His description of allegory as an aesthetic art form and his privileging of a more direct form of communication parallel the Romantics' reaction against the ornamental artificiality of preceding generations' literary output. But he does not share their esteem for metaphor understood as language coming alive.[159] Metaphor is indeed not solely ornamental for Jülicher; it prompts and enriches;[160] nevertheless it remains on the same side of his great divide as allegory, as an artificial device rather than a fundamental of language. Jülicher does not envisage that the great 'passion' of Jesus might find expression in metaphor, which is too indirect a mode; only simile will do. Romantic influences, then, do not swamp Jülicher, or fully account for his approach to the parables. To understand that approach more fully we must turn, paradoxically perhaps, to the great 'vertical' influence of Christian tradition.

We note first that the fact that Jülicher belonged to an age that was discovering emancipation from the *dogmatic* Christ does not preclude his holding a 'high' view of Jesus. Indeed, many Christian theologians who were experiencing this emancipation *needed* to maintain that esteem for Jesus and therefore, consciously or otherwise, sought different grounds from the dogmatic on which to base it. Jülicher was a pastor.[161] There was no question of throwing all veneration for Jesus to the winds until assumptionless historical research could establish what sort of person he really was. This is seen in the assumptions about Jesus which Jülicher brings from Scripture to his work.[162] He clearly accepts John's witness to Jesus as the λόγος, and the synoptic gospels' emphasis on the Kingdom of God as the dominant subject of Jesus' teaching. The accent is especially on human qualities: the personal originality of Jesus is stressed more than his divine Sonship; his possession of wisdom[163] rather than his 'being' divine Wisdom; but the Scriptural framework remains.

It is post-biblical Christian interpretation against which Jülicher inveighs and rebels, and yet, I suggest, this is the most overwhelming influence upon him. The strength of the rebellion seems to be in direct proportion to the anxiety this influence induced. Bloom adapts Sigmund Freud's use of the story of Oedipus - as symbolic of a psychological phenomenon - to describe a literary one, of which Jülicher appears to be a good example: 'The strong poets have followed [Oedipus] by transforming their blindness towards their precursors into the revisionary insights of their own work.'[164] As Oedipus unwittingly killed his father and equally unwittingly married his mother, Jülicher (blind to what he is doing) slays the 'Fathers' and yet also joins himself to the tradition which gave him birth. In other words, much of Jülicher's second chapter, which seems quite dramatically to misread the tradition, seems as much about his struggle to find his own voice as his search for that of Jesus.

Jülicher finds himself in a historical bind. On the one hand he is committed to the 'objective' standards of historical scholarship. On the other hand, although loosed from a whole tradition of interpretation, he must still make his own construction of the ancient figurative text. The anxiety generated by this situation shows itself in Jülicher's antagonism to the whole idea of the *interpretation* of the parables. Even the Evangelists, in his view, to a greater or lesser extent misread the parables, and are thus contrasted with Jesus' sparkling freshness. The church misread them still more, and thus the need is to return to the plain text itself beyond the claims to inspiration of particular 'interpreters'.

The great irony in *Die Gleichnisreden Jesu* is that Jülicher himself is offering his own interpretation. He admits as much, quite freely, when he recognizes ruefully the impossibility of attaining a goal such as every scholar in the tradition of the Enlightenment aspires to:

> Our real wish would be so to tell the history of parable-understanding, that *our interpretation* would emerge as the result, as the single possibility still remaining after many failed attempts . . . this goal is placed too high, because for a start judgements about 'failed' and 'possible' are too different . . .[165]

But he seems not to feel the force of his own words. *His* reading is not (he thinks) a *Deutung*, but it is nevertheless an *Auffassung*, an interpretation, an attempt to grasp, just as all previous readings have been. Indeed, it is an even more intense attempt than earlier readings, precisely because Jülicher *is* seeking to 'catch' the meaning and tone of Jesus, not just meditating on the resonances of the text.

Jülicher fears the uncertainty that an acknowledgement of this truth might open up. So he vigorously asserts the essential clarity of Jesus' words and projects himself as its champion against obscurantist interpreters of every generation. Others have offered a *Deutung*; *he* simply attends to the natural force of the text. The essential points of The Good Samaritan 'offer themselves unmediated out of the story to the hearer, they fall into our lap'.[166] We should not miss the startling nature of this claim. Jülicher pretends to an immediate insight into the mind of Jesus in a far bolder way than the Fathers, medievals or Reformers ever contemplated. Of course he presents it as the response of 'everyone', and in the opposition he draws between the plain text and the individual interpreter with his dangerous pietistic claim to inspiration he aligns himself very firmly with the text itself. But this surely cannot blind us to what is going on. He has not only aimed to understand Jesus better than the Evangelists themselves; he concludes that he has done so. From the great opponent of *Scharfsinn*, here is a claim to *Scharfsinn - par excellence*.

But it should by now be no surprise to the reader when I assert that we should not dismiss the 'insight' of Jülicher just because it is 'insight'. There can be no understanding of parables without insight. The insight of Jülicher was won through creative wrestling with his precursors. The genuine insight, however, was not into a Jesus who spoke in similes, but a Jesus who was passionate about communication, who wanted his message to be heard and understood. It was insight accompanied by blindness. In Albert Schweitzer's words, 'Jülicher has an incomparable power of striking fire out of every one of the parables, but the flame is of a different colour from that which it showed when Jesus pronounced the parables before the enchanted multitude.'[167] There was blindness to the fact that his predecessors' focus was not the historical intention of Jesus. There was blindness, too, to the specificity they discerned in the parables, which Jülicher replaced with generality. The 'general truth' understanding was an escape route from what he saw as the enslavement of different generations to interpretations reflecting their own concerns. He did not want to find that the parables directly addressed heretics, monks or popes, and therefore he did not find that they addressed specific situations or people in the ministry of Jesus.

There also seems to have been blindness to the fact that in the fundamental content of what his precursors' interpretations suggested (despite themselves) about Jesus, there was continuity between their readings and his own, much more striking than the disjunction. Jülicher, like the tradition before him, found in the parables moral exhortation and doctrine about God. The influence of the tradition was far more overwhelming than he knew and wished, yet in his protest against it he found not only his own voice, but also a fresh hearing of the voice of Jesus.

NOTES

1. Stuhlmacher, *Criticism*, 22.
2. Bloom, *Anxiety*, 10.
3. W. G. Kümmel, *The New Testament: The History of the Investigation of Its Problems* [*Das Neue Testament: Geschichte der Erforschung seiner Probleme*, 1970] (London: SCM Press, 1973), 186, 433, 479. Jülicher's work has never been translated into English. Translation of the title itself is problematic, since Jülicher deliberately avoided the German *Parabel* because of its associations with riddle or allegory (Jülicher, *Gleichnisreden* I, 30f.). His title reflects his emphasis on the essentially comparative character of Jesus' parables (the basic meaning of *Gleichnis* is 'simile').

4. Kissinger (*Parables*, xvii) refers to an earlier Dutch work which, had it been in German, might have had an impact like Jülicher's: C. E. van Koestveld, *De Gelijkenissen van den Zaligmaker*, 2nd ed. (Schoonhoven: 1869).

5. Neill characterizes the mindset out of which nineteenth-century criticism was breaking free: 'Traditional Christian reverence held a view of Biblical inspiration which separated it off from every other book . . . all awkward questions were supposed to be stilled by the protection of inspiration': Neill and Wright, *Interpretation*, 33.

6. The idea of the 'mythopoeic' outlook of the ancient sources goes back to David Friedrich Strauss's epochal *Life of Jesus* [1835]: see Neill and Wright, *Interpretation*, 13f.

7. Jülicher, *Gleichnisreden* I, 1-24.

8. Ibid., 1.

9. Ibid.

10. On the Romantic hermeneutics of 'divination' cf. Wolterstorff, *Divine Discourse*, 183.

11. Kümmel, *New Testament*, 369.

12. Jülicher, *Gleichnisreden* I, 2-11.

13. Ibid., 11.

14. Ibid. On Jülicher's moderate stance in relation to the 'Tübingen School' of Baur see Kümmel, *New Testament*, 174-8.

15. Jülicher, *Gleichnisreden* I, 16.

16. Ibid., 18.

17. Ibid., 19f.

18. 'The one who seeks, finds': ibid., 20.

19. Ibid., 22.

20. Ibid., 22f.

21. Ibid., 23f.

22. Ibid., 25-118.

23. Ibid., 49.

24. Ibid., 80, 98.

25. He acknowledges that example-stories are picture-language ('Bildrede', ibid., 113); they are not 'uneigentlich' (non-literal), but then nor, for him, are the figures of speech *Gleichnis* and *Fabel*. Jülicher maintains the distinction between figures and tropes, though he does not explicitly expound it; a trope is always 'uneigentlich', a figure need not be.

26. This challenge, which is posed by historical 'data' of all kinds, becomes particularly acute when dealing with the history of a person such as Jesus. I am grateful for Professor James Dunn's historical insight at this point.

27. Stuhlmacher, *Criticism*, 45, expounding the work of Ernst Troeltsch.

28. Jülicher, *Gleichnisreden* I, 26.

29. Ibid., 41.

30. Ibid., 25-8.

31. Ibid., 32-42.

32. See especially ibid., 38, 52, 69ff., 94f.

33. Ibid., 42.

34. Ibid., 30f.
35. Ibid., 57, 66, 101.
36. Ibid., 69f.
37. Ibid., 88.
38. Ibid., 63, 86, 100f.
39. See Kissinger, *Parables*. For a summary of positions supportive of, and opposed to, Jülicher's, see Hermann Binder, *Das Gleichnis von dem Richter und der Witwe: Lukas 18,1-8* (Neukirchen-Vluyn: Neukirchener, 1988), 61-5. A useful brief critique of Jülicher is found in Caird, *Language*, 162.
40. Jülicher, *Gleichnisreden* I, 105.
41. See Dodd, *Parables*, and Jeremias, *Parables*. The new awareness of the 'apocalyptic' background of Jesus' kingdom-language had been heralded by the appearance in 1892 of *Die Predigt Jesu vom Reiche Gott* by Johannes Weiss. Thus, as Albert Schweitzer pointed out, by the time Jülicher's second volume appeared 'the eschatological question' was 'already in possession of the field' - but 'in general the new problem plays no very special part in Jülicher's exposition': Albert Schweitzer, *The Quest of the Historical Jesus* [*Von Reimarus zu Wrede: Eine Geschichte der Lebens-Jesu-Forschung*, 1906], 3rd ed. (London: A. & C. Black, 1954), 263.
42. ' "Die Deutung der Parabel kann nur in einer allgemeinen Wahrheit liegen, die aus der Uebertragung der dargestellten Regel auf das Gebiet des religiös-sittlichen Lebens, auf die Ordnungen des Gottesreiches sich ergiebt" ': Jülicher, *Gleichnisreden* I, 105.
43. For a review of positions supportive of and opposed to Jülicher's 'one-point' approach, see Craig L. Blomberg, *Interpreting the Parables* (Leicester: Apollos, 1990), 29-74. Blomberg himself opts for a restrained multi-point understanding; to speak of 'points' at all in connection with the parables may be reductive (it was certainly not, of course, the method of the earlier interpreters).
44. For instance, Martin proposes that simile and metaphor should not be distinguished as to cognitive function: 'Metaphor', 61. Cf. Kjärgaard, *Metaphor*, 198-216.
45. Cf. especially Boucher, *Mysterious Parable*.
46. See particularly Wilder, *Rhetoric*; Robert W. Funk, *Language, Hermeneutic, and Word of God: The Problem of Language in the New Testament and Contemporary Theology* (New York, Evanston, and London: Harper & Row, 1966); Crossan, *In Parables* and *Cliffs of Fall: Paradox and Polyvalence in the Parables of Jesus* (New York: Seabury Press, 1980); Ricoeur, 'Biblical Hermeneutics'; Frederick Houk Borsch, *Many Things in Parables: Extravagant Stories of New Community* (Philadelphia: Fortress Press, 1988); Scott, *Hear*.
47. For a caricature of Jülicher's view, saying that he presents the parables as 'picturesque stories to enforce prudential platitudes', see Hunter, *Interpreting*, 39.
48. 'Die opferfreudige Liebesübung verschafft in Gottes und der Menschen Augen den höchsten Wert, kein Vorzug des Amtes und der Geburt kann sie ersetzen. Der Barmherzige verdient, auch wenn er ein Samariter ist, die Seligkeit eher als der jüdische Tempelbeamte, der Selbstsucht fröhnt': Jülicher, *Gleichnisreden* II, 596.
49. Ibid., 598.
50. Ibid., 596.
51. Ricoeur, 'Biblical Hermeneutics', 131.

52. '[I]n dem Beispiel eines Vaters, der den mit Schuld beladenen aber reuig heim
gekehrten Sohn liebewarm empfängt und seine Freude auch dem Zorn des älteren,
immer treu gebliebenen, Sohnes gegenüber rechtfertigt, soll Jesus gerechtfertigt werden,
der die Zöllner und Sünder annimmt, obwohl die Pharisäer und Schriftgelehrten darüber
murren': Jülicher, *Gleichnisreden* II, 359.
53. 'Wie ein Vater zweier Söhne, dem der eine davongeht, um Gut und Ehre, fast auch
das Leben zu verschleudern, diesen, sobald er reuig wiederkehrt, mit Herzlichkeit, ja
nun mit einer nach langem Glimmen fast lodernden Liebesglut empfängt, ohne dass dem
andern Sohn, der allewege seine Pflicht gethan, dadurch ein Unrecht geschähe und er
sich der Liebe seines Vaters minder teilhaftig fühlen dürfte, so steht der Weg zu Gottes
Vaterherzen auch dem verrottetsten Sünder, wenn er nur Zugang dahin haben will,
immer offen, und ist die Wiederaufnahme an Kindes Statt ihm gewiss, ohne dass dies je
eine Zurücksetzung des Gerechten bedeutete, und den von Gottes Liebe irgendwie
ausschlösse': ibid., 362.
54. E.g. Jeremias, *Parables*, 132; Scott, *Hear*, 122.
55. '[I]st nicht sowohl eine Verteidigung des sünderfreundlichen Jesus gegen Angriffe
dünkelhafter Superfrommen, als - und das erhöbt ihren Wert - eine erhabene
Offenbarung über eine Grundfrage der Religion, nämlich die: darf der Gott der
Gerechtigkeit die Sünder in Gnaden aufnehmen?': *Gleichnisreden* II, 363. Linnemann
comments that '[t]his view of the proclamation of Jesus, which makes of him a
systematic theologian, can hardly be right': *Parables*, 154.
56. Cf. his protest against the dogmatic usage of the parable in support of the doctrine of
justification by faith: *Gleichnisreden* II, 334.
57. '[I]n dem Bewusstsein, an seinem Herzen seines Vaters Herz recht zu erkennen,
malt er den Menschen des Vaters Bild: weil er, Jesus, ohne sich Mangel an
Wertschätzung der Gerechten vorwerfen zu müssen, doch so viel mehr sich hingezogen
zu denen fühlt, Freude zu denen hat, die ihn nötig haben, für die er etwas leisten kann,
die ohne ihn der Hölle gehören würden, muss auch sein Vater so empfinden, kühnlich
proklamiert er Gott als den echten Sündervater': ibid., 363.
58. 'Nach Jesus Begriffen hat Gott so vergeben, wiederaufgenommen, sich gefreut auch
schon vor Jesus; er hätte es seit Anfang der Welt an jedem Verworfenen so gern gethan:
die neue Aera des Evangeliums hebt mit Jesus nicht an, weil erst sein Sühnetod eine
Begnadigung der Sünder für Gott möglich machte, sondern weil erst er durch sein Leben
und seine Verkündigung diesen Gott den Menschen enthüllte, nahe brachte, ihnen das
Vertrauen auf Gottes Gnade, d.h. den Glauben schuf, und sie mutig machte auf Gott zu
hoffen': ibid., 365.
59. See Chapter 5 below.
60. 'Damit würde der Haushalter als ein Vorbild der Klugheit für die Gläubigen
hingestellt, und auf Empfehlung der Klugheit liefe die Parabel hinaus': *Gleichnisreden*
II, 509.
61. Ibid., 510.
62. 'Ich sehe in der Parabel vielmehr veranschaulicht, wie jemand rechtzeitig die
geeigneten Mittel ergreift, um seinen Zweck zu erreichen, wie er aus scheinbar
hoffnungsloser Notlage sich doch noch rettet, weil er überlegt und handelt, solange ihm
beides noch nützen kann, so lange er noch Mittel in Händen hat': ibid., 510f.

63. 'Nicht die rechte Verwendung des Reichtums, sondern die entschlossene Ausnützung der Gegenwart als Vorbedingung für eine erfreuliche Zukunft sollte an der Geschichte des Haushalters eingeprägt werden, die je nach dem Anlass, der sie hervorrief, mehr ernst warnenden Charakter haben konnte: hütet Euch vor dem Zuspät, denn wenn erst die neue Zeit angebrochen ist, kann man nichts mehr für sie thun . . . so lang es noch heute heisst, giebt es Mittel das Morgen günstig für Euch zu gestalten': ibid., 511.

64. See above, p. 90.

65. 'Jesus erzählt, was ihm zuerst eingefallen ist, und ihm fällt ein, was er erlebt; er sprach, um unmittelbar auf seine Landsleute zu wirken, um den Geschmack moderner Bibelleser unbekümmert': Jülicher, *Gleichnisreden* II, 514.

66. '[A]n etwas mehr als an Almosengeben gedacht hat': ibid.

67. '[D]ie ärgste Verkennung . . . war der Wahn, sie sei gedichtet, um neue Offenbarungen über die Zustände in der andern Welt zu proklamieren': ibid., 623.

68. See above, p. 94.

69. Jülicher, *Gleichnisreden* II, 638.

70. Ibid., 640.

71. 'Freude an einem Leben im Leiden, Furcht vor dem Genussleben': ibid., 638.

72. See *Gleichnisreden* I, 56, where Jülicher states that unlike simile which enlightens the reader's understanding, metaphor 'presupposes an existing understanding, it suggests briefly, instead of showing' ('setzt bei ihm schon Verständnis voraus, sie deutet kurz an, statt zu zeigen').

73. Jülicher, *Gleichnisreden* II, 283f.

74. Ibid., 289.

75. Ibid.

76. Ibid., 289f.

77. Fitzmyer cites Is. 42:1; 43:20; 65:9; Ps. 105:6,43; Sir. 47:22: *Luke*, 1180.

78. 'Allegorization' was emphasized by Jeremias as a 'principle of transformation' by which the parables were adapted in the early church: *Parables*, especially 66-89.

79. 'Jesus wollte lehren, dass unter allen Umständen die Demut Gotte willkommener ist als die Selbstgerechtigkeit': Jülicher, *Gleichnisreden* II, 609.

80. Ibid.

81. See further below, p. 136.

82. 'Wie ein Samariter, der Liebe übt, der höchsten Ehren bei Gott und Menschen würdiger ist als unbarmherzige Priester und Levit, so ist der Zöllner, der in bussfertiger Demut um Gnade fleht, dem Himmelreich näher als ein aufgeblasener Pharisäer: Gott siehet allein das Herz an . . .': Jülicher, *Gleichnisreden* II, 609.

83. '[Er] . . . die Weisheit nicht in der Unklarheit zu suchen nötig hatte': Jülicher, *Gleichnisreden* I, 41.

84. 'Jesus hatte zu viel Logos in sich, um den klaren λόγος hinter solch dunkler Gestikulation zurückzusetzen': ibid., 56.

85. '[E]ine rätselhafte Antwort von seiner Seite hätte als Ausflucht genommen werden müssen': ibid., 86.

86. 'Die Redeform ist eben zu schwer, um seinen heiligen Eifer, um überhaupt ein hohes Pathos zu vertragen. Die Leidenschaft, reine wie unreine, schafft sich ihren Ausdruck

unwillkürlich; das Bedacht, Ueberlegte einer Allegorie ist ihrem Ansturm nicht gewachsen': ibid., 63.

87. Ibid., 64.

88. 'Es wäre bei ihm höchlich überraschend, wenn er in seiner Lehre eine Kunstform mit dominierendem Einfluss ausgestattet hätte, die wohl ästhetisch, aber nicht didaktisch wirksam ist': ibid.

89. '[J]edes Wort Jesu der Erziehung zum Himmelreich galt': ibid., 104f.

90. '[D]ie παραβολή der hellenistischen Schriftgelehrsamkeit, wie wir sie aus Sirach kennen, die Zwillingsschwester des αἴνιγμα, mit dem Maschal der Schrift in all seiner Weite und Natürlichkeit, der zugleich der Maschal Jesu gewesen sein wird, verwechselt haben': ibid., 42.

91. '[T]iefsinnige Verhüllung absonderlich hoher Gedanken': ibid., 44. For Jülicher, the Evangelists regarded the words of the parables as a 'cloak' ('Verhüllung', a word he uses frequently) which was 'deep-sensed' ('tiefsinnige'), i.e. contained a hidden meaning that could be revealed to the initiated while being concealed from the outsiders.

92. Ibid., 45.

93. '[S]elbst für die Eingeweihtesten einer Auflösung bedurften': ibid., 46.

94. '[E]ifriger Ueberarbeiter', ibid., 49.

95. Ibid., 90f.

96. 'Jesu Parabeln waren auf sofortige Wirkung berechnet, Kinder des Augenblicks, tief eingetaucht in die Eigenheit der Gegenwart, der Zauber der Unmittelbarkeit liess sich bei ihnen durch keinen Buchstaben fortpflanzen': ibid., 91.

97. '[E]s ist sehr möglich, dass jene Schriftsteller aus ihrem Bildungskreise gewisse Vorurteile auch an die Parabeln herangebracht haben, von denen Jesus in seiner hohen Originalität ganz frei war': ibid., 68.

98. Ibid., 11.

99. 'Den Grad von perspicuitas, den das Dogma für die hl. Schrift verlangt, können Allegorien ohne beigefügte Deutung ihrem Wesen nach nie besitzen': ibid., 62. On Luther's view of the inner and outer clarity of Scripture cf. Stuhlmacher, *Criticism*, 34; on the possible implication of this doctrine that hermeneutical endeavour is hardly necessary, cf. Thiselton, *New Horizons*, 179.

100. 'Wer auf ein Verstehen verzichtet, wer ohne Phrase dabei verharrt, dass solche Parabellösung bis heute niemandem gelingt, als wem der Herr von oben her durch Offenbarung die gewähre, dass also dieser Teil der Schriftexegese nicht der Wissenschaft und methodisch gelehrten Forschung, sondern dem Glauben und der Inspiration allein zugänglich ist, für den freilich enthält jenes Dilemma nichts, was ihm eine andre Auffassung des Wesens der Parabeln nahelegte': Jülicher, *Gleichnisreden* I, 62f. Cf. Stuhlmacher, *Criticism*, 37 on the pietists' aim to revive 'the insight and missionary courage of faith'.

101. '[B]is zu diesem Tage der allegorisierenden Parabelauslegung nichts fest und sicher . . . nichts unmöglich ist': Jülicher, *Gleichnisreden* I, 63.

102. 'Man könnte ja einwenden . . . dass jedes Geschlecht und jede kirchliche Partei in ihnen das gelesen habe, was ihnen gerade am Herzen lag': ibid.

103. Ibid., 105f.

104. '[O]hne ein deutendes Wort': ibid., 62.

105. Ibid., 90f.

106. Cf. Thiselton, *New Horizons*, 143.

107. '[E]tsi figmentum veritatis in imagine est, imago ipsa in veritate est sui. Necesse est esse prius sibi, quo alii configuretur. De vacuo similitudo non competit, de nullo parabola non convenit': Tertullian, *De Resurrectione* 30, cited in Jülicher, *Gleichnisreden* I, 216f.

108. '[I]n dem falschen Parabel-Begriff seiner Zeitgenossen': ibid., 217.

109. Ibid., 227-30.

110. Ibid., 236.

111. Ibid., 252.

112. Ibid., 252-4.

113. Ibid., 256-62.

114. Ibid., 220-25.

115. '[J]eder Gedanke an die Einheitlichkeit der Parabel ist aufgegeben; Wort für Wort werden ihre Begriffen ohne alle Rücksicht auf Zusammenhang übertragen': ibid., 224f.

116. '[D]ass er sich nicht zutraue, alle Tiefen des Parabelsinnes ergründet zu haben, aber weniges sei besser denn nichts': ibid., 223.

117. 'Die Unsicherheit aller Parabelexegese ist hiermit prinzipiell anerkannt; nur der darf über sie mitreden, den Jesus mit dem Licht der Erkenntnis erleuchten will - wer stellt fest, ob die angebliche innere Erleuchtung nicht eine Illusion ist?': ibid.

118. Ibid., 242.

119. *Notes*, 17.

120. If Jülicher still holds to some notion that divine meaning is to be found in Scripture, I have found no instance where he discusses this as an issue in his reception of older interpreters. Claude Welch, *Protestant Thought in the Nineteenth Century*, 2 vols. (New Haven and London: Yale University Press, 1972) describes the view of Herder that 'the more fully the truly human character of Scripture is discerned, the more fully the living divine spirit may be recognized' (I, 54). If such views influenced Jülicher at all, it is not apparent.

121. Gerald L. Bruns makes a similar point when he writes that the dismissal of allegory as pseudo-exegesis 'maps onto allegory the structure of romantic hermeneutics in which a subject deploys itself analytically against an object': 'Midrash', 640.

122. 'Die vorreformatorische Kirche hat denn auch ziemlich einstimmig den Begriff der Evangelisten festgehalten und sich abgemüht mit immer neuem Scharfsinn die eigentliche, volle Bedeutung all dieser vieldeutigen Rätselreden zu ergründen, am glücklichsten immer, wenn sie inkonsequent genug war in der Exegese statt von dem Parabelbegriff sich von einem gesunden Taktgefühl leiten zu lassen': Jülicher, *Gleichnisreden* I, 48.

123. See above, 91.

124. There seems to be some inconsistency in Jülicher's view in *Gleichnisreden* on this point. On I, 59 he writes that the outward form of the allegory should ideally be 'complete' ('vollkommen') in itself, offering pleasure ('Wohlgefallen') even to those who do not perceive that there is an inner meaning. But on I, 65 he writes that an allegory always points beyond itself because 'its wording does not satisfy' ('ihr Wortlaut nicht befriedigt').

125. '[N]atürlich muss jeder Punkt der gegebenen Ebene gleich weit von der gesuchten entfernt sein. Das Ideal von Allegorie ist hiernach, etwas zu berichten, was dem eigentlich Gemeinten so ausgezeichnet entspricht, dass, wer an einem Punkte des Berichtes das Gemeinte erkannt hat, nun auch sofort die transposition des Ganzen in die höhere Lage vornehmen könnte': ibid., 58.

126. '[W]eder Mc noch Mt noch Lc selber ihr Prinzip der Parabeldeutung konsequent bei allen Exemplaren von Parabeln Jesu, die sie besassen, durchgeführt haben': ibid., 61.

127. '[M]it ihrer naiven Willkür haben sie die Parabeln da immerhin weit besser behandelt als die Kirchenväter, die für die Allegorese begeistert in diesen Reden nun kein eigentliches Jota mehr duldeten': ibid.

128. '[S]owie sie unter Bespöttelung ihrer Vorgänger aber versichern, diese Dinge bedeuten das und das und nichts andres, so dürfen wir im Blick auf Mc 4 34 fragen: Wer hat Euch denn dies alles κατ' ἰδίαν aufgelöst?': ibid., 62.

129. '[I]n verbis ludit, in sententiis dormitat': cited in Plummer, *Commentary*, lxxxi.

130. See above, p. 100.

131. See above, p. 78.

132. Kermode, *Secrecy*, 36. Aquinas unashamedly put differing exegetical opinions side by side in his *Catena Aurea in Evangelica*: Stein, *Parables*, 48.

133. 'Wer sich das ὅμοιον irgend eines Vergleiches von ganz fremden Schriftstellern oder doch aus ganz anderm Zusammenhange zeigen lässt, der ist auf den Standpunkt des Origenes zurückgesunken': Jülicher, *Gleichnisreden* I, 77.

134. More recently a movement with some affinities to Origen, the 'biblical theology' movement that was prominent in the 1950's, received a critique that is, roughly speaking, a more sophisticated development of Jülicher's position against Origenism, in James Barr, *The Semantics of Biblical Language* (London: SCM Press, 1961).

135. 'Welch ein grober Fehler ist es dann, einzelnen Begriffen innerhalb einer Parabel à tout prix die metaphorische Bedeutung zuzuschreiben, die sie an andern Stellen der heiligen Schrift haben': Jülicher, *Gleichnisreden* I, 77.

136. E.g. Bonaventure's distinction between different senses of 'bosom' in Scripture, with reference to Lk. 16:22: *Enarratio*, 355b, 356a.

137. 'Der Parabeldichter erkläre oft selber sein Gold für Rechenpfennige; er lasse seine Erzählung als die Schale ohne Wert sofort fallen, sowie er an den Kern, an die Anwendung gelange; es sei schon viel, wenn man einer Parabel nicht gleich zu Beginn anmerke, wo sie hinaus wolle, wenn das kalte Sturzbad der Anwendung recht unversehens und überraschend über uns komme': *Gleichnisreden* I, 101. The subjunctives here indicate that Jülicher is talking about the impression the Fathers *give* of the *Parabeldichter*. Trench considered the 'shell and kernel' image an appropriate one to characterize a parable, citing Jerome: *Notes*, 5, 31.

138. Jülicher, *Gleichnisreden* I, 101.

139. Jülicher, *Gleichnisreden* II, 596-8.

140. 'An diesen Klippen ist die Methode der allegorischen Parabelauslegung immer kläglich gescheitert; den thörichten Reichen für etwas andres als einen thörichten Reichen und den Zöllner für mehr als einen armen Sünder auszugeben glückte ihr nicht; hier ist das Deuten doch gar zu schwer gemacht. Auch eine Vergleichung der Einzelzüge hat gar keinen Sinn; denn wenn man den Pharisäer als Bild alter

Hochmütigen bezeichnet, kann man im Ernst alle Hochmütigen mit einem Hochmütigen, also die Gattung mit dem ihr zugehörigen Individuum vergleichen?': *Gleichnisreden* I, 112.

141. See above, p. 76.

142. See above, p. 91.

143. 'Kein Mittel hat er unversucht gelassen, kein Mittel des Wortes, um das Wort seines Gottes an und in die Herzen seiner Hörer zu bringen, nur die Allegorie, die nicht verkündigt, sondern verhüllt, die nicht offenbart, sondern verschliesst, die nicht verbindet, sondern trennt, die nicht überredet, sondern zurückweist, diese Redeform konnte der klarste, der gewaltigste, der schlichteste aller Redner für seine Zwecke nicht gebrauchen': Jülicher, *Gleichnisreden* I, 118.

144. For a more balanced view of the nature of allegory see Blomberg, *Interpreting*, 49-58.

145. Friedrich Schlegel, *Athenaeum* 3:15, cited in Welch, *Protestant Thought* I, 52.

146. Welch, *Protestant Thought* I, 53.

147. Ibid., 52.

148. Anthony Thorlby (ed.), *The Penguin Companion to Literature*, vol. 2: European Literature (Harmondsworth: Penguin, 1969), 362.

149. Ibid.

150. Ibid., 363. Cf. William Wordsworth's famous statement that 'all good Poetry is the spontaneous overflow of powerful feelings': W. J. B. Owen (ed.), *Wordsworth and Coleridge: Lyrical Ballads, 1798*, 2nd ed. (Oxford: Oxford University Press, 1969), 157f.

151. Jülicher, *Gleichnisreden* I, 63.

152. Contrast Wordsworth in Owen (ed.), *Ballads*, 167, on the necessity of the poet's giving pleasure, with Jülicher's view of the unlikelihood of Jesus' using a form of speech that was aesthetic but not didactic (*Gleichnisreden* I, 64).

153. Hawkes, *Metaphor*, 23-7, 34-56.

154. Ibid., 33.

155. Critically discussed in Charles Hayes, 'Symbol and Allegory: A Problem in Literary Theory', *Germanic Review* 44 (1969), 273-88.

156. In Owen (ed.), *Ballads*, especially 156f.

157. Hawkes, *Metaphor*, 39.

158. *Parables*, 50, referring to Hayes, 'Symbol', 276. Blomberg also notes here that by stressing the parables' specific *Sitz im Leben,* Dodd and Jeremias in fact moved back in the direction of allegory.

159. It will be left to twentieth-century writers to explore this Romantic construal of metaphor in relation to the parables: see especially Crossan, *In Parables*, 11-13: metaphor is 'irreplaceable and irreducible' (11).

160. Jülicher, *Gleichnisreden* I, 57.

161. Cross (ed.), *Dictionary*, 753. Drury notes the religious interest which made the approach to the parables adopted by Jülicher and his successors 'attractive and satisfactory to them': *Parables*, 2.

162. Schleiermacher wrote: 'The more we learn about an author, the better equipped we are for interpretation' (*Hermeneutics*, 113, cited in Thiselton, *New Horizons*, 221), and

Jülicher depends on a good deal of 'knowledge' of Jesus in order to interpret the parables he authored.

163. Jesus was 'im Besitze der Weisheit': Jülicher, *Gleichnisreden* I, 41.

164. Bloom, *Anxiety*, 10.

165. My italics. '[G]erne würden wir die Geschichte des Parabelverständnisses so erzählen, dass unsre Auffassung als das Resultat herausspränge, als die einzige nach vielen missglückten Versuchen noch übrig bleibende Möglichkeit . . . dies Ziel zu hoch gesteckt ist, schon weil die Urteile über "missglückt" und "möglich" zu verschieden sind': Jülicher, *Gleichnisreden* I, 203.

166. '[Sie] ergeben sich unmittelbar aus der Erzählung für den Hörer, sie fallen uns in den Schoss': Jülicher, *Gleichnisreden* II, 596.

167. Schweitzer, *Quest*, 264.

CHAPTER 5

The Age of the Reader: The Parable Interpretation of Bernard Brandon Scott

The art of understanding is more complicated, and richer, than an attempt to isolate the earliest fragments and to seek to understand them in a conjectured 'original' context: we hear the voice and the echoes and re-echoes, and it is as we hear that harmony that we come to understanding.[1]

The strong reader . . . is . . . placed in the dilemmas of the revisionist, who wishes to find his own original relation to truth.[2]

1. The Escape from 'Severe History'

The scene for the main discussion of this chapter, which concerns one work on the parables published a century after Jülicher's *Die Gleichnisreden Jesu*, must first be set with reference to some important works of the intervening years.

Jeremias's *The Parables of Jesus* is the work through which many students today encounter the massive shift in parable interpretation established by Jülicher. I have already noted Jeremias's emphasis (of a still-optimistic, modernist kind) on returning to the voice of Jesus.[3] Though his focus on the urgent situation of the kingdom's arrival, much sharper than in Jülicher, is of great importance, for our purposes the most significant aspect of his work is that he approaches the parables with Jülicher's literary eyes. Everywhere it is evident that Jeremias is not seeking to deny the insight of Jülicher into the parables as clear teaching, but follow it through further. For him, the hallmark of all the parables is their expression of the good news, an urgent summons relating to the new situation that has broken in upon the world with the coming of Jesus. Of particular interest is the fact that though he distances himself from Jülicher's 'general truth' readings, he introduces his own kind of generality. The application of the parables to the gospel of the kingdom distances them from application to *specific* moral and social issues in the world of Jesus' hearers. This can be illustrated from his treatment of The Shrewd Steward and The Rich Man and Lazarus. In making the former parable turn entirely on Jesus' commendation (as he reads it) in Luke 16:8a, Jeremias makes its message strangely vague. The steward 'recognized the critical nature of the situation . . . he acted . . . boldly, resolutely and prudently, with the purpose of making a new life for himself'.[4] The economic situation which the parable presupposes - rather obscure though it may be to us now - is not seen to have any relevance for its real message. Curiously, through his *withholding* of real significance from the details of the parable, it becomes in Jeremias's hands almost an 'allegory' of something unexpressed - faith in the kingdom's arrival.[5] The Rich Man and Lazarus, similarly, is read as a warning that '[i]n the face of this challenge of the hour, evasion is impossible'.[6] Again this warning is to be construed in the most general terms: 'Jesus does not want to comment on a social problem.'[7] In these interpretations Jeremias seems, in fact, to have taken a backwards step from Jülicher. He has heightened the parables' atmosphere of urgency by stressing the context of the arriving kingdom, but at the cost of further relegating the significance of individual figures and elements ('Lazarus is only a secondary figure introduced by way of contrast'[8]) and thus blunting their moral and social force.

The parables were central texts for the 'new hermeneutic': its advocates, theologically-motivated, intended to demonstrate that Jesus not only *spoke* about, but *brought* about, the kingdom, through powerful speech-acts.[9] However, the literary assumption (mediated by the influence of existentialist philosophy) is that Jesus' message was directed to the deepest and therefore most general level; so the continuity with Jülicher remains. This can be seen in the work of Linnemann, *Parables of Jesus*. 'Jesus, by compelling his listeners to a decision through telling a parable, gives them the possibility of making a change of existence, of understanding themselves anew from the depths up, of achieving a "new life".'[10] Note the general, indeed universal import ascribed to The Pharisee and the Customs Officer: 'Every man who has been bowed down by the burden of guilt knows for sure that here not just *something but everything,* in fact he himself, has been called in question . . . here the whole of his existence is exposed to a radical challenge . . .'[11]

The potential of the parables for transcending their own time and culture was further explored by Dan Otto Via through his proposal to treat them as 'aesthetic objects'.[12] His work sounded the retreat from too intense a search for the intention of Jesus, what he called the 'severely historical' approach. He was clearly under the influence of the literary vogue known as the 'New Criticism'. Since written texts are in the public domain (so the argument runs), loosed from their moorings in the authorial mind, the intention of the critic should be to seek the 'meanings' created by the configuration of the work itself. It is one of the strongest arguments for Via's case that the parables of Jesus have much in common with the Hebrew *mashal*, the proverbial saying which can be used in a variety of different circumstances.[13] The history of the parables' usage indeed demonstrates both their versatility, and the fact that their usefulness does not depend entirely on knowledge of the precise original circumstances of their speaking, or the particular intention of the speaker in those circumstances. But it does not follow from Via's view of the parables as 'aesthetic objects' that one should not ask questions about what an original speaker may have meant by them. Further, it is an essentialist fallacy to define a text as an 'aesthetic object' *to the exclusion* of its being another kind of object. Parables may be described, from different angles, as aesthetic, historical, sociological, or theological objects - or in still other ways. Hence my preference for speaking, rather, of the necessity for an aesthetic *response to* such texts.

Via is not ahistorical in a thoroughgoing way. He writes: '[A]s aesthetic objects [the parables] have a *relative* autonomy and detach themselves from [Jesus'] history in a way that his other sayings do not . . . the parables belong *not only* to the history of the covenant people but to the artistic tradition as well'.[14] Nor does he deny that in them we may find 'a clue to Jesus' understanding of his own existence'.[15] The fact that he insists, nevertheless, on the parables' nature as 'aesthetic objects' can be explained in part by the continuing powerful influence of Jülicher: he wants to make Jülicher's protection of the parables against the danger of allegorization more impregnable still. He is not saying that there is *no* 'outside' meaning, only that the meaning must not be sought in simple one-to-one correspondences between elements of the parable and some external reality. It is the 'configuration' of the parable, its internal patterning, which is crucial. However, Via's proposal leaves the door open to a view of Jesus that Jülicher would strenuously have denied, viz. that he was the maker of finely-honed works of art.[16] Via opened up real possibilities for insight into the parables through his use of the ancient categories of tragedy and comedy,[17] but the message they are found to yield remains one of existential generality (on Luke 16:1-8: 'The parable in itself says that the present is a crisis because the future is threatening.'[18])

Two volumes on the parables by Crossan, like Via a member of the Parables Seminar of the Society of Biblical Literature,[19] display the same kind of philosophical move as that undergone a little earlier in the literary criticism of continental Europe. From a structuralist approach which he sought to tie in with a still intense concern to uncover the true message of Jesus (in *In Parables*) he shifted (in *Cliffs of Fall*[20]) to a mood of post-structuralist uncertainty in which the controlling paradigm or 'mega-metaphor' for all textual study is 'play'.[21]

Crossan is deeply influenced (like Rudolf Bultmann) by the existentialist thought of Martin Heidegger. In *In Parables*, he uses Heidegger's understanding of *time* as a key to unlock the meaning of Jesus' announcement of the kingdom. Crossan discerns in the speech of Jesus not language about past, present and future but 'a deeper and more ontological simultaneity of three modes in advent-reversal-action'.[22] Texts do reflect and express deeply-rooted structures and patterns of thought: to accuse Crossan of too readily *imposing* patterns on texts would be unfair, and would maintain the illusion of an ideal approach in which personal aesthetic apprehension played no part. When Crossan confidently claims that those patterns represent the mind of Jesus,[23] we should recognize it as a claim of insight into an intention[24] - ironically, for the secular literary critics who adopted structuralist models from anthropology had no illusions about their ability to recover the mind of the author from texts by these means. Crossan's use of structural analysis should not deceive us into thinking that there is a kind of objective security about his historical conclusions.

Nevertheless, though historically flawed, *In Parables* marked a significant step in parable studies, for it sought to keep pace with secular literary criticism through the adoption of a structuralist approach, as Via's *Parables* had done in the adoption of New Critical insights. Above all, though, the influence of Jülicher keeps flowing. The 'Jesus' discerned in *In Parables* seems to be an example of a universal principle, a figure who acts as the gathering-point for certain philosophical ideals. But the book points in the direction of a true sensitivity to the voice of Jesus, insofar as its literary structuralism directs attention away from the outward form of the text (the focus of the New Criticism, seen in Via) towards the patterns which structure it on a deeper level.

In *Cliffs*, Crossan shows his awareness of the limitations of his earlier work. His stance becomes more radical, though he does not directly confront the question of how the shifting sands in secular literary criticism can ground or advance the *historical* quest. As Stephen D. Moore indicates, Crossan's posture, asserting the ultimate playfulness of language and its lack of reference to anything 'real', does not sit easily with historical-critical methods.[25] There is incongruity in the juxtaposition of Crossan's affirmation of plurivocity in the parables and his insistence on his own interpretation.

Central to *Cliffs* is the view that *all* language is metaphorical.[26] Already in *In Parables* Crossan had characterized the parables as metaphorical, highlighting the creative power and renewability of metaphor, and casting Jesus implicitly as a Romantic poet.[27] In *Cliffs* Crossan draws especially on the work of Ricoeur,[28] though its view of language has a long pedigree.[29] When language is seen in this way, structuralism with its system of codes and oppositions looks decidedly too rigid a framework for interpretation:

texts are seen to take on instead a slippery, elusive quality, where nothing can be pinned down, and there is an endless playful interplay of signs. By showing the self-referential quality of The Sower as a parable about parabling,[30] Crossan opens up the parables as a quintessential example of the ludic character of language.

I would go in one respect further than Crossan, in affirming not simply the *metaphorical*, but the *tropical* structure of language generally.[31] But unlike Crossan, who under Derrida's influence assimilates all 'world' to 'text', I see no need to link this view of language with a non-realist philosophy, or with a literary criticism which foregoes all claim to the detection of real human voices other than one's own.[32] The recognition of the presence of tropes deep in the structure of discourse implies to me a recognition of the presence of real human agency in constant interaction with the real, conventional world of signs.

The work on which I will now focus, Bernard Brandon Scott's *Hear then the Parable*, is influenced by Crossan, especially in the adoption of metaphor as the controlling figurative key. Scott remains within the dominant historical-critical framework of parable scholarship established by Jülicher, with the major extra resource of recent social-scientific studies of the ancient world on which to draw. But attention has shifted away from the *consilium Christi*, what Jesus meant, to the other aspect of 'voice': how he was *heard*. Jülicher exemplifies the shift from seeking divine meaning to seeking the meaning of Jesus (though, as we saw, that is not how he presents his project himself). Scott exemplifies the shift away from seeking any intentional meaning at all - though, as we shall see, there is considerable nostalgic longing for this search.[33]

2. The Intention of Scott

Scott is interested in the parables *of Jesus,* and the *Jesus of* the parables, as the subtitle of his book (*A Commentary on the Parables of Jesus*) makes plain. It soon becomes clear that a sophisticated 'historical-critical' procedure will be applied to determine first which of the *soi-disant* parables of Jesus can truly be attributed to him, and then how much of the extant text represents the 'structure' of Jesus' parable and how much is editing, gloss and so forth. Scott uncritically adopts the methods of source-, form- and redaction-criticism which characterized historical study of the gospels for much of the twentieth century. The gospel context is seen as an aid to our understanding of the parables but also as a distortion of them;[34] criteria are laid out for assessing the 'authenticity' of particular tales.[35] Scott compares his task with the restoration of old paintings.[36] Central to this quest, for Scott, is attunement to the originating 'voice' of the parables, a voice which he believes has 'a tendency to play in minor keys',[37] that is, to be somewhat unconventional. The reader is thus invited to listen carefully for the accents of the parables' speaker. Jesus' actual *words*, of course, are irretrievably lost to us.[38] It might seem therefore as if Scott (in the tradition of Jülicher) were seeking to lead us back to Jesus' *intention,* 'what he really meant', by blazing a trail through the thicket of ecclesiastical interpretations.

But Scott's enterprise turns out to be rather different from Jülicher's. The words of the parables in the gospel texts are contrasted not with their original *intention,* but with their original *structure:*[39] that is the entity regarded as both potentially accessible, and of interest. This distances the investigation from a direct involvement with the personality of the speaker and his meaning. Then, as soon as Scott has announced his plan to look for the 'voice' of the parables - a notion implying, as he acknowledges, 'a distinctive, creative presence' - he disclaims any hope of a direct encounter with that presence, stating that

> this is not the historical Jesus in the sense of Jesus as author of the parables. Rather, it is a reconstruction of the implied speaker / author of the corpus of parables.[40]

Such a reconstruction is possible on the basis of the parables' mutual consistency, but Scott is adamant that '[t]he implied author is not to be identified with the real author'.[41] Here Scott's literary sophistication is coming into view,[42] as well as a sense of the necessary mediating role of language,[43] of the impossibility of an immediate encounter with an 'other'.

This careful distancing of the reader from any sense that we are going to meet the real Jesus, the original author of the parables, continues when we move from the introductory chapters to the expositions themselves. Scott takes his readers through each parable line by line, inviting us to imagine how an original audience would have heard it, the expectations it might have aroused, the resonances of tradition it would have evoked. This hearer / reader-centred approach has the effect of pushing to the background the matter of what the speaker - even if it is only the 'implied speaker' - intended. The concern is with 'the effect on the hearer'[44] and the subject of the sentence in these readings is never the speaker, or Jesus, but frequently the text or some attribute or analogue of it: 'line 1 outlines the general possibilities open to the story'[45], '[t]he initial scene presents a hearer with a tragic situation',[46] 'the parable is remarkably restrained in what it says about the Priest and Levite . . .'[47], and so on.

However, the speaker remains a presence, if a shadowy one, in Scott's text. He appears with particular force, but still not in unveiled fashion, when Scott delineates the threads that bind the parables together with each other and other gospel texts, as he often does at the end of a chapter. Thus

The Good Samaritan and The Pharisee and the Customs Officer are connected through the theme that '[t]he kingdom does not separate insiders and outsiders on the basis of religious categories'.[48] Such bonds of coherence do indeed imply a common author, as Scott himself argues.[49] He even relates The Shrewd Steward to what is known of Jesus' activity: with its equation of 'justice and vulnerability' it 'coheres with Jesus' association with the outcast, as well as, e.g., his use of leaven in the parable The Leaven'.[50] But he holds back from a direct exposition of Jesus' outlook or aim as speaker / author; it is characteristic of his conclusions to keep the text as the subject of the sentence: for instance, '[t]he three parables . . . test that part of the social and religious map where boundaries indicate who is inside and who outside'.[51]

Apparently, then, it is Scott's purpose to reconstruct the way that the parables worked upon their hearers, not the intention in the mind of their speaker; but it is difficult for him to evade the issue of the speaker's intention. It is a particular surprise when we reach the Epilogue to find Scott making bold, unambiguous statements about Jesus. After the sensitive ebbing of confidence, the drawing back from listening for the voice of Jesus to listening for the implied speaker of the parables, from discerning the intention of the author to discerning the response of the hearer, from affirming the one mind behind the parables to affirming the coherence of a group of texts, we do not expect to find this: 'Jesus was both antiwisdom and antiapocalyptic, although ironically the tradition confessed him as both rabbi and messiah'.[52] After the mood of hesitancy which has pervaded his work, one senses that the foundation has not been laid for this assertion:[53] the burden of the book is not that *Jesus was like this*, but that this was the impression we can imagine him to have made on others. What of the possibility that even if the careful reconstruction of the likely reception of his words is right, his hearers were sometimes mistaken about his intention? This is surely the possibility implied by Scott's reluctance in the body of the volume to entertain the issue of what Jesus meant.[54] This 'Jesus' of Scott's epilogue is a *trope* for the 'implied Jesus' of his commentary, behind which lie the intention and motivation to reach out and make contact, to 'divine', despite the painful awareness of the limitations of historical research. It is like a Romantic moment of vision - sudden sublime encounter or supreme self-delusion, depending on your point of view. By the same token, the 'implied Jesus' through the book, the one heard by the ideal hearer whose impressions Scott conjures up, is now seen, in retrospect, as a trope for the real Jesus of the epilogue, the one Scott really wants to write about.

There is a skill and beauty in the deployment of this device of the implied speaker. From one angle it presents itself as sadly necessary understatement, inducing a sense of the near-unknowability of the real speaker. Yet this reticence about the shadowy author-figure behind the parables evokes a sense both of reverence towards, and curiosity about him. If this reticence is thrown to the winds in the Epilogue, it can be read as an interesting modulation of the ancient dialectic between silent awe before the God whom no one has ever seen and the compulsion to speak of what one has seen and heard.

Scott intends, then, to discover how the voice of Jesus *was heard* in the parables - though he casts significant glances backwards at what he *meant*. The central means of insight he uses is the trope of metaphor.

3. Scott's Interpretative Key: Metaphor

For Scott, the parables of Jesus are all to be interpreted as being 'about' the kingdom of God, not only those explicitly linked to the kingdom in the gospels. Alluding to Rabbinic texts which refer to Solomon's parables or proverbs as 'handles' on the Torah, enabling it to be understood, he writes of parables in the Jesus tradition as being 'handles on the symbol of the kingdom of God'.[55] There is a more powerful literary key at work than the comparison with the Rabbis, however. If for him the parables are handles on the kingdom, then *metaphor* is the handle on the parables.[56]

Just as Jülicher proposed that the parables in their original form possessed a simile structure, such that his reconstructions involved fitting stories like The Prodigal Son into a 'just as . . . so also' framework absent from the gospel text, so Scott proposes that in their original form the parables possessed a metaphorical structure, such that his reconstructions press deeper than simile-formulations such as 'the kingdom of God is like' even when they *are* present in the text. Even when the simile-form is there on the surface, the deeper linguistic movement is a metaphorical exchange between the kingdom of God and some everyday reality. Thus in the parable The Leaven (Matthew 13:33 / Luke 13:20f.), the parable works not simply as a comparison between the kingdom and leaven, but as a rather startling *identification* of the kingdom and leaven.[57]

Moreover, Scott is at one with the emphasis of various recent works on the cognitive value of metaphor: that is, metaphor does not merely illustrate a known truth, it yields a new insight.[58] In particular, he follows Ricoeur in perceiving the creative metaphorical function of narrative, as 'a model for redescribing reality'. Such redescription 'exposes something new, not simply copying the already known'.[59] This means that we need to pay careful attention to the literal sense of the stories, the conventional associations of their language, so that we can discern the new insight that is being offered into the kingdom. Otherwise, the parables lose their subversive edge. Scott points out how the conventional associations of leaven are usually ignored in interpreting the parable. Although 'leaven in all known examples from the ancient world stands for moral corruption', commentators agree that 'in this parable it cannot signify that because this is a parable about the kingdom (i.e., something good)'.[60] Rather, we should let the ancient connotations of leaven alert us to the startling nature of what Jesus is saying about the kingdom, his overturning of expectations about purity. The parables use the language of the everyday human world, and, as Scott convincingly argues, we need to feel the force of Jesus' use of this world to speak of God and his rule.

The point is further developed with reference to metaphor's exposure of dissimilarity as well as similarity, its power to hide some aspects of the referent even while it reveals others:

> Similarity can block remembrance of what metaphor hides; dissimilarity highlights what previously was hidden . . . in narratives where there is strong dissimilarity to the expected values of the referent, as there frequently is in Jesus' parables, dissimilarity may well be a way of redefining and subverting a hearer's vision of the referent so as to redescribe reality.[61]

To expand Scott's point, if 'the kingdom of God' were referred to by (say) the metaphor of a human empire, the metaphorical expression would be so close to the referent as to be in danger of obscuring completely the real difference between the two entities. But when 'the kingdom of God' is referred to by the metaphor of leaven, the disjunction between metaphorical expression and referent is so sharp that previously hidden similarities leap into view. Through this understanding of Jesus' parables as metaphors, Scott takes further Jülicher's insight into Jesus the man of insight. Jesus appears as the one who sees that to which others are blind, or which they have forgotten.

Scott's treatment of the parables as metaphors highlights again the necessity for the interpreter to make her own aesthetic choices when dealing with figures. He himself states that a parable 'provides no explicit instructions for its hearer / reader to employ in relating narrative to referent'.[62] Not only in the discernment of the relationship between narrative and referent, we might add, but also in the very assumptions that the referent of all Jesus' parables is invariably 'the kingdom',[63] and that metaphor is the best interpretative key, Scott's own aesthetic choosing is apparent. The awareness of an inevitable plurality in contemporary responses, as well as a sense of the possible variety of original hearers' responses, ought naturally lead to a greater caution in the reconstruction of the voice of Jesus than is evident in Scott's work.

As we turn now to Scott's interpretations of the individual parables, I shall suggest ways in which his genuine and important insights into hearer-responses might be enhanced by liberation from the restrictions he places on them. At the same time, we shall see how he cannot escape from the issue of the *intention* of Jesus. It is, I suggest, the inevitable presence of such an intention looming behind the parables which drives his desire to fix their meanings.

4. Scott's Parable Interpretations

According to Scott, the parables function as redescriptions of the kingdom - understood previously by Jesus' hearers in some kind of apocalyptic or nationalistic sense, or perhaps just as 'a cipher for obedience to the law'[64] - as a universal reality which dissolves all boundaries. He is anxious to keep the parables as 'redescriptions' without allowing them also to be examples or exhortations. This is partly because, as we shall see, Scott selects from 'the possibilities suggested by the metaphor / parable'[65] an understanding of the kingdom in contemporary social-scientific terms. This continues, with a different twist, the Jülicher tradition of reading the parables as statements of general truth. Further, we shall see how there is a mismatch between these interpretations and how original hearers might be expected to have responded to such metaphorical language.

The Good Samaritan

In the opening sentence of his exposition Scott sets The Good Samaritan in a universal socio-cultural context: 'All cultures, modern and ancient, draw boundaries between themselves and others'.[66] The cognitive value of the parable, its meaning as a metaphor, is stated as follows:

> Utterly rejected is any notion that the kingdom can be marked off as religious: the map no longer has boundaries. The kingdom does not separate insiders and outsiders on the basis of religious categories.[67]

The parable 'subverts the effort to order reality into the known hierarchy of priest, Levite and Israelite'[68] - a lay Israelite being the expected third member of the story's triad, rather than the surprising Samaritan.

Scott has earlier cited the work of Funk[69] as being significant in exposing the metaphorical character of the story. Funk challenged the traditional designation of the parable as an 'example story' on the grounds that a Samaritan would have been an unacceptable example of neighbourliness for a Jewish audience. As Scott rightly summarizes, 'the literalness of the *Samaritan* turns the *story* into a metaphor'.[70] The shock of the Samaritan's appearance points to the parable's being something other than a simple tale of loving behaviour that is to be imitated. For Funk, the parable proposes that 'one become the victim in the ditch who was helped by an enemy' and that '[i]n the kingdom mercy is always a surprise'.[71]

In similar vein, Scott differentiates his interpretation from that of Luke, who (he thinks) has used the parable as a simple example story for his Gentile readership[72] and was the originator of the kind of sorry stereotypical contrast between 'the unloving Jews and the loving Samaritan' made by Bultmann.[73] Scott believes that on the lips of Jesus the story was more radical and subversive, implicitly breaking down *all* racial barriers. Though this is less than fair to Luke (as we saw in Chapter 2 and will note further below), it catches well a fresh metaphorical tone in the tale, recognizing that Jesus is not merely replacing one stereotype with another.

The problem, paradoxically, is with Scott's stated plan of envisaging the original hearers' responses. Would they have realized that Jesus was speaking about 'the kingdom of God', and furthermore that he was saying that the kingdom cannot 'be marked off as religious'?[74] These sound more like the responses of a twentieth-century interpreter to considered reflection on the parable than the immediate reactions of an original hearer. And indeed we find Scott making an ambiguous transition from his account of original hearers' responses, to his final section entitled 'From Story to Kingdom'.[75] That is, we are left unsure as to whether he is saying that *the hearers* would have drawn the conclusions about the kingdom which *he* is drawing, or simply that, on reflection, this is what the text of the parable is pointing to (whether or not the hearers got the point, at first or subsequently). Again paradoxically, Scott's interpretation, opening up the grand and universal implications of the parable, would make more sense (notwithstanding certain anachronisms of language) as an interpretation of *Jesus' intention* than an account of hearers' responses, though (as with Jülicher) we would still miss the sharp sense of Jesus' location in a particular context.

An implication of reading a story such as this as *metaphor*, particularly the kind of fresh and challenging metaphor which Scott persuasively makes it, is precisely that its hearers would have needed time for its wider purport to dawn on them. Even the lawyer in Luke's setting, we may imagine, though he saw clearly enough whose behaviour was exemplary, would have needed some considerable time to come to terms with what Jesus was saying, and above all with the fact that the exemplary figure was a Samaritan. In particular, hearers would surely have asked rather more precise questions about the significance of individual characters in the parable. In the tradition of Jülicher, Scott treats the parable as a whole, and (in continued reaction against the Fathers) is reluctant to assign tropical significance to individual elements. But in fact even for Scott the Samaritan seems to be a synecdoche for the 'outsider' or the 'nonreligious', and the priest and Levite seem to be synecdoches for the 'insider' or the 'religious'.

It is difficult to imagine that the significance of these characters to the ears of Jesus' audience - or in the mind of Jesus - would have been so wide. The immediate impact of the story, though one of puzzlement, would also have been one of more forcible shock than Scott implies. Before any synecdochic or metaphorical reference dawned, they would have been stirred by the startling nature of the literal words. A *priest and a Levite* passed by on the other side; a *Samaritan* stopped and cared. Only gradually would they begin to ask what the wider ramifications of these portrayals might be, and they might have come to a range of different conclusions. Was Jesus implying a condemnation of the entire hierarchy, or was he just asking hearers to recognize that, sometimes, outward piety and true love did not go together? Was he really suggesting that Gentiles and Jews were on an equal footing in their ability to keep the law, or only that sometimes a person on the racial fringes might offer a good example?

On the one hand, the ghost of Jülicher seems to be forbidding the imputation of semi-mysterious speech to Jesus. The audience, it is suggested, get the point straightaway. On the other hand, Scott's conclusions nevertheless imply that the parable requires a *knowing* audience: but what they are assumed to know is not the literal associations of 'priests' or 'Samaritans', but a reflective doctrine of the kingdom of God couched in the language of twentieth-century social science.

The Prodigal Son

In The Prodigal Son, Scott writes, '[t]he metaphor for the kingdom is the father's coming out, both for the younger son and for the elder'.[76] His literary analysis highlights the parallelism between the two sections of the story. The father 'comes out' to both sons.[77] Scott emphasises what most traditional readings (including, in his view, Luke's) have played down or even obliterated - the father's affirmation of, and love for, the *elder* son: 'Son, you are always with me, and all that is mine is yours' (Lk. 15:31).[78]

His reading contains important insights into the ways that the parable may have resonated with its hearers, and draws attention to features that are often overlooked. The problems again revolve around his belief that the parable is a metaphor for the kingdom, a kingdom understood in twentieth-century categories.

Scott believes that Luke has woven the parables of ch. 15 into his narrative in such a way that his readers, like Jesus' 'fictional audience' of scribes and Pharisees, will identify the younger son with the 'customs officers and sinners' of v. 1, and the elder son with the 'Pharisees and scribes' of v. 2. He believes that Luke's readers will *themselves* identify 'with the call to rejoice at the repentance of those lost' and 'condemn those who do not so rejoice'. He further reads the Lukan setting as implying the 'rejection' of the elder son, and contrasts this with the parable narrative itself, where 'there is no rejection: he inherits all'.[79] He notes, however, that 'the parable is a less than perfect example of Lukan soteriology'; the elder son's fate 'does not correspond to the eventual rejection of Judaism envisioned by Lukan ideology'.[80] That is, Luke has allowed to stand a parable of Jesus which does not seem (to Scott) to fit with Luke's overall framework, though Luke does 'draw attention away from the nonrejection of the elder son . . . by repeating the conclusion of the episode of the younger as the conclusion for the episode of the elder son'.[81] Scott continues:

> In the parable's second part, Jesus hopes to move the Pharisees to accept the gospel. But why should they if they indeed are always with the father and have inherited all? Now we see the power of Luke's fiction and likewise its ultimate inability to account for the parable itself. The identification of Pharisees with the elder brother, suggested not by the parable but by the primary Gospel narrative, has miscued the parable.[82]

Having thus sought to unmask the misreading which he believes the parable's gospel context has bequeathed to us, Scott proceeds, in his detailed reading, to describe how Jesus' original hearers would have responded to the parable. His key assertion is that the hearers would not have identified with the elder son, as he thinks Luke wants us to believe, but with the younger son.[83] This is because the OT contains a number of stories involving a pair of brothers, and the younger ones 'frequently leave the house of their father to find their wealth; there is something slightly scandalous or off-color in their stories; and they are the favorites'.[84] Knowing that such initially dubious characters in the tradition usually end up on top, an audience is prepared for the same thing to happen in the parable. They are, as it were, rooting for the younger son despite his misdemeanours. Especially significant is the use of this 'mytheme' in Scripture to explain 'why God has continually chosen his people even when they have apparently wandered from his way'.[85] Scott gives Malachi 1:2f. ('I have loved Jacob, but I have hated Esau') as an example of a text where 'The story of Jacob and Esau is called on to indicate that God loves (chooses) freely'.[86] The subversion of this ancient mytheme, the shock to the parable's hearers, comes with the end of the parable, in which the elder is *not* rejected: 'both are chosen'.[87]

By this reading of the brothers as metaleptically allusive to a whole tradition, Scott skilfully breaks down the woodenness with which it has been customary to read it - the younger son as the blackguard who is wonderfully changed, the elder as the self-righteous prig who excludes himself from the party - and shows that the actual play of expectation and surprise would have been much richer. Nevertheless, he again presents the response of the hearers in an implausible way.

First, when Scott writes that the fictional audience of scribes and Pharisees 'see themselves' in the role of the elder brother,[88] it would be more convincing to write in terms of the *intention* of (the implied) Jesus than the *response* of (the fictional) audience. The response of the hearers is left open by Luke. It is true that Luke tells us that on one occasion the scribes and the chief priests perceived that Jesus had told a parable against them (20:19), but there is no similar indication here. Luke does not clearly imply that the scribes and Pharisees drew a correspondence between themselves and the elder brother, but he *does* surely imply *that Jesus intended* that correspondence. By focusing on the hearers' putative response rather than Jesus' putative intention Scott incidentally softens somewhat his claim that Luke misread and even falsified Jesus, though he does not eliminate it.

Secondly, does the text indicate the nature of the intended readership to the extent that Scott thinks? Does Luke expect his readers to be 'repentant sons' who will see the prodigal as 'one of them'? Might this chapter not equally imply (if we *were* to read a strong Lukan polemic into it, which is open to question) that Luke wished to address, and reach out to, equivalents of the scribes and Pharisees in his own context (within or on the edges of the church)? Might we not ascribe to Luke the same openness to such 'scribes and Pharisees' as that which is implied by the open ending of the parable? Why should we think that Luke wished, rather, to reinforce the prejudices of a Christian community whose penitence had already hardened into exclusivism?

The question of the 'identifications' made by Luke's readers or Jesus' hearers is a complex one. Luke may imply a *readership* containing some who would see themselves as the younger son before his about-turn; some who would see themselves as the younger son after his about-turn; some who would see themselves as the elder son still refusing to come in; some who would see themselves as an 'elder son' who had earlier refused to come in but had now had a change of heart; some who had thus far steadfastly refused to see themselves reflected in any character in any parable, but for whom parable might seem the only means of conversion. Likewise, the *'fictional audience'* of scribes and Pharisees seem *intended* by Jesus to identify with the elder son, with the aim that they should be stung by the portrayal of him and 'join the celebrations'. But perhaps

Luke's Jesus implies that after this initial identification their heart *should* be so changed as to 'identify' with the younger too - in the sense not only of sharing in his joy, but also of seeing clearly their *past* selves in the elder son's refusal to rejoice. Or maybe the hope of Luke's Jesus is that his audience will *immediately* want to 'identify' with the younger son, not just because of the two-sons mytheme but because the sense of joy at his return to the father will be sufficient to overcome their reluctance to place themselves in the category of rebels needing a change of heart. Maybe the parable was heard by as many 'sinners' as Pharisees: what would *they* have made of it? As Nicholas Wolterstorff points out, 'by way of a single locutionary act one may say different things to different addressees.'[89] Scott tries to reduce the range of possible original responses, both to Jesus' words and to Luke's text, but it is better to try to imagine the extraordinary possible variety. Luke's context naturally implies a particular application of the parable, but that does not mean that he closes off its applicability to different groups among his readers or Jesus' hearers.

Thirdly, Scott's referral of the parable to the kingdom gives it a *general* conclusion which distances it from the territory (perceived as dangerous?) of what specific identifications Jesus might have intended, and his hearers might have made, between people in the story and people in their experience. For Scott it yields a radical, universal message about the breakdown of the distinction between chosen and rejected: 'the kingdom is not something that decides between but something that unifies'. Without denying the universal *implications* readily seen in the story, we note that again Scott passes too swiftly from how Jesus was understood to how we can appropriate his teaching today. How credible is the dichotomy which Scott repeatedly presents between Luke's specificity, with connotations of stereotype and other malign kinds of rhetoric, and Jesus' generality, with his wonderfully broad and subversive vision? A historically credible Jesus might surely, sometimes, have stereotyped groups like the Pharisees, warned them in pungent terms. A historically credible Luke might surely, sometimes, have wanted to give his readers a general perspective on the ministry of Jesus and all the possibilities, challenges and new means of self-identification that it opened up.

What if we do propose that Jesus might have had specific groups in mind when he told the story? Are we then just swallowing Luke's line? And are we dismissing the two-sons mytheme as background to the parable? Scott believes that the parable 'radically rejects Israel's self-understanding of itself as the favored, younger son'.[90] But the parable focuses not only on the father's attitude to the two sons, but also on their behaviour. It is not just self-understanding that is at stake, but how to live. The clear implication is that even the favoured (the younger son, according to the mytheme) must return to the father, and that the unfavoured (the elder) has the opportunity to join in the celebration when that happens. On this view Israel's *self-understanding* is not basically challenged: they are still the 'younger son', but their *behaviour* is mirrored in his rebelliousness. Moreover, the emphasis on behaviour inevitably brings the parable close to the real situation and invites more specific comparisons. Who are those who *are,* now, turning back to the father? Who are those who *need* to? Who are those who have the opportunity to rejoice with the penitent, and are not taking it? Who exactly is Jesus talking about, and getting at? Such, surely, would have been the questions beginning to form in the hearers' minds as the parable started to do its work.

The Shrewd Steward

Scott sees the relationship of The Shrewd Steward to the kingdom in 'the sense of justice normally implied in the symbol of the kingdom of God'; the parable 'implements the metaphorical network of the kingdom as an accounting'.[91] In keeping with his readings of other parables, he sees it as overthrowing hearers' expectations. The master does not settle matters with the steward. Although the steward as a 'comic' character has won an audience's sympathy, the mention of the master's praise in v. 8a *both* gives the storyteller's verdict that the steward was 'unjust' *and* removes any hostility towards the master. This leads to the conclusion:

> [T]he parable's ending deconstructs its own metaphorical structure . . .
> The hearer now has no way to navigate in the world; its solid moorings
> have been lost. Are masters cruel or not? Are victims right in striking
> back? By a powerful questioning and juxtaposition of images, the parable
> breaks the bond between power and justice. Instead it equates justice and
> vulnerability. The hearer in the world of the kingdom must establish new
> coordinates for power, justice and vulnerability. The kingdom is for the
> vulnerable, for masters and stewards who do not get even.[92]

This is ingenious. But in order to reach his conclusion Scott has to assume that the hearers would automatically have made a connection between the patron-client world evoked in the parable, and the kingdom of God. This is implausible. And is the 'equation' of 'justice and vulnerability' a suspiciously general, and contemporarily applicable theme to draw from the story, which may again dull our ears to the sharp resonances of the individual characters and situation?

The Rich Man and Lazarus

In The Rich Man and Lazarus it is the village setting, according to Scott, which reflects the kingdom. The kingdom 'replicates the village . . . in reverse'.[93] The parable exposes the rich man's failure by the kingdom's standards. Scott brings out well the importance of the linked imagery of the gate and the gulf:

> In the parable, the kingdom provides a gate to the neighbour; if God must help ('Lazarus'[94]), then the gate disappears. Grace is the gate. The parable subverts the complacency that categorizes reality into rich and poor or any other division. The standard is not moral behavior as individual, isolated acts but the ability to go through the gate, metaphorically, to the other side, solidarity.[95]

We then find one of the clearest instances of Scott's reading of the parables as expressions of universal truth:

> The gate is not just an entrance to the house but the passageway to the other . . . In any given interpersonal or social relationship there is a gate that discloses the ultimate depths of human existence. Those who miss that gate may, like the rich man, find themselves crying in vain for a drop of cooling water.[96]

Scott's first step towards this conclusion is to remove Luke 16:27-31, concerning the rich man's brothers, as having been 'appended to relate the parable to Jewish disbelief in Jesus' messiahship'.[97] We note the element of circularity in the argument: 'Once Abraham pronounces the chasm, the great dividing line, the story has reached its conclusion, for as we shall see in an analysis of the narrative proper, the story is about boundaries and connections'.[98] We see what is excluded if the ending is relegated to secondary status: the references to Moses and the prophets, to repentance, and to resurrection. This allows Scott to focus more on social constructs ('boundaries and connections') than on biblical context.

He then explores the issue of hearers' sympathies during the imagined narration by Jesus of the story in vv. 19-26. He makes the point that in contrast to other ancient tales that have been adduced as parallels, in this parable 'there is no objective third person for the reader to identify with', someone who puts the question about the relationship of 'God's justice . . . to the here and now', and that therefore 'the hearer is forced to confront both Lazarus and the rich man as images of the hearer'.[99] But what he does not make explicit is that the two characters also become synecdoches, inviting hearers to ask not only how they might be tropes for themselves, but also how they stand for particular classes or groups in society.

The story is described as 'a metaphor for the unnoticed menace that Jesus' announcement of the kingdom of God places on ordinary life'.[100] That may accurately represent our contemporary understanding; it might conceivably represent the intention of Jesus. But it is doubtful if the revelation that '[i]n any given interpersonal or social relationship there is a gate that discloses the ultimate depths of human existence' would have flooded unmediated upon a Galilean or Judean peasant or Pharisee.

The Judge and the Widow

Scott believes that The Judge and the Widow, rather than being a lesson in prayer as Luke presents it, confounds expectation by ignoring 'the justice associated with the kingdom'.[101] The story as a whole 'is an anti-metaphor'[102], and this, it turns out, depends on the discernment of a significant figurative connotation in one of the characters: not the judge, for he, being unjust, 'is neither a metaphor nor a metonymy for God'.[103] Instead attention is directed to 'the widow's continual coming', her 'shamelessness':

> The kingdom keeps coming, keeps battering down regardless of honor or justice. It may even come under the guise of shamelessness (lack of honor) . . . A hearer of the parable discovers the kingdom under the guise not of a just judge but of a pestering widow who exposes her own shamelessness in continually pressing her cause on a dishonorable judge.[104]

But though we may be able to relate the widow's persistence to other elements of Jesus' teaching which suggest that the kingdom may be discerned in surprising ways, and though reflective listeners in Jesus' own time may gradually have seen such connections, this is surely a somewhat distant aspect of signification in the parable. Scott implies that the constructs of 'honour' and 'shame' and their conjunction with the (unmentioned) 'kingdom of God' would have controlled hearers' responses, rather than the more obvious questions of how the characters in some way stood for groups in the world they knew. Again, Scott evokes a generalizing voice. The widow appears not as one of Israel's poor but as a universal 'outsider'.[105]

The Pharisee and the Customs Officer

Scott's interpretation of The Pharisee and the Customs Officer depends, as in the other cases, upon stripping away the Lukan frame. Luke's introduction (18:9) 'sets up the character to be rejected as false, untrue to his religiosity'. Scott further notes that Luke's conclusion in v. 14b, strengthened by its close proximity to Jesus' authoritative 'I say to you' in v. 14a, has invited readers to see the Pharisee 'as not righteous and therefore the one who is self-righteous, a despiser of others, haughty, and to be humbled - literally, in the history of Christianity, in pogrom after pogrom'.[106] In place of 'Luke's use of the parable as an example story', thus sweepingly tarred with the brush of all Christian anti-Judaism down the centuries, Scott proposes that we see the original parable as subverting 'the metaphorical structure that sees the kingdom of God as temple':

> Given this metaphorical system, things associated with the temple are holy and in the kingdom, and things not associated with the temple are unholy and outside the kingdom. In the parable the holy is outside the kingdom and the unholy is inside the kingdom.[107]

The parable's real scandal, though, according to Scott, is that there is no reason for the justification of one man and not the other; neither is an example.[108] But is the metaphorical link between parable and kingdom as convincing as Scott thinks?

Scott rightly emphasises the great symbolic significance of the temple. It would have reminded many Jews powerfully, almost instinctively, of their identity as God's people. In social terms, according to Scott, the temple 'conjures up a religious standard that gives value to both the characters'; it is 'the map, the metaphor, that stands for the insiders and outsiders'.[109] But Scott makes two surprising leaps from this perception of the temple's importance.

First, though he might be right that the very mention of the temple would have heightened awareness of the Pharisee's righteousness by contrast with the life of the customs officer, this does not necessarily mean that the Pharisee is thereby defined as one of those on the 'inside' and the tax-collector as one of those on the 'outside'.[110] The very beginning of the parable might equally suggest to a hearer that *both* characters are on the inside, from the start. The customs officer stands 'far off', but he is certainly in the temple along with the Pharisee. The presence of *both* men in the sacred precincts means that we cannot say decisively that for Jesus' hearers the parable tears up the social map defining insiders and outsiders. The two men's relative positions, and the Pharisee's prayer, certainly stress that both are aware of a distance: the Pharisee from the customs officer, the customs officer from God. But if we are to use the social terminology, we could equally well say they are *both insiders.*

Secondly, although the symbolisms of temple and kingdom no doubt fertilized each other at many points, Scott is again misleading when he implies that the parable's hearers would have made this connection. Why should they have thought that Jesus was speaking *here* about the kingdom of God? It almost begins to look like the kind of obscure allegory on which twentieth-century parable scholarship had turned its back. Combined with the previous point, this makes the statement that in the parable 'the holy is outside the kingdom and the unholy is inside the kingdom' rather strange. In the parable the two men are *both inside* the temple, and *both* then go home. If the temple were somehow transparent upon the kingdom, one might equally conclude that both ended up *outside* of the kingdom! The acceptance of one and not the other has nothing to do with their physical locations in the story. But 'maps' and 'boundaries' are controlling the understanding of both temple and kingdom here, and forcing them into an unnatural alliance.

Rather than such grand generalities, the immediate questions a listener might pose would surely, once again, be 'what, and who, is he getting at'? And again, a range of answers might suggest themselves over time, as people saw themselves and others in the guise of either the Pharisee or the customs officer.

Scott's conclusion concerning this parable aptly illustrates his whole approach:

> There is no lesson to learn! The hearer cannot imitate the behavior of one or the other. The parable's message is simpler. The map has been abandoned . . . [111]

No 'lesson', but a 'message'. The uneasiness of this distinction betrays the vulnerability of an interpretative strategy which rightly stresses the subversiveness of the parables, but on a general level which fails to imagine their slowly working yet sharp persuasiveness towards a particular way of living.

5. From Influence to Insight: The Voice of Jesus in Scott

Scott's insight into the voice of Jesus in its synchronic sense is of a stance radically subversive of contemporary presuppositions about the kingdom of God. But this subversion remains on a general level. The parables are not perceived as implying the necessity of any specific course of action. They propose, rather, a different view of the world, and leave it at that.

On account of his concentration on the immediate context of the parables' reception, Scott's references to Jesus' voice within its longer, diachronic setting are more oblique and occasional. Nevertheless, the hints are quite clear that Jesus is to be seen as subverting not only contemporary understandings of the kingdom, but more ancient, OT 'mythemes' such as that of the favoured younger son.

This picture of a radical Jesus, standing over against his contemporaries and his ancestors, is closely bound up with the use of metaphor as Scott's interpretative key, and with the particular accent he has placed on metaphor's potential to create new perceptions through the conjunction of terms or images normally regarded as disparate - such as the kingdom of God and a shameless widow. We need now to evaluate Scott's position with reference to the influences upon him; and to achieve greater clarity in this we first need to draw out two underlying oppositions in his work, fundamentally similar to two of those we found in Jülicher.

First, again, is the opposition between *speaker and transmitters*. We noted above that Scott's tactic of distancing his exposition from the question of Jesus' intention gives the figure of Jesus a kind of mystical aura that draws the reader towards him (whether intentionally or not) despite all the emphasis on text and hearer. We may go further than this. Scott is clearly in deep sympathy with the common thrust he finds in the parables, and is therefore not only exponent but also advocate of this thrust to his readers. One senses the element of personal commitment in his discernment, in Jesus' sayings, of (for example) 'the radical identification of God's kingdom with community and the demand to provide for the needs of others'.[112] But this unmistakable, though often veiled, exaltation of the speaker of the parables comes at a price: the denigration of those who handed them on and wrote them down.

No reverence is evinced for Luke, the other Evangelists and their sources such as is evinced for Jesus. Until the epilogue, the issue of the intention of Jesus is not even broached. The intention of the Evangelists, however, is regarded as plain for all to see: 'The problem with allegory in the parables is not allegory per se, but the ideological reading of the parables with an ideology that is *manifestly* later.'[113] Luke's particular 'ideology' is seen as embracing a schema of salvation history which 'relies on the rejection of the Jews in favour of the Gentiles'.[114] The 'additions' to The Shrewd Steward in Luke 16:8-13 are regarded as an 'attempt to impose sense (consistency) on the parable by diverting attention from the story's roguish character'.[115] Luke is credited with considerable literary skill, seen in the 'fictional' setting he has given to the parables in chapter 15, but it is a skill that leads to The Prodigal Son being 'miscued'.[116] His application of The Judge and the Widow 'has weakened, not eliminated, the parable's scandal'.[117] Worst of all, his framing of The Pharisee and the Customs Officer has helped turn it 'into an anti-Pharisaic and anti-Semitic story' which has bequeathed a 'harsh history'.[118] Scott has little doubt about the intention of the *writer*, and little sympathy with it or him. He ignores the possibility that Luke's discourse may be presentational rather than authorial:[119] that is, that Luke may genuinely be trying to *represent* the parables as told by Jesus, rather than to invest them with his own sinister freight of meaning. The opposition between speaker and transmitters seen in Jülicher's writing has hardened.

This leads us to the second opposition, between *text and interpretation*. If the intention of Jesus is kept at arm's length, and that of his early interpreters is scorned, where for Scott is the locus of meaning in the parables? The *text* is given a place of considerable esteem;[120] we have already noted its frequent appearance, in various guises, as the subject of sentences. Though considerable attention is given to the *hearer*, that must throw an interpreter back upon the text itself, which is our only basis for reconstructing a hearer's responses. This leads to the interesting fiction of the text 'creating meaning'. In his Epilogue Scott writes:

> Instead of accenting what the parable means, I have chosen to describe how it creates meaning . . . To underscore further the polyvalence of parables, I have paid close attention to how each parable functions in its extant contexts in the various Gospels. But these versions are only performances of the parable, layings-beside, in an effort to create new meaning.[121]

In the distinction between 'meaning' and 'creating meaning', and in the language of 'performance', Scott further distances himself from the quest for the speaker's intention, but also covers over the necessity of interpretation. To speak of a parable 'creating meaning' and of the 'new meaning'[122] attempted by successive 'performances' is to imply that the parable itself starts a process of creativity in which successive generations, inspired by the parable, trope it to their own ends. This is similar to the argument of this book that a stream of influence can be traced from Jesus himself through the generations of his interpreters. But what it ignores is the fact that interpreters, by and large (and certainly including the Evangelists) have not been interested in simply lifting a parable from its historical setting and creating new meaning for it in their own. Wolterstorff offers a good critique of the kind of 'performance interpretation' that Scott believes was practised on the parables by the early church (and, by implication, should continue to be practised today). He comments that '[w]hat performance interpretation ignores, by its very nature, is the actual acts of discourse' - promise, testimony and so on.[123] Scott turns the

Evangelists into 'creative writers' in a modern sense, when, I suggest, they would have been precisely concerned with *Jesus' acts of discourse*, not simply with 'performing' the parables. The Fathers and their successors, too, retained the sense of the parables' location at a turning point in history: this was indeed bound up with their perception of the parables' 'divine meaning'.

But in presenting the parable texts as the triggers for repeated new creations of meaning - seeds, we might say, bearing thirty-, sixty- or a hundredfold - Scott betrays uneasiness with the part played by the interpreters themselves, and with the inevitable variety of their insights. This is strange, given his emphasis on the hearing of the parables. Pointing out that reading the parables as metaphors precludes there being only one point of comparison, as stated by Jülicher - since metaphor implies a fertile interpretative conjunction of dissimilar things, a conjunction which may be read differently by different people - he writes that '[t]o select only one out of all the possibilities suggested by the metaphor / parable is manipulative of reality, ideology in its negative sense'.[124] Yet he himself makes exactly such a selection in his interpretations.

Near the end of the book he shows awareness of the inconsistency:

> After writing a commentary on all the parables, I am faced with a curious contradiction: much more remains to be written about the parables, and I have written too much . . . The parable as employed by Jesus is an open genre . . . The parable does not seek closure, regardless of how often during its transmission various interpreters have sought closure. For precisely this reason the parabolic narrative is always primary and can never be replaced by its supposed meaning.[125]

The desire for 'closure' is indeed as strong in Scott as it was in Jülicher, and certainly far stronger than in the premodern period which allowed such rich variety. But if the parabolic narrative is really to remain primary, interpreters must remain open, and that means that they must fully acknowledge the part played by their own insight. They must not shuffle off responsibility for the act of interpretation on to a text which has supposedly 'created meaning'.

These two oppositions - between speaker and transmitters, text and interpretation - are of course closely connected. There is a fault-line in Scott's work between the obviously (to him) pragmatic use of the parables by the early church, dictated by its particular historical context, and the universally available 'polyvalence' of Jesus' original parables. The meaning of Luke appears to Scott as accessible but dismissible; the meaning of the speaker appears inaccessible, but the 'texts' he bequeathed are seen to have endlessly renewable meaning.

We note at this point that the greatest opposition found in Jülicher's work - that between Jülicher himself and the tradition of interpretation - is not really paralleled in Scott's. The Fathers do not need to be taken on again: Jülicher's demolition job proved more than satisfactory for twentieth-century interpreters. Jülicher himself and his twentieth-century followers are treated with respect by Scott. Nevertheless, as we have seen, the interpreter's urge to offer the final, definitive reading, over against the inadequate attempts of one's predecessors, is still evident.

We turn, then, to the influences which can be discerned in Scott's position. In the synchronic dimension of contemporary influence, two sources stand out: philosophical and sociological.

Scott, as we have seen, makes use of the reader-response methodology developed by Wolfgang Iser.[126] This provides helpful insights into distinctions such as that between the 'real' audience of Luke and the 'fictional' audience of Jesus suggested by Luke's text. It is a methodology amenable to combination with the traditional historical-critical methods to which Scott remains attached, for Scott's central concern is with *how the stories were heard* rather than with how we hear them today. However, behind his interpretations seems to lie not just a methodology but also a philosophy of the reader: the postmodern reader as autonomous agent, loosed from ecclesiastical constraints and the historical community of interpretation.[127] Especially in the rather slippery transition between his detailed accounts of hearer-response and his closing 'From Story to Kingdom' sections, there seems to be a desire to affirm - more strongly than the objectified historical-critical discourse will allow - the fact that here indeed, in the entire enterprise, Scott the reader *is* making his own response, though with a measure of uneasiness.

The sociological influence can be discerned not just in the enriching way Scott draws on studies of the first-century Near Eastern social world, but also more fundamentally in his use of the category of 'common' or 'conventional' 'wisdom'. His central criterion for determining authentic parable-material is that it should 'play against the expectations of common wisdom'.[128] This notion is expounded as follows by Marcus J. Borg. Conventional wisdom, he writes,

> is an exceedingly useful notion, illuminating our own lives and illuminating the Christian message, important for our self-understanding and as a hermeneutical tool. Conventional wisdom is the heart or core of every culture. It consists of a culture's taken-for-granted understandings about how things are . . . Though its specific content varies from culture to culture, conventional wisdom has a number of general features in

common across cultures . . . embodies the central values of a culture . . . is intrinsically based on rewards and punishments . . . creates a world of hierarchies and social boundaries . . . When the notion of God is integrated into a system of conventional wisdom, God is imaged primarily as lawgiver and judge . . . this way of being [i.e. conventional wisdom] is not unusual . . . it is normal adult consciousness, both in Jesus' time and in our own time.[129]

The danger of placing such a (supposedly) universally applicable grid over the ancient texts is that a suspiciously neat result can easily be allowed to emerge: Jesus' teaching simply reverses the conventional wisdom. Whatever traces we have in the gospel texts of words spoken against universal common wisdom as twentieth-century social science understands it, become the definitive hallmarks of Scott's Jesus.

It is true that Scott acknowledges that reconstructing the common wisdom of a period, and discerning an individual voice that stands out from it, is not a straightforward matter, and that the imagination must come into play.[130] He declares his intention to adopt a *literary* method primarily, since 'the social context is subsumed into the literary, fictional world of the parable'.[131] Nevertheless, this social-scientific construct plays a significant part in his work. He writes that the 'cultural context' of first-century Judaism is 'critical for the parables' interpretation':[132] it is only (he says) the search for a specific *Sitz im Leben* in the ministry of Jesus which is misguided. Yet it seems that it is precisely not the feel of a particular cultural strangeness but the tone of a universal, 'radical', culture-transcending voice that characterizes, for Scott, the authentic accents of Jesus.

Diachronically, the influence on Scott of parable scholarship from Jülicher onwards has already been suggested in the opening section of this chapter. The influence of Jülicher's work is a paradoxical one. The replacement of simile with metaphor as the interpretative key signals a decisive move away from the picture of Jesus as appealing to obvious phenomena to teach people about God's kingdom; instead, he is seen as telling surprising stories which imply that God's kingdom is very different from contemporary conceptions. Yet this reaction against Jülicher may divert our attention from a more fundamental continuity. The Jesus who emerges from Scott's commentary is, like the Jesus of Jülicher, one who speaks in general, universal terms - understood in sociological categories rather than Jülicher's 'religious' ones. Despite the emphasis on hearer-response, the fear of 'allegory' will not allow Scott to imagine sharp and specific identifications between the situations of parables and those of Jesus' hearers.

Wherein, then, lies any genuine insight offered by Scott into the voice of Jesus? On the one hand, it may appear that his 'radical' Jesus is none other than a reflection of the 'radical' Scott, the product of an autonomous reader's parable 'performance', the reversal of a convenient construct of 'conventional wisdom', the exemplar *par excellence* of metaphor at its most striking and fresh; a Jesus who speaks to today not because his words had an original sharpness of application, but because his stories were 'about' the crossing of boundaries and the upsetting of conventions. What Scott 'knows' of Jesus through the key of metaphor may seem, in Sally McFague TeSelle's phrase, nothing other than 'the metaphors or projections of the self',[133] a self which wants to be radically uprooted from its ancestry and set apart from its contemporaries.

On the other hand, the picture of a Jesus who speaks in metaphors, with a teasing indirectness, is surely an important refinement of Jülicher's picture of Jesus the passionate communicator of plain truth. The intention of Jesus to get a message across is upheld, while the dynamics of his indirect *method* of speaking in parables are taken more seriously. Scott implies that the subversive message would have been received by Jesus' hearers more immediately than is likely. But we cannot dismiss Scott's Jesus as a mere projection of the late twentieth century, any more than we can dismiss Jülicher's as a mere projection of the late nineteenth. The insight is the more convincing because it emerges at least in part *despite* Scott's intention, as Jülicher's had emerged in part despite his. Both commentators illustrate that there is no escaping the fact that figures of speech invite the receiver to make a response to an intentional shaping of language. Jülicher wanted to find the intention of Jesus, and to escape from a merely personal response; what he offers is precisely a personal response, but one which discloses real insight into the voice of Jesus. Scott wants to find how people responded to Jesus, and to escape from the quest for his intention; he nevertheless offers insight into intention of Jesus, arising from his personal response to his words.

The voice of specific moral challenge which echoed through the early centuries, and whose sharpness was toned down by Jülicher's generalities, is now more muted still. But other tones are awakened whose origin may be equally ancient. It is our task now to see whether other interpretative keys for understanding the parables as figures can provide us with windows of insight which will allow a simultaneous vision of the communicative and the mysterious, the didactic and the subversive, the specific and the general aspects of the stance of Jesus in relation to his own society and the tradition in which he stood, earpieces through which the different tones of his voice can sound in harmony.

NOTES

1. Louth, *Discerning*, 108.
2. Bloom, *Map*, 3f.
3. See above, p. 1.
4. Jeremias, *Parables*, 182.
5. Thus illustrating the truth of Blomberg's comment that 'almost all commentators who actually expound a selection of the parables wind up with some allegorical interpretations, as the anti-Jülicher tradition defines them, regardless of what they may say about their method': *Interpreting*, 47.
6. Jeremias, *Parables*, 182.
7. Ibid., 186.
8. Ibid.
9. '*Die Basileia kommt im Gleichnis als Gleichnis zur Sprache*' ('the kingdom comes to expression in the parable as parable'): Jüngel, *Paulus*, 135. Cf. Funk, *Language*.
10. Linnemann, *Parables*, 31.
11. Ibid., 61.
12. Dan Otto Via, *The Parables: Their Literary and Existential Dimension* (Philadelphia: Fortress Press, 1967).
13. On the mashal see further below, pp. 203, 230.
14. *Parables*, 204.
15. Ibid., 193.
16. Cf. Parker, *Painfully Clear*, 20.
17. Via, *Parables*, 110-76.
18. Ibid., 161.
19. Norman Perrin discusses the output of this Seminar in the late 1960's and early 1970's: *Jesus and the Language of the Kingdom* (Philadelphia: Fortress Press, 1976), 168-81.
20. Although Crossan says in *Cliffs* (67) that he is seeking to move his view of language 'more resolutely into a structuralist viewpoint' away from the 'primarily romanticist' view of *In Parables,* the move does seem to me to be one from romantically-tinged structuralism to post-structuralism.
21. Crossan, *Cliffs*, 73. It could be argued that Crossan's introduction of the category 'play' has given Via's serious category 'aesthetic object' an unnecessarily bad name, as when Birger Gerhardsson combines the two and denies that the narrative parables are 'playful, literary products, *aesthetic objects*': 'Frames', 330f.
22. Crossan, *In Parables*, 32.
23. This attempt at penetrating the mind of Jesus is what is in view when Crossan writes of the 'primarily romanticist view of language' within which he had operated in *In Parables* (*Cliffs*, 67).
24. Drury's comment, directed particularly at Crossan, is therefore partially but not wholly fair: 'The Jesus whose parables could not be certainly isolated from the Christian gospels or his Jewish milieu, by being isolated from them nevertheless, became the receptacle of the wishes of the exegetes': 'Parable', 510.

25. Stephen D. Moore, *Literary Criticism and the Gospels: The Theoretical Challenge* (New Haven and London: Yale University Press, 1989), 137-51. Moore notes the incongruity in ch. 2 of *Cliffs*, where a standard historical-critical treatment of The Sower is followed by Crossan's 'playful' reading.
26. Crossan, *Cliffs*, 1-12.
27. Crossan, *In Parables*, 10-16.
28. Particularly Ricoeur, *Rule*.
29. Cf. Soskice, *Metaphor*, 74f.
30. Crossan, *Cliffs*, 25-64.
31. Cf. p. 9 above.
32. Crossan discusses in *Cliffs*, 98f., the distinction made by Rosemond Tuve between mimetic and ludic allegory. 'In mimetic allegory one is enjoying layers of divinely caused structural order mirroring the divine mind or will. One is viewing with great pleasure, as Tuve says, the "nature of the world" placed there by God to be discovered by ourselves. But *in ludic allegory one is enjoying the playful human imagination creating isomorphic plot as an act of supreme play* . . . I find mimetic allegory closed to me forever and I find in ludic allegory the way I must reread the past, interpret the present and propose the future. At least for now.' I do not find 'mimetic allegory' (or other mimetic figures) closed to me; I still believe in the possibility of discerning the real, though I would agree with Crossan that 'play' lies deep in human motivation, whether we think we are doing history, literary criticism, or anything else.
33. For a critical account of Scott's approach see Wolfgang Harnisch, 'Beiträge zur Gleichnisforschung (1984-1991),' *Theologische Rundschau* 59 (1994), 346-87, here 357-63.
34. *Hear*, 55. Cf. Ricoeur, 'Biblical Hermeneutics', 106.
35. *Hear*, 63-68.
36. Ibid., 19.
37. Ibid., 65f.
38. Ibid., 40.
39. Ibid.
40. Ibid., 65.
41. Ibid.
42. He eschews Schleiermacher's hermeneutics of divination and draws on the reader-response methodology of Wolfgang Iser's *The Act of Reading* (Baltimore: John Hopkins University Press, 1978) and *The Implied Reader* (Baltimore: John Hopkins Press, 1974).
43. Cf. James Fodor, *Christian Hermeneutics: Paul Ricoeur and the Refiguring of Theology* (Oxford: Clarendon Press, 1995), 143f.
44. *Hear*, 148.
45. Ibid., 133.
46. Ibid., 193.
47. Ibid., 195.
48. Ibid., 202.
49. Ibid., 65.
50. Ibid., 266.
51. Ibid., 187.

52. Ibid., 423.

53. It is not that a movement from the 'implied' to the 'real' speaker or author is logically impossible. Mark Allan Powell has noted the possibility (in relation to the gospel narratives) of making a small hermeneutical 'leap' entailing 'acceptance of the unprovable premise that the authors of our Gospels succeeded in creating narratives that would have the effects they wanted them to have': *What is Narrative Criticism?* (Minneapolis: Fortress Press, 1990), 97. Scott has made a leap of this kind from the Jesus *implied* by the parables, and the likely way in which they were understood, to the *real* Jesus, on the assumption that Jesus succeeded in creating parables that had the effect he desired. The fact that Scott jumps from 'implied speaker' to 'real speaker' without making this leap explicit seems to betoken an anxiety about the whole process, a tension between doubt and desire.

54. On at least one occasion, though, Scott betrays the quite unwarranted presuppositions that Jesus' audience must immediately have understood him, that they understood his intention aright, and that he *intended* such immediate understanding. He writes, with reference to The Wicked Tenants (Mk. 12:1-12 and parallels): 'If the son is Jesus, it is impossible to understand how the parable can go back to Jesus. Who, after all, in the original audience would have understood the allusion?' (*Hear*, 65). This implies that the response of the hearers must necessarily have mirrored the intention of the speaker.

55. Ibid., 61; and see 53, quoting *Midrash Rabbah* on the Song of Songs 1.1.8 and *m. Erub.* 21b.

56. The notion of the parables as metaphors has been recently influential in Europe too: see Hans Weder, *Die Gleichnisse Jesu als Metaphern: Traditions- und redaktionsgeschichtliche Analysen und Interpretationen* (Göttingen: Vandenhoeck & Ruprecht, 1980); Kjärgaard, *Metaphor*; Chris Hermans, *Wie werdet Ihr die Gleichnisse verstehen? Empirische-theologische Forschung zur Gleichnisdidaktik* (Kampen: Kok Publishing House, 1990), discussed in Harnisch, 'Beiträge', 380f.; Heininger, *Metaphorik*.

57. Scott, *Hear*, 49.

58. Ibid., 47.

59. Ibid., 48.

60. Ibid., 49.

61. Ibid., 51.

62. Ibid., 49. Jülicher argued that there must originally have been a *tertium comparationis*, a point of comparison around which the parables pivoted, but his case was weakened by the general absence of such explicit points in the texts. Scott here acknowledges that the discernment of the point of metaphorical identification, his equivalent of the *tertium comparationis*, must be a matter of the interpreter's insight.

63. Ibid., 48.

64. Ibid., 59, citing *Sifra* on Lev. 18:1.

65. *Hear*, 50.

66. *Hear*, 189.

67. Ibid., 201f.

68. Ibid., 201.

69. Funk, *Language*, 213; idem, *Parables and Presence: Forms of the New Testament Tradition* (Philadelphia: Fortress Press, 1982), 29-34.
70. Scott, *Hear*, 29 (my emphasis)
71. Funk, *Parables*, 34.
72. Scott, *Hear*, 200.
73. Rudolf Bultmann, *History of the Synoptic Tradition* [*Geschichte der synoptischen Tradition*, 1921] (New York: Harper & Row, 1963), 178.
74. Scott, *Hear*, 202.
75. Ibid., 200. Hedrick (*Parables*, 98f.) also notes this feature in Scott's readings, as well as in Crossan's.
76. Scott, *Hear*, 125.
77. Ibid., 120.
78. Ibid., 121f., 125.
79. Ibid., 103.
80. Ibid., 105.
81. Ibid.
82. Ibid.
83. This is stated unambiguously on ibid., 104. On 113 Scott is more nuanced: 'On the one hand, the younger son's request for his share of the property, especially the right of disposition, effectively announces his father's death . . . On the other hand, the mytheme of elder-and-younger-brother stories encourages an audience to expect the younger to be something of a rogue and the favorite.'
84. Ibid., 112. Scott also gives an example of this tradition from the *Midrash* on Ps. 9:1.
85. Scott, *Hear*, 123.
86. Ibid.
87. Ibid., 125.
88. Ibid., 103.
89. Wolterstorff, *Divine Discourse*, 55.
90. Scott, *Hear*, 125.
91. Ibid., 265.
92. Ibid., 265f.
93. Ibid., 158.
94. Scott has already noted the significance of Lazarus's name, 'he whom God helps' (ibid., 149).
95. Ibid., 159.
96. Ibid.
97. Ibid., 146.
98. Ibid.
99. Ibid., 158.
100. Ibid., 159.
101. Ibid., 187.
102. Ibid., 175.
103. Ibid., 186.
104. Ibid., 187.
105. Ibid.

106. Ibid., 93.

107. Ibid., 97.

108. Ibid.

109. Ibid., 94.

110. Ibid., 94ff.

111. Ibid., 97.

112. Ibid., 140.

113. Ibid., 44 (my italics).

114. Ibid., 104.

115. Ibid., 265.

116. Ibid., 105.

117. Ibid., 187.

118. Ibid., 93.

119. Cf. Wolterstorff, *Divine Discourse*, 55.

120. The focus on the text itself (rather than an author) constitutes a strong link between the early and contemporary periods of interpretation: see above, Chapter 3, and Wolterstorff, *Divine Discourse*, 16ff. The crucial difference between these periods is that in the earlier, the text was seen as transparent upon *divine* meaning.

121. Scott, *Hear*, 420.

122. Scott exemplifies here the postmodern ethos, with its origins in the work of Marx, Nietzsche and Freud, who created 'a mediate *science* of meaning, irreducible to the immediate *consciousness* of meaning': Paul Ricoeur, *Freud and Philosophy* [1965] (New Haven: Yale University Press, 1970), 34.

123. *Divine Discourse*, 181, and see the section 171-82.

124. Ibid., 50.

125. Ibid., 419.

126. See note 42 above.

127. For a clear assertion of such readerly autonomy see David J. A. Clines, *The Bible in the Modern World* (Sheffield: Sheffield Academic Press, 1997), especially 15-18.

128. *Hear*, 67.

129. Borg, *Jesus*, 149f.

130. *Hear*, 67f.

131. Ibid., 74.

132. *Hear*, 42.

133. TeSelle, *Speaking*, 147.

CHAPTER 6

Parables and Persuasion: The Voice of Jesus in his Contemporary Context

[T]he tone of his message had a sharper edge than a witty mocking of convention. The kind of passion one hears in Jesus' social critique suggests more of the social prophet . . . Jesus was not simply concerned with the individual's freedom from the prison of convention, but with a comprehensive vision of life that embraced the social order.[1]

It is not reasonable historical explanation to say that Jesus believed in a whole list of non-controversial and pleasant abstractions (love, mercy, and grace) and that his opponents denied them.[2]

1. The Synchronic Context of Jesus: Society and Faith

My aim in this chapter is to imagine the voice of Jesus in his contemporary context, by asking how the six parables might have functioned as figures of speech when told by him. The chapter thus focuses on the 'far side' of the text, Chapter 2 having focused on the 'near side'.[3]

Anyone approaching any aspect of the study of Jesus today has a wealth of up-to-date historical scholarship on which to draw, and an array of 'portraits of Jesus' from which to choose as a framework.[4] It is impossible here to enter into detailed interaction with different options concerning the overall aims of Jesus and the shape of his career. It will be sufficient for my purpose, of demonstrating the insight that may be yielded through the application of a particular trope, to set the discussion in the context of two affirmations about Jesus' setting which command wide assent. These aspects of his setting may be seen as the central synchronic influences upon him, affecting him in both conscious and pre-conscious ways.

First, the *social world* of Palestine, in which Jesus' ministry was rooted, can be understood as dominated, in Borg's formulation, by peasantry, purity and patriarchy.[5] Scholarship has been reaching an increasingly clear picture of the stark disparities at the time between a wealthy élite and a poor majority oppressed by the power structures both of Rome and of Jewish officialdom.[6] I shall draw upon various studies of the social background of individual parables.[7]

Secondly, the *thought-world* of contemporary Judaism, in which Jesus was deeply immersed, was fundamentally shaped by the Torah of Moses.[8] More specifically, it may be seen as strongly coloured by what E.P. Sanders terms 'covenantal nomism'.[9] Contrary to the earlier view of Pharisaism, or of Judaism in general, as intent on 'earning salvation' by means of the law (a view which seems to derive from reading Paul through Lutheran eyes), it is now widely held that the intense focus of some groups of Jews (such as the Pharisees) on observance of the law was intended not as a means of winning God's approval, but as a public form of *expression* of belonging to God's covenant people, and the way to true life within that people.[10] Such an expression was especially important in first-century Palestine, where many Jews felt their very identity to be under threat from the domination of Rome. The idea of obedience to the law as an expression of belonging to the covenant, as the means of life, and as a response to God's grace, is fully consonant with the OT,[11] and can be taken as a central motif among the variety of expressions of Judaism in this period. In discussing the functioning of the parables this, like the social context of Jesus, will be a vital sounding board against which we may try to hear his voice.[12]

The key question for us, then, is the way that the parables functioned as figures, tokens of a particular individuality within this context. As I suggested in Chapter 1, this is as much a matter of detecting tone or mood as of determining precise meaning. Germane to this enterprise are two particular features of the parables' narrative texture: realism and surprise.

Many scholars have seen in the parables a *realistic* portrayal of the world of Jesus.[13] Jülicher wrote of the parables' 'natural colouring',[14] and this sense of the parables' homely reflection of life has given strong support to the view that their figural mood is one of plain similitude: as it is in the world, so it is - in higher register - in the kingdom. Dodd went so far as to claim that the parables could be used as source-material for first-century Palestinian life: they give, he wrote, 'probably a more complete picture of petit-bourgeois and peasant life than we possess for any other province of the Roman Empire except Egypt, where papyri come to our aid'.[15] This is an interesting instance of an aesthetic judgement: Dodd did not bring forward from other sources evidence of practices reflected in the parables in order to back the claim that they were realistic: this is simply how they struck him. There has, however, been a steady stream of scholars who point to features in the parables that disrupt otherwise realistic tales.[16] From the latter perspective the parables can be seen as embodying a dissonance between a real world and a possible world, and thus as 'metaphorical'.[17]

The main element of the parables that seems to disrupt realism is that of *surprise*.[18] Would a father behave like that? Would a master praise such a steward? Hedrick, however, shows convincingly that realism and surprise can go together. Discussing Erich Auerbach's *Mimesis*,[19] Hedrick makes the point that 'realism does not require that the actions of characters be predictable':[20] that is, realism must not be equated with the presentation of stock behaviour and stereotyped figures. If the real world is strange, so will be a realistic portrayal of it.[21] We must clarify now the sense in which our six parables are indeed realistic, and the significance of the element of surprise they contain.

It is a commonplace of current parable scholarship to say that the parables are invitations to new insight into the world.[22] This may in fact true of all stories, perhaps realistic ones especially. When a storyteller selects, orders and portrays events, characters, and behaviour, the resulting narrative is more than simply a mirror of the real world. It has become *suggestive*, provocative perhaps. We can describe this as the *figurative* essence of realistic narrative fiction.[23] Stories have a suggestive penumbra which belies Hedrick's insistence that the parables need not point beyond themselves.[24] One direction in which they surely point is towards their author. A story is a figure, a signal of individuality. Funk put it like this: 'Jesus belongs to the parable, not as a figure in it, but as author of the situation depicted by the parable';[25] with reference to The Good Samaritan, he wrote that Jesus is in the parable's 'penumbral field . . . the parable is permission on the part of Jesus to follow him, to launch out into a future that he announces as God's own'.[26] Maurice Baumann, who denies that the parables have a metaphorical character, tacitly admits this general figurative essence when he writes that 'the surprising effect of the parables cannot but excite the desire to profile the identity of their author'.[27] Figures as figures launch the quest for the 'voice'. The questions or statements in which a narrator's person becomes more visible (Lk. 10:36; 16:8b,9; 18:6-8,14) only serve to make explicit what is implicit in the other stories, which is that the narrative is not to be taken as a simple account of something that happened, but as a story with another dimension of meaning, a story with implications. While such questions and statements (like other elements of the texts as we have them) naturally reflect the interpretation of the communities which transmitted them, and of the Evangelist himself, it is arbitrary and fallacious to separate them off from the stories themselves as 'secondary' simply because they somehow intrude on the purity of the story.[28]

What figure, then, best describes these parables' particular tone of surprising realism or realistic surprise? In what ways does their story-world simply mirror the thought and society of Jesus and his contemporaries, and in what ways does it suggest unusual possibilities? I will not consider further the idea that these particular parables originally functioned as similes; the 'like / as' construction is missing from all of them, and to impose it on them as Jülicher did rests, as I have shown, on dubious foundations. The question then is which *trope* or tropes best describe the voice of these stories within the world of Jesus. We shall investigate this first by considering the possibly misleading nature of a number of tropes if used to describe these parables, and then proposing one as a more insightful interpretative key.

2. Inadequate Interpretative Keys

When consideration is given to the operation of tropes in a living oral context, it will readily be seen that speech is full of them,[29] on both surface and deep-structural levels; and that it is fallacious to assume that tropical words, phrases or longer units of discourse can be categorized under the heading of one trope alone. Nevertheless, it is possible to detect some false trails, and find more promising ones which make better sense of the data of text and context.

In considering the reasons for the inadequacy of various tropes as keys, I shall draw attention especially to the parables' *characters*. Characters are the agents of a story's momentum, and can offer important clues as to its tropical significance.[30]

Metaphor

In an obvious sense, these narrative parables can be considered as metaphors uttered by Jesus, if they are thought to be fictitious.[31] They say 'this happened', but do not necessarily mean that it *happened*; they mean 'imagine that this happened'.[32] To say that these stories are metaphorical in this sense need not involve us in saying what the metaphor precisely *means*, tying it down to a referent such as 'the kingdom of God'.[33] Their metaphoricity may simply consist in their fictionality.

However, the popular designation of the parables as metaphors can be misleading. Metaphor implies a transference between two spheres, involving a contrast that is originally more or less striking. We think, for instance, of the humour, insult and insight engendered by the bringing-together of human and animal worlds (Herod is a fox; a sailor is an old sea-dog). But we should consider carefully whether we do in fact find such a bringing-together of different spheres in the parables I am considering. On one level, as has often been noted,[34] they are clearly different from animal- or plant-fables, in which the bestial or vegetable world in thinly-veiled fashion and sometimes humorously reflects the human. On a deeper level, though, metaphor may imply that the 'everyday' sphere of life they present stands for the sphere of the 'kingdom' as something essentially different. This is the thought behind the standard assumption that in such parables as Luke 16:1-8 and 18:1-8 disciples are being exhorted to learn 'new age' lessons from 'old age' examples.[35] I believe rather that we should see the situations pictured in these stories as surprising instances of the new age itself. Although writers such as Scott stress that the parables by metaphor show the kingdom in a new and surprisingly 'everyday' light,[36] 'metaphor' still assumes that two different *spheres* are being brought together; an earthly scene is picturing, and giving new insight into, a transcendent one. Ruth Etchells' sensitive reading proposes a 'crossing' of metonymic ('horizontal') and metaphoric ('vertical') dimensions in the parables.[37] That is, they are stories of the everyday world, but contain clues (the elements of 'extravagance' or surprise) which point in a transcendent direction. While her reading opens up rich possibilities for theological meditation on the parables, I am not convinced that for Jesus and his hearers, such a crossing of spheres would have been either intended or detected. Their language - even in Luke's edition! - is too thoroughly this-worldly. Further, the construal of the parables as metaphors could imply that the parables' characters are *disguises,* mere masks or *personae* concealing a true self beneath. They seem, rather, to be realistic figures drawn from life.

Metonymy

We argued in Chapter 2 that metonymy best expressed the function of the parables in the context of Luke-Acts, where they substitute for and express the gospel message through presenting vivid aspects of its outworking. But it does not seem appropriate as a way of describing their oral operation in Jesus' ministry, before the time when 'the gospel' was a clear concept in people's minds. This trope is associated with *symbol*[38] and with *static* representation. The parables' realism and dynamism preclude their working by means of symbols, whether established ones ('the crown' for 'the monarchy', for instance) or newly invented ones which the hearer is expected to decipher for herself.[39] Put another way, the characters in the parables are not *personifications,* as would be implied if we read them as metonymies in which the person expressing the characteristic substitutes for the characteristic itself, the 'real' subject of the discourse.[40] The Samaritan does not simply personify 'goodness', nor the father 'love', nor the steward 'shrewdness', nor the widow 'persistence', nor the customs officer 'humility'. The development, briefly drawn though it is, which takes place in some characters - the prodigal son, the steward and his master, the judge - and the action in which most are involved, are not consistent with static symbolism such as this. Etchells' understanding of the parables' 'metonymic' structure[41] is closer to what I will describe as 'synecdoche'.

Irony

Scholars have become increasingly attuned to the possible presence of irony in biblical writings, but there is a danger that it becomes just a convenient and unimaginative escape-route from problematic texts. Irony 'ensues from the juxtaposition or clash of incommensurate levels of powerful realities'.[42] The Shrewd Steward is a parable where irony has been suggested as an interpretative tool.[43] But though I have argued that a certain irony is present in the parable when read in the context of Luke-Acts, and especially in the word 'unrighteous',[44] on what grounds would we call the story ironic in the context of Jesus' world? Irony in that context would entail *a sense that such things would never happen*. I have the sense, rather, that such things might well have happened: accusations of sharp practice, hasty dismissal, bleak prospects, resourceful reaction. Even the master's praise, though surprising, need not be seen as ironically described, for it reveals a kind of credible connivance, a relaxation of stringency which makes him a rounded figure, not a sheer two-dimensional hard man. The hearers, it seems, are to think of the occurrence as a *real possibility*, of such things as actually happening.

The same is true of The Judge and the Widow, thought to be ironic by Wolfgang Harnisch.[45] If the characters in these parables, or the others, were ironic representations, they would be *fancies*, either wistful ('if only there were such people!') or complacent ('thank God such people don't exist!'). But in fact, what you see is how things are. The working of irony depends on a mutual knowingness between speaker and hearer. I find here no wistful awareness that notwithstanding their stories, such actions as the Samaritan's compassion, the son's return, the father's forgiveness, the judge's relenting, could not possibly happen. Equally, there is no *complacent* awareness that such dire contrasts as those between the rich man and Lazarus or between the Pharisee and the customs officer, the situations of social oppression and corruption which can readily be imagined as standing behind all the parables,[46] are inconceivable. Even where the designation of the character is surprising (the compassionate man is a *Samaritan*, the unjustified man is a *Pharisee*), that designation is not given ironically. The point is that a Samaritan, or a Pharisee, *might in fact be like that*.

Hyperbole

It is necessary to spend a little longer on hyperbole. This trope is rather subtly different from irony: where irony hints at an incommensurability through dry understatement, hyperbole presses it in our face through exaggerated expression. Given the element of 'extravagance' in the parables,[47] it would be a natural conclusion to say that they were hyperbolic, that they exaggerated the way the world was, for a particular effect. For example, Hedrick thinks that the Samaritan is a 'parody' or 'caricature' of the late Jewish ideal of righteousness, such that one cannot take this compassionate figure seriously as an example.[48] But this is unconvincing; the parable becomes a teasing story but loses its edge. Similarly, the father's welcome of his wayward son is striking, but not incredible; the image would not have shown such enduring power if it were. The landowner's praise of his cunning steward is surprising, but not hyperbolic. The rich man's lifestyle is indeed lavish, but that only makes him one of a small class, not beyond the bounds of any class at all. The widow's persistence and judge's response are remarkable, but believable. The Pharisee and the customs officer likewise are credible figures. Would a judgement on this question of characters' credibility have to wait until historical evidence turned up actual examples of first-century people from these various classes behaving in such ways? Do we not see here how a twenty-first-century response *can* cross two millennia and affirm that here is human nature in its roundedness, ambiguity, and capability of change?

The exclusion of hyperbole entails that we do not see the characters as either *ideals* or *grotesques*. The positive characters are *models,* but the drawing of them is too restrained to make them into implicitly unattainable ones. This point needs to be developed in some detail, since recent parable scholarship has tended to 'discover' ideal, parodic and grotesque elements.[49] The characters in our parable-stories, however, are presented in restrained fashion. They are not so much described, as *discovered* in their musings[50] and behaviour.[51] These parables approximate closely to Auerbach's famous description of the story of Abraham and Isaac in Genesis 22: we find here

> the externalization of only so much of the phenomena as is necessary for the purpose of the narrative, all else left in obscurity; the decisive points of the narrative alone are emphasized . . . thoughts and feeling remain unexpressed, are only suggested by the silence and the fragmentary speeches; the whole, permeated with the most unrelieved suspense and directed toward a single goal . . . remains mysterious and 'fraught with background'.[52]

Let us see how this mode of restrained character-portrayal dominates in each of the parables.

Nowhere in the text is the Samaritan given so much as the adjective 'good', but the hearer learns in detail about what he did: moved with compassion, he attended to the wounded man's immediate and longer-term needs, in a sequence of actions captured in nine main verbs or participles in Luke 10:34f. In Luke's setting the lawyer is then left to make his own judgement on this behaviour and its contrast with that of the passers-by. (The priest and Levite are also shown graphically, in action - or rather inaction). To be *told* that a character is righteous or exemplary can give him or her an air of ideal unattainability. To be *shown* what such a description might mean in practice, to have character earthed in *behaviour,* can be more persuasive, communicating a sense that imitation might be possible.[53]

Something similar applies to the father in The Prodigal Son. After the single word describing his deep feeling, ἐσπλαγχνίσθη ('he was moved with compassion', 15:20[54] - and note that this is a feeling-word as much as a moral marker, perhaps the one element which distinguishes these parables from Auerbach's description of Genesis 22), the father's character is then made clear, not abstractly via descriptive statement but concretely in a sequence of actions (including commands), recounted in vv. 20 and 22. Actions speak louder than words. The narrative does not tell us that the father was overwhelmingly forgiving. It *shows* us that he was, through recounting his feeling and his deeds. This, again, militates against a reading of the parable as hyperbolic. It is *understated*, not overstated. We discover the characters of the two brothers, also, in what they say and do, not in anything the narrator tells us in a general or abstracted way about them.

We find this pattern in The Rich Man and Lazarus also. The rich man's iniquity is not directly mentioned, but the appalling injustice of the situation is amply *revealed* in the vivid description of the two men's conditions of life. In this parable, indeed, more clearly perhaps than in any of the other five, the focus is on the characters as *types.*[55] It is not their *individual* morality which is at issue, but the injustice of the society in which they live.[56] Borg rightly comments that when we read Jesus' sayings in the knowledge that his was a peasant society, '[p]overty and wealth cease to be abstractions or metaphors . . . [t]hey also cease to be primarily qualities of individuals.'[57] Thus the *post-mortem* scene, which suggests that injustice will not for ever rule, can be read as a vindication not so much of Lazarus in his personal behaviour (the moral aspect of which is never mentioned in the story), but as a righting of *society's* inequalities.[58] The skilful restraint of the parables, in which characters and situations are not so much labelled as evoked, contributes considerably to their rhetorical power as realistic stories and contrasts sharply with the rather garish way that commentators have sometimes painted their characters.[59]

This dramatic principle of character emerging realistically in action, seen I believe quite clearly in the three parables just mentioned (The Good Samaritan, The Prodigal Son and The Rich Man and Lazarus) can give us a better grasp of the other three parables where the issue of character has been more problematic. Nowhere has this problem been felt more acutely than with The Shrewd Steward. We have seen the way that exegetes have often sought to defend this parable against the impression given by 16:8f. that the steward's behaviour is meant to be exemplary. τὸν οἰκονόμον τῆς ἀδικίας ('the steward of unrighteousness', 16:8) has been taken as a totally blackening designation[60] and controlled the interpretation. However, it is necessary both to understand the nuance of that phrase and to see how the man's character emerges from the story as a whole.

Ellis helps us to capture the right connotations for the word ἀδικίας ('unrighteousness'). He demonstrates that the word (used also in 16:9 and 18:6)

> does not refer to individual ethics but to the universal character of 'this age'. 'Dishonest steward' and 'unjust judge' (18:6 AV) are both misleading translations; these men are neither better nor worse than other 'sons of this world'. The description . . . means only that they belong to this age and order their lives according to its principles.[61]

David Daube rightly says that the steward is called unrighteous because 'up to now, he has willingly executed a wealthy oppressor's bidding'.[62] He is caught up in an unrighteous system. Further, as already suggested, 'unrighteous' may well have been a term of social stigmatization used by the Pharisees.[63] When we return to read the story from the beginning, we find that the *action* of the story does not present him as a wicked man. He *was falsely accused* (διεβλήθη) of wasting his master's goods (16:1).[64] Even if we soften the meaning to 'accused', excluding the notion of calumny, it is still only an unproven charge.[65] If there is any character blackening by the narrator in vv. 1f., it is of the *master*, whose justice seems summary in the extreme.[66] He pronounces the steward's dismissal without any checking of the reports. The steward's resolute action is then recounted. Again, there is no abstract description of him ('he was a wise man'). His cleverness and determination are *revealed* to us through the vivid device of the interior monologue, and through the tale of how he actually carried through his plan. The fact that his tactics are clearly self-regarding makes many commentators assume that his ruse with the debtors was also an act of defiant rebellion against the master, a further instance of the supposed 'squandering' of v.1.[67] But here we need the help of historical imagination to grasp the realistic logic of the story. William R. Herzog II writes:

> [The steward] is familiar with back-stabbing and has probably survived a few episodes of witch-hunting to reach his present position. Given the

master's frame of mind, he can see that it would be useless to fall into the familiar role by protesting his innocence. All that would do is confirm the master's hasty judgment. If he is to survive, he must develop a different strategy and employ different tactics. To the steward, the question of whether he is innocent or guilty is not even a consideration. Guilty of what? Taking too large a cut? Failing to achieve usurious profit margins? Not covering his backside as well as he usually does?[68]

The act of reducing debts was an act which benefited the poor[69] and fulfilled the Torah's requirements by cancelling the illegal interest normally covertly charged to the master's benefit.[70] The steward took the initiative to do something that was just and community-minded, and aimed at securing his own future into the bargain.[71] The master cannot help but recognize this, and praises the steward, seeing that his just action towards the debtors has put them in a heightened relationship of obligation to the master.[72] This saves the narrative from descending into the hyperbole of surreal madness, as is almost implied by Scott's reading.[73] The parable reflects all too familiar an environment. The way is open for us to see the steward as a genuine example put forward by Jesus; the story is not merely 'comedy'.[74]

As in the case of the steward, the judge in 18:6 is described (in this case after the end of the story) as ὁ κριτὴς τῆς ἀδικίας ('the judge of unrighteousness'), and in this case too Ellis's explanation of the phrase helps us to see the realism of the character-portrayal. The judge is no worse than other children of the old age. This is seen also in the opening description of v. 2. Hedrick attempts to *whiten* the judge's character by making this description refer to lack of religious or human prejudice.[75] This overstates the case, but helps redress an imbalance in conventional interpretations. Hedrick is right to take the verb ἐντρέπομαι, which appears in vv. 2 and 4, as 'to show partiality', on the basis of the LXX passages he cites (Wis. 6:7; Sir. 4:22; Job 33:21). The judge is his own man and is not going to bow to pressure just on account of a person's poverty; such impartiality is indeed commanded, as Hedrick shows, in the OT (Dt. 1:17, and I would add especially Lev. 19:15, where partiality to the poor is specifically mentioned as something to be avoided, along with favouritism to the rich). But Hedrick is wrong to try to turn 'not fearing the Lord' into a good quality. As he notes, Luke especially uses the phrase in a traditional, positive sense.[76] Instead of making this an exception, saying that Luke has taken over the phrase from a source, and that it retains a different sense from its normal one in his gospel,[77] I suggest that we see in the two character descriptions together ('neither feared God nor regarded man') the realistic portrayal of a devil-may-care outlook on life. The judge is not wholly villainous at the outset; his lack of 'regard' for people preserves an important quality anciently enjoined on administrators of the law. But his failure to fear God puts him beyond the pale for the pious Jew, and means that his strong impartiality is not tempered by a concern for mercy - a concern that was also enjoined in the law and the prophets.[78]

The judge appears to be exceptional in the cast of the parables in that his character is *described* at the beginning of the story (Lk. 18:2).[79] However, it is the narrative presentation of his motivation (seen in his interior monologue in vv. 4f.) and implied action, not this description, which ultimately controls the reading of his character. Just as he is not totally villainous at the beginning, nor does he become a paragon of virtue by the end. For a while he ignores the widow's pleading, and then, like the prodigal and steward, he reasons within himself. Though he does not fear God (and therefore feels under no obligation to do justice or mercy), and though he is no respecter of persons (and therefore feels positively justified in not paying the widow particular attention), he will adjudicate for her in order to stop her bothering him.[80] When he decides to turn his mind to her case, it can be dealt with expeditiously; 'I will vindicate her' (v. 5) implies that the judge knows very well that she is in the right. He has simply been ignoring her - whether through idleness, pressure of work or sheer callousness is left to the imagination. The judge's final resolve is not a matter of his being 'willing finally to be compromised for the sake of his own comfort', as Hedrick asserts.[81] The absence of any fear of God means that he would have had little sense of being compromised, and his impartiality, though rooted in an important principle, had simply been a convenient escape from demands for mercy. Yet even though his motives were mixed - like those of the prodigal son when he returned - the conclusion of the story is that he did what was just and merciful, like the master in 16:8. This complicated human being seems remarkably credible, not 'hopelessly ridiculous'; the story is not 'burlesque'.[82]

The problems that have been raised by scholars recently with reference to characterization in The Pharisee and the Customs Officer concern Luke's introduction (18:9) and what is regarded as his conclusion (v. 14b). We have seen how Scott thinks that Luke prejudices our view of the two characters.[83] We need, again, to see how the story itself presents them in their own words and deeds.

Once more it is best to see them as *realistic* portrayals. That is, they are not exaggerated, but believable figures from Jesus' social world. Many have noted the genuineness of the Pharisee's acknowledgement of God as the source of his goodness.[84] Our knowledge of similar prayers in the Talmud and Tosephta[85] suggests that the Pharisee in the story would have been a recognizable person to Jesus' hearers. The customs officer says no more or less than the words of Psalm 51:1, which no doubt would have been equally familiar. The presentation of character here by means of showing people in action is highly effective. It is simultaneously understated (there is no direct description of the characters within the tale itself) and vivid, and through its realism would draw a hearer or reader in and makes her feel that this truly is her own world, opened up before her. The notes of the two men's posture - the Pharisee standing by himself (Lk. 18:11),[86] the customs officer standing afar off (v. 13) - speak volumes, as does the contrast between the two prayers: especially noteworthy is the Pharisee's awareness of the customs officer, which does not seem to be reciprocated. There is no need for the speaker to say more in order to crystallize their characters and attitudes.[87] V. 14a gives the startling denouement. As in The Rich Man and Lazarus, we find out enough about the character of the protagonists from the picturing of their state and the announcement of their end; we do not need any explicit description.[88] (To exclude v. 14a from the 'story proper', as Hedrick does on the grounds that the 'I tell you' intrudes on the fictional world of the parable as happens in no other parable,[89] is simply to leave the story without an ending, conducive to a portrait of Jesus as a mere teaser, but otherwise unwarranted).

So are Luke's introduction in v. 9, and the conclusion in v. 14 (whoever may be responsible for it), fair to these two men, or an exaggerated, moralizing caricature, reductively removing the radical subversiveness of the story? They seem to be a reasonable summary of the picture painted in the story itself. The Pharisee, though he thanks God, certainly trusts that he is righteous, and appears to look down on the customs officer. His 'trusting in himself that he is righteous' is best described as 'self-deception' rather than 'self-righteousness'. This can appropriately be seen as 'exalting oneself' in one's own eyes before God: he has an inflated conception of his own righteousness. The vignette of the customs officer, beating on his breast and crying for mercy, is certainly a picture of humility.[90] In any case, Luke in v. 9 is writing about those to whom the parable was told; his description of the men does not have to be an exact mirror image of the presentation of the Pharisee in the parable in order for him to convey the pointed effectiveness of Jesus' teaching. Luke's framework does not turn either character into an unbelievable hyperbole for a real person.

3. Synecdoche as an Interpretative Key

Having pointed to the possibly misleading consequences of treating the six parables as metaphoric, metonymic, ironic or hyperbolic, I suggest now that the best insight into their rhetorical power and tone as parables of Jesus can be won by reading them as *synecdoches*.[91] They are stories of specific everyday events, which suggest something about the world as a whole. They do not discourse about another sphere of existence under the *guise* of talking about everyday life. They present, rather, a narrowly focused, in some way representative, part of the same sphere about which their speaker intends to talk.

Quintilian 'equate[d] synecdoche with ellipsis, which occurs "when something is assumed which has not actually been expressed" '.[92] Noting the connection of such an ellipsis with narrative fiction, Fletcher comments that the 'inferential process' such a figure requires 'is a natural response to any fiction that is elliptical or enigmatic in any way'.[93] A diagram may help us to grasp the working of synecdoche in the parables.

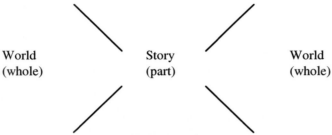

World   Story   World
(whole)   (part)   (whole)

    At its simplest synecdoche is seen in a single word, as in the example given in Chapter 1, the Hebraism 'many' for 'all', found in Mark 10:45.[94] The working of the trope is in two stages. The speaker - in this case probably as a matter of pure linguistic convention, of which he may not even be conscious - substitutes 'many' for 'all'; and the hearer must then make the substitution in reverse. The speaker turns the whole into the part, and the hearer turns the part into the whole again. The entire exchange in its original context probably took place on a completely instinctive, near-instantaneous, unreflective level.

    The telling of a realistic story can encompass essentially the same process. The storyteller recounts a lifelike occurrence. And as he does so, his *claim* is that *this is not a mere isolated incident among a myriad of unconnected and meaningless events, but somehow focuses or represents 'how things are' on a wider canvas.*[95] The hearer senses that this is the claim (cf. Lk. 10:37; 20:19). Therefore her natural response (though seldom, of course, articulated like this) is to ask: of *what whole is this a representative part?*

    However, in the case of an original *story,* that process of discernment is not so instinctive or instantaneous as it usually is with a single *word* used in a synecdochic way. Here Dodd was exactly right to say that a parable leaves the hearer's mind 'in sufficient doubt about its precise application to tease it into active thought'.[96] With synecdochic parables, the element of doubt revolves especially around the dimensions of 'world' in the diagram above. How *universally* representative does the speaker wish the story to be?

I suggest that in these six stories Jesus was saying to his hearers 'This is how the world is' - not merely presenting a new *possibility*, as Harnisch thinks.[97] Their realism lies not only in their location in familiar surroundings but in their portrayal of the kind of hopeful event that Jesus saw happening around him. Jesus wished his hearers to see that the world on a wider scale was a world in which such things take place, and to adapt their lives to this reality.[98] That is, his words did indeed have universal implications. But they were not grand, general, universal words. He pointed to parts of the whole, specific suggestive instances which invited further reflection. The hearers' task, the work of insight demanded of her, was to draw the lines out from the part and see what shape the resulting whole would take.

We turn therefore to examine in more detail the two stages of synecdoche in our parables: the focusing of the 'world' (on the left hand side of the diagram) in the story (the centre), and the 'retranslation' of that part into a whole again (the right hand side). As in the previous section, we shall concentrate especially on the parables' characters.

Whole to Part: world into story

In excluding the other tropes, we discussed what the characters are *not* (disguises, personifications, ciphers, fancies, ideals / grotesques). What then *are* they if the operative trope is *synecdoche*? They are, I believe, *examples*.[99] Although the brevity of their presentation naturally does not allow for the development of character which we can find, for instance, in a modern novel, this brevity is not a challenge to their exemplary function; indeed, that function is fulfilled the more sharply on account of it. *Jesus focused the world in realistic stories of characters intended as exemplary.*

The Good Samaritan, The Rich Man and Lazarus, and The Pharisee and the Customs officer are generally recognized as example-stories; they present behaviour to be imitated or avoided.[100] I wish to extend this description to the other three parables in the group not normally thought of in this way (The Prodigal Son, The Shrewd Steward and The Judge and the Widow). It seems to me that this is a natural way to read them, when their close parallels with the three traditionally-named 'example stories', as well as their Lukan context, is taken into account.

The reasons for the neglect of the exemplary dimension of the three parables are not far to seek. In the case of The Prodigal Son, the identification of the father with God has been pervasive in interpretation. This has inevitably caused the parable to be read primarily as a disclosure about God, rather than an exemplary tale.[101] It is a curiosity of the history we have recounted that while modern scholarship since Jülicher has decisively repudiated the traditional identification of the good Samaritan with Christ, Jülicher himself (like many since) was happy to see the father in this parable as an image or similitude for God. As I will make clear at the end of the chapter, I am not suggesting that God was *absent* from these stories - just as, indeed, Jesus the maker of the figures is in a sense figured within them. However, they seem to have had an immediate practical purpose which depended primarily on the social, not theological resonances of their characters.

The Prodigal Son holds forth the tableau of a moderately well off landowner yielding up his dignity and honour, and writing off his financial losses, out of overwhelming yearning for his wayward son. The father's behaviour is contrasted with that of his elder son, who is presented as clinging to dignity and property in preference to restored relationship. As in The Good Samaritan, both positive and negative examples are presented. There is the additional exemplary dimension of the return of the prodigal: the wounded man of 10:30-37 is merely a victim, but this younger son takes action. It is a rounded picture of a new order of things, of a world where reconciliation does sometimes triumph, carrying with it an invitation to *be* the father in his forgiveness, as well as to *be* the younger son in his return, rather than the elder in his resentment.

With The Shrewd Steward, as we have seen, commentators have sought various ways of evading the exemplary implications of Luke 16:8f., which say that the 'unrighteous' steward was commendable. Even if v. 9 were to be excluded from consideration as possibly (though obscurely) a later attempt to distil the parable's lesson - a hypothesis which seems no more than another evasion of difficulty - we should still be left with the master's commendation of the steward in v.8a and the narrator's comment in v.8b that 'the sons of this world are more shrewd in dealing with their own generation than the sons of light'. In fact, when the use of the word 'unrighteous' is understood as explained above,[102] and the just and merciful quality of the steward's reduction of the debts is seen, there is no problem about seeing him as an example. Moreover, there is no difficulty with seeing the master's praise as exemplary too. Like the father in the previous parable, he models an attitude of forgiveness, the reverse of the grasping spirit that exacts the pound of flesh. We should note too the similarity between the ending of this parable and those of the classic 'example-stories' in 10:30-37 and 18:9-14. The story, in the person of the master,[103] affirms the goodness of what the steward has done, just as the narrator draws attention to the exemplary qualities of the Samaritan and the customs officer.

Of the three parables, The Judge and the Widow seems at first glance to be a story more obviously metaphorical, in that the Lukan context presents it as a lesson in persistent prayer to God. To turn it into an example-story that stays on the level of human interchanges would appear to entail a more violent rupturing from its context than with the other two; though even if the judge is taken as somehow figurative of God, the widow is still an example. However, we should recognize that even if the story is read as a lesson in prayer, it depends for its rhetorical power on the fact that this is the kind of event that could happen, indeed was actually happening. A story of human justice being dispensed (even belatedly) would be no encouragement to disciples to continue praying if Jesus knew that there was no hope of widows and the like getting a fair deal, and therefore no point in their continuing to hammer on the courtroom door. I suggest that in fact on the lips of Jesus this was another story giving an instance of a new order of things in this world, an encouragement through its exemplary figures to be a part of that new order, boldly seeking justice and delivering it. (Nor does this mean that God is necessarily to be relegated entirely to the level of the early church's understanding of the parable; I shall return to this below.)

These six parables, then, can be seen as portraying a new world order by means of specific instances of its manifestation, through characters who fulfil an exemplary function. The fact that it is a *new* world order is seen in the *surprise* element they contain. We may usefully recall at this point Kjärgaard's distinction between present, imperfect and perfect metaphors,[104] and transfer it to synecdoche.[105] This can give us a language to describe their shock-value more precisely.

We could say that the Samaritan is a *present synecdoche*. The association of such a person with the behaviour depicted in the story would surely have been intended as striking: 'a *Samaritan* can typify *compassion*!' The case of the Pharisee in Luke 18:9-14 appears at first somewhat different: for Jesus would have known that the depiction of his *behaviour* would have raised no eyebrows, but his *end* in the story is shocking. But since it is the end of the story which opens our eyes to the man's true nature, he also emerges as a present synecdoche, a startling proposal that *even a Pharisee* could be at risk of not being vindicated by God. The portrayal of the customs officer's attitude in prayer, indeed of his very presence in the Temple,[106] would probably have been intended as more surprising than the portrayal of the Pharisee; his happy end and the Pharisee's unhappy one are perhaps equally striking.

Other situations seem to be *imperfect synecdoches*. The father and his two sons, the master and the steward, the widow and the judge, are probably not designed to shock to the extent that the Samaritan or customs officer are.[107] One can more easily imagine that others before and besides Jesus might have used a judge or an estate manager as types of a canny self-regard which nevertheless serves others, than one can imagine others using a Samaritan as a type of compassion. The rich man and Lazarus at the start

of their story are perhaps already *perfect synecdoches*: Jesus would have
known that the kinds of contrasting people they stand for (and the contrast
itself) would have been painfully familiar.[108] Nevertheless they are not
'dead' as figures, mere clichés; their vividness sees to that; and their
respective ends would no doubt have been designed to surprise many.[109] I
am not sure of the status of the priest and Levite on this continuum. I
suspect that Jesus would not have intended to shock his audience so much
by their *inaction* as by the Samaritan's *action*.[110]

I am not trying to argue here for the precise 'tense-status', on
Kjärgaard's scale, of any of these figures. We should not, for instance, fall
into the offensively stereotypical 'idealism' which severs Jesus from his
background to the extent of suggesting that no Jew before him had so much
as thought of a compassionate Samaritan or a complacent Pharisee. My aim
is simply to show that sensitivity to the nuances of tropical language can
give us a clearer insight into Jesus' possible intention in drawing such
characters and the particular kind of surprising realism he was using.

The surprise element in the parables (along with the development which
takes place in some characters) means that the characters are not
stereotypes, nor need they turn into them. As (mainly) *present* or *imperfect*
synecdoches they do not *need* to pass eventually into the 'perfection' of
literal usage implied by 'stereotype'. The Samaritan of 10:30-37 and the
Pharisee of 18:9-14 have *through history* become stereotypical figures, but
it is not required by the parables that they should do so. Whether or not
Kjärgaard is right to say that *metaphor* has self-abolition as its inevitable
goal,[111] I do not think we can say this of synecdochic suggestivity, such as
is involved in the parables. There is no inner necessity of language by
which the proposal of a 'part' ('consider a compassionate Samaritan, a
complacent, unjustified Pharisee') must turn into a statement of a 'whole'
('all Samaritans are compassionate, all Pharisees are complacent and
unjustified'). The parables can and do remain *suggestive*: 'imagine a world
where Samaritans can be compassionate, and Pharisees can be complacent
and unjustified!' To state this is simply to cast another light on the widely
accepted view that we shall miss the power of the parables if we do not
delve beneath their familiarity and try to reconstruct the original dynamics
of their telling.[112]

The design of the parables as synecdoches will be more fully grasped if
we recognize that it is not simply in the characters considered individually,
but in their *relationships*, that the suggestive, provocative reflection of the
world, with its exemplary implications, takes place. Righteousness in
Judaism was bound up with relationship.[113] The parables offer vignettes of
relationships made and restored: the Samaritan stopping to help the
wounded man, the son returning to the father and the father running out to
meet him, the steward making friends with the debtors and the master being

reconciled to the steward. They offer also vignettes of stark division and alienation: the priest and Levite passing by on the other side, the older brother out in the field, the rich man and Lazarus both before death and after,[114] the widow and her adversary, the Pharisee standing apart from the customs officer. These pictures of human closeness and distance are focused in Luke's telling of the parables by the use of words meaning 'far off'. The rich man beheld Abraham 'from afar' (μακρόθεν, 16:23); the customs officer stood 'at a distance' (μακρόθεν, 18:13), presumably from the Pharisee, and perhaps also from the inner court of the temple where sacrifice was being offered.[115] A contrast appears between an enforced and tormenting distance and a self-imposed but ultimately salutary one. Further, the father sees his returning son while he is still 'a long way off' (μακράν, 15:20). This image complements the other two: in the sight of the father distance is overcome. In story, Jesus proclaims that such restoration of relationship is taking place in the world; righteousness according to Torah is happening.

We may also gain insight into the working of the parables as synecdoches through noting certain *differences* between them. First, there is a distinction in *the presentation of exemplary characters*. In three parables (The Prodigal Son, The Shrewd Steward and The Judge and the Widow) two characters are seen as exemplary: prodigal and father, steward and master, widow and judge. This gives a special power to the new world-picture and the moral challenge offered by the stories, for one character's action is validated by another. The prodigal's decision to return is vindicated by the father's decision to have him back; the steward's decision to reduce the debts is vindicated by the master's praise. Both parables are thus propositions of the reality of a new social order, and exhortations to be part of it by the adoption of its key attitudes of forgiveness of others' debts (first of all in a literal sense: and note that in The Shrewd Steward, both steward *and* master exemplify a spirit of forgiveness) and the readiness to seek an escape-route from the impasse caused by personal folly and societal exigencies. The widow's cry for justice is vindicated by the judge's granting of it, and this parable too is thus a proposition of such an order, and an exhortation to be part of it by *both* doing justly *and* hopefully seeking justice.

In two other parables, however, only one character appears to be exemplary (the Samaritan, and the customs officer) while in The Rich Man and Lazarus only a negative example is shown. These differences and comparisons are instructive. In The Good Samaritan, the question has been raised of the role of the victim in the story. Funk has argued that Jewish hearers would have identified with this victim, and that the challenge of the story is therefore that they should accept the gospel as this victim accepted

help, even from a hated outsider.[116] However, a half-dead man who
probably had no idea what was happening to him or who was helping him
cannot strictly be seen as an *example*. In his utter inactivity and
helplessness the victim in this story is analogous to Lazarus, who is seen
purely as a poor man in need of justice and compassion, not as an example
of piety or trust.[117] So 10:30-37 and 16:19-31 are related to each other, and
contrasted to the three parables just dealt with, in respect of their emphasis
on the call to show compassion regardless of any prior trust, worthiness, or
even capability of response on the part of the recipient (how was the
Samaritan to know if he would be successful in his ministrations and one
day receive the victim's gratitude?) It is interesting, though, that the
validation of one character's action by another, which we noted in the other
three parables, is present obliquely, or in reverse, in these latter three also.
Jesus the narrator draws from the lawyer's mouth the declaration that the
Samaritan was obedient as a neighbour, and himself declares that the
customs officer went home justified. In a reversal of this, Abraham declares
that there is no crossing the gulf for the rich man who, it is implied, had
neglected the law and the prophets as his brothers were continuing to do.

Secondly, we may note a distinction among these parables in the
characters' *motivation*. The prodigal, the master, the steward, the judge, the
widow, even the customs officer, have an earthy self-regard in their actions.
This leads them nonetheless to do the right thing, and the instinctive human
desire for life and security is therefore central to the rhetoric of their stories,
as we shall see further shortly.[118] (Similarly, Lazarus is motivated by
desperate hunger; but he is poignantly beyond the point of taking any
action.) These characters are set apart on the one hand from a group who
appear to be motivated purely by nobler ends, and on the other hand from a
group who are also self-regarding, but whose self-regard leads them in the
wrong direction.

In the first group, the Samaritan and the prodigal's father appear to be
motivated by disinterested compassion, but we ought to reflect that this may
simply be the impression given by the brevity of the stories. The word for
their compassion is a feeling-word,[119] and we ought not to idealize these
figures. If the other characters appear in the stories as fallible mixed-up
humans, Jesus would presumably not have intended the Samaritan and the
father to appear as idealized persons. The point is that the stories present
their *actions* as being of key importance, whatever may have been their
motivations. In the second group, the priest and Levite, the older brother,
the rich man and the Pharisee are all concerned for their own interests but in
a wrong (and in the case of the rich man, finally disastrous) manner. Again
this forces us to look away from *motivation* to *action*. A check is placed
upon the incentive of self-interest which the parables set before their

hearers in their appeal for right living. It is what you *do,* not your motivation, which ultimately counts.[120]

We may now return to our summary statement with more precision: *Jesus intended to focus the world in realistic but surprising stories of characters and their relationships, which he intended as exemplary.* At this point we are ready to move to a consideration of the second stage of the synecdochic operation, in which the hearer makes a 'whole' out of the 'part' with which the story has presented her (the right hand side of the diagram on p. 194 above).

Part to Whole: story into world

If indeed these stories, their characters and relationships, were synecdoches as used by Jesus, they carried with them a claim to stand for the way the world is, as part for the whole. The receiver of the tale senses that she is meant *somehow* to generalize from it: but to what extent? How does one draw out the lines from part to whole? This is where the insight of the hearer comes into play. The thought process can be imagined: if a *Samaritan* can obey the law, who else might be able to? If a *Pharisee* is not justified, who else might be in danger? Would customs officers be included in the class suggested by 'a Samaritan', for instance - the different categories of outcast being lumped together in common thinking? Would priests be included in the class suggested by 'a rich man', or vice versa?[121] For example, leading priests were (in the context of their society) rich,[122] but the question of whether, in the common mind, 'priesthood' and 'wealth' were inevitably associated, must remain more uncertain.[123] Here the issue raised in Chapter 2 concerning the mutual suggestiveness of stories *within a text* is transposed into the issue of the mutual suggestiveness of class designations *within society.* We can be sure that the stories of Jesus upset many an easy stereotype: the most obvious case is that the wealthy appear both as heroes and as villains.[124]

Crossan overstates the case, however, when he writes that in the parables Jesus announced God as the one who 'shatters world, this one and any other before or after it'.[125] So does Scott, writing about the social 'map' being 'abandoned'.[126] (This kind of interpretation, linked to a view of the parables as metaphors, echoes the standpoint of Friedrich Nietzsche, who recognized in connection with metaphor 'that probably every linkage was open to destruction by the perspectives of a planned incongruity':[127] metaphor is able to do all kinds of strange things with our picture of the world, but that does not mean that Jesus, or anyone else, *in fact* destroyed every linkage, by metaphor or any other trope). For instance, the grounds on which the people in Luke 18:9-14 are accepted and rejected are quite clear, via the indirect method of character *portrayal* rather than the direct one of character *description*. The world is not shattered; the hearer is not totally disoriented, but invited to stretch conventional categories and imagine new possibilities. Scott sees that the parable is not merely overturning one set of stereotypes by the proposal of another. But the right conclusion from this is not that the world is completely subverted; simply that hearers were to be surprised by the choice of examples and invited to perceive a new order of things. I dissent here also from Ricoeur's statement that the parables 'dislocate . . . our project of making a whole of our lives - a project which St Paul identifies with the act of "self-glorification", or, in short, "salvation by works" '.[128] I am proposing precisely that these parables invited hearers to make a whole of their lives, but a *newly conceived* whole.

To envisage the way that the synecdoche is 'completed' as the receiver turns the part into a whole is closely allied to the important enterprise of envisaging where the receiver's sympathies would have lain, explored by Scott. In both cases a sense of historical reality must force us to imagine a range of different responses. But I suggest that to conceive this process of response by the receiver in terms of *troping* captures more profoundly the power of the parables than to stay with the question of sympathy. The real impact of the story comes when a hearer or reader says not just, 'I sympathise with that man', or 'my sympathies have been disoriented', but 'I *am* the man' or 'I *must be* the man' or 'I *want to be* the man'. In saying that, he is showing that he has reconverted part into the whole, that he has grasped the impact of the story on the real world in its concrete particulars - above all on that which is most real to him, his very self.[129] And as we have seen, the distinction between parables proper and example stories ultimately does not hold.[130] The father and younger son, the master and steward, the widow and even the judge, are in their way examples just as much as the Samaritan and the customs officer; the hearer might find any one of them a direct exemplary challenge. So, also, might the hearer be convicted through seeing herself mirrored in an over-cautious Levite, a self-indulgent man of wealth or a Pharisee who trumpets his righteousness.

Thus the stories *always* had a wide range of application beyond the original context in which they were spoken. Jesus' immediate situation must surely have been at the forefront of his mind. But the fact that the synecdochic process *must be completed by the receiver* - even the first time a parable is told! - means that there are no 'proper' limits on the application of the story. To put the point as sharply as possible, if the story was *intended* to be synecdochic, *suggestive and not prescriptive*, we cannot argue for one 'proper' or 'historical' application on the grounds that we believe it to be the 'intentional' one.[131] Even when we have tried to answer the question, 'what scope of application would the hearers have seen in the parable?' in as historically accurate a manner as we can, we have not succeeded in outlining the 'proper' limits of application, because the parable itself, like the *mashal*, is a form of speech designed to be useful in different contexts. Here is the kernel of truth in Jülicher's statement that the meaning of a parable 'falls into our lap', his sense that it applies so readily to later times. Here also, though, is the falsehood of his belief that no interpretation is necessary. It only falls into our lap because, like the first hearers, we carry out the second stage of the synecdochic process *ourselves* and turn the part into the whole again.

What, though, of the original reception of these parables? We may consider the matter under the headings of the two facets of Jesus' contemporary context set out at the start of the chapter, social setting and thought-world. First, their applicability to the hearers of Jesus in their social setting can be readily imagined. Drury is right to say that the parables of Luke 15 and 16, the climax in Luke of Jesus' prophetic summons of Israel to national repentance, 'are not aimed only or chiefly at private persons',[132] and that summons (like those of the OT prophets) seems to have been issued with the social realities of Palestine clearly in view. It is artificial to set aside some parables, such as The Good Samaritan and The Prodigal Son, as being less rooted in these realities than others where the theme of wealth is more obvious on the surface.[133] We may illustrate the range of possible responses with reference to the three structures of society outlined by Borg: peasantry, purity and patriarchy.[134]

In a peasant culture, the hard facts of wealth and poverty are never far from view. The man on the Jericho road was *robbed,* and the Samaritan gave him not only first aid but also financial provision. The father in 15:11-32 had an inheritance to divide and a fatted calf to kill. He is closely connected to the rich master in 16:1,[135] though the link is often overlooked through seeing the father as an image of God. But we should probably not see this father and master as part of the very wealthy élite, but rather as lower-stratum members, 'free farmers with relative prosperity'.[136] Both are implicitly praised for not being ultimately tight-fisted. This would have been encouragement and challenge for the peasants and landowners of Galilee or Judea.[137] They would have heard the advocacy of a revolutionary attitude to money, for the purpose of transcending family and social divisions, not perpetuating them. Those who had already set out on this revolutionary path would have been encouraged as they saw themselves in the Samaritan, the father, the wise steward, even the (at first reluctant) judge; those who were resisting would have been warned (if they were prepared to listen) as they saw themselves in the rich man of 16:19-31, or the self-deceptive Pharisee of 18:9-14 whose prayer masked his complicity in the oppressive system of temple taxation.[138] Those without hope, at the bottom of the pile, could take heart not only from Lazarus's destiny beyond death, but from this-worldly scenes: the Samaritan's nurturing of the victim into life, the prodigal's return from the jaws of starvation to a welcome beyond all expectation, the steward's dogged and successful determination to avoid utter penury,[139] the widow's vigorous tactics and victory. These stories would surely not have been received as mere fancies about a world of which the poor could only dream. People would have recognized their own world in them, and been invited to discern the signs of a just and gracious revolution which was already beginning, which was being given added momentum through the stories themselves,[140] and which called for their participation.

I have already noted the theme of purity and defilement in the parables.[141] Suffice it to indicate at this point how Jesus' hearers might have converted the specific cases depicted there into a newly defined world. The reluctance of the priest and Levite to risk tainting themselves by contact with the possibly-dead man is exposed so starkly in its tawdriness against the foil of the Samaritan's compassion that the whole purity system is radically relativized: a piercing stab for those to whom it was so valuable, an open door to relief for those to whom it was so oppressive. Echoes of the Scriptures reinforce the point: when the Samaritan shows mercy, not sacrifice (Hos. 6:6), with 'oil and wine' - elements of the daily temple offerings (Lev. 23:13) - he becomes an example (in ironic contrast to the temple functionaries) of true obedience to the law.[142] This parable also proposes to dismantle in startling fashion the social walls built by the purity system, for not only is the hated Samaritan held up as an example, but it is shown that in this case the victim's only hope lay in himself being defiled through his contact with his rescuer. A world is held forth in which purity considerations *must* not stand in the way of life itself.[143] The Prodigal Son and The Pharisee and the Customs Officer extend hope to those hopelessly 'corrupted' through contact with Gentiles[144] or through failure to pay tithes,[145] and warn those who think they are pure; the elder son may join the party, but at the cost of becoming tainted by association with his younger brother. The Shrewd Steward suggests a view of things in which 'dirty money' may nevertheless be handled righteously; The Widow and the Judge, one in which scruples about impure magistrates and shameless women are irrelevant beside justice sought and dispensed. The Rich Man and Lazarus shows the eternal and horrific cost of maintaining ritual-social separation (Lazarus was not only poor, but unclean[146]).

What of patriarchy? It is a question of great interest and importance whether the dominance of males among the characters of these six parables (the widow of 18:1-8 is the only female mentioned[147]) would have made the stories seem inapplicable, or *less* applicable, to women. Pointedly, could a woman say 'I am the woman' in response to one of the parable's male characters with the same force with which a man might say 'I am the man'?

This opens up a huge area in anthropology, sociology, psychology, gender studies and no doubt other disciplines besides, at which we can do little more than glance here.[148]

The fact that women are largely absent from the explicit level of the stories can be seen simply as another function of the stories' realism: they do indeed reflect a patriarchal society.[149] So would a woman have felt the *impact* of the stories to the same extent as a man? The aesthetic judgement involved in deciding the question carries more weight coming from a woman than from a man. Jane Schaberg writes that although The Good Samaritan is a story about the world of men, and the male experience 'is presented here as universal human experience', most women can easily imagine themselves as *women* in the ditch.[150] But how would women have related to characters like the Samaritan and the father? Were they so accustomed to living under the shadow of men, with their identity bound up with that of male kin, that they instinctively wrote themselves into the stories as assumed and unmentioned adjuncts of the men?[151] Alternatively, might the male characters turn out to be failed, or ideologically compromised synecdoches,[152] aiming at including women but in fact setting a gender-boundary round the whole to which they point as parts? Is any startling element of 'presentness' (on Kjärgaard's tense-scale), by which *men* might be brought up short (e.g. the *Samaritan* as an example of compassion) dulled for women, because eclipsed by the overriding, clichéd 'perfection' of a man standing for the whole race (the Samaritan as *just another male model*)? For the stories to have been truly striking to women, would they have needed a substantial female cast with whom they might immediately identify - an innkeeper's wife, a prodigal's mother, worshippers in the Court of the Women?

Scott's reading of The Prodigal Son points to maternal resonances in the portrayal of the father.[153] The hint is that Jesus is overthrowing gender-stereotypes. But I suggest that females among the ancient audiences would more probably have accepted the story, consciously or unconsciously, and no doubt with a variety of equanimity-levels, as confirming the *status quo* in gender relationships. The father's expressions of affection may indeed have been striking for the culture, but that may only (though significantly) have invited an enlarged view of what a man could be like,[154] and not addressed the issue of women's suppression. Returning to the tropes, one might put the question like this: would a man in the story who showed (traditionally) feminine qualities have been heard as a synecdoche for 'all fathers' or 'all men' (who *could* be like this!), or for 'all mothers *and* fathers', 'all men *and* women'? My hunch is that women would have received the impression that there *was* an application to them, but that like much else in life it was being mediated to them through a man.[155] Scott's

The Voice of Jesus

reading tends towards an artificial lifting of Jesus above the patriarchalism of his day.[156] Moreover, it tends to imply that women (like the poor who may have heard The Rich Man and Lazarus) would have simply received encouragement and affirmation from the parable. It overlooks that there might also have been wayward women who *were* challenged by seeing themselves in the younger son, or unforgiving women who were challenged by seeing themselves in the elder or in the father - even if that 'seeing' was more indirect than would have been the case with male hearers.

So much for the response of Jesus' hearers in terms of their *social setting*. With respect to their *thought-world*, we have seen how the parables present a vision of true righteousness according to the law, the righteousness of restored relationship. The premise of 'covenantal nomism' that obedience to the law is the way to life within God's gracious covenant is not challenged. Where the individuality of Jesus' figures, the 'presentness' of the synecdoches, becomes clear is in the surprising examples he uses. Jesus opens up the possibility of exemplary or non-exemplary behaviour to a wider range of people than conventionally expected, and thus helps a great variety of hearers to find themselves in the parables and in the new order of things they represent. By showing a Samaritan, a steward or judge generally classed as 'unrighteous', a profligate son or a customs officer as acting in commendable ways, Jesus was indeed dismantling the boundaries which artificially restricted the scope of the covenant people. Careful listeners would have recognized that he was challenging a hardened attitude which pretended to obedience where there was none, and which excluded from the possibility of obedience those outside a rigidly defined pure race.

To summarize, I have outlined in this section the way that I believe the six parables would have worked as synecdoches on the lips of Jesus and in the minds of his hearers. Jesus gave his hearers a provocatively expressed segment of life which implicitly claimed to represent a wider reality, and carried with it an invitation to refashion a whole out of the part they had been given. Within that segment the key elements are the human figures, and their relationships. Within the new whole that the hearers make they see themselves, their acquaintances, their social situation, with new eyes. Their world is given a new and encouraging shape. It is a world in which Samaritans can keep the law, wayward sons are welcomed home, even worldly-wise stewards and judges can do the right thing, the poor are exalted (even if sometimes they have to wait till death) and customs officers are justified. And given the proposal that the world *is* like this, a moral challenge emerges, and the characters appear as examples.[157] Hearers can only become a part of this world by learning from the characters. They must imitate the Samaritan in his costly compassion, the prodigal in his return and the father in his lavish forgiveness, the steward in his just reduction of debts and the master in his commendation, the judge in his vindication of the widow and the widow in her tenacious trust that she will be vindicated,[158] the customs officer in his humility. They must heed the warning represented by the priest and Levite, the elder brother, the wealthy magnate of Luke 16:19-31, and the Pharisee. The parables do not dictate precise identifications.[159] People would have made many links, impossible for us now to delineate precisely, between the stories with their various characters and plots, and the world that they knew and were being invited to see with new insight.[160]

For such synecdoches to 'work' requires a willingness on the part of the hearer to reorient her perspective, to make the connections.[161] Even given that willingness, the adjustment of viewpoint, we may suppose, may take some time; indeed, it may continue for a lifetime. That is the peculiar power of a parable, and these parables in particular. But it is not essentially a *mystifying* process or one that requires arcane knowledge; nor is it an intellectual exercise like the cracking of a code. They may ultimately, to borrow Andrew Parker's title, become 'painfully clear', but their full implications can seldom have been instantly obvious. The insight they yield grows brighter the more one looks at the world through their lenses.[162]

4. The Voice of Jesus in Synchronic Perspective: Gracious Wisdom

In arguing that these parables not only reflect the world, in ways surprising to Jesus' hearers, but also carry an exemplary force, I imply that they offer a new incentive for right living.[163] I am therefore taking the side of those who place the parables in the category of persuasive rhetoric, implied argument,[164] against those who prefer to see them as poetry or mere provocation.[165] I also distinguish my position on these parables from Herzog's view that some, at least, of Jesus' stories (including Lk. 16:19-31) were intended simply to 'unmask' or 'codify' oppression, to facilitate conversation about it among the peasants, without necessarily involving any persuasive thrust.[166] What then is the heartbeat of their persuasive power? The answer, I suggest, is their appeal to *wisdom*.

An exemplary figure alone may remain distant, unattractive, unattainable. The fact that the exemplary figures of the parables are not like this is due partly to the stories' rootedness in the life of Jesus' culture, but also to the fact that righteousness is made *attractive*. Each of the six parables exhibits, either within itself or in its surrounding context, a concern that one or more people (in the story, or among Jesus' hearers) take action that in their own best interests, as well as being right.[167] This is the classic OT appeal to wisdom: fearing the LORD and turning away from evil is the way of healing and refreshment, the sensible and successful way to live.[168] Furthermore, the synecdochic form of the parables reflects that of many a proverb, in which a specific instance of wisdom is pointedly used to make a statement about wisdom more generally.[169]

In responding to a lawyer's question about the identity of his neighbour, Jesus is helping him with the answer to his prior question: what must he do to inherit the life of the age to come (Lk. 10:25)? The Samaritan is given as his example. In the context of that first question, it is clear that the passage invokes *self-interest* (the incentive of inheriting eternal life is mooted by the lawyer, and implicitly accepted as a valid incentive by Jesus), although the action implicitly enjoined involves *self-giving*.

The Prodigal Son also involves an encouragement to obedience with the incentive of self-interest. The father's welcome is no mere cool, detached act of righteousness. It involves an overwhelming emotion and joy; it is good, it is wonderful to behave like this. Moreover, the throwing of the feast is a necessary gesture for the restoration of the entire family's honour in the eyes of the community.[170] By contrast, the story concludes with the scene of the father's invitation to the elder son to come and join the party. It will be *good* for him to do so; out in the field he is the picture of miserable self-exclusion. Yet it is clear that to come in would also, conversely, be an act of obedient love. The dynamics of righteousness and self-interest are seen in the younger son's story too. 'His stomach induced his return';[171] truly he came to 'life' in a sense no less than physical (15:24,32). Scott is right to remark that in 'coming to himself' the lad 'begins to overcome his self-destructive pattern of behaviour',[172] but is wrong to drive a wedge between this self-interested motivation and the idea of repentance. Whether or not 'to come to oneself' represents an Aramaic idiom meaning 'to repent',[173] the thrust of the younger son's story is surely that *he did the right thing, even while he was seeking his own safety.*[174]

The shrewd steward is plainly concerned for his own future, yet he is not condemned for his actions, but rather praised (16:8). Indeed, what he did is seen as exemplary (vv. 8b,9).[175] The master's praise in v. 8a, commendable for its compassionate and conciliatory spirit, is in *his* interests too, for in sanctioning the reduction of debts that has taken place behind his back he will win popularity[176] and a new sense of indebtedness in his clients.[177]

The Rich Man and Lazarus is a tale of fearful warning. The rich man ends up in torment not because he was too self-interested, but because he was in one sense not self-interested enough. The way to bliss would have been the sharing of his bounty. It might be objected that lack of generosity is nowhere mentioned as the reason for his punishment.[178] But the stark picture of contrast drawn in 16:19f. is enough in itself. Jesus does not describe the rich man's personal wickedness, but he does portray the ugly reality of injustice.[179] The rich man wants his brothers to be warned, and urged to repent (16:27f., 30); but the great incentive he wishes to be held out to them is not high-minded remorse for sin against God, or compassion for the poor, but this sole overwhelming motive, uttered from the agonies of Hades: 'lest they also come into this place of torment' (16:28). It is an incentive not to be lost on Jesus' audience.

In 18:1-8, the judge only wants to stop being nagged;[180] yet this motivation impels him to a just decision.[181] The widow sought redress for her own cause, and obtained it; simultaneously she sought *justice*. The same dynamic is reflected in the 'application': the elect will gain that for which they cry - vindication for themselves (vv. 7f.), but the crying is not mere selfishness: it is precisely the faith for which the son of man will be looking (v. 8).

Our final parable, 18:9-14, holds out two possible ends: being justified, or not justified. The incentive is offered. Do not be over-confident in your acts of piety; humbly confess your sin; and it will be well with you.

The appeal of the six parables can be seen more lucidly still if we highlight some of the words and concepts linking them together in the description of motivations or goals. The lawyer desired life ($\zeta\omega\dot{\eta}\nu$, 10:25), and it was *life* to which The Prodigal Son had returned ($\dot{\alpha}\nu\dot{\epsilon}\zeta\eta\sigma\epsilon\nu$, 15:23; $\ddot{\epsilon}\zeta\eta\sigma\epsilon\nu$, 15:32). It was the life *of the age to come* ($\alpha\dot{\iota}\dot{\omega}\nu\iota o\nu$, 10:25) which the lawyer sought, and it is the tabernacles *of the age to come* ($\alpha\dot{\iota}\omega\nu\dot{\iota} o\upsilon\varsigma$, 16:9) which disciples are exhorted to seek. The prodigal and Lazarus both 'yearned to be filled' ($\dot{\epsilon}\pi\epsilon\theta\dot{\upsilon}\mu\epsilon\iota$ / $\dot{\epsilon}\pi\iota\theta\upsilon\mu\hat{\omega}\nu$ $\chi o\rho\tau\alpha\sigma\theta\hat{\eta}\nu\alpha\iota$, 15:16 / 16:21.).[182] The widow cries *vindicate* me ($\dot{\epsilon}\kappa\underline{\delta\iota\kappa}\eta\sigma o\nu$ $\mu\epsilon$, 18:3), and it is *vindication* ($\dot{\epsilon}\kappa\underline{\delta\iota\kappa}\eta\sigma\iota\nu$, 18:7) which God will bring about for his elect; the customs officer is *justified* ($\delta\epsilon\underline{\delta\iota\kappa}\alpha\iota\omega\mu\dot{\epsilon}\nu o\varsigma$, 18:14). These parables, then, have a powerful appeal to the individual's strongest instincts for security, peace and joy, in the standard Jewish framework of expectation (the hope for life, the age to come, vindication), as they encourage right living to be expressed in specific, practical ways: love, forgiveness, use of money, the bestowal of and search for justice, penitent humility.

Already in OT times, of course, it was recognized that 'obey, and you will be blessed' was a one-sided view of the way life worked. Passages such as Psalm 73 and the book of Job put very sharply the question of why the righteous suffer. In this connection it is interesting to note that the righteousness seen in these parables, righteousness which is so beneficial to the practitioner as well as others, is not a righteousness without cost. There is the courage of crossing boundaries and risking life, not to mention the expense of time and money (the Samaritan). There is the father's throwing of patriarchal dignity to the winds in acceding to his son's initial request, then in running to greet him as he returned, as well as his reaching-out to the community in laying on the feast, risking refusal[183] - a refusal actually encountered in the final scene of the parable in the person of his older son.[184] There is the humbled recognition of a disgraced underling's worth (the master), the abandonment of safe detachment to respond to the cry of the poor (the judge). There is the risk of daring to return home (the son), of seeking a secure future through a righteous act in an unrighteous environment (the steward), of pleading openly and against custom for justice (the widow), of entering the hallowed Temple courts a defiled figure and pleading for mercy (the customs officer). Moreover, the characters who are negative examples should not be hastily condemned, for the cost of acting *otherwise* than they did should be recognized. Like the Samaritan, the priest and Levite might well have wondered about the continued vicinity of the robbers;[185] the contemplation of the disruption of their secure and familiar purity-system may also have contributed to their decision to hasten on their way. What would it have cost the elder brother to come in from the field? Or the rich man to reach out and share his wealth with Lazarus? Or the Pharisee to come to the Temple in the same attitude as the customs officer?

The way of wisdom adumbrated by these parables, therefore, is no easy option, notwithstanding its attractiveness. The stories reflect the pain of different social situations, and the hope they suggest is no glib optimism that bypasses the pain.[186] It is a hope inextricably bound up with a righteousness that goes beyond mere correctness - in fact, with love.

Where, finally, is God in these parables? It might appear from their realistic quality as synecdoches that he was absent altogether. To overlook their realism and jump straight to a metaphorical identification of the father, the master or the judge with God would be to miss their depth of focus in Jesus' intention and to fail to imagine the natural responses of the original hearers. Nor does the structure of these parables allow for Jülicher's view that Jesus was somehow *arguing* from realistic human situations to the divine order.[187] Nevertheless, it would be erroneous to suppose that this concentration of the parables on this world means that a divine dimension in the original telling and hearing is to be overlooked. I suggest two ways in which we may conceive of this.

First, we may see the figures of the father, the master and the judge as *metalepses*. This figure, we recall, is the trope of a trope.[188] This gives it, even more than other tropes, the air of evocation, of suggestion as opposed to statement. Undoubtedly 'father', 'master' and 'judge' were established ways of speaking about God.[189] But the *realism* of the stories of Jesus puts a certain distance between these characters and that connotation. Although the plots of the parables can be explored as reflecting, in a highly suggestive way, God's dealings with Israel and the world,[190] it is best to think of them as arousing such thoughts as evocative echoes, rather than making metaphorical statements to be decoded point by point. What they evoke, by way of linguistic signs that have often pointed to God, is the sense of the interlinking of human and divine worlds, the ancient and instinctive description of God in human language and the belief (perhaps almost equally ancient) that human affairs somehow mirror divine order.

And this leads to the second way of conceiving the parables' divine dimension. Quite apart from any particular metaleptic figures, the justice and wisdom exemplified in the narratives are indeed the justice and wisdom of God. Rather than overemphasising the 'secularity' of the parables,[191] we should recall that they come from a milieu where the assumption that the world was God's, and worked according to his laws, was taken for granted.

When in the OT human beings did what was just and wise, God himself was regarded as present and at work in *his* justice and wisdom.[192] Clearly the mercy and compassion seen so clearly in the Samaritan and the father are reflections of the חסד (loving kindness) of the God of Israel.[193] But God may be seen not only in the father, but also in the wisdom of the returning son, who had previously alienated himself (as the Fathers correctly saw) not only from his human father but also from God.[194] Similarly, we may see God not in *either* the judging then praising master *or* the accused and canny steward, but in *both* (and perhaps in the debtors too);[195] not in *either* the judge eventually administering justice *or* the widow hopefully seeking it, but in *both*.[196] This is the converse of asserting that we see *human* folly and frailty in many of these characters too. Not apparently in the Samaritan: he has no prehistory in the story, he undergoes no conversion. But the father in The Prodigal Son is initially guilty of folly according to the advice of Sirach 33:19-23 not to divide an inheritance before one's death.[197] The steward, his master, and the judge, are caught up in systems of human corruption, though they ultimately find themselves executing God's wisdom and justice. These two stories make sense in the ultimate context of God as judge, vindicating those whom human justice and judges have failed.[198] In The Rich Man and Lazarus, rather than being seen in a character, God is the unseen presence in the story, hiding perhaps behind Abraham, but ultimately set apart from all, because here, for these characters, the time when his justice can be worked out *in this world* is over. In Luke 18:9-14 God is present in the unlikely guise of the breast-beating customs officer, who has found the way of wisdom, yet also stands apart from and above both characters in the 'divine passive' of 'this man went down to his house justified rather than the other' (18:14).

Therefore, though God is scarcely mentioned in the parables, they would have been heard as chiming with his character and order. In them righteousness is practised in sometimes surprising ways by sometimes surprising people; but it remains *his* righteousness. Furthermore, God may have been seen here not only in the attractiveness of the way of wisdom, but also in its cost. A thoughtful listener, over time, may have wondered not only at the joy of God in the restoration of relationship and the establishment of righteousness, but also at the pain which made it possible.[199]

We come back to the heart of our subject: the parables as figures are signs of an individual voice. Though, on the suggested interpretation of this chapter, these stories did not employ everyday language merely as a code for God's order or the activity of Jesus, that order and activity are woven into their fabric; and those who listened to and pondered them would have heard and seen not only glimpses of a new order of things into which they were being invited to enter, but a speaker who embodied and inspired the righteousness and wisdom of which he spoke.

NOTES

1. Borg, *Jesus*, 116.
2. E.P. Sanders, *Jesus*, 339.
3. Cf. Drury, *Parables*, 2.
4. See the catalogue of 'portraits' in Borg, *Jesus*, 19-34.
5. Ibid., 101-112.
6. This picture, of course, can be considerably nuanced in various ways. For a full recent overview see Stegemann and Stegemann, *Jesus Movement*. On the social background of the parables see especially Herzog, *Parables*; Shillington (ed.), *Jesus*.
7. In addition to the works mentioned in note 6, I am indebted particularly to Jeremias, *Parables*; Bailey, *Poet* and *Peasant Eyes*; Scott, *Hear*; Hedrick, *Parables*.
8. Cf. Shillington, preface to Shillington (ed.), *Parables*, xv.
9. E.P. Sanders, *Jesus*, 335ff.
10. Cf., on Paul against this background, N.T. Wright, *The Messiah and the People of God: A Study in Pauline Theology with Particular Reference to the Argument of the Epistle to the Romans* (D.Phil. Thesis, University of Oxford, 1980), 85-92; James D. G. Dunn and Alan M. Suggate, *The Justice of God: A Fresh Look at the Old Doctrine of Justification by Faith* (Carlisle: Paternoster, 1993), 27f.
11. Cf. Dunn and Suggate, *Justice*, 14ff.
12. Some contemporary parable interpreters still adopt an older view of Pharisaic legalism as the background against which the parables contrast: see Maurice Baumann, 'Les Paraboles Evangéliques et Le Langage de Changement', *Etudes Theologiques Et Religieuses* 68, no. 2 (1993), 185-202; Harnisch, 'Beiträge', 366; Walther Bindemann, 'Ungerechte als Vorbilder? Gottesreich und Gottesrecht in den Gleichnissen vom "ungerechten Verwalter" und "ungerechten Richter",' *Theologische Literaturzeitung* 11 (1995), 956-70.
13. Notably Jülicher, *Gleichnisreden*; Dodd, *Parables*; Jeremias, *Parables*; recently Herzog, *Parables*; Hedrick, *Parables*. Cf. also Oliver Chase Quick, *The Realism of Christ's Parables* (London: SCM Press, 1931).

14. 'Naturfarbe': Jülicher, *Gleichnisreden* I, 66.

15. Dodd, *Parables*, 21.

16. Cf. e.g. Linnemann, *Parables*, 10, on elements of 'stage-production' (though on 29 she makes the balancing point that the reflective reader sometimes sees as obstacles to 'realism' elements which do not so strike the *listener* caught up in the flow of the story); Ricoeur, 'Biblical Hermeneutics', 99f., 114-18, and Borsch, *Parables*, on 'extravagance' in the stories; Harnisch, 'Ironie', 426f.; Drury, *Parables*; Heininger, *Metaphorik*, 15f. An often-noted element of 'extravagance' in the parables is the size of monetary sums: see Mt. 18:24; 25:15. A good summary of accepted wisdom on both realism and strangeness in the parables is found in Donahue, *Gospel*, 13-17.

17. Wolfgang Harnisch, 'Language of the Possible: The Parables of Jesus in the Conflict between Rhetoric and Poetry', *Studia Theologica* 46, no. 1 (1992), 41-54. Cf. my discussion of Scott in Chapter 5 above.

18. Another apparently non-realistic element is that of mythology, especially the *post-mortem* scene in 16:23-31. But here features of the after-life (Abraham's bosom as the place of bliss, punishment as fire) seem simply to have been taken over from conventional beliefs; the story can still be seen as realistic in that it reflects the *thought-world* of Jesus and his hearers.

19. Hedrick, *Parables*, 40-43, discussing Erich Auerbach, *Mimesis: The Representation of Reality in Western Literature* [1946] (Princeton, NJ: Princeton University Press, 1953).

20. Hedrick, *Parables*, 42.

21. Drury deals well with the human realism of the parables peculiar to Luke. '[T]he L parables are more human than anything in Matthew in the sense that the characters are far more subtly drawn. Instead of Matthew's black and white contrasts we get the *chiaroscuro* of ambivalent human beings: doing good out of self-interest, calculating profit and loss, finding the way home out of despair, doing no more than their duty or acknowledging their shortcomings . . . Luke's people have understandable motives, they are something more interesting than sons of light or sons of darkness, and they have the limited but critical freedom of decision which we all exercise': *Parables*, 115f.

22. Funk writes that parable 'as a paradigm of reality unfolds the "logic" of the everyday world' such that it is . . . 'brought to the surface, and . . . shattered', that it ' "cracks" the shroud of everydayness lying over mundane reality in order to grant a radically new vision of mundane reality': *Language*, 194f. Borg writes that the longer narrative parables 'invite the hearer to enter and experience the world of the story and then to see something in the light of that story': *Jesus*, 148. Both aphorisms and parables 'address the imagination, which is both that "place" within us where our images live (images of reality, of ourselves, and of life itself) as well as our capacity to imagine things being different . . . They invite a different way of seeing': ibid. Cf. the slightly different emphasis of Baumann on the parables as 'language of change': the parabolic drama 'n'est pas un faire-valoir . . . d'une autre réalité ou d'une vérité générale; elle est la structure qui va permettre an déstinataire d'entrer dans la communication': 'Paraboles', 201.

23. Ricoeur ('Biblical Hermeneutics', 75-106) explores the connection between the categories narrative and *metaphor,* but not that between narrative and *figure.*

24. 'They mean what they say - and maybe more': Hedrick, *Parables*, 35. Hedrick's literary precursors seem to be nineteenth-century realists; they believed that 'the specific, being its own end, should represent nothing beyond itself': Hayes, 'Symbol', 275.
25. Funk, *Language*, 196f. Funk is discussing The Great Banquet (Lk. 14:16-24) but clearly has his eye on the parables in general. Cf. Jüngel: 'Die Gleichnisse führen uns . . . nicht nur in das Zentrum der Verkündigung Jesu, sondern verweisen zugleich auf die Person des Verkündigers, auf das Geheimnis Jesu selbst' (*Paulus*, 87).
26. Funk, *Language*, 216.
27. '[L]'effet surprenant des paraboles ne peut que susciter la volonté de profiler l'identité de leur auteur': Baumann, 'Paraboles', 201.
28. As Hedrick, for instance, does in the case of Lk. 18:14: *Parables*, 209ff.
29. Cf. p. 53 above.
30. Heininger sees in the parables Luke's use of a kind of rhetorical *Figurenlehre*, the classical device of *sermocinatio* or character portrayal: *Metaphorik*, 79. I wish to try to avoid the weakness in Bailey's *Poet*, noted by Crossan, of focusing on the characters to the detriment of attention to the action: John Dominic Crossan, 'Review of K.E. Bailey, *Poet and Peasant*', *Journal of Biblical Literature* 96.4 (1977), 606-8.
31. Cf. Hedrick, *Parables*, 5. The judgement concerning historicality or fictionality is one of the central *aesthetic* decisions that must be made about any narrative text. A recent writer who believes that the stories Jesus told must have been true is Parker: he writes that that there is a 'natural weight of authenticity' behind actual examples from life, and that '[t]he idea of asking people to model their behaviour on fictitious characters would have struck the evangelists (to say nothing of Jesus) as absurd in the same way that we would find someone who modelled himself or herself on Batman': *Painfully Clear*, 41. Parker does not make any distinction between realism and historicality. It may be sufficient for their suggestive power that the stories be credibly located in the world of Jesus' hearers, not that actual incidents be recounted; though the latter is often quite a plausible possibility with the parables.
32. It is thus fallacious to exclude metaphor from the operation of the parables, as Baumann does, on the grounds that they do not speak of another reality concurrent with the everyday world: 'Paraboles', 187. Metaphor can be seen as inherent in any kind of fictive statement.
33. Scholars have recently stressed the polyvalence of the notion 'kingdom of God' - it would have meant different things to different speakers and hearers. See Perrin, *Jesus*, 20-29, an important influence on Scott: *Hear*, 56-61. But even to postulate a polyvalent 'kingdom of God' as the referent of parables *where it is not mentioned* is too restrictive. The parables can be connected to the idea of the kingdom without in some way 'meaning' the kingdom.
34. See e.g. M. D. Goulder, 'Characteristics of the Parables in the Several Gospels', *Journal of Theological Studies* 19 (1968), 51-69, here 51; Jeremias, *Theology*, 29f.
35. E.g. Green, *Luke*, 641, on Lk.18:4b-6: 'The phrase "unjust judge" is also reminiscent of the analogous phrase in 16:8, a reminder that Jesus' followers may learn profound lessons about discipleship (oriented toward the coming age) from worldly examples (oriented to this age).'

36. E.g. Scott, *Hear*, 47ff.
37. Etchells, *Reading*, passim.
38. See Jülicher, *Gleichnisreden* I, 56 note 1. Jülicher rejected the presence of symbol in the parables outright, for he took their *comparative* nature to exclude metonymy. The example he gives is of an ox as a symbol of strength. There is no question of a *comparison* between 'ox' and 'strength': 'strength appears manifestly in the ox, is one of its attributes' ('die Kraft erscheint im Stier sinnenfällig, ist eines seiner Attribute'). The nature of symbols is a complex matter upon which I cannot enter here; in Coleridge, symbol is associated with synecdoche: A. Fletcher, *Allegory*, 17.
39. For some qualification of this point see p. 210 on metaleptic echoes.
40. Caird discusses metonymy and personification in *Language*, 136f. Note especially his insistence that 'to personify is to treat as a person that which is not a person' (137), which means that it would be very misleading to call the figures in the parables 'personifications'. Cf. A. Fletcher, *Allegory*, 86.
41. Etchells, *Reading*. Indeed, Etchells reverses the usual definitions of these two tropes, saying that the traditional understanding of metonymy is 'the use of the part to represent the whole' and that in synecdoche ' "the attribute" stands for the thing it describes' (8). However, her *example* of metonymy ('sceptre' for 'authority') better fits the normal definition of metonymy as attribute or adjunct standing for the object itself (which suggests that her definition may reflect an inadvertent error). In general terms, Etchells follows the bipolar division of trope between metonymy as coherent combination (which can be seen as encompassing both synecdoche and 'metonymy' more narrowly defined) and metaphor as selective substitution, found in Jakobson, 'Aphasia', and David Lodge, *The Modes of Modern Writing* (Leeds: Arnold, 1977).
42. Bloom, *Poetics*, 410.
43. See D.R. Fletcher, 'Riddle'; Porter, 'Unjust Steward'. I find Porter's reading most unconvincing. It will not do simply to use irony as a 'key' in such a way as to say that Jesus actually meant the opposite of whatever we find surprising or uncomfortable (in this case, 16:8f). Porter says that in v. 8b 'the sons of this age are unfavourably contrasted with the sons destined for God's kingdom of light' (147f.), but in fact the sons of light are told to *learn* from the sons of this age. Porter's attempts to blacken the steward through parallels with the prodigal of 15:11-32 and the rich man of 16:19-31 are also misguided. The prodigal and steward have surely not been 'consistently bad in their judgment' (150 - though the rich man was); at the centre of the stories are thoroughly wise moves. On v. 9 Porter writes: 'The irony is found on two planes: dishonest wealth cannot be expected to produce earthly friendship, as the prodigal realizes, but more than that, this means of ingratiation cannot be used to buy eternal friends, as the rich man so painfully learns' (149). I would respond that (a) there is no indication in 16:1-8 that the steward's plan to make friends is not going to be successful, (b) it is a strained parallel to see the prodigal as trying to use 'dishonest wealth' to gain 'earthly friendship', and (c) since the rich man has made no effort to use his money to buy eternal friends, he cannot have learned that it is a useless tactic. Porter writes that steward, prodigal and rich man 'all hope to use the things of this world to secure a place for themselves in the kingdom' (151), but none of them seem in the slightest degree concerned about anything

that could be called 'the kingdom', and are certainly not trying to use their worldly goods to get there.

44. See above, p. 46, and p. 59 note 62.

45. Harnisch, 'Ironie', 430-36.

46. Cf. Herzog, *Parables*.

47. Cf. note 16 above.

48. Hedrick, *Parables*, 115f. The possibility of genuine righteousness, on the part of Gentiles as well as Jews, had long been envisaged in Jewish tradition: see for instance the stories of Naaman the Syrian (2 Kgs. 7) and the Ninevites' repentance at the preaching of Jonah (Jon. 3).

49. Especially Hedrick, *Parables*; cf. Baumann, who writes of 'grotesquerie' in connection with Lk. 16:1-8 ('Paraboles', 198).

50. Cf. Sellew, 'Monologue'. Sellew is sceptical that these characters can be taken as exemplary (242); Heininger, however, comments on the power of the monologues to motivate the hearer to follow the character's example: *Metaphorik*, 224f.

51. Cf. Bultmann, *History*, 189; Donahue, *Gospel*, 24.

52. Auerbach, *Mimesis*, 11f.

53. Cf. Powell, *Criticism*, 52f., on 'showing' and 'telling', a distinction drawn from Wayne Booth, *The Rhetoric of Fiction*, 2nd ed. (Chicago: University of Chicago Press, 1983), 3-20.

54. Cf. 10:33.

55. Cf. Johnson, *Function*, 142.

56. Cf. the vivid exposition of Herzog, *Parables*, 117-20, 128.

57. Borg, *Jesus*, 104.

58. Richard J. Bauckham comes to the same conclusion: 'What is wrong with the situation in this world . . . is the stark inequality in the living conditions of the two men': 'The Rich Man and Lazarus: The Parable and the Parallels', *New Testament Studies* 37 (1991), 225-46, here 232.

59. Cf. Calvin on Lk. 12:16-21: 'Christ does not . . . condemn [the rich fool] precisely for acting as a careful householder in setting aside a store for the future, but for wanting to swallow up and devour many barnfuls in his greedy cupidity like a bottomless pit, and therefore for not understanding the true use of plentiful possessions' (*Harmony* II, 93). Is this really fair to the man as the parable presents him to us? There is an extremism about some kinds of biblical exegesis which projects convictions about the absolute importance of Scriptural subject-matter into colourful, hyperbolic readings of individual texts. But the diminishing of realism diminishes also the moral challenge. This is precisely the weakness (but also, maybe, the desired effect) of Hedrick's reading of The Good Samaritan.

60. Cf. the conventional title of the parable, 'The Unjust Steward'.

61. Ellis, *Luke*, 199: ἀδικία is 'a Greek equivalent of *'awel*, a term used technically at Qumran for the principle and reality of evil in the end time'.

62. Daube, 'Nuances', 2335. Daube draws the parallel with the 'unrighteous judge' in 18:6, where 'the pejorative characterizes his habitual unscrupulousness and not his overdue, proper act.'

63. See above, p. 46.

64. Cf. Daube, 'Nuances'. See Herzog, *Parables*, 243f., for a longer exposition of the social background: the steward 'is constantly susceptible to back-stabbing and calumny from disgruntled debtors or tenants. Of course, they would not complain to the master that the steward is too severe; the master would take that as testimony to the steward's thoroughness . . . Instead, they would accuse the steward . . . The steward is always caught in a cross fire between the master's greed and excessive demands, on the one hand, and the tenants' or debtors' endless complaints, on the other . . . The master will always keep a suspicious eye on his steward, and the tenants will continuously envy the steward's power over them.'

65. A similar ambiguity of characterization marks the beginning of The Prodigal Son. Linnemann (*Parables*, 74f. and 150f.) cites commentators on both sides of the argument as to whether the son's request for his share of the inheritance, and subsequent departure, were reprehensible; she herself thinks that they were not. Scott, however, believes that in 15:12 the father 'has put his family honor in jeopardy' and the son 'has in effect pronounced his father dead': *Hear*, 111.

66. *Contra* Bailey, who thinks that the master was merciful in only dismissing the steward and not punishing him further: *Poet*, 97. At this point the highly culture-sensitive Bailey seems driven by the desire to draw a parallel between the master and God.

67. Herzog is precisely to the point when he writes that much commentary 'assumes a simple moral code and judges the steward by it. Most of the sins ascribed to him are those that belong properly to a capitalist framework': *Parables*, 245.

68. Ibid.

69. Ibid., 258; Bindemann, 'Ungerechte', 963ff.; Daube, 'Nuances', 2335. Herzog believes that the debtors would have been merchants who transported and sold the master's goods, and the initial accusations may have come either from them or the peasants who worked the land and paid large rents to the master: *Parables*, 249ff.

70. Herzog, *Parables*, 247-52.

71. Herzog thinks that the security for which the steward is aiming through his remission of the debts is not mere hospitality, but another job (*Parables*, 256); cf. Bailey, *Poet*, 98.

72. Herzog, *Parables*, 257.

73. Cf. his comment about the parable's ending deconstructing its own metaphorical structure: *Hear*, 265.

74. As suggested by Via, *Parables*, 155-62.

75. Hedrick, *Parables*, 194-97.

76. See Lk. 1:50; 12:5 (cf. Mt. 10:28, the only occurrence of the phrase in the gospels outside Luke); 23:40; Acts 10:2; 13:16,26; 22:35.

77. As Hedrick does in *Parables*, 197.

78. See e.g. Mic. 6:8.

79. Cf. Bultmann, *History*, 189.

80. Cf. p. 209.

81. Hedrick, *Parables*, 197.

82. Ibid., 203.

83. See above, p. 169. Cf. Hedrick, *Parables*, 209ff.

84. E.g. Jeremias, *Parables*, 143.

85. b. Ber. 28b, t. Ber. 7.18: cited in Scott, *Hear*, 95.

86. With Scott, I take πρὸς ἐαυτόν with σταθείς: *Hear*, 94.

87. Linnemann argues against the significance of characterization in the story (*Parables*, 144ff.), for fear of 'transferring the parable on to the level of moralizing' (145). Her point, foreshadowing Scott's emphasis on there being 'no lesson' (*Hear*, 97) is that the paradox of God *declaring the wicked just* is removed if 'justify' is simply taken to mean 'forgive'. I am not arguing that 'justify' here means no more than 'forgive', but I am arguing that there is no paradox, that the Pauline tenet of God justifying the ungodly (Rom. 4:5) is not the issue here. God declares as righteous the one who behaves with true righteousness (and implicitly, declares as unrighteous the one who does not). The characters are, precisely, examples, and their respective ends are an incentive.

88. In Luke's context, as I have shown (above, pp. 46ff.), the claims of the Pharisee are shown up as flawed. On the lips of Jesus the question of the validity of those claims would have remained hanging in the balance as the story unfolded, and the conclusion would have decided it but not explained it: just *why* was the Pharisee not justified? But we should not exaggerate this understatedness; those who may have heard polemic from Jesus' lips against the Pharisees (e.g. that reflected in Lk. 11:42) would not be in any doubt about Jesus' view of why such a man was not justified.

89. Hedrick, *Parables*, 209ff.

90. Contra Linnemann who writes of 'the lack of correspondence between application and parable', simply stating, without arguing, that 'it is not true either that the tax-collector has "humbled himself" or that the Pharisee has "exalted himself" ': *Parables*, 18.

91. Herzog recognizes that if the parables are called 'realistic', that implies the necessity of reconstructing 'the social whole of which the fleeting glimpses are a part': *Parables*, 48. He means the necessity *for the modern historian*. I am exploring here the synecdochic process as it would have taken place specifically *between Jesus and his hearers*.

92. A. Fletcher, *Allegory*, 85, citing Quintilian, *Institutes*, VIII.6.21.

93. *Allegory*, 86. Interestingly Fletcher sees this process as 'the essence of interpretive *allegory*' (my emphasis).

94. See above, p. 7.

95. 'In the relationship of *connection* [implied by synecdoche], two objects "form an ensemble, a physical or metaphysical whole, the existence or idea of one being included in the existence or idea of the other" ': Ricoeur, *Rule*, 56, citing Fontanier, *Figures*, 87. The 'existence or idea' of the occurrences depicted in these parables includes and implies the 'existence or idea' of such occurrences in the wider sphere of the world itself.

96. Dodd, *Parables*, 16.

97. Harnisch, 'Possible'.

98. Ernst Fuchs argued that some parables (e.g. Lk. 16:1-8) appealed to a typical situation, while a few (e.g. Lk. 15:11-32) presented a situation not typical but already shaped by the hope of the gospel ('alles in ihnen wird durch eine nicht selbstverständliche, dafür aber um so entschiedenere Hoffnung getragen'): 'Die Analogie', in Wolfgang Harnisch (ed.), *Die neutestamentliche Gleichnisforschung im*

Horizont von Hermeneutik und Literaturwissenschaft (Darmstadt: Wissenschaftliche Buchgesellschaft, 1982), 1-19, here 14. My proposal is that both these parables, and the other four in my group, present situations which though unusual were not unknown or unimaginable, situations that Jesus wants to *proclaim* typical, situations such as he sees already occurring in the time of his ministry.

99. The parables called by Jülicher 'example-stories' are described as 'extended synecdoches' by Boucher: *Mysterious Parable*, 22. Blomberg thinks that Sider's use of the word 'example' to designate these stories fits them better than 'extended synecdoche', 'since exemplary characters in the parables . . . are not really parts of some larger whole but examples of a particular category of people': *Interpreting*, 46, citing John W. Sider, 'The Meaning of *Parabolē* in the Usage of the Synoptic Evangelists', *Biblica* 62 (1981), 453-70, here 460. The appropriateness of any such term is measured by its explanatory and illuminating power; it is not a question of establishing whether the language 'is' this or that rhetorical manoeuvre in an absolute, deliberate or determinative sense. As Gerhardsson rightly says, '[O]ur texts are meshalim, not designed on the basis of clear-cut rules from ancient rhetoric or modern literary criticism': 'Frames', 333.

100. The fourth so-called 'example-story' in the traditional classification is The Rich Fool (Lk. 12:16-21).

101. A recent writer who treats the father as an example, linking him both to the Samaritan and to Jesus' command in Lk. 6:35 to be 'kind to those who are ungrateful and evil', is Thielman (*Law*, 148). Oakman calls The Prodigal Son an 'example story' (*Jesus*, 171).

102. Pp. 190f.

103. The ambiguity of ὁ κύριος in Lk. 16:8 ('the master', or 'the Lord', i.e. Jesus) may well have been felt, therefore, by Luke and his readers as well as us: the master praises the steward, but his praise fulfils the same function as Jesus' implicit praise of the Samaritan and the customs officer.

104. See above, p. 9.

105. I would gladly acknowledge that there is not much difference between my proposal here and what Harnisch expounds as the 'metaphorical tension between the real and the possible' which 'drives towards a new insight which overcomes the tension': 'Possible', 51f. But I am suggesting that what the parables stress, more than a tension between real and possible worlds, is the already existing presence of a new reality, as if Jesus is saying: 'look around and you will see that people are already behaving like this'.

106. Cf. Herzog, *Parables*, 192.

107. On the elements of the expected and unexpected in The Prodigal Son, cf. Iver K. Madsen, *Die Parabeln der Evangelien und die heutige Psychologie* (Copenhagen / Leipzig: Levin & Munksgaard / Ejnar Munksgaard / Verlag von Johann Ambrosius Barth, 1936), 166-74. Madsen points to the behaviour of the father towards his younger son as the unusual dimension (170f.); cf. Bailey, *Poet*, 181, on the father's running out to greet his son in 15:20. Quick, however, believed that '[t]he father does no more than many human fathers have done for their children': *Realism*, 32. The public and vocal appearance of the widow in 18:3 would have been startling: Donahue, *Gospel*, 182.

Donahue thinks the persistent widow and the running father would have been as originally shocking as the compassionate Samaritan: ibid., 183.

108. See the remarks about the stark realities of oppression in a peasant society in Borg, *Jesus*, 101-5.

109. Cf. Herzog, *Parables*, 129, and the surprise of the disciples at Jesus' words about the rich, reported in Mk. 10:24,26. Herzog also points (130) to the shock-value of the figure of Abraham, whose legendary wealth and hospitality 'had been reinterpreted [by Jesus' contemporaries] into a form of condescending almsgiving whose purpose only reinforced the distinction between clean (the wealthy) and unclean (the poor)'.

110. Linnemann, *Parables*, 139, cites Hermann Strack and Paul Billerbeck, *Kommentar zum Neuen Testament aus Talmud und Midrasch*, 5 vols., vol. IV, 2nd ed. (München: C.H. Beck'sche Verlagsbuchhandlung, 1956), 182, and *T. Levi* 17, to the effect that Jesus' hearers would not have had a high opinion of the moral status of priests and Levites.

111. Kjärgaard, *Metaphor*, 218.

112. Cf. Walter Wink's description of how modern readers, knowing the story so well and identifying with the customs officer as the positive character, miss the force of Lk. 18:9-14: *The Bible in Human Transformation: Toward a New Paradigm for Biblical Study* (Philadelphia: Fortress Press, 1973), 42f., cited in Thiselton, *Two Horizons*, 14. Cf. also James D. G. Dunn, 'Historical Text as Historical Text', in J. Davies, G. Harvey, and W. Watson (eds.), *Words Remembered, Texts Renewed* (Sheffield: JSOT Press, 1995), 340-59.

113. Cf. P. J. Achtemeier, 'Righteousness in the New Testament', in George Arthur Buttrick (ed.), *The Interpreter's Dictionary of the Bible* (Nashville: Abingdon Press, 1962), 91-9. I am especially grateful to Professor James Dunn for drawing my attention to this point and this reference. It is more satisfactory to understand these parable-relationships in the light of this Jewish context than in terms of modern sociological categories concerning boundaries, as Scott does.

114. Herzog notes that though the rich man calls Abraham 'father', he has not seen that Lazarus is therefore his brother: *Parables,* 123f. The connection with 15:11-32 is reinforced, for there too the elder son is reluctant to accept his brother as a brother. Note also that the word τέκνον ('dear child') is used both by the father to his elder son (15:31) and by Abraham to the rich man (16:25), emphasising the connection between the two scenes.

115. Bailey, *Peasant Eyes*, 152f.

116. Funk, *Language*, 212f.

117. Cf. Herzog, *Parables*, 128; contra the ancient interpretation which saw him as someone 'rich in faith' or 'rich toward God', e.g. Ambrosius, *Expositio*, VIII, 135-141.

118. Therefore though Bultmann was right to say that the motivation of the parable-characters is not *expounded,* he is wrong to say that motivation is 'irrelevant to the point': *History*, 190.

119. See above, p. 189.

120. This represents the kernel of truth in Bultmamn's point about motivation's irrelevance (see note 118 above).

121. Sider approaches the same issue through discussion of *example* as one type of *analogy*. 'Example invites *synthesis*: ostensibly it cites a specimen to represent a species; in effect it puts us on the lookout for other specimens which we may not previously have thought of connecting': 'Meaning', 466.

122. Bailey, *Peasant Eyes*, 43.

123. On the comparative poverty of many priests see Stegemann and Stegemann, *Jesus Movement*, 123.

124. The Samaritan and the father are clearly people of means; the 'rich man' of 16:1-8 appears callous to begin with, but compassionate at the end; but the rich man of 16:19-31 is condemned, implicitly for his obscene and utter neglect of Lazarus. But 'the wealthy' should not in any case be lumped together as a single group: see p. 203 below on the issue of comparative wealth. It may be that the rich man of 16:19-31 is the only true member of the élite in our parables (Stegemann and Stegemann, however, place even him in the prosperous end of the *lower* stratum: ibid., 133).

125. Crossan, *In Parables*, 27.

126. Scott, *Hear*, 97.

127. K. Burke, *Permanence*, 91.

128. 'Biblical Hermeneutics', 125. The continuing persuasiveness of this view is seen in Donahue's approving citation: *Gospel*, 16.

129. One might even say that the recognition 'I am the man' implies yet a *third* stage of synecdoche. Having turned the part into the whole again, the receiver has focused the 'whole world' on which the story made its impact on to one 'part' once more, by saying 'I am the man' - as if no one else was implicated. This is the case with the phenomenon sometimes reported in which a member of a congregation attests that it seemed as if the preacher (or God) were speaking for her benefit alone.

130. Heininger comments that on the level of Lukan redaction 'ist die Grenze zwischen Parabel und Beispielerzählung praktisch aufgehoben': *Metaphorik*, 223. I argue that the distinction was never there in the first place.

131. 'There is no literary reason to suppose that Jesus did not have both particular and general intentions': Sider, 'Meaning', 465.

132. Drury, 'Luke', 421. I am making a statement about *Jesus* here which Drury would avoid.

133. Johnson (*Function*, 159ff.) notes the importance of possessions as symbolic of relationships in The Prodigal Son, but when he writes 'No one would claim that the story is "about" possessions' (160) he is perpetuating the spiritualization of the parables noticeable since Jülicher. This parable, like the others, is clearly 'about' much more than possessions, but the transformations which the stories dramatize are played out on a severely practical level; the father's willingness to write off his losses is striking.

134. Borg, *Jesus*, 101-12.

135. Cf. the use of διασκορπίζω in both 15:13 (of the prodigal) and 16:1 (of the steward): see above, p. 57 note 37.

136. Stegemann and Stegemann, *Jesus Movement*, 133.

137. Borg cites the view of Richard Horsley that Jesus' sayings about forgiveness of debts were 'intended as guidelines for ordinary people in local communities': *Jesus*, 29. Herzog greatly illuminates The Pharisee and the Customs Officer by showing the place

of both characters within oppressive social systems: the Pharisee was implicated in the system of temple tithes which kept the poor in poverty, while the customs officer was a minor official in the complex system of Roman toll-collection: *Parables*, 180ff. In the parable the one who penitently recognizes his complicity is justified, the one who fails to see it is not.

138. Herzog, *Parables*, 178-84; Farris, 'Tale'.

139. 'To lose his stewardship and join the work force of day laborers is to drop out of the class of retainers into the class of the expendables . . . His dismissal from the stewardship is a death sentence that has nothing to do with his refusal to accept honest work': Herzog, *Parables*, 242.

140. Cf. ibid., 193: '[Jesus'] pedagogy of the oppressed was designed . . . so that the peasants could name oppression as a prelude to renaming their world': Herzog, *Parables*, 193. But there is no reason to restrict Jesus' 'pedagogy' to the oppressed; there is every sign that he was addressing oppressors as well - even if it was the smaller-scale agents of oppression among whom he mainly moved.

141. See above, p. 51.

142. Donahue, *Gospel*, 132.

143. On the purity issue in this parable see also Dunn, 'Historical Text'.

144. Herzog thinks that customs officers may in fact have been despised more for their arbitrariness and dishonesty than for their contact with Gentiles: *Parables*, 187.

145. Cf. ibid., 184f.

146. Ibid., 118.

147. She would have been alone at the place of judgement, too: 'In the midst of all the male voices heard at the gate, a domain where men alone are in control, one woman's voice continually cries out for justice': ibid., 229.

148. In Judaism there has been considerable debate about the applicability or otherwise of sections of the Torah to women. In the sense of being exempt from certain precepts, women in early Judaism were regarded as being in the same category as minors and slaves (Rabbi Professor Louis Jacobs, seminar in the University of Lancaster, 1991).

149. It is interesting to note, however, the balancing of men and women as protagonists *in Luke's narrative*, reflecting perhaps the newly important status of women in the early church: Donahue, *Gospel*, 135. Especially see the juxtapositions of The Good Samaritan with the story of Mary and Martha (10:38-42), The Prodigal Son with The Lost Coin (15:8-10), and The Judge and the Widow with The Pharisee and the Customs Officer.

150. Jane Schaberg, 'Luke', in Carol A. Newsom and Sharon H. Ringe (eds.), *The Women's Bible Commentary* (London: SPCK, 1992), 275-92, here 282. 'Most of the poor in every age are women and the children who are dependent on them': ibid., 277.

151. Such would be the implication of Richard L. Rohrbaugh's comment that the prodigal's departure would have meant far more in terms of loss of security to his mother than to his father: 'A Dysfunctional Family and Its Neighbours (Luke 15:11b-32): The Parable of the Prodigal Son', in Shillington (ed.), *Jesus*, 141-64, here 151f., citing J.G. Peristiany (ed.), *Mediterranean Family Structures* (Cambridge: CUP, 1976), 14.

152. We may compare our current convention of 'inclusive' language. I have chosen to avoid pedantry by alternating freely between 'he' and 'she' rather than say 'he or she'

every time that is what I mean. 'He' on its own would have been read as a failed or compromised synecdoche, an adoption of an older 'sexist' linguistic convention. My synecdochic use of 'she' in the same discourse in which I make synecdochic use of 'he' renders the latter acceptable.

153. Entitled '1 Remember Mama': Scott, *Hear*, 89-125. He mentions the father's affectionate kissing (κατεφίλησεν, 15:20) and his address to his elder son, 'dear child' (τέκνον, 15: 31) (117). Schaberg calls this the parable of 'the missing mother': 'Luke', 282.

154. Sandra Schneiders sees the parable as 'a radical challenge to patriarchy'; in it '[t]he divine father . . . is revealed as the one who refuses to own us, demand our submission or punish our rebellion': *Women and the Word* (New York: Paulist Press, 1986), 47, cited in Donahue, *Gospel*, 161. Crossan adds a different twist: 'is the *ambiguity* of the three males [in Lk. 15:11-32] more congenial to the female reading than the *reversal* of the three males in the Good Samaritan story?': 'Review of B.B. Scott, *Hear then the Parable: A Commentary on the Parables of Jesus*', *Catholic Biblical Quarterly* 54, no. 2 (1992), 377-8.

155. Donahue has suggested an interesting possible reversal of sexual stereotypes in 18:1-14. The threat to the widow is described by the judge with a metaphor from the boxing ring (ὑπωπιάζη, v.5) while the customs officer beats his breast, a gesture said to be more characteristic of women in ancient Near Eastern culture than of men (v. 13): *Gospel*, 190f.

156. More credible is Schaberg's opinion that the picture of Jesus as a revolutionary feminist pitted against Jewish tradition is not supported by research: 'Luke', 279.

157. Donahue again catches this well, writing of The Prodigal Son: the parable 'creates an imaginative world which makes *metanoia* possible': *Gospel*, 158.

158. 'The hearers are confronted with a new vision of reality . . . where victims will claim their rights and seek justice - often in an unsettling manner': ibid., 184. Donahue's use of the word 'rights' is anachronistic and perhaps misleading, but again he is close to the mark.

159. It is in this leaving of the hearer free to make the appropriate response that we can best see why 'allegory' is an inappropriate way to describe these parables' tropical operation, notwithstanding the multiplicity of points at which story reflects world. 'Allegory does not accept doubt; its enigmas show instead an obsessive battling with doubt': A. Fletcher, *Allegory*, 323.

160. 'The realism of Luke's parables shows that the consequences of conversion touch all areas of human life - family life, the use and danger of wealth, legal disputes and banquets, journeys and the management of estates . . . "every man and every woman" realize that salvation is at stake precisely in the everyday unfolding of human life': Donahue, *Gospel*, 208. On the 'revolutionary' implications of Jesus' words, see Oakman, *Jesus*, 141-69.

161. Cf. Harnisch, 'Possible', 51f.: the insight offered by the parables 'is realized only when the addressee allows him- or herself to become involved in the movement of the scenic development, and to be carried beyond the conceivable'.

162. This is close to Drury's view, citing the OT term *mashal*, that parable belongs 'at the same time both to secrecy and revelation, hiddenness and openness': *Parables*, 42.

163. Cf. the formulation of Donahue: the parables present 'a *vision of reality which becomes a presupposition to ethics*': *Gospel*, 17. Gerd Petzke uses the phrase 'narrative Ethik': *Das Sondergut des Evangeliums nach Lukas*, Zürcher Werkkommentare zur Bibel (Zürich: Theologischer Verlag, 1990), 217ff.

164. E.g. Madeleine Boucher and Corbin S. Carnell, 'Parable', in Jeffrey (ed.), *Dictionary*, 581ff.: the parables are 'heterotelic', with a purpose beyond themselves, not 'autotelic', designed like works of art to be appreciated for their own sake.

165. E.g. Harnisch, 'Possible', 47, adducing the poetic character of *fable* with which the genre parable is connected. Harnisch believes that Jesus was seeking to blow apart the old theological frameworks altogether, through a *reductio ad absurdum* of the opposition between sinners and righteous: 'Beiträge', 366, countering Eckhard Rau, *Reden in Vollmacht: Hintergrund, Form und Anliegen der Gleichnisse Jesu* (Göttingen: Vandenhoeck und Ruprecht, 1990). Cf. Baumann, 'Paraboles', 199: '[L]a parabole n'enseigne rien, elle crée une mise en mouvement de son auditeur vers des comportements et des compréhensions qui échappent à la pesanteur religieuse. En ce sens, elle n'a pas de message; elle est une procédure de langage dont la principale caractéristique est d'être éphémère.' Cf. too the anti-persuasive thrust of Hedrick, *Parables*, and Scott, *Hear*. For a wise warning against overdrawing the distinction between rhetoric and poetry see John W. Sider, 'Proportional Analogy in the Gospel Parables,' *New Testament Studies* 31 (1985), 1-23.

166. Herzog, *Parables*, 77, 129f.

167. Cf. Drury on the link between Lk. 15:11-32 and 16:1-8: both concern 'the same doctrine of repentance in the interests of self-preservation': *Tradition*, 78. Daube discusses 11:5-8, 16:1-8 and 18:1-6 as linked by the presence of 'behaviour externally meritorious, yet flowing from a contaminated source', and draws attention to the debate in Judaism about the motivation for actions: 'Nuances', 2329ff.

168. Cf. Prov. 3:7f. and passim.

169. On this see further below, pp. 230ff.

170. Rohrbaugh, 'Dysfunctional Family', 157f.

171. Scott, *Hear*, 116.

172. Ibid., 115f.

173. Jeremias, *Parables*, 130.

174. Contra Linnemann, who de-emphasises the fact that the son did what was *right* in returning, reading the story rather as a challenge to those who 'had put in question the unconditional nature of God's forgiveness by the demands which they attached to repentance': *Parables*, 152.

175. Drury catches the self-regarding mood that characterizes the steward, but does not give weight to the benefit that accrued to the debtors as a result of his action. He writes that the parable 'commends shrewdness and cunning, favourite qualities of the earthy or realistic wisdom tradition of the Old Testament as opposed to the apocalyptic. Moral principles take a back seat. The art of coping is supreme': *Parables*, 148.

176. Bailey, *Poet*, 101f.

177. Herzog, *Parables*, 257.

178. Scott believes that the rich man's condemnation 'without evidence of evident wrongdoing' would have provoked a Jewish audience: *Hear*, 155.

Parables and Persuasion 225

179. 'Wealth [in a peasant society] was not the result of being an ambitious hard-working individual striving to advance in the world, but the product of being part of an oppressive social class that extracted its wealth from peasants': Borg, *Jesus*, 104.

180. Or perhaps threatened, if we take ὑπωπιαζῇ με in v. 5 literally as 'gives me a black eye': e.g. Hedrick, *Parables*, 200.

181. I do not believe that Hedrick's emphasis on the meaning of ἐκδίκησον (v. 3) as *avenge* rather than simply *execute justice for* (ibid., 198f.) undermines the argument that the widow's cause was just. As he himself states, the normal procedure would have been for trial and judgement to precede punishment; so the story should not be taken to imply that in satisfying the widow's thirst for revenge (if we are to read ἐκδίκησον so strongly) the judge had not also done the *just* thing. As to the widow, it is entirely credible that she should be spoken of as crying out for vengeance without making a nice distinction between 'give me a fair hearing' and 'avenge me'. Hedrick remarks that had the widow wanted to be declared 'right' or 'just' in court she should have used δικαιοῦν (as Luke does at 10:29 and 16:15)': ibid. This betrays pedantry on Hedrick's part. Why *should* a poor widow, even (or especially?) in a deliberately crafted story, have used the 'right' Greek (or even Aramaic!) word? Hedrick wants to read the story as 'burlesque' (ibid., 203) and this involves making the widow's demeaning of herself, her upsetting 'the stereotype of vulnerability that led to her protected status in Israel and Judaism' (ibid., 201), more important than the basic fact of her cry for justice. If she wanted rather more than justice, she would be only human; but there is no suggestion that she wanted *less*.

182. Cf. Donahue, *Gospel*, 170.

183. Rohrbaugh, 'Dysfunctional Family', 158, comparing Lk. 14:16-24.

184. Ibid., 159f.

185. Scott, *Hear*, 195.

186. Harnisch feels that though the parables start with the everyday, suggesting 'a norm according to which one's fate corresponds to one's actions' (e.g. raising the expectation that the prodigal would have starved to death), this norm is overthrown by the strangeness of their outcomes: 'Possible', 49f. I suggest that in the outcome of the stories, surprising and hopeful though they are, we can still see the pattern of wisdom in which behaviour and fate are related, but it is a refined wisdom which takes account of, and involves, suffering and cost.

187. This is also the position of Quick, *Realism*, 34.

188. See above, p. 8.

189. See, e.g., Ps. 68:5; 89:26; 103:13; Is. 63:16; Mal. 1:6; Ps. 7:11; 96:13.

190. As proposed, in different ways, by Heininger, *Metaphorik*, 26-30, 161ff., 174, 204f.; N. T. Wright, *Jesus*, 125-31, 175. For a critique of Wright's treatment of parables in this book see Klyne R. Snodgrass, 'Reading and Overreading the Parables in *Jesus and the Victory of God*' in Carey C. Newman (ed.), *Jesus and the Restoration of Israel: A Critical Assessment of N.T. Wright's* Jesus and the Victory of God (Downers Grove, Ill. / Carlisle: IVP / Paternoster, 1999), 61-76. Kurt Erlemann has shown that the parables, if taken together, yield a 'picture of God' that is full of contradictions, on account of the varied metaphorical language used: *Das Bild Gottes in den synoptischen Gleichnissen* (Stuttgart: W. Kohlhammer, 1988). Harnisch comments that 'picture of

God' seems to be a concept that Erlemann projects on to the texts, not one which arises out of them: 'Beiträge', 352.
191. As in Wilder, *Rhetoric*, 82ff.
192. R.W.L. Moberly, 'Solomon and Job: Divine Wisdom in Human Life', in Stephen C. Barton (ed.), *Where Shall Wisdom be Found? Wisdom in the Bible, the Church and the Contemporary World* (Edinburgh: T. & T. Clark, 1999), 3-17, citing for instance Dt. 1:17: 'You shall not be partial in judgement . . . for the judgement is God's.'
193. Cf. the fine exposition of McDonald, 'Alien Grace', 49f.
194. Cf. Donahue on 15:13: 'By dissipating the property, the younger son severs the bonds with his father, with his people, and hence with God; he is no longer a son of his father and no longer a son of Abraham': *Gospel*, 154. Drury's account is therefore too neat: 'The father stands for God, the older son is orthodox unreconstructed Judaism, and the prodigal who has put himself beyond the orthodox Jewish pale by his fornicating and swineherding is typical of the sinners and Gentiles who were welcome to Luke's Church': *Parables*, 117. Such a reading is reductive, even in terms of Luke's setting: not only does it not sufficiently take account of how the parable could be heard differently by different groups or individuals, it misses the overall framework of divine order within which it is told by making the direct allegorical correspondences.
195. M. Ball sees in the welcoming friends of Lk. 16:4,9 'an alternative way of expressing the solidarity of God with the needy' found in Mt. 25:31-46: 'The Parables of the Unjust Steward and the Rich Man and Lazarus', *Expository Times* 106, no. 11 (1995), 329-30. The subject of δέξωνται in v.9 would then not be *either* the friends made by the steward, *or* an impersonal periphrasis for God, but *both:* but in both cases it is a welcome in *this* world which is to be sought.
196. A statement like this of Hans Weder is therefore too limited: 'Zur Identifikation angeboten wird nicht die leitende Figur, sondern die geleitete': 'Wirksame Wahrheit: Zur Metaphorischen Qualität der Gleichnisrede Jesu', in idem (ed.), *Einblicke ins Evangelium: Exegetische Beiträge zur neutestamentlichen Hermeneutik* (Göttingen: Vandenhoeck & Ruprecht, 1992), 151-66, here 163. Insofar as God is seen in the justice and wisdom of the different characters, so each of those characters becomes one to be identified with and imitated.
197. The background in Sirach is mentioned by Drury, *Parables*, 145, but without drawing this conclusion.
198. Drury notes the background to Lk. 18:1-8 in Sir. 35:13-18: *Parables*, 153. We might add Ps. 82, where God appears as judge of the judges. By evoking this tradition the parable is a reminder that God will vindicate the poor, even if human judges do not, but also a sign of hope that vindication is already happening through the action of his appointed judicial representatives.
199. Cf. Eduard Schweizer's highly suggestive exposition of The Prodigal Son in terms of the suffering of the father: *Jesus, das Gleichnis Gottes: was wissen wir wirklich vom Leben Jesu?* (Göttingen: Vandenhoeck & Ruprecht, 1995), 66-70. With reticence we may wonder how much this thought was in Jesus' own mind as he told this parable on the way to Jerusalem.

CHAPTER 7

Parables and Precursors: The Voice of Jesus and the Voices of Scripture

So many songs of triumph, read close, begin to appear rituals of separation.[1]

A man who has truly mastered the utterances of Jesus will also be able to apprehend His silence.[2]

1. The Diachronic Context of Jesus: Scripture

In the last chapter, our focus was on the intention and reception of Jesus in his contemporary context. It should now be clear that any discussion of his 'voice' which does not attend to what he intended and how he was received is bound to be inadequate. Nevertheless, such a discussion cannot end there. As with his interpreters, so with Jesus himself: it is important to think also in terms of influences upon him, of which he may or may not have been fully conscious. An awareness of these can enable us to characterize his 'voice' more fully.

There were, of course, synchronic influences on Jesus, a conditioning by what A.E. Harvey has called historical 'constraints',[3] and I sketched aspects of these in Chapter 6. But it is especially in the discernment of diachronic influence upon him that this fuller hearing of his voice will take place. In this discernment we go beyond his intention to the maybe unconscious ways in which he both reflects and reacts to earlier voices; we go beyond imagining the insight of his first hearers to a more direct insight from our own longer perspective. I aim, therefore, in this chapter to suggest how we might set the parables in the context of Scripture, Jesus' great precursor.[4] I ask how his voice *now sounds* to us when heard against the background of earlier voices.

To consider the parables 'in the context of the OT' could mean a number of different things. Such consideration, of course, was a significant aspect of what the early interpreters were doing when they interpreted the parables as part of the framework of 'divine meaning'. We may mention five types of more recent scholarly approach to the OT's relationship to the NT, in order to clarify the distinct purpose of the present chapter.

Four of these types are described by Willard M. Swartley. First, there has been study of the use of key OT texts and themes in the NT.[5] Secondly, attempts have been made to understand more broadly, under the umbrella of some kind of 'biblical theology', the relationship of the early Christians and their writings to the OT.[6] Especially since James Barr's introduction of Saussurian linguistics into biblical scholarship,[7] 'diachronic' readings of Scripture under the sign of such a 'biblical theology' have been under suspicion; the synchronic context of a speaker or writer is seen as being decisive for their 'meaning'. Thirdly, the gospels or sections of them have been read in the light of the liturgical use of Scripture, or as structurally modelled on specific parts of it.[8] Fourthly, Swartley's own work proposes that 'key Old Testament theological traditions influenced the structure and theology of the synoptic gospels',[9] i.e. that story shaped story. The fifth avenue is represented by the literary critic Northrop Frye, who has stressed the rhetorical unity of the biblical writings in both Testaments in their influence on western culture.[10]

In distinction from these approaches, I am concerned with a language to characterise the newness of Jesus' speech. Claus Westermann[11] and John Drury[12] have both written on the relationship of the gospel parables to the OT (they stand in the tradition of Jülicher's great critic Paul Fiebig).[13] Both writers operate with an implicitly generic model, invoking a 'plausibility structure' of family likeness in the way they demonstrate the continuities between older texts and newer ones: Westermann stressing the cognitive power of metaphor, Drury the tradition of allegory. One may acknowledge such continuities, and yet still not have properly appraised what it is that marks off the parable texts from their precursors.

To assess the particular quality of newness possessed by a text is first a matter of simple, careful comparison with other texts with which it appears to share some family likeness, whether in language, form or function. Then a model for describing the relationship is required. Swartley outlines schemata of John Hollander and T.M. Greene.[14] I turn, however, to a model from Bloom. His diachronic understanding of the tropes as twistings of older forms of language,[15] arising from a deeper than conscious level, can be a means of insight into the relationship of Jesus to Scripture, the precursor which (as we may now recognize) he sought both to affirm and to transcend.

Bloom argues that in the study of poetry, the context within which all tropes should be understood is that of the tradition of creative writing in which the poet stands. The trope is the mark of the poet's assertion of his own voice, reflecting a perhaps unconscious repression, sublimation or other such dealing with the influence of his precursors.[16] In this context the foil against which figures stand out, the 'proper' against which they 'deviate', is not merely some quasi-impersonal construct like 'convention' or 'tradition'[17] but the human vision of a precursor or precursors, revealed in their work. The present 'voice' not only echoes, but may also contend with the voices of the past. The names of individual 'figures of speech' can thus not only describe the relationship of a writer's language to the language and culture of her contemporaries (in the way explored in Chapter 6 above), but the relationship of her writing to that of her precursors. The writing may be a tropical statement of substitution, implicitly seeking to displace the precursor's work. The poem can, through its silences as much as its expressions,[18] hint at an awareness of lesserness or loss by comparison with the predecessor, or of heightened intensity. An entire poem can stand towards a precursor poem in a relation of irony, hyperbole, metaphor or another kind of trope.[19]

Mutatis mutandis, Bloom's understanding of influence can be applied much more widely than 'poetry'.[20] In applying it to the relationship between Jesus and the voices of Scripture, I will first draw out the parables' continuity with the ancient voices, by drawing attention to their structural precursors in some of the great forms of OT literature,[21] which function similarly as exemplary synecdoches, in the synchronic sense I expounded in the last chapter. I shall then briefly suggest how the six tropes when understood in Bloom's 'diachronic' sense, as assertions against the influence of a precursor, may illuminate the marks of newness which the parables exhibit when read beside the OT.

2. The Parables' Continuity with Scripture

My focus here, as just hinted, is not so much on individual texts, not even on famous OT 'parables' like Jotham's or Nathan's or Ezekiel's,[22] obvious precursors for those of Jesus, but on the forms of Scriptural discourse more widely: sacred story, law, wisdom, prophecy.

It should be apparent that the parables possess important links with all four of these great OT genres. They are stories with significance, like sacred history. They encourage certain types of behaviour as the way to true life,[23] as do Torah and wisdom.[24] They are directed to specific social conditions, like prophecy.[25]

The connection comes into still clearer focus if we recognize that just as these dimensions are all bound up *together* in the parables, so they are all bound up *together* in the OT. The conventional divisions break down. Stories are told to encourage obedience to Torah; much of 'Torah' consists of story.[26] The appeal of wisdom is an appeal to fear the LORD (who gave

Torah) and so find life;[27] the law itself contains such appeals on the basis of the incentive of 'life'.[28] Wisdom implies an overarching story,[29] that of a world created by God - a story that emerges from the shadows in the poem of Proverbs 8:22-31. The vivid imagery which characterizes the *meshalim* of Proverbs is similar to the comparative language with which the prophets make their powerful points.[30] Part of prophecy's rhetoric, in turn, is to remind Israel of its story,[31] and its goal is to recall her to obedience to Torah.[32] 'The Former Prophets' (Joshua-2 Kings) are narrative books. The great genres are as intertwined in Scripture as they are focused in the parables.

By closer attention to both the 'old' and the 'new' texts we can become more precise. I proposed that the working of the parables in question in their synchronic context comes into clear focus for us if we read them as synecdochic examples, focusing the world in a specific event and inviting audiences or readers to 'translate' that event into a 'world' again, a 'world' in which they are drawn to participate. Synecdochic example is fundamental also to the structure of OT genres, as I shall now seek to show.[33]

Synecdoche and Wisdom

For greatest clarity we may begin with wisdom-sayings, for here the similarity with parables, already noted in Chapter 6,[34] is most apparent. We have seen how the parables, like wisdom sayings, show the benefits of righteousness, making it attractive. We may now consider the structural similarity between the two forms in a little more detail.

Many wisdom sayings imply an original focusing-down of experience into one, typical instance, and invite application of that instance to a range of other circumstances.[35] Proverbs 15:17 may serve as an example. 'Better is a dinner of herbs where love is than a fatted ox with hatred in it' is a specific and vivid statement which intends a wider application concerning riches and poverty. As a 'part' it replaces a wider 'whole', such as 'it is better to be poor than to live in an atmosphere of hatred - if one has to choose'. It is much more effective rhetorically to use a specific instance as the proverb does, than to couch the statement in more 'literal' but general terms. So viewed from the perspective of its *first expression,* the proverb can be seen as a part-for-whole synecdoche. But having thus turned the whole into the part, the saying encourages people to 'complete' the synecdoche by turning it into a 'whole' again, and then applying it to different situations. In the actual *use* of proverbs in the situations in which they arise and through which - from repetition - they acquire the 'feel' of accepted wisdom, they function as whole-for-part. Thus a proverb like the one just quoted, when *used* on different occasions, would express a *general* truth by way of an interpretative framework for understanding a particular instance. In a period when the proverb was current, one can imagine someone saying it either ruefully at a feast where a family row had erupted, or encouragingly at a homely gathering where rations were short. In either case it links the individual situation to the wider world. This is the way that the parables of Jesus, too, have been used in the illumination of many a specific circumstance. This understanding of the proverb is closely related to general scholarly understanding of the category *mashal*. The Hebrew title of Proverbs is *Meshalim* and the word is used in 1:1. *Mashal* is used of various forms of figurative speech, 'insofar as they originally express something specific, but which then, as a general symbol, is applied to everything of a like kind and to this extent stands as a picture . . . insofar as [the form] sets forth general truths in sharply contoured miniatures'.[36] The Vulgate entitled the book of Proverbs *Liber Proverbiorum Salomonis,* but interestingly the word it used for 'proverbs' in 1:1 was *parabolae.* It has been an important insight of scholars to see Jesus' parables as *meshalim*.

Synecdoche and Sacred History

I suggested just now that even 'wisdom' collections imply a narrative, that of the world created by God. It is a meaningful world in which character is linked to end or goal: fearing the Lord leads to life. The glimpse of that world in a one-verse proverb is necessarily much more compacted than that which is seen in the longer gospel parables. However, many overtly narrative sections of the OT can be read as offering the same kind of synecdochic wisdom as both the proverbs and the parables. They tell a story which is pregnant with signification, with possibilities for wide application. Whether or not the 'lessons' are spelled out (usually they are not), characters are often portrayed with a striking realism, often (as in the parables) revealed more by actions than adjectives. Especially, we note that OT stories (like the parables) do not merely offer examples of action to be imitated or avoided, but present a world, an order, whose maker and guarantor (whether explicitly stated or not) is God. Drury notes the echoes of the Joseph cycle in The Prodigal Son,[37] and we may make our present point with reference to this section of Genesis.

Joseph is never said to have been 'foolish' or 'conceited' as a youth, but readers see that this was the case, and that his brothers' reaction when he told of his dreams of domination might have been expected (Gen. 37:5-11). The brothers are never said to have 'cruelly overreacted', but that is what the reader *sees* in the story (Gen. 37:18-28). Joseph is never said to have learned humility through his experiences, but this is discovered when he reveals himself to his brothers again and speaks words of forgiveness to them (Gen. 45:3-15). Likewise, the brothers are never described as 'penitent', but the reader discovers it by means of their conversation about their past guilt (Gen. 42:21f.) and their attitude of humility before Joseph and his steward (Gen. 43:19-22, 26-28). The manifold suggestiveness of the story is nowhere slavishly spelled out in terms of detailed 'lessons', yet it is fraught with suggestive and exemplary significance. The real world (whether we think of the story as historical reportage or realistic fiction) is reflected in the story, and the story invites its readers to see and live in the real world differently as a result.

The only 'lesson' that is drawn out of this story comes, not directly from the pen of the narrator, but via the mouth of a character, Joseph himself (Gen. 50:20). But this 'lesson' is highly significant, for it concerns not specific 'morals' arising from the behaviour of characters, but the overarching order of God. And when Joseph tells his brothers in this verse, 'you meant evil against me; but God meant it for good . . .' it is not an attempt to limit the rich signification of the long chain of events in its various stages, but rather a highly compacted, suggestive interpretation of those events which invites the brothers to recall, and the readers to reread, and see everything with new eyes. It is so also with the master's praise of his canny steward in Luke 16:8. We have to go back and read the story afresh.[38] Like the parables, the OT narratives assume a fundamental divine purpose and moral order, worked out in the vicissitudes of real human behaviour.

Sometimes the narrator himself draws out the 'message' of the story, the connection between behaviour and consequences, as does the writer of 2 Kings when he explains the reasons for the Assyrian conquest of the northern kingdom (17:7-18). It is still noteworthy that the implications for his readers (that they should take the warning to heart for their own times) are not spelled out, yet are pointedly clear. The specific events suggest a wider pattern or principle, a principle which can be characterized as the justice of God. At whatever precise period the book took the shape it now has, its readers or hearers would be left in no doubt of the consequences of disobedience, or the causes of disaster.[39]

Synecdoche and Law

A law-code also involves synecdoche, for it may specify particular cases but imply a more general application; conversely, when the law is couched in general terms, decisions must be made as to how it is to be applied in specific cases. It would be of interest to explore the extent to which debate in Judaism about the application of law may be seen to revolve around these two issues: how to generalize particular laws and how to particularize general ones. The question of the law's application to women is a good instance of the first issue.[40] Does a law clearly addressed to men (e.g. 'you shall not covet your neighbour's wife') apply, as part for whole, to the entire population of each gender? The matter of Sabbath observance is a good instance of the second. The law says 'in it you shall do no work', but what is work? The law appears to have been too general for the Pharisees;[41] or rather, they saw the only way of trying to encourage its observance in a hostile environment as being the way of detailed specification.[42] A consequence of observing synecdoche in the operation of law is that like parable, law appears to need 'completion' or insight beyond the surface into its intention. 'Law' is not so unambiguous, and therefore 'parable' is not so unlawlike, as they may at first appear.[43]

We have already seen the link between the parables and the incentive of 'life' held out by Torah.[44] One passage of Torah, Leviticus 18:1 - 19:37, may exemplify for us in more detail the continuity between the law and these parables.[45] The fundamental principle of this 'holiness code' is that the people of Israel were to be holy like God (19:1) and thus differentiated from those among whom they had lived and would live (18:3). Care for the poor, so central to the six parables, is enjoined (19:9f.). Oppression, robbery, injustice, an unforgiving spirit, all implicitly or explicitly warned against in our parables, are all forbidden (19:13-18, 35-37). The Israelites were to love their neighbours as themselves (19:18), and the parallelism of that verse shows that 'neighbour' is equivalent to 'a son of their own people', but they are specifically told also to love as themselves the strangers who sojourned among them (19:34). Moreover, those strangers were themselves under an obligation to keep the law (18:26), so from this long historical perspective Jesus was not proposing anything new by his use of a Samaritan as an example of obedience in Luke 10:30-37.[46]

A further link between this Leviticus passage and the parables is found in the motivation held out to the Israelites for loving strangers: 'for you were strangers in the land of Egypt' (19:34). This is an invitation to the people of Israel to identify with the strangers, to put themselves in their shoes, by recalling the humbling they had known through their Egyptian sojourn. That recollection would entail a realization that God's gift of the promised land implied no intrinsic superiority of one race over another. The message is strengthened further in Deuteronomy 10:18f.: just as *God* executes justice for the fatherless and widow, *he* also loves the sojourner. Such an invitation to place oneself in others' shoes is just what we have seen in the parables. The lawyer is invited to follow the steps of a Samaritan, and thus not only love the needy but humble himself (and moreover to imitate the just compassion of God). Pharisees are invited to see themselves *not just* as the standoffish elder brother, but also as money-loving wastrels like the younger, and then to return to God. If they would be justified, they must put themselves in the fullest possible sense in the shoes of the customs officer. As they do so, self-inflation is pricked. They find themselves as parts of the whole of which the parable-characters are also part, just as Israelites would find themselves parts of the same whole as the sojourners, if they but remembered Egypt.

Synecdoche and Prophecy

Prophecy was not simply repetitive of Torah, though it did reiterate Torah's commands, incentives and sanctions. It *applied* the law in new situations. Especially, it showed the *extent* of its application in ways that seem designed to have shocked the hearers. In this respect it is similar to the parables (particularly Lk. 10:30-37 and 18:9-14) which seem designed to have stretched people's conception of who might be a positive or negative example. Two passages from Amos may illustrate this. 6:4-7 announces a great reversal:

> Woe to those who lie upon beds of ivory, and stretch themselves upon their couches, and eat lambs from the flock, and calves from the midst of the stall; who sing idle songs to the sound of the harp, and like David invent for themselves instruments of music; who drink wine in bowls, and anoint themselves with the finest oils, but are not grieved over the ruin of Joseph! Therefore they shall now be the first of those to go into exile, and the revelry of those who stretch themselves shall pass away.

The biting sarcasm of the prophet stuns the hearers into a new outlook: those who now seem most prosperous will be the first to go into exile. The scene and its outcome are not only a part-for-whole 'slice of life' (no doubt Amos intended to 'sting' others besides those displaying the specific marks of idle luxury that he mentions) but, like some parables, a *present* synecdoche, a *shocking* slice of life (to think that the wealthy and successful might stand as representatives of the wicked!) Then in 9:7f. there is a shock of a different kind:

> 'Are you not like the Ethiopians to me, O people of Israel?' says the LORD. 'Did I not bring up Israel from the land of Egypt, and the Philistines from Caphtor and the Syrians from Kir? Behold, the eyes of the Lord GOD are upon the sinful kingdom, and I will destroy it from the surface of the ground; except that I will not utterly destroy the house of Jacob,' says the LORD.

This is another sort of vision-stretching. Not only, as in the previous passage, are surprising people to be the first to suffer. Surprising people also are the objects of God's care. Other nations have had their exodus; perhaps other nations might be Torah-keepers, too. It is the same rhetorical dynamic as we have found in The Good Samaritan and The Pharisee and the Customs Officer.[47] More deeply yet, it is synecdoche that TeSelle (without naming it) links with prophecy when she writes of the prophetic 'double vision, simultaneously keeping in focus the universal implications of a particular present as well as the potential particularization of the universal and eternal'.[48]

Jesus and 'Conventional Wisdom'

I will conclude this necessarily brief outline of these parables' relationship to different OT forms by setting it alongside Borg's discussion of Jesus' relationship to 'conventional wisdom'.[49] Though the thrust of Jesus' parables would certainly have been 'unconventional' in his time, his message and method here were not truly 'original', indeed were deeply traditional. Several of the features of the social-scientific construct 'conventional wisdom' as described by Borg are in fact also features of OT 'wisdom', broadly understood. 'Rewards and punishments', 'God . . . as lawgiver and judge':[50] are these not part of the fabric of Scripture? Conversely, is the 'gracious and generous'[51] God spoken of by Jesus absent from OT thinking? Yet according to Borg, a 'gracious and generous' God is not to be seen as part of the normal inherited way of thinking, for Jesus, who spoke of such a God, is defined as the antithesis of conventional wisdom.[52] A comparison of the structure and content of these parables with OT genres suggests rather that Jesus was deeply and positively influenced by the Scriptural heritage of law and prophecy, narrative and wisdom: by those texts which could speak on one page of the sanctions of God the lawgiver and on the next of God the forgiving and compassionate, who could indeed *command compassion.* But since the parables have nevertheless struck many a reader as something new when placed alongside their precursor the OT, it is necessary now to try to assess more precisely in what that newness consists.

3. Interpretative Keys: The Parables' Troping of Scripture

Bloom, as we have seen, uses tropes in his diachronic sense as a way in to the apprehension of intertextual relationships between earlier and later writings.[53] It is a means of thinking ourselves into the manner in which a new assertion can be made despite an inescapably influenced condition. The later writer does not merely add his voice to those of his precursors; whether consciously or unconsciously, he seeks to displace and replace them. This process of diachronic 'troping' is a subtle one, for sometimes the assertion will be made by *appearing* (modestly) to say 'less' than the precursor, when in fact the trope is just as significant an attempt at supplanting the precursor as when it appears overtly to say more. Bloom, indeed, sees the six tropes alternating between tropes of *limitation* (appearing to say less than a precursor) and tropes of *representation* (appearing to say more).[54] What he means should become clearer as we turn to suggest different ways in which the parables might be seen as 'supplanting' their precursor texts via the various tropical modes.

Irony and normality

The first trope of limitation is *irony*. Bloom finds in 'belated' poetry an ironic awareness of loss, often especially evident at the start of the poem - a sense that it is not what its precursor was. Yet it turns this awareness, as it were, to its own advantage; its very difference from the precursor is a part of its own statement, its clearing of the ground.

Where might we find this ironic sense in the parables? Especially, I think, in the absence of any authorizing word, any 'thus says the Lord'.[55] By such a formula the prophets had claimed a hearing from the people, asserting an authority linked to that of Moses himself, regarded as the greatest of the prophets.[56] No such words introduce the parables, according to the Evangelists. Jesus has something to say, and his challenge (as we saw in the previous section) has a ring similar to that of the prophets, yet it is not *exactly* a prophetic word. This, I believe, is Scott's true insight when he writes that the parable is 'ironically appropriate for the kingdom',[57] and Crossan's when he writes of the parables' 'normalcy'.[58] They *seem* to possess a lesser authority than their great precursors, yet perhaps they possess a greater.

Synecdoche and narrativity

The second trope, *synecdoche*, is (specifically now in its diachronic manifestation) a trope of representation. It aims at restating a position of the precursor, but in such a way that the precursor's position is made to look partial while the poet's own position appears as a whole. It 'completes' the precursor. I suggest that the parables do this in relation to the wisdom tradition and to laws. We have seen the parables' structural similarity to short proverbs and laws, and their similar appeal to the incentive of 'life' in the summons to obedience. But there is a fullness in these six parables which is absent in the short proverbs and individual precepts of Torah. The parables are short, yet they are rounded narratives. They can, indeed, be seen as a kind of 'narrative exegesis' of Torah.[59] They appear as wholes against the miniature, partial vignettes collected in Proverbs, and against commandments stated in summary form. They give us the opportunity to see the principles of wisdom and law at work in a situation with lifelike characters, in a story with beginning, middle and end. It was precisely this *difference* of parables from the short OT *meshalim* which Jülicher failed to expound: he saw the general truth stated in the specific instance, but did not explore the suggestive narrative manner in which that statement was made.

Metonymy and brevity

The next trope, one of limitation, is *metonymy*. In Bloom's scheme this is linked to the 'revisionary ratio' he calls '[k]enosis, or repetition and discontinuity'.[60] Here the poet seems to limit himself by replacing a term of the precursor's with a mere attribute or adjunct of the term, yet in this movement, apparently one of banal repetition, he asserts his discontinuity with the precursor. The parables as stories with lessons seem at first to repeat on a rather trivial scale the great stories of the OT, its histories pregnant with meaning and with application for the future. They seem in their brevity very self-limiting; rather than the grand saga of a nation, they seem merely to deal with tiny individual incidents. What power can they possess beside those mighty narratives? Crossan notes the significance of the parables' brevity, using Jorge Luis Borges' illustration of a coin: 'it is clear that coins are small because they point elsewhere, their true content is always somewhere else'.[61] This very self-limitation becomes a part of their self-assertion, betokening newness and difference.

Hyperbole and humanity

The fourth trope, *hyperbole*, seeks representation again. This is where the poet aims to *go beyond* the precursor, to open himself to something that inspired the precursor but of which the precursor himself was not fully conscious.[62] In what way could the parables be seen as going beyond their precursors? Perhaps, again, in their relationship to the sacred histories of the OT. Although, as we have just seen, in one respect their brevity marks them as self-limiting metonymies beside these great histories, in another respect their sphere of interest goes wider and deeper. As we have seen, there are many echoes in the Lukan parables of stories in the OT that are full of human interest, like the Joseph cycle.[63] But those stories were handed down within the framework of a narrative heavy with theological freight and community function. The parables, by contrast, seem to stand on their own, above even their gospel contexts; they seem to shake off other agendas and assert that the human *per se* is the sphere of God's interest.

With their cast of natives and foreigners, fathers and sons, masters and stewards, rich and poor, powerful and oppressed, pious and impious, they as it were press back *through* the pageant of such characters in Israel's history, *through* even Moses and Abraham, to Adam and Eve, to the creation of the world, and assert that the world and humanity are of greater importance even than Israel's history.

Metaphor and fictionality

The fifth trope, the last trope of limitation, is metaphor. It relates to a movement of '[a]skesis' or 'purgation'.[64] The later poet here comes closer to the earlier than ever, and seeks to win his own voice by an act of metaphorical substitution that somehow claims his own vision as more 'real' than the precursor's. It may look like a yielding-up of the 'real' for the 'merely metaphorical', but in fact it is the proposal of a new 'real'. Maybe it is the parables' fictionality which makes them metaphors in this diachronic sense. Much, though not all, of OT narrative asks to be read as history.[65] But this central speech-form of Jesus gives out the air of fiction. More precisely, it gives out the air of *not mattering* whether it is fiction or history. It may be that in giving up the discourse of what *really happened* for that of *the kind of thing that has happened, is happening and may happen,* in exchanging ἱστορία (history) for ποίησις (making), the most fundamental shift has occurred.   Here I am dissenting from Hedrick's project of imagining how the parables 'as freely invented fiction narratives' would have been heard 'in the context of the fictional narrative constructs that Palestinian Judaism developed for making sense of its own existence'.[66] Palestinian Judaism certainly told *stories* to make sense of its own existence,[67] but the most significant of those stories, gathered in our OT, were cherished as history, not fiction. These parables of Jesus, though, seem to be *fictions* which as such relativize even the importance of the sacred history for defining the identity of the people of God.

Metalepsis and allusiveness

The final trope of representation is *metalepsis* or transumption, the trope of evocation, or the trope of a trope. Diachronically a metaleptic text 'seeks to end-stop allusiveness by presenting its own formulation as the last word, which insists upon an ellipsis rather than a proliferation of further allusion'.[68] Such a text aims that *it* henceforth will be the one to be reckoned and wrestled with, rather than the precursor texts. '[B]y troping on a trope, you enforce a state of rhetoricity or word-consciousness.'[69] Bloom writes that it was this 'farfetchedness' in Milton's poetry, his rich allusiveness, that 'gave similitudes the status and function of complex arguments'.[70] Metalepsis summarizes the whole operation of a 'strong' poem, one that succeeds in its self-assertion. Through evocation of the precursors the poet seeks to scale the heights of their attainment while simultaneously speaking his own word. One might say that the precursor is *evoked*, but only in order to be *revoked*. The later text tropes the earlier one in metaleptic fashion by proposing a whole new configuration of old visions, terms, voices. The proof of its success is the desire that other, later poets have in turn to stand in the same place, and the difficulty with which they wrestle to find *their* own message in that place.

The quality of the six parables which makes them 'strong' in this sense, relating metaleptically to their precursor text, is precisely their rich allusiveness. The echoes of earlier texts which they contain, echoes of saga and wisdom, law and prophets,[71] impossible to pin down and cash out in terms of precise intention on Jesus' or Luke's part, brought together in stories so simple yet so hard-hitting, do indeed have the effect of 'end-stopping allusion', at least in Christian tradition which has preserved them. Here, gathered in the tersest of narratives (as the Fathers saw so clearly) are the great themes of Eden and fall, exodus and redemption, exile and return. This is another way of putting what Crossan calls the paradox in the pragmatics of Jesus' parables. He writes that it is almost as if the parables displaced the scriptures as text: 'Authority, situation or setting, and "text" for teaching are all paradoxically different with Jesus.'[72] For Christians they have both superseded as a reference-point the older texts to which they allude, and remain unsurpassed as embodiments of a vision of life. The parables have been endlessly *interpreted,* but they have not been *imitated* with any success.[73]

These parables' power to generate interpretations is the mark of their strength. Drury puts this in terms of Luke's achievement:

> Luke's achievement was to make a new sort of parable [less allegorical than earlier ones] by bringing in to the genre the kind of realism, moral ambivalence, excitement and common sense which he learned from Old Testament storytellers. So this was not an unprecedented achievement. But it was a fine one big with consequences for art, literature, drama and theology in Christendom and beyond it - not to mention the exegesis of the gospel parables in the twentieth century.[74]

I suggest that between the OT storytellers and Luke stands Jesus himself, and a creative wrestling with the voices of his ancestors that went beyond consciousness, and must remain beyond our imagining.

The influence of his parables, and the simultaneous difficulty interpreters have in truly encapsulating their message or imitating their style, may be illustrated with an example from art. A stained-glass window in St John the Baptist's Church in the village of Quebec, near Durham, portrays the story of The Good Samaritan. The figure on whom the picture of the Samaritan is based is the local doctor in whose memory the window was given. It is an instance of insight and blindness, of both hearing the parable aright as an endlessly renewable *mashal* (*the doctor* was such a man!) and deafness to its shocking tones (where is the exemplary Samaritan's *strangeness*? where is the story's troping of precursor voices?) The window tropes Jesus, or Luke, but it is what Bloom would call a 'weak misreading' - as, perhaps, any static visual representation of an oral narrative must inevitably be. The original parable remains to be wrestled with.

4. The Voice of Jesus in Diachronic Perspective: New and Old

A comparison of genres and a schema of intertextual tropes such as I have sketched in this chapter, though far from being either exhaustive or prescriptive, may give us a better insight into the true newness of these six parables than can be gained by mere observation of other texts whose forms or messages bear some superficial similarity to them. Viewing the parables in this way may enable us to catch the strange blend of antiquity and novelty which they display.

The parables stand in a long-established tradition in which a narrative of a world directed by the purpose of God shaped a people's thought and life. The many sub-plots of this narrative had God for the central actor, but were also rich in suggestive examples for living. The narrative was also reflected obliquely in wisdom-sayings and laws grounded in the belief that obedience was the way to life. It found new and often startling expression in prophecies which sought to remove complacency by inviting Israel to see herself as part of a larger whole, of a world under both judgement and grace.

Within and over against this tradition, however, the parables stake out their own space. Reticent in authoritative claim, reluctant even to name God, the world they show us is nevertheless more infused with the presence of God. Rounded in their narrative form, they display the fullness of a new order as law and proverb could not do. Brief in compass, they may seem from one angle almost trivial, yet their concern is with humanity as a whole. As fictions they say that truth is more than history; rich in allusion, they forestall imitation yet provoke endless interpretation. The voice of Jesus, echoing variously in countless interpreters of his work, was itself a voice in which the echoes of its past resounded in remarkable counterpoint.

NOTES

1. Bloom, *Anxiety*, 110.

2. Ignatius of Antioch, *Eph.* 15, in Andrew Louth (ed.), *Early Christian Writings*, revised ed. (London: Penguin, 1987), 65.

3. A. E. Harvey, *Jesus and the Constraints of History* (London: Duckworth, 1982).

4. Drury writes that first-century Jews 'gave to their tradition and above all to their holy Scripture, the Old Testament, a dedicated and rapt attention which it requires an effort of historical imagination to recapture': *Parables*, 41. The applicability of this statement to the full social range of first-century Jews, lesser- as well as better-educated, would be disputed (I owe this observation to Dr Loren Stuckenbruck). I think it can be safely assumed, however, that Jesus was well-versed in Scripture. Drury, who doubts whether we can say if these stories go back to Jesus, rightly says that even if they do (as I believe), 'it still allows for Jesus himself, whose humanity precluded total creation *ex nihilo*, to have spun them out of ideas known to him as a scripture-learned Jew': *Tradition*, 75.

5. Swartley, *Scripture*, 10-13, citing especially works by Dodd, Lindars, Juel, Piper, Mauser and Hobbs.

6. Ibid., 13-16, citing especially works by von Rad, Gese and Dahl.

7. Barr, *Semantics*.

8. Swartley, *Scripture*, 16-21, citing especially works by Daube, Bowman, Goulder, Evans, Moessner, Derrett and Roth.

9. Ibid., 1.

10. Northrop Frye, *The Great Code: The Bible and Literature* (New York and London: Harcourt Brace Jovanovich, 1982). See the endorsement of Frye's position in Jeffrey, *People*, 42.

11. Westermann, *Parables*.

12. Drury, *Parables*.

13. On the influences of both the OT and Hellenism on the parables, see Detlev Dormeyer, *The New Testament among the Writings of Antiquity* [*Das Neue Testament im Rahmen der Antiken Literaturgeschichte*, 1993] (Sheffield: Sheffield Academic Press, 1998), 156-60.

14. Swartley, *Scripture*, 31 note 86.

15. For Bloom's proposal of a 'diachronic' view of rhetoric, i.e. a study of figures as playing against anterior figures through literary history, see 'The Breaking of Form' in Geoffrey H. Hartman (ed.), *Deconstruction and Criticism* (New York: Seabury Press, 1979), 1-37, here 11f. Cf. de Bolla, *Bloom*.

16. 'In poetry, a "place" [i.e. a 'topos'] is *where* something is *known*, a figure or trope is *when* something is willed or desired': Harold Bloom, *Agon: Towards a Theory of Revisionism* (New York and Oxford: Oxford University Press, 1982), 69.

17. As in the classic essay by T. S. Eliot, 'Tradition and the Individual Talent' [1919], in Frank Kermode (ed.), *Selected Prose of T. S. Eliot* (London: Faber and Faber, 1975), 37-44.

18. 'A strong authentic allusion to another strong poem can be only by and in what the later poem does not say, by what it represses': Bloom, 'Breaking', 15.

19. Bloom, *Map*, 94f.

20. I am grateful for Dr Seán Burke's insight at this point.

21. I will not discuss psalmody or apocalyptic. The difference between many of Jesus' earthy parables and the latter genre is notable, though some, like Scott, make more of the difference than is warranted, as when the parables *en bloc* are taken as evidence that Jesus was 'antiapocalyptic': *Hear*, 423.

22. Jotham: Judg. 9:7-15; Nathan: 2 Sam. 12:1-7; Ezekiel: Ezek. 17:1-10. Drury has suggested some plausible antecedents for specific parables of Jesus: e.g. for The Good Samaritan, 2 Chron. 28:14f. (*Parables*, 134f.); for The Prodigal Son, Gen. 39 - 45 (ibid., 144); for The Shrewd Steward, 2 Kings 7 (ibid., 148); for The Judge and the Widow, Sir. 35:13-18 (ibid., 153).

23. Swartley notes the connection between 'inheriting eternal life', the subject of the lawyer's question in 10:25, and 'inheriting the land', the goal towards which Deuteronomy looks: *Scripture*, 132. The concerns of Luke in this section are those of Deuteronomy in its exhortations to a kind of life which will ensure that the land can be truly enjoyed once it is entered. 'The way to inherit eternal life is marked specifically by love for the neighbour, even the enemy, and using wealth for the benefit of the poor' (ibid.). Such an understanding of the lawyer's question and its background is to be preferred to that of Bailey, who sees it as reflecting a wrong Rabbinic idea that salvation can be earned: *Peasant Eyes*, 35f., 55.

24. David Daube comments that '[t]he difficulty theologians have with the three parables [Lk. 11:5-8; 16:1-9; 18:1-8] would be greatly mitigated if the wisdom input were appreciated': 'Shame Culture in Luke', in M. D. Hooker and S. G. Wilson (eds.), *Paul and Paulinism* (London: SPCK, 1982), 355-72, here 366.

25. '[I]n Jesus, it is as though many ancient tributaries of speech, many styles, merged in him. The discourse of prophet, lawgiver and wise man meet in him. He unites in himself many roles': Wilder, *Rhetoric*, 86. Cf. Witherington, *Sage*, 158f.

26. The entire Pentateuch is in a narrative framework, and stories occupy nearly all of Genesis and much of Exodus, as well as being sprinkled through Leviticus and Numbers. Deuteronomy opens with Moses' retelling of the story of the wilderness wanderings (ch. 1 - 3).

27. E.g. Prov. 1:7; 8:13,35.

28. E.g. Dt. 31:15f.

29. Cf. W. A. Beardslee, 'Uses of the Proverb in the Synoptic Gospels', *Interpretation - A Journal of Bible and Theology* 24 (1970), 61-76, here 65.

30. See Drury, *Parables*, 14-20, on the *mashal* as a prophetic oracle; Westermann, *Parables*, 9-12, on the 'comparative sayings' in Proverbs, and 25-112 on those in the prophetic books.

31. E.g. Ezek. 23.

32. E.g. Mic. 6:8, which emphasises that the LORD has *already* shown 'what is good', i.e. in Torah.

33. Wolterstorff comments that when Scripture is read as divine discourse, 'a relation of *specificity / generality*' often obtains between the injunction, story etc. given by the human author, and what God is presumed to be saying through it - that is, God makes the historically-conditioned human discourse more universally applicable: *Divine*

Discourse, 215. My point is slightly but significantly different. I am arguing that these ancient texts possess synecdochic features even as human discourse, whether or not one reads them also as products of a divine author.

34. See above, p. 208.

35. '[A proverb] is a statement about a particular kind of occurrence or situation, an orderly tract of experience which can be repeated': Beardslee, 'Proverb', 65.

36. '[I]nsofern sie ursprünglich etwas Besonderes ausdrücken, welches aber dann, als allgemeines Symbol, auf alles andre Gleichartige angewendet wird und insofern bildlich steht . . . insofern [dieser] allgemeine Wahrheiten in scharf umrissenen Kleingemälden darstellt': Jülicher, *Gleichnisreden* I, 34, citing Franz J. Delitzsch, *Kommentar zu Proverbia Salomonis* (Leipzig: 1873), 43f.; in the first part of the citation Delitzsch is himself quoting Fleischer.

37. Drury, *Parables*, 144.

38. Drury comments on the background of The Shrewd Steward in OT narrative wisdom: ibid., 148.

39. On biblical narrative as felt by most readers to be making a 'point', cf. Wolterstorff, *Divine Discourse*, 214.

40. See above, p. 222 note 148.

41. See Alfred Edersheim, *The Life and Times of Jesus the Messiah*, 2 vols. (London, New York and Bombay: Longmans, Green, and Co., 1900) II, 56-60.

42. Cf. N. T. Wright, *The New Testament and the People of God* (London: SPCK, 1992), 187-90.

43. Weder's bald statement that the parables are not law, but gospel ('Wahrheit', 166) therefore needs nuancing. Linnemann, also, is wrong to contrast so sharply the 'purely general' demand of the law with the 'authentic demand' of the 'concrete situation', the challenge 'to the movement of authentic living' represented by a parable such as The Good Samaritan: *Parables*, 55. General laws demand specific applications, while the challenge of a parable in a specific situation carries with it more general implications. Conversely, the danger of saying that parables should be preached 'in an open-ended fashion' (Donahue, *Gospel*, 215) is precisely that the *specificity* of Jesus' synecdoches, the power they possess by virtue of representing the world in a concrete situation, may be lost; they empty out again into the moral generalities of Jülicher. Harman has an interesting discussion of the dialogue form of The Good Samaritan, suggesting that it reflects two modes of thought: legal discussion (in Jewish terms, Halakah) and an appeal to the imagination (Haggadah). He points out that in the exchange with the lawyer Jesus affirms *both* modes: *Parables*, 61f.

44. See above, p. 208.

45. Herzog finds a contradiction between the parts of Torah that enjoined justice for the poor (the 'debt code') and the parts (the 'purity code') which effectively excluded them (*Parables*, 125) and sees Jesus as affirming the former while rejecting the latter. I suggest here that attention to the Leviticus holiness code, where purity and care for the poor are bound up together, exposes such a contradiction as too simple. On p. 184 Herzog puts it more luminously: the scribal Pharisees made the debt code subservient to the purity code, whereas the purity code should have been subservient to the debt code.

46. Contra W. E. O. Oesterley, *The Gospel Parables in the Light of their Jewish Background* (London: SPCK, 1936), 166.

47. I agree with Blomberg that Jesus appears as no more and no less radical than the Old Testament prophets in his denunciation of Israel's leaders: *Interpreting*, 313. On this vision-stretching within the Old Testament, the breaking down of stereotypes, e.g. of the enemies of Israel or Judah, cf. the 'good Samaritans' of 2 Chron. 28:14f., noted by Drury (*Parables*, 134), and especially Drury's comment on the two-sons theme which he describes as 'a favourite trope of Old Testament narrative': although Dt. 21:15-21 defended the first-born's right of inheritance and commanded death for rebellious sons, '[t]here is a sneaking distrust of older brothers and fondness for the younger, even when less meritorious. It gave the excitement of reversal to many tales - and more scope to God': ibid., 145.

48. TeSelle, *Speaking*, 137.

49. See above, p. 174.

50. Borg, *Jesus*, 149f.

51. Ibid., 151.

52. Funk is more circumspect than Borg on the question of law and parable. Discussing The Good Samaritan, it is the traditional interpretation of the law, not the law itself, that he contrasts with parable: 'Jesus attempted nothing less than to shatter the whole tradition that had obscured the law . . . Jesus had to interpret the law in parable': *Language*, 222.

53. Bloom's main exposition of the tropes in this light is in *Map*, ch. 4 - 7. He also links the six tropes with the six 'revisionary ratios' that he had introduced in *Anxiety*, 14-16, and with six psychological defences.

54. *Map*, 94f. Crossan remarks on 'limitation' as a quality in Jesus' parables, citing Ricoeur's formula 'the extraordinary in the ordinary': *Cliffs*, 14. As will be seen below, Crossan attempts to pinpoint what gives the parables their unique character in his chapter 'Paradox and Metaphor' (ibid., 1-24) but without real attention to their large diachronic context.

55. Cf. Witherington, *Sage*, 155.

56. See Dt. 34.

57. Scott, *Hear*, 425.

58. Crossan, *In Parables*, 15.

59. Cf. Green, *Luke*, 426.

60. Bloom, *Anxiety*, 78. Donahue writes of the *realistic* language of the parables as a 'scandal', and that it is this which is the counterpart to the emptying (kenosis) of Jesus in the incarnation: *Gospel*, 14. But this is perhaps to overlook the very realistic language of much of the OT.

61. Crossan, *Cliffs*, 5.

62. Cf. Bloom, *Anxiety*, 15, on 'daemonization', the 'revisionary ratio' associated with hyperbole in *Map*.

63. Cf. Drury, *Parables*, 115f.

64. Bloom, *Anxiety*, 15.

65. Cf. Wolterstorff, *Divine Discourse*, 243; like him, I take it that Job and perhaps Jonah are fiction. Naturally the few short parables present in the Old Testament (see note 22 above) ask to be read as fiction.

66. Hedrick, *Parables*, 5.

67. See N.T. Wright, *New Testament*, 67, on the importance of stories in first-century Judaism.

68. Bloom, *Poetics*, 400.

69. Idem, *Map*, 138.

70. Ibid., 143, where Bloom gives 'far-fetching' as an earlier English name for metalepsis.

71. See Drury, *Parables*, especially 139-52. Naturally there are verbal echoes of the LXX in the Greek text of the parables (cf. Drury, *Tradition*), and these would not have sounded in the Aramaic or Hebrew spoken by Jesus; but echo works as much through theme, mood and tone - and even silence - as through words.

72. Crossan, *Cliffs*, 17. The weakness of Crossan's treatment is that he does not properly explore the question 'different from what?' When one starts to treat the parables in their diachronic context, and notice their strong links to the OT, one discovers the true subtlety of their 'difference'.

73. Cf. the lack in early Christian literature of anything really comparable to the parables of Jesus, noted at least since Jülicher: *Gleichnisreden* I, 22f.

74. Drury, *Parables*, 155. By his last comment Drury is referring to the tendency seen particularly in Jeremias to make the more realistic parables of Luke the touchstone for authentic Jesus-material (see ibid., 111).

CHAPTER 8

The Story of a Voice

The quest of the historical Jesus may be for ever elusive, yet resonating through the mists of tradition and antiquity is a discernible, authentic voice, speaking in parables.[1]

Les mots ont changé, le livre est différent, mais la parole dérangeante, celle qui remet en question notre ordre humain pour rendre l'espoir à celui qui l'avait perdu, cette Parole est là, vivante, actuelle, toujours surprenante. C'est elle qui a défié les siècles et fait encore du Nouveau Testament un livre de notre temps.[2]

We are now in a position to survey the insights into the voice of Jesus that have emerged through a study of the parable interpretation of different periods, through an attempt to enter imaginatively into his contemporary setting and through seeing the distinctiveness of his stance with respect to that of his Scriptural precursors. The story that emerges may be briefly told.

The voice of Jesus, as it may be detected in the six parables we have considered, was in profound continuity with Israel's tradition of law, sacred history, wisdom and prophecy.[3] Yet it also sounded a different note in the important respects that we saw in the last chapter, implicitly transcending and seeking to replace these genres of discourse. His voice is figural in the diachronic sense, standing out from his precursors, 'troping' them in a variety of subtle ways, maybe largely unconscious and unintentional.

In his contemporary setting also the voice of Jesus was figural, individual, as witnessed by the striking parables which have come down to us. In the synchronic sense, as in the diachronic, these six parables appear to work as tropes. By synecdoche, they offer glimpses into a newly ordered world - one that is not only possible, but already coming into being. Jesus intended to invite hearers to see themselves in this world, in which relationships are restored and the way is open for all kinds of people to discover life through generous, wise and costly obedience. The realism of the stories makes their voice sharp, specific and exemplary in practical ways, but also provocative of ongoing reflection, as hearers draw out the lines from 'part' to 'whole'. This was a voice of hope for the ending of ugly societal divisions of many kinds, for a new way of life which would not be bound by the artificial restrictions of purity codes. It was a voice imbued with the sense of a newly intensified gracious divine ordering of the world, to which the language of the parables gives metaleptic pointers.

Our earliest witness to the voice of Jesus in these parables is Luke. I argued that he has preserved both their rich suggestiveness - not forcing them into some stereotypical straitjacket to fit his authorial ends - and their practical force - not 'spiritualizing' their material demands. His incorporation of them into his gospel entails a reading of them as metonymies, summaries or miniature embodiments of the gospel message of judgement and grace, the wondrous reversals seen in the entire story of Jesus' life, death, resurrection and continued doings through the church. The move from synecdoche (in Jesus' own context) to metonymy (in Luke) is not a big one, but it is significant. The essential difference can be put in the words of Werner Kelber:

> [T]he narrative gospel . . . deprived aphorisms and parables of their oral status by subordinating them, together with a good deal of additional materials, to the literary ordering of narrative . . . Orality, the voice of the living Jesus, the ground and life of the tradition, and the very gospels of Jesus' proclamation were overruled by the more complex ordering of narrative textuality.[4]

The distinction is precisely Luke's 'narrative textuality'. In the gospel the parables have a definite function as expressing and substituting for the gospel message, as metonymic reductions. But in the ministry of Jesus, the parables open out on to the world he and his hearers inhabit, inviting a de-forming and re-forming of their vision. The hearers have to remake the whole from the part themselves. In Bloom's words: 'A metonymy *names*, but a synecdoche begins a process that leads to an *un-naming*.'[5] Yet the tone changes little from synecdoche to metonymy. As would be expected from the fact of continuing oral transmission of the gospel alongside written forms,[6] it seems as if 'the voice of the living Jesus' - proclaiming good news of relationships transformed, a transformation undergirded by the order of a gracious God, and suggestively yet persuasively inviting people to join the transformation - continues to echo clearly in the gospel of Luke.

Luke had specific historical intentions in writing. For the commentators of the patristic and medieval periods, the voice of the historical Jesus was not the main object of their interpretations. There was an unstressed assumption that the parables they were dealing with were parables of Jesus; but the controlling framework of their readings - so I have argued - was the *divine* meaning of all Scripture, indeed of all creation. This opened up to them many metaphorical and metonymic dimensions of the parables, some of them now appearing very fanciful. Nevertheless, their comments are far from being without value for an inquiry into the voice of Jesus. Indeed, in view of their high estimation of the value of tradition,[7] not so much a body of knowledge as a tacit, nurturing spiritual atmosphere, we may well expect that the tone of the one they called Lord was by no means lost entirely. The stress on the moral, practical and specific impact of the parables - to be sure, received directly as messages for their own situation - is an impressive witness, consistent with a view of the parables as synecdoches, which ought to be given its due weight, instead of allowing the interpretation of this period to be tarred with the all-covering brush of 'allegory'.

The Reformation brought a new focus on the intention of Jesus, and with it a sensitivity to the nature and variety of his language, literal and figurative. In this tradition, Jülicher argued persuasively against the parables being seen as deliberately mystifying stories with arcane meanings accessible only to the insight of the initiated - though as I have tried to show, few interpreters probably ever believed that anyway. Jülicher appears to react against the older metaphorical mode of reading by his insistence on the parables' character as plain similes, but the much profounder reaction is found in the dislodgement of interpretation from the framework of divine meaning. The interpretations of Jülicher, despite their idealistic and generalized colouring, allow us to hear the clarity of a voice which brought eternal divine truth to new and vivid expression, with plain implications for human behaviour.

Developments in parable interpretation in the century since Jülicher have been marked by increasing sophistication in historical and sociological awareness of the conditions of Jesus' life. Our particular focus, however, has been on the return of the literary key of metaphor as a means of unlocking the parables' meaning. Their strange, counter-cultural, mysterious quality has been highlighted afresh, in the works of Crossan, Scott and others. But again, there has been a more profound shift. If Jülicher exemplified the retreat from divine meaning to human intention, what we have now seen has been the retreat from human intention to a text-based interpretation which seeks to know how Jesus 'was heard'. Again, notwithstanding a measure of idealism, anachronism, and confusion between ancient and contemporary 'hearing', such interpretations too may enable us to hear the authentically subversive and surprising tones of Jesus.

And so to the present work. A neat conclusion would be to close the circle, and refer the reader back to the start of the story above: implying - as even Jülicher was too cautious to claim[8] - that one's own interpretation was the natural, logical and unavoidable outworking of the history of scholarship. Such a conclusion, however, would fly in the face of all I have tried to do.

I have sought to show that the interpretation of the parables has not been a matter of different generations dispassionately seeking accuracy, but of succeeding interpreters revealing and responding to the influence of the parables upon them, even as the parables themselves can be seen as revelations of and responses to the influence of the Scriptures upon Jesus. The natural implication of this is that no interpreter can claim finality; a multiplicity of interpretative voices must be allowed.[9]

The hearing or reading of a figure of speech involves *both* the insight or personal response of the interpreter who reads or 'hears' it, *and* the claim to penetrate an intention beyond the conventional meaning of the words. Perhaps the offensiveness of early parable readings to some modern ears lies in the fact that both these elements were so obviously present (though the 'intention' being penetrated was wider than that of a historical person). Jülicher, who focused on Jesus' intention but feared 'insight', both exemplifies insight in his own work and reveals the inadequacy of parable interpretation which fails to ask how Jesus was *heard*, to inquire what were the sharp and specific identifications suggested by the parables. Scott, who focuses on how Jesus was heard but tries (unsuccessfully) to withdraw from 'intention', exemplifies the inadequacy, indeed impossibility, of parable interpretation which fails to ask what Jesus *meant*, at the same time as hesitancy about owning up to the presence of his own insight as an interpreter.

A single interpreter, then, ought not to present his insight as the last word, for it is truly *his*, and it is truly *insight*. This book represents simply an attempt to 'hear' Jesus afresh: to hear what he meant, how he sounded to his contemporaries, how he sounds to us now amidst the voices of his precursors and interpreters. I have abjured the standard historical-critical methods, and the modernist quest for verification, but I have sought to show that to focus on figures of speech is not to turn one's back on history, but rather to be deeply attuned to its texture. Neither the modernist aspiration to definitive historical readings, nor the frequent postmodernist denial of human intentionality as an appropriate literary concern, is adequate to the nature of 'figures of speech'. What I have written, then, intends no claim to a position of detached objectivity. My reading of Jesus' figures in their synchronic and diachronic contexts is consciously an act of imagination. My telling of the story of his echoing voice is necessarily and gladly perspectival and partial - in texts covered, interpreters read, tools used. The goal is to emphasise the permission we all have to respond to the voice of the parables, but also to alert us to the fact that as we do so we are not necessarily just hearing the echo of our own voice, but that of their human speaker.

To some extent any interpretation of the parables today is likely, despite all such good intentions, to bear the stigmata of modern individualism, the solitary interpreter's desire to stake out her own territory. Yet at the same time I have tried to employ both a postmodern 'hermeneutics of suspicion' and a premodern 'hermeneutics of trust' which, as Thiselton shows, 'equally recognize, as modernist individualism does not, the importance of the trans-individual frame within which understanding and interpretation operate'.[10] By the 'hermeneutic of suspicion' I have sought to go beyond the conscious intentions of interpreters, and of Jesus himself, in order to heighten the true nature of their insights. By the 'hermeneutic of trust' I have accepted that each interpreter from Luke onwards may mediate something of the voice of Jesus to us. I have, then, sought a 'trans-individual frame' in which to understand the parables; and it would be quite in keeping with this if any insights into the voice of Jesus which the reader finds in this study are not those which I think I have gained myself, but are disclosed despite my conscious or stated intentions. The important thing is that the speaker of the parables should be heard. And if fresh insights dawn upon us, over and above those disclosed via earlier readers, we may after all wish, like Bede, to attribute them to the author of light himself.

NOTES

1. McDonald, 'Alien Grace', 51.
2. 'The words have changed, the book is different, but the disconcerting word, that which puts into question our human order to give hope to the one who has lost it, this Word is there, living, real, always surprising. It is that which has defied the centuries and makes the New Testament once more a book of our time:' Christian-B. Amphoux, 'Les Manuscrits du Nouveau Testament: Du Livre A La Parole', *Etudes Theologiques Et Religieuses* 67, no. 3 (1992), 345-57, here 357.
3. From what influence did these Scriptural forms themselves arise? Strictly theological questions have been excluded from my inquiry. I have discussed texts in terms of human voices and influences. But an eminent *literary* critic has warned us that ultimately '[t]he separation . . . between a theological-religious experiencing of Biblical texts and a literary one is radically factitious . . . the plain question of divine inspiration - of orders of imagination and composition signally different from almost anything we have known since - must be posed . . . the voice and that which it speaks can never be considered as separate': George Steiner, 'Review of *The Literary Guide to the Bible*', *The New Yorker* (11 January 1988), 94-8, here 97f.
4. Werner H. Kelber, 'Narrative as Interpretation and Interpretation as Narrative: Hermeneutical Reflections on the Gospels', *Semeia* 39 (1987), 107-33, here 118. The

written medium was responsible for transforming Jesus 'from the speaker of kingdom parables into the parable of the kingdom of God': idem, *The Oral and the Written Gospel* (Philadelphia: Fortress Press, 1983), 220, cited in Thomas J. Farrell, 'Kelber's Breakthrough', *Semeia* 39 (1987), 27-45, here 41.

5. Bloom, 'Breaking', 11.
6. Cf. Farrell, 'Kelber's Breakthrough', 38.
7. See Louth, *Discerning*, 73-95.
8. See above, p. 140.
9. Cf. Jeffrey, *People*, 10: 'What gets voiced, always partially even when truly, presumably continues to deserve diverse voicing because it is repeatedly found, in multiplied encounters, to be incomplete in itself, yet in some proper sense of the term meaning-full.'
10. Thiselton, *New Horizons*, 146. Cf. Bruns, 'Midrash', 630.

Bibliography

Achtemeier, P.J., 'Righteousness in the New Testament', in George Arthur Buttrick (ed.), *The Interpreter's Dictionary of the Bible* (Nashville: Abingdon Press, 1962), 91-9.

Aland, Barbara, Kurt Aland, Johannes Karavidopoulos, Carlo M. Martini, and Bruce M. Metzger (eds.), *The Greek New Testament*, 4th revised ed. (Stuttgart: Deutsche Bibelgesellschaft / United Bible Societies, 1994).

Aland, Kurt, *Synopsis of the Four Gospels*, 6th revised ed. (Stuttgart: United Bible Societies, 1983).

Alter, Robert, *The Art of Biblical Narrative* (London: George Allen & Unwin, 1981).

– *The World of Biblical Literature* (London: SPCK, 1992).

Alter, Robert, and Frank Kermode (eds.), *The Literary Guide to the Bible* (London: Collins, 1987).

Ambrosius Mediolanensis, *Expositio Evangelii Secundum Lucam*, Corpus Christianorum (Series Latina) XIV (Turnhout: Typographi Brepols Editores Pontificii, 1957).

Amphoux, Christian B., 'Les Manuscrits du Nouveau Testament: Du Livre A La Parole', *Etudes Theologiques Et Religieuses* 67, no. 3 (1992), 345-57.

Aquinas, Thomas, *Summa Theologiae*, 60 vols., vol. I, ed. Thomas Gilby O.P. (London: Eyre & Spottiswoode, 1964).

Aristotle, 'On the Art of Poetry', in T.S. Dorsch (ed.), *Aristotle, Horace, Longinus: Classical Literary Criticism* (Harmondsworth: Penguin, 1965), 29-75.

Armstrong, Robert P., *The Affecting Presence: An Essay in Humanistic Anthropology* (Urbana: University of Illinois Press, 1971).

Auerbach, Erich, *Mimesis: The Representation of Reality in Western Literature* [1946], trans. Willard R. Trask (Princeton, NJ: Princeton University Press, 1953).

Bailey, Kenneth E., *Poet and Peasant* (Grand Rapids: Eerdmans, 1976).

– *Through Peasant Eyes* (Grand Rapids: Eerdmans, 1980).

Ball, M., 'The Parables of the Unjust Steward and the Rich Man and Lazarus', *Expository Times* 106, no. 11 (1995), 329-30.

Barr, James, *The Semantics of Biblical Language* (London: SCM Press, 1961).

Barthes, Roland, *The Semiotic Challenge* [*L'aventure sémiologique* (Paris: Editions du Seuil, 1985)], trans. Richard Howard (New York: Hill and Wang, 1988).

– 'The Death of the Author' [1977], in Seán Burke (ed.), *Authorship: From Plato to the Postmodern* (Edinburgh: Edinburgh University Press, 1995), 125-30.

Bartholomew, Craig, Colin J.D. Greene and Karl Möller (eds.), *Renewing Biblical Interpretation* (Carlisle / Grand Rapids: Paternoster Press / Zondervan, forthcoming).

Barton, John, *Oracles of God: Perceptions of Ancient Prophecy in Israel after the Exile* (London: Darton, Longman and Todd, 1986).

Bauckham, Richard J., 'The Rich Man and Lazarus: The Parable and the Parallels', *New Testament Studies* 37 (1991), 225-46.

Baumann, Maurice, 'Les Paraboles Evangéliques et Le Langage de Changement', *Etudes Theologiques Et Religieuses* 68, no. 2 (1993), 185-202.

Beardslee, W.A., 'Uses of the Proverb in the Synoptic Gospels', *Interpretation - A Journal of Bible and Theology* 24 (1970), 61-76.

Beda Venerabilis, *In Lucae Evangelium Expositio*, Corpus Christianorum (Series Latina) CXX (Turnhout: Typographi Brepols Editores Pontificii, 1960).

Bell, Michael, 'The Metaphysics of Modernism: Aesthetic Myth and the Myth of the Aesthetic', in David Fuller and Patricia Waugh (eds.), *The Arts and Sciences of Criticism* (Oxford: Oxford University Press, 1999), 238-56.

Bindemann, Walther, 'Ungerechte als Vorbilder? Gottesreich und Gottesrecht in den Gleichnissen vom "ungerechten Verwalter" und "ungerechten Richter" ', *Theologische Literaturzeitung* 11 (1995), 956-70.

Binder, Hermann, *Das Gleichnis von dem Richter and der Witwe: Lukas 18,1-8* (Neukirchen-Vluyn: Neukirchener, 1988).

Blaise, Albert (ed.), *Lexicon Latinatis Medii Aevi* (Turnhout: Typographi Brepols Editores Pontificii, 1975).

Blomberg, Craig L., 'Midrash, Chiasmus, and the Outline of Luke's Central Section', in R.T. France and D. Wenham (eds.), *Studies in Midrash and Historiography*, Gospel Perspectives 3 (Sheffield: JSOT Press, 1983), 217-61.

— *Interpreting the Parables* (Leicester: Apollos, 1990).

— 'Poetic Fiction, Subversive Speech and Proportional Analogy in the Parables: Are We Making Any Progress in Parable Research?', *Horizons in Biblical Theology* 18, no. 2 (1996), 115-32.

Bloom, Harold, *The Anxiety of Influence: A Theory of Poetry* (New York: Oxford University Press, 1973).

— *Kabbalah and Criticism* (New York: The Seabury Press, 1975).

— *A Map of Misreading* (New York: Oxford University Press, 1975).

— 'The Breaking of Form', in Geoffrey H. Hartman (ed.), *Deconstruction and Criticism* (New York: The Seabury Press, 1979), 1-37.

— *Agon: Towards a Theory of Revisionism* (New York and Oxford: Oxford University Press, 1982).

— *The Breaking of the Vessels* (Chicago and London: University of Chicago Press, 1982).

— *Poetics of Influence* (New Haven: Henry R. Schwab, Inc., 1988).

— *Ruin the Sacred Truths* (Cambridge, MA and London: Harvard University Press, 1989).

— *The Western Canon* (London: Papermac, 1995).

de Bolla, Peter, *Harold Bloom: Towards Historical Rhetorics* (London and New York: Routledge, 1988).

Bonaventura, *In sacrosanctum Jesu Christi Evangelium secundum Lucam Elaborata Enarratio* (Venice: Apud Petrum de Francisci et nepotis, 1574).

Booth, Wayne, *The Rhetoric of Fiction*, 2nd ed. (Chicago: University of Chicago Press, 1983).

Borg, Marcus J., *Jesus in Contemporary Scholarship* (Valley Forge, PA: Trinity Press International, 1994).

Borsch, Frederick Houk, *Many Things in Parables: Extravagant Stories of New Community* (Philadelphia: Fortress Press, 1988).

Boucher, Madeleine, *The Mysterious Parable: A Literary Study*, The Catholic Biblical Quarterly Monograph Series 6 (Washington, D. C.: The Catholic Biblical Association of America, 1977).

– *The Parables*, New Testament Message 7 (Wilmington, Del.: Michael Glazier Inc., 1981).

Boucher, Madeleine, and Corbin S. Carnell, 'Parable', in David Lyle Jeffrey (ed.), *A Dictionary of Biblical Tradition in English Literature* (Grand Rapids: Eerdmans, 1992), 581ff.

Bovon, François, 'Parabel des Evangeliums - Parabel des Gottesreichs', in Hans Weder (ed.), *Die Sprache der Bilder* (Gütersloh: Gerd Mohn, 1989), 11-21.

Brown, Francis, S.R. Driver, and Charles A. Briggs (eds.), *A Hebrew and English Lexicon of the Old Testament* [1906], revised ed. (Oxford: Oxford University Press, 1951).

Bruns, Gerald L., 'Midrash and Allegory: The Beginnings of Scriptural Interpretation', in Robert Alter and Frank Kermode (eds.), *The Literary Guide to the Bible* (London: Collins, 1987), 625-48.

Bullinger, E.W., *Figures of Speech Used in the Bible Explained and Illustrated* [1898] (Grand Rapids: Baker, 1968).

Bultmann, Rudolf, *History of the Synoptic Tradition* [*Geschichte der synoptischen Tradition*, 1921], trans. J. Marsh (New York: Harper & Row, 1963).

Burke, Kenneth, *Permanence and Change* (Los Altos: Hermes, 1954).

Burke, Seán, *The Death and Return of the Author: Criticism and Subjectivity in Barthes, Foucault and Derrida* (Edinburgh: Edinburgh University Press, 1992).

– (ed.), *Authorship: From Plato to the Postmodern* (Edinburgh: Edinburgh University Press, 1995).

Caird, G.B., *The Language and Imagery of the Bible* (London: Duckworth, 1980).

Calvin, Jean, *Institutes of the Christian Religion*, Library of Christian Classics XX, 2 vols., ed. John T. MacNeill, trans. Ford Lewis Battles (Philadelphia: Westminster Press, 1960).

– *A Harmony of the Gospels Matthew, Mark and Luke*, 3 vols., trans. T.H.L. Parker (vol. II) and A.W. Morrison (vol. III) (Edinburgh: The Saint Andrew Press, 1972).

von Campenhausen, Hans, *The Fathers of the Latin Church* [*Lateinische Kirchenväter*, 1960], trans. Manfred Hoffmann (London: A. & C. Black, 1964).

Carabine, Deirdre, 'A Dark Cloud: Hellenistic Influences on the Scriptural Exegesis of Clement of Alexandria and the Pseudo-Dionysius', in Thomas Finan and Vincent Twomey (eds.), *Scriptural Interpretation in the Fathers* (Dublin: Four Courts Press, 1995), 61-74.

Childs, Brevard S., *The New Testament as Canon: An Introduction* (Philadelphia: Fortress Press, 1984).

Clines, David J.A., *The Bible in the Modern World* (Sheffield: Sheffield Academic Press, 1997).

Combrink, H.J. Bernard, 'Structuralism', in Bruce M. Metzger and Michael D. Coogan (eds.), *The Oxford Companion to the Bible* (New York and Oxford: Oxford University Press, 1993), 715-8.

Cooper, David E., 'Science, Interpretation and Criticism', in David Fuller and Patricia Waugh (eds.), *The Arts and Sciences of Criticism* (Oxford: Oxford University Press, 1999), 60-70.

Cross, F.L. (ed.), *The Oxford Dictionary of the Christian Church* (London, New York and Toronto: Oxford University Press, 1957).

Crossan, John Dominic, *In Parables: The Challenge of the Historical Jesus* (San Francisco: Harper & Row, 1973).

– 'Review of K.E. Bailey, *Poet and Peasant*', *Journal of Biblical Literature* 96.4 (1977), 606-8.

– *Cliffs of Fall: Paradox and Polyvalence in the Parables of Jesus* (New York: Seabury Press, 1980).

– 'Review of B.B. Scott, *Hear then the Parable: A Commentary on the Parables of Jesus*', *Catholic Biblical Quarterly* 54, no. 2 (1992), 377-8.

Daube, David, 'Shame Culture in Luke', in M.D. Hooker and S.G. Wilson (eds.), *Paul and Paulinism* (London: SPCK, 1982), 355-72.

– 'Neglected Nuances of Exposition in Luke-Acts', *Aufstieg und Niedergang der römischen Welt* II.25.3 (1984), 2329-56.

Dawsey, James, *The Lukan Voice: Confusion and Irony in the Gospel of Luke* (Macon: Mercer University Press, 1986).

Delitzsch, Franz J., *Kommentar zu Proverbia Salomonis* (Leipzig: 1873).

Dibelius, Martin, *From Tradition to Gospel* [*Die Formgeschichte des Evangeliums*, 1919], revised ed., trans. B.L. Woolf (London: Ivor Nicholson and Watson, 1934).

Dodd, C.H., *The Parables of the Kingdom* (Nisbet & Co.: London, 1936).

Donahue, John R., *The Gospel in Parable: Metaphor, Narrative and Theology in the Synoptic Gospels* (Philadelphia: Fortress Press, 1988).

Dormeyer, Detlev, *The New Testament among the Writings of Antiquity* [*Das Neue Testament im Rahmen der Antiken Literaturgeschichte* (Darmstadt: Wissenschaftliche Buchgesellschaft, 1993)], trans. Rosemarie Kossov (Sheffield: Sheffield Academic Press, 1998).

Dorn, K., *Die Gleichnisse des lukanischen Reiseberichts aus Sondergut und Logienquelle* (Diss. theol., Marburg, 1988).

Douglas, J.D. (ed.), *The Illustrated Bible Dictionary*, 3 vols. (Leicester: Inter-Varsity Press, 1980).

Douglas, J.H., Denis Girard, and W. Thompson (eds.), *Cassell's Compact French-English English-French Dictionary* (London: Cassell & Co., 1968).

Downing, F. Gerald, 'Theophilus's First Reading of Luke-Acts', in C.M. Tuckett (ed.), *Luke's Literary Achievement: Collected Essays*, JSNT Supplement Series 116 (Sheffield: Sheffield Academic Press, 1995), 91-109.

Drury, John, *Tradition and Design in Luke's Gospel* (London: Darton, Longman & Todd, 1976).

– *The Parables in the Gospels: History and Allegory* (London: SPCK, 1985).

– 'Luke', in Robert Alter and Frank Kermode (eds.), *The Literary Guide to the Bible* (London: Collins, 1987), 625-48.

– 'Parable', in R.J. Coggins and J.L. Houlden (eds.), *A Dictionary of Biblical Interpretation* (London: SCM Press, 1990), 509-11.

Dunn, James D.G., 'Historical Text as Historical Text', in J. Davies, G. Harvey, and W. Watson (eds.), *Words Remembered, Texts Renewed* (Sheffield: JSOT Press, 1995), 340-59.

Dunn, James D.G., and Alan M. Suggate, *The Justice of God: A Fresh Look at the Old Doctrine of Justification by Faith* (Carlisle: Paternoster Press, 1993).

Edersheim, Alfred, *The Life and Times of Jesus the Messiah*, 2 vols. (London, New York and Bombay: Longmans, Green, and Co., 1900).

Eliot, T.S., 'Religion and Literature' [1935], in Frank Kermode (ed.), *Selected Prose of T.S. Eliot* (London: Faber and Faber, 1975), 97-106.

– 'Tradition and the Individual Talent' [1919], in Frank Kermode (ed.), *Selected Prose of T. S. Eliot* (London: Faber and Faber, 1975), 37-44.

Elliger, K., and W. Rudolph (eds.), *Biblica Hebraica Stuttgartensia* (Stuttgart: Deutsche Bibelgesellschaft, 1967/1977).

Ellis, E. Earle, *The Gospel of Luke*, The New Century Bible Commentary, revised ed. (London: Marshall, Morgan & Scott, 1974).

Erlemann, Kurt, *Das Bild Gottes in den synoptischen Gleichnissen*, Beiträge zur Wissenschaft vom Alten und Neuen Testament, Siebente Folge (Stuttgart: W. Kohlhammer, 1988).

Etchells, Ruth, *A Model of Making: Literary Criticism and its Theology* (Basingstoke: Marshall Morgan & Scott, 1983).

– *A Reading of the Parables of Jesus* (London: Darton, Longman & Todd, 1998).

Evans, Craig A., 'Luke 16:1-18 and the Deuteronomy Hypothesis', in Craig A. Evans and James A. Sanders (eds.), *Luke and Scripture: The Function of Sacred Tradition in Luke-Acts* (Minneapolis: Fortress Press, 1993), 121-39.

Evans, Craig A., and James A. Sanders, 'Gospels and Midrash: An Introduction to Luke and Scripture', in Craig A. Evans and James A. Sanders (eds.), *Luke and Scripture: The Function of Sacred Tradition in Luke-Acts* (Minneapolis: Fortress Press, 1993), 1-13.

– *Luke and Scripture: The Function of Sacred Tradition in Luke-Acts* (Minneapolis: Fortress Press, 1993).

Evans, G.R., *The Language and Logic of the Bible: The Earlier Middle Ages* (Cambridge: Cambridge University Press, 1984).

– *The Language and Logic of the Bible: The Road to Reformation* (Cambridge: Cambridge University Press, 1985).

Farrell, Thomas J., 'Kelber's Breakthrough', *Semeia* 39 (1987), 27-45.

Farris, Michael, 'A Tale of Two Taxations (Luke 18:10-14b): The Parable of the Pharisee and the Toll-Collector', in V. George Shillington (ed.), *Jesus and His Parables: Interpreting the Parables of Jesus Today* (Edinburgh: T. & T. Clark, 1997), 23-33.

Fearghail, Fearghus O., 'Philo and the Fathers: The Letter and the Spirit', in Thomas Finan and Vincent Twomey (eds.), *Scriptural Interpretation in the Fathers* (Dublin: Four Courts Press, 1995), 39-59.

Fernandez, James W., *Persausions and Performances: The Play of Tropes in Culture* (Bloomington: Indiana University Press, 1986).

– (ed.), *Beyond Metaphor: The Theory of Tropes in Anthropology* (Stanford: Stanford University Press, 1991).

Finan, Thomas, 'St Augustine on the "mira profunditas" of Scripture: Texts and Contexts', in Thomas Finan and Vincent Twomey (eds.), *Scriptural Interpretation in the Fathers* (Dublin: Four Courts Press, 1995), 163-99.

Finan, Thomas, and Vincent Twomey (eds.), *Scriptural Interpretation in the Fathers* (Dublin: Four Courts Press, 1995).

Fitzmyer, Joseph, *The Gospel According to Luke*, Anchor Bible 28A, 2 vols. (Garden City, New York: Doubleday & Company, 1985).

Fletcher, Angus, *Allegory: The Theory of a Symbolic Mode* (Ithaca and London: Cornell University Press, 1964).

Fletcher, Donald R., 'The Riddle of the Unjust Steward: Is Irony the Key?', *Journal of Biblical Literature* 82 (1963), 15-30.

Fodor, James, *Christian Hermeneutics: Paul Ricoeur and the Refiguring of Theology* (Oxford: Clarendon Press, 1995).

Fontanier, Pierre, *Les figures du discours* [1830] (Paris: Flammarion, 1968).

Fowl, Stephen, 'Reconstructing and Deconstructing the Quest of the Historical Jesus', *Scottish Journal of Theology* 42, no. 3 (1989), 319-33.

Frye, Northrop, *The Great Code: The Bible and Literature* (New York and London: Harcourt Brace Jovanovich, 1982).

Fuchs, Ernst, *Hermeneutik*, 4th ed. (Tübingen: J.C.B. Mohr, 1970).

– 'Die Analogie', in Wolfgang Harnisch (ed.), *Die neutestamentliche Gleichnisforschung im Horizont von Hermeneutik und Literaturwissenschaft* (Darmstadt: Wissenschaftliche Buchgesellschaft, 1982), 1-19.

Fuller, David, and Paticia Waugh (eds.), *The Arts and Sciences of Criticism* (Oxford: Oxford University Press, 1999).

Funk, Robert W., *Language, Hermeneutic, and Word of God: The Problem of Language in the New Testament and Contemporary Theology* (New York, Evanston, and London: Harper & Row, 1966).

– *Parables and Presence: Forms of the New Testament Tradition* (Philadelphia: Fortress Press, 1982).

– 'The Issue of Jesus', *Forum* 1, no. 1 (1985), 7-12.

Gerhardsson, Birger, 'If we do not cut the parables out of their frames', *New Testament Studies* 37, no. 3 (1991), 321-35.

– 'Illuminating the Kingdom: Narrative Meshalim in the Synoptic Gospels', in Henry Wansborough (ed.), *Jesus and the Oral Gospel Tradition* (Sheffield: JSOT Press, 1991), 266-309.

Gingrich, F. Wilbur, and Frederick W. Danker (eds.), *Shorter Lexicon of the Greek New Testament* (Chicago and London: University of Chicago Press, 1983).

Glare, P.G.W. (ed.), *The Oxford Latin Dictionary* (Oxford: Clarendon Press, 1968-82).

Goulder, M.D., 'Characteristics of the Parables in the Several Gospels', *Journal of Theological Studies* 19 (1968), 51-69.

Green, Joel B., *The Gospel of Luke*, The New International Commentary on the New Testament (Grand Rapids: Eerdmans, 1997).

Harman, Theodore A., *New Testament and Modern Parables: Their Relationship and Literary Character: A Reader's Response* (M.A. Thesis, University of Durham, 1990).

Harnisch, Wolfgang, 'Die Ironie als Stilmittel in Gleichnissen Jesu', *Evangelische Theologie* 32 (1972), 421-36.

– (ed.), *Die neutestamentliche Gleichnisforschung im Horizont von Hermeneutik und Literaturwissenschaft* (Darmstadt: Wissenschaftliche Buchgesellschaft, 1982).

– 'Language of the Possible: The Parables of Jesus in the Conflict between Rhetoric and Poetry', trans. W. Kahl, H. Boers and W. Whedbee, *Studia Theologica* 46, no. 1 (1992), 41-54.

- 'Beiträge zur Gleichnisforschung (1984-1991)', *Theologische Rundschau* 59 (1994), 346-87.

Harvey, A.E., *Jesus and the Constraints of History* (London: Duckworth, 1982).

Hawkes, Terence, *Metaphor*, The Critical Idiom 25 (London: Methuen & Co., 1972).

Hayes, Charles, 'Symbol and Allegory: A Problem in Literary Theory', *Germanic Review* 44 (1969), 273-88.

Hays, Richard B., *Echoes of Scripture in the Letters of Paul* (New Haven and London: Yale University Press, 1989).

Hedrick, Charles W., *Parables as Poetic Fictions: The Creative Voice of Jesus* (Peabody, MA: Hendrickson, 1994).

Heidegger, Martin, *Unterwegs zur Sprache*, 2nd ed. (Pfüllingen: Neske, 1960).

Heininger, Bernhard, *Metaphorik, Erzählstruktur und szenisch-dramatische Gestaltung in den Sondergutgleichnissen bei Lukas*, Neutestamentliche Abhandlungen, Neue Folge 24 (Münster: Aschendorff, 1991).

Hermans, Chris, *Wie werdet Ihr die Gleichnisse verstehen? Empirische-theologische Forschung zur Gleichnisdidaktik*, Theologie und Empirie 12 (Kampen: Kok, 1990).

Herzog II, William R., *Parables as Subversive Speech: Jesus as Pedagogue of the Oppressed* (Louisville, KY: Westminster / John Knox Press, 1994).

Hill, David, *The Gospel of Matthew*, The New Century Bible Commentary (Grand Rapids / London: Eerdmans / Marshall, Morgan and Scott, 1972).

Hirsch, E.D., *Validity in Interpretation* (New Haven: Yale University Press, 1967).

Holgate, David A., *Prodigality, Liberality and Meanness: The Prodigal Son in Graeco-Roman Perspective*, JSNT Supplement Series 187 (Sheffield: Sheffield Academic Press, 1999).

Holladay, Carl R., 'Contemporary Methods of Reading the Bible', in Leander E. Keck et al. (ed.), *The New Interpreter's Bible* (Nashville: Abingdon Press, 1994), 125-49.

Hollander, John, *The Figure of Echo: A Mode of Allusion in Milton and After* (Berkeley: University of California Press, 1981).

Hooker, M.D., 'On Using the Wrong Tool', *Theology* 75 (1972), 570-81.

Huizinga, J., *The Waning of the Middle Ages: A Study of the Forms of Life, Thought, and Art in France and the Netherlands in the Fourteenth and Fifteenth Centuries* [1924], trans. F. Hopman (Harmondsworth: Penguin, 1955).

Hunter, A.M., *Interpreting the Parables* (London: SCM Press, 1960).

Jakobson, Roman, 'Linguistics and poetics', in Thomas A. Sebeok (ed.), *Style in Language* (Cambridge, MA / New York and London: M.I.T. Press / John Wiley & Sons, Inc., 1960), 350-77.

- 'Aphasia as a linguistic problem' [1956], in Roman Jakobson and Morris Halle, *Fundamentals of Language* (The Hague: Mouton, 1980), 69-96.

Jasper, David, *The New Testament and the Literary Imagination* (Basingstoke: Macmillan, 1987).

Jeffrey, David Lyle (ed.), *A Dictionary of Biblical Tradition in English Literature* (Grand Rapids: Eerdmans, 1992).

- *People of the Book: Christian Identity and Literary Culture* (Grand Rapids: Eerdmans / Institute for Advanced Christian Studies, 1996).

Jeremias, Joachim, *The Parables of Jesus* [*Die Gleichnisse Jesu*, 1947], revised ed., trans. S. H. Hooke (London: SCM, 1963).

- *New Testament Theology* [*Neutestamentliche Theologie I. Teil: Die Verkündigung Jesu* (Gütersloh: Verlagshaus Gerd Mohn, 1971)], trans. John Bowden (London: SCM Press, 1971).

Johnson, Luke T., *The Literary Function of Possessions in Luke-Acts*, Society of Biblical Literature Dissertation Series 39 (Missoula: Scholars Press, 1977).

Jülicher, Adolf, *Die Gleichnisreden Jesu*, 2 vols. [1886/1898], 2nd ed. (Freiburg I.B., Leipzig & Tübingen: J.C.B. Mohr [Paul Siebeck], 1899).

- *Itala: Das Neue Testament in Altlateinischer überlieferung*, vol. III (Lucas-Evangelium), 2nd ed. (New York: Walter de Gruyter, 1976).

Jüngel, Eberhard, *Paulus und Jesus: Eine Untersuchung zur Präzisierung der Frage nach dem Ursprung der Christologie* (Tübingen: J.C.B. Mohr [Paul Siebeck], 1962).

Kelber, W.H., *The Oral and the Written Gospel* (Philadelphia: Fortress Press, 1983).

- 'Narrative as Interpretation and Interpretation as Narrative: Hermeneutical Reflections on the Gospels', *Semeia* 39 (1987), 107-33.

Kermode, Frank, *The Genesis of Secrecy: On the Interpretation of Narrative* (Cambridge, MA: Harvard University Press, 1979).

Kim, Kyoung-Jin, *Stewardship and Almsgiving in Luke's Theology*, JSNT Supplement Series 155 (Sheffield: Sheffield Academic Press, 1998).

Kissinger, Warren S., *The Parables of Jesus: A History of Intepretation and Bibliography*, American Theological Library Association Bibliography Series 4 (Metuchen, NJ: Scarecrow Press, 1979).

Kjärgaard, Mogens Stiller, *Metaphor and Parable: A Systematic Analysis of the Specific Structure and Cognitive Function of the Synoptic Similes and Parables qua Metaphors* (Leiden: E.J. Brill, 1986).

Klauck, Hans-Josef, *Allegorie und Allegorisierung in synoptischen Gleichnistexten*, Neutestamentliche Abhandlungen 13 (Münster: Aschendorff, 1978).

van Koestveld, C.E., *De Gelijkenissen van den Zaligmaker*, 2nd ed. (Schoonhoven: 1869).

Kümmel, W.G., *The New Testament: The History of the Investigation of Its Problems* [*Das Neue Testament: Geschichte der Erforschung seiner Probleme*, 1970], trans. S. McLean Gilmour and Howard C. Kee (London: SCM Press, 1973).

Leibniz, Gottfried Wilhelm, *New Essays on Human Understanding*, trans. and ed. P. Remnant and J. Bennett (Cambridge: Cambridge University Press, 1981).

Lentricchia, Frank, *After the New Criticism* (Chicago: University of Chicago Press, 1980).

A Lexicon Abridged from Liddell and Scott's Greek-English Lexicon (Oxford: Clarendon Press, 1871).

Lindemann, Andreas, 'Literatur zu den Synoptischen Evangelien 1984-91', *Theologische Rundschau* 59 (1994), 41-100, 113-85, 252-84.

Linnemann, Eta, *Parables of Jesus: Introduction and Exposition* [*Gleichnisse Jesu: Einführung und Auslegung*, 1961], trans. John Sturdy (London: SPCK, 1966).

Little, William, H.W. Fowler, Jessie Coulson, and C.T. Onions (eds.), *The Shorter Oxford English Dictionary*, 2 vols. [1933], 3rd ed. (Oxford: Clarendon Press, 1973).

Loader, William, 'Jesus and the Rogue in Luke 16: 1-8a: The Parable of the Unjust Steward', *Revue Biblique* 96 (1989), 518-32.

Lodge, David, *The Modes of Modern Writing* (Leeds: Arnold, 1977).

Longenecker, Richard N. (ed.), *The Challenge of Jesus' Parables*, McMaster New Testament Studies 4 (Grand Rapids: Eerdmans, 2000).

Louth, Andrew, *Discerning the Mystery: An Essay on the Nature of Theology* (Oxford: Clarendon Press, 1983).

– (ed.), *Early Christian Writings*, revised ed. (London: Penguin, 1987).

Madsen, Iver K., *Die Parabeln der Evangelien und die heutige Psychologie* (Copenhagen / Leipzig: Levin & Munksgaard / Ejnar Munksgaard / Verlag von Johann Ambrosius Barth, 1936).

de Man, Paul, *Blindness and Insight* [1971], 2nd ed. (Minneapolis: University of Minnesota Press, 1983).

Marshall, I. Howard, *The Gospel of Luke: A Commentary on the Greek Text* (Exeter: Paternoster Press, 1978).

– (ed.), *New Testament Interpretation* (Exeter: Paternoster Press, 1979).

Martin, J., 'Metaphor amongst Tropes', *Religious Studies* 17 (1981), 55-66. (= Soskice, *Metaphor*, ch. IV.)

McDonald, J. Ian H., 'Alien Grace (Luke 10:30-36): The Parable of the Good Samaritan', in V. George Shillington (ed.), *Jesus and His Parables: Interpreting the Parables of Jesus Today* (Edinburgh: T. & T. Clark, 1997), 35-51.

McEvoy, James, 'The Patristic Hermeneutic of Spiritual Freedom and Its Biblical Origins', in Thomas Finan and Vincent Twomey (eds.), *Scriptural Interpretation in the Fathers* (Dublin: Four Courts Press, 1995), 1-25.

Metzger, Bruce M., and Michael D. Coogan (eds.), *The Oxford Companion to the Bible* (New York and Oxford: Oxford University Press, 1993).

Meyer, Marvin (ed.), *The Gospel of Thomas: The Hidden Sayings of Jesus* (New York: Harper San Francisco, 1992).

Milavec, Aaron A., 'A Fresh Analysis of the Parable of the Wicked Husbandmen in the Light of Jewish-Catholic Dialogue', in Clemens Thoma and Michael Wyschogrod (eds.), *Parable and Story in Judaism and Christianity* (New York and Mahwah, NJ: Paulist Press, 1989), 81-117.

Miles, M.R., 'Review of Stephen L. Wailes, *Medieval Allegories of Jesus' Parables*', *Speculum - A Journal of Medieval Studies* 65, no. 4 (1990), 1074-6.

Minnis, A.J., *Medieval Theory of Authorship: Scholastic literary attitudes in the later Middle Ages* (London: Scolar Press, 1984).

Mitchell, W.J.T. (ed.), *Against Theory: Literary Studies and the New Pragmatism* (Chicago and London: The University of Chicago Press, 1985).

Moberly, R.W.L., 'Solomon and Job: Divine Wisdom in Human Life', in Stephen C. Barton (ed.), *Where Shall Wisdom be Found? Wisdom in the Bible, the Church and the Contemporary World* (Edinburgh: T. & T. Clark, 1999), 3-17.

Moore, Stephen D., *Literary Criticism and the Gospels: The Theoretical Challenge* (New Haven and London: Yale University Press, 1989).

Morgan, Robert, and John Barton, *Biblical Interpretation* (Oxford: Oxford University Press, 1988).

Moule, C.F.D., *An Idiom Book of New Testament Greek* [1953], 2nd ed. (Cambridge: Cambridge University Press, 1959).

Moxnes, Halvor, *The Economy of the Kingdom: Social Conflict and Economic Relations in Luke's Gospel* (Philadelphia: Fortress Press, 1988).

Neill, Stephen, and Tom Wright, *The Interpretation of the New Testament 1861-1986* (Oxford: Oxford University Press, 1988).

Newsom, Carol A., and Sharon H. Ringe (eds.), *The Women's Bible Commentary* (London: SPCK, 1992).

Nietzsche, Friedrich, 'On Truth and Falsity in their Ultramoral Sense', in Oscar Levy (ed.), *Collected Works* (London and Edinburgh: T.N. Foulis, 1977).

Nolland, John, *Luke 9:21-18:34*, Word Biblical Commentary 35B (Dallas: Word Books, 1993).

Oakman, Douglas E., *Jesus and the Economic Questions of His Day*, Studies in the Bible and Early Christianity 8 (Lewiston, NY / Queenston, Ontario: Edwin Mellen Press, 1986).

Oesterley, W.E.O., *The Gospel Parables in the Light of their Jewish Background* (London: SPCK, 1936).

O'Neill, Michael, 'Poetry as Literary Criticism', in David Fuller and Patricia Waugh (eds.), *The Arts and Sciences of Criticism* (Oxford: Oxford University Press, 1999), 117-36.

Ong, Walter J., *Ramus, Method and the Decay of Dialogue* (Harvard: Harvard University Press, 1958).

Owen, John, *The Death of Death in the Death of Christ* [1650] (Edinburgh: The Banner of Truth Trust, 1959).

Owen, W.J.B. (ed.), *Wordsworth and Coleridge: Lyrical Ballads, 1798*, 2nd ed. (Oxford: Oxford University Press, 1969).

Parker, Andrew, *Painfully Clear: The Parables of Jesus*, The Biblical Seminar 37 (Sheffield: Sheffield Academic Press, 1996).

Peristiany, J.G. (ed.), *Mediterranean Family Structures* (Cambridge: Cambridge University Press, 1976).

Perrin, Norman, *Jesus and the Language of the Kingdom* (Philadelphia: Fortress Press, 1976).

Petzke, Gerd, *Das Sondergut des Evangeliums nach Lukas*, Zürcher Werkkommentare zur Bibel (Zürich: Theologischer Verlag, 1990).

Pittner, Bertram, *Studien zum lukanischen Sondergut: Sprachliche, theologische und formkritische Untersuchungen zu Sonderguttexten in Lk 5-19*, EThS 18 (Leipzig: St Benno Verlag, 1991).

Plummer, Alfred, *A Critical and Exegetical Commentary on the Gospel According to St Luke*, International Critical Commentary (Edinburgh: T. & T. Clark, 1910).

Porter, Stanley E., 'The Parable of the Unjust Steward (Luke 16:1-8): Irony is the Key', in David J.A. Clines, Stephen E. Fowl, and Stanley E. Porter (eds.), *The Bible in Three Dimensions* (Sheffield: JSOT Press, 1990), 127-53.

Powell, Mark Allan, *What is Narrative Criticism?* (Minneapolis: Fortress Press, 1990).

Proust, Evelyne, 'Vigeois (Corrèze): un ensemble de chapiteaux historiés en Bas-Limousin', *Cahiers De Civilisation Médiévale* 35, no. 1 (1992), 49-63.

Quick, Oliver Chase, *The Realism of Christ's Parables* (London: SCM Press, 1931).

Rau, Eckhard, *Reden in Vollmacht: Hintergrund, Form und Anliegen der Gleichnisse Jesu*, FRLANT 149 (Göttingen: Vandenhoeck & Ruprecht, 1990).

Ricoeur, Paul, *Freud and Philosophy* [1965], trans. Denis Savage (New Haven: Yale University Press, 1970).

- *The Conflict of Interpretations: Essays in Hermeneutics* (Evanston: Northwestern University Press, 1974).
- 'Biblical Hermeneutics', *Semeia* 4 (1975), 29-145.
- 'Phenomenology and Hermeneutics', *Nous* 9, no. 1 (1975), 85-102.
- *Interpretation Theory: Discourse and the Surplus of Meaning* (Fort Worth: Texas Christian University Press, 1976).
- *The Rule of Metaphor: Multi-disciplinary Studies of the Creation of Meaning in Language* [*La métaphore vive* (Paris: Editions du Seuil, 1975)], trans. Robert Czerny with Kathleen McLaughlin and John Costello SJ (Toronto): University of Toronto Press, 1977).
- 'Schleiermacher's Hermeneutics', *Monist* 60, no. 2 (1977), 181-97.
Rohrbaugh, Richard L., 'A Dysfunctional Family and Its Neighbours (Luke 15:11b-32): The Parable of the Prodigal Son', in V. George Shillington (ed.), *Jesus and His Parables: Interpreting the Parables of Jesus Today* (Edinburgh: T. & T. Clark, 1997), 141-64.
Rollinson, Philip, *Classical Theories of Allegory and Christian Culture* (Pittsburgh / London: Duquesne University Press / Harvester Press, 1981).
Ryken, Leland (ed.), *The New Testament in Literary Criticism* (New York: Frederick Ungar, 1984).
Sanders, E.P., *Jesus and Judaism* (London: SCM Press, 1985).
Sanders, James A., 'Sin, Debts, and Jubilee Release', in Craig A. Evans and James A. Sanders (eds.), *Luke and Scripture: The Function of Sacred Tradition in Luke-Acts* (Minneapolis: Fortress Press, 1993), 84-92.
de Saussure, Ferdinand, *Course in General Linguistics* [*Cours de linguistique générale*, 1916], trans. Wade Baskin (London: Peter Owen, 1974).
Schaberg, Jane, 'Luke', in Carol A. Newsom and Sharon H. Ringe (eds.), *The Women's Bible Commentary* (London: SPCK, 1992), 275-92.
Schleiermacher, Friedrich D.E., *Hermeneutics: The Handwritten Manuscripts*, trans. J. Duke and J. Forstman (Missoula: Scholars Press, 1977).
Schmoller, Alfred (ed.), *Handkonkordanz zum griechischen Neuen Testament* [1869], 14th ed. (Stuttgart: Württembergische Bibelanstalt, 1968).
Schneiders, Sandra, *Women and the Word* (New York: Paulist Press, 1986).
Schweitzer, Albert, *The Quest of the Historical Jesus* [*Von Reimarus zu Wrede: Eine Geschichte der Lebens-Jesu-Forschung*, 1906)], 3rd ed., trans. W. Montgomery (London: A. & C. Black, 1954; reissued London: Xpress Reprints, SCM Press, 1996).
Schweizer, Eduard, *Jesus, das Gleichnis Gottes : was wissen wir wirklich vom Leben Jesu?* [*Jesus, the parable of God - what do we really know about Jesus?* (Allison Park, PA: Pickwick, 1994)] (Göttingen: Vandenhoeck & Ruprecht, 1995).
Scott, Bernard Brandon, *Jesus, Symbol-Maker for the Kingdom* (Philadelphia: Fortress Press, 1981).
- *Hear then the Parable: A Commentary on the Parables of Jesus* (Minneapolis: Fortress Press, 1989).
Sellew, P., 'Interior Monologue as a Narrative Device in the Parables of Luke', *Journal of Biblical Literature* 111, no. 2 (1992), 239-53.
Shillington, V. George (ed.), *Jesus and his Parables: Interpreting the Parables of Jesus Today* (Edinburgh: T. & T. Clark, 1997).

Sider, John W., 'The Meaning of Parabole in the Usage of the Synoptic Evangelists', *Biblica* 62 (1981), 453-70.
- 'Proportional Analogy in the Gospel Parables', *New Testament Studies* 31 (1985), 1-23.
Siebald, Manfred, 'Dives and Lazarus', in David Lyle Jeffrey (ed.), *A Dictionary of Biblical Tradition in English Literature* (Grand Rapids: Eerdmans, 1992), 208ff.
Siebald, Manfred, and Leland Ryken, 'Prodigal Son', in David Lyle Jeffrey (ed.), *A Dictionary of Biblical Tradition in English Literature* (Grand Rapids: Eerdmans, 1992), 640-4.
Smalley, Beryl, *The Gospels in the Schools*, c.1100 - c.1280 (London: Hambledon Press, 1985).
Smith, C.W.F., *The Jesus of the Parables* (Philadelphia: Westminster Press, 1948).
Smith, Sir William, *A Smaller Latin-English Dictionary* [1855], 3rd ed. (London: John Murray, 1933).
Snodgrass, Klyne R., 'Reading and Overreading the Parables in *Jesus and the Victory of God*', in Carey C. Newman (ed.), *Jesus and the Restoration of Israel: A Critical Assessment of N.T. Wright's Jesus and the Victory of God* (Downers Grove, Ill. / Carlisle: IVP / Paternoster Press, 1999), 61-76.
- 'From Allegorizing to Allegorizing: A History of the Interpretation of the Parables of Jesus', in Richard N. Longenecker (ed.), *The Challenge of Jesus' Parables*, McMaster New Testament Studies 4 (Grand Rapids: Eerdmans, 2000), 3-29.
Soskice, Janet Martin, *Metaphor and Religious Language* (Oxford: Clarendon Press, 1985).
Stegemann, Ekkehard W., and Wolfgang Stegemann, *The Jesus Movement: A Social History of Its First Century* [*Urchristlich Sozialgeschichte: Die Anfänge im Judentum und die Christusgemeinden in der mediterranean Welt* (Stuttgart: W. Kohlhammer, 1995)], trans. O.C. Dean, Jr. (Edinburgh: T. & T. Clark, 1999).
Stein, Robert H., *An Introduction to the Parables of Jesus* (Philadelphia: Westminster Press, 1981).
- 'Parables', in Bruce M. Metzger and Michael D. Coogan (eds.), *The Oxford Companion to the Bible* (New York and Oxford: Oxford University Press, 1993), 567-70.
Steiner, George, 'Review of The Literary Guide to the Bible', *The New Yorker* (11 Jan 1988), 94-8.
St-Jacques, Raymond, 'Good Samaritan', in David Lyle Jeffrey (ed.), *A Dictionary of Biblical Tradition in English Literature* (Grand Rapids: Eerdmans, 1992), 315f.
Strack, Hermann, and Paul Billerbeck, *Kommentar zum Neuen Testament aus Talmud und Midrasch*, 5 vols., vol. IV, 2nd ed. (München: C.H. Beck'sche Verlagsbuchhandlung, 1956).
Stuhlmacher, Peter, *Historical Criticism and Theological Interpretation of Scripture: towards a hermeneutics of consent* ['Historische Kritik und theologische Schriftauslegung' in *Schriftauslegung auf dem Wege zur biblischen Theologie* (Göttingen: Vandenhoeck & Ruprecht, 1975)], trans. Roy A. Harrisville (Fortress Press: Philadelphia, 1977).
Swartley, Willard M., *Israel's Scripture Traditions and the Synoptic Gospels: Story Shaping Story* (Peabody, MA: Hendrickson, 1994).

Swete, Henry Barclay (ed.), *The Old Testament in Greek according to the Septuagint*, 3 vols. (Cambridge: Cambridge University Press, 1887/1891/1894).

Swinburne, Richard, 'Meaning in the Bible', in S.R. Sutherland and T.A. Roberts (eds.), *Religion, Reason and the Self: Essays in honour of H.D. Lewis* (Cardiff: University of Wales Press, 1989), 1-33.

Tannehill, Robert C., *The Narrative Unity of Luke-Acts: A Literary Interpretation*, 2 vols., vol. I (Philadelphia: Fortress Press, 1986).

Terrell, Peter, Veronika Scnorr, Wendy V.A. Morris, and Roland Breitsprecher (eds.), *Collins German-English English-German Dictionary* [1980], 2nd ed. (Glasgow and New York / Stuttgart: HarperCollins / Ernst Klett Verlag für Wissen und Bildung, 1991/1993).

TeSelle, Sallie McFague, *Speaking in Parables: A Study in Metaphor and Theology* (Philadelphia: Fortress Press, 1975).

Thielman, Frank, *The Law and the New Testament: The Question of Continuity* (New York: Herder & Herder, 1999).

Thiselton, Anthony C., 'Semantics and New Testament Interpretation', in I. Howard Marshall (ed.), *New Testament Interpretation* (Exeter: Paternoster Press, 1979), 75-104.

– *The Two Horizons: New Testament Hermeneutics and Philosophical Description with Special Reference to Heidegger, Bultmann, Gadamer and Wittgenstein* (Exeter: Paternoster Press, 1980).

– *New Horizons in Hermeneutics: The Theory and Practice of Transforming Biblical Reading* (London and New York: HarperCollins, 1992).

Thorlby, Anthony (ed.), *The Penguin Companion to Literature*, 4 vols., vol. II: European Literature (Harmondsworth: Penguin, 1969).

Tillich, Paul, *Perspectives on 19th and 20th Century Protestant Theology*, ed. Carl E. Braaten (London: SCM Press, 1967).

Tinsley, E.J., 'Parable and Allegory: Some Literary Criteria for the Interpretation of the Parables of Christ', *Church Quarterly* 3 (1970), 32-9.

Tolbert, Mary Ann, *Perspectives on the Parables: An Approach to Multiple Interpretation* (Philadelphia: Fortress Press, 1979).

Torrance, T.F., *Divine Meaning: Studies in Patristic Hermeneutics* (Edinburgh: T. & T. Clark, 1995).

Trench, Richard Chenevix, *Notes on the Parables of our Lord* [1840], 5th ed. (London: John W. Parker and Son, 1853).

Trueblood, Elton, *The Humour of Christ* (San Francisco: Harper and Row, 1964).

Tucker, Jeffrey T., *Example Stories: Perspectives on Four Parables in the Gospel of Luke*, JSNT Supplement Series 162 (Sheffield: Sheffield Academic Press, 1998).

Via, Dan Otto, *The Parables: Their Literary and Existential Dimension* (Philadelphia: Fortress Press, 1967).

Wailes, Stephen L., *Medieval Allegories of Jesus' Parables* (Berkeley and London: University of California Press, 1987).

Wansborough, Henry (ed.), *Jesus and the Oral Gospel Tradition* (Sheffield: JSOT Press, 1991).

Watson, Gerard, 'Origen and the Literal Interpretation of Scripture', in Thomas Finan and Vincent Twomey (eds.), *Scriptural Interpretation in the Fathers* (Dublin: Four Courts Press, 1995), 75-84.

Weber, Robertus, and Roger Gryson (eds.), *Biblia Sacra Iuxta Vulgatam Versionem*, 4th ed. (Stuttgart: Deutsche Bibelgesellschaft, 1994).

Weder, Hans, *Die Gleichnisse Jesu als Metaphern: Traditions- und redaktionsgeschichtliche Analysen and Interpretationen* (Göttingen: Vandenhoeck & Ruprecht, 1980).

– 'Wirksame Wahrheit: Zur Metaphorischen Qualität der Gleichnisrede Jesu', in Hans Weder (ed.), *Einblicke ins Evangelium: Exegetische Beiträge zur neutestamentlichen Hermeneutik* (Göttingen: Vandenhoeck & Ruprecht, 1992), 151-66.

Welch, Claude, *Protestant Thought in the Nineteenth Century*, 2 vols., vol. I (1799-1870) (New Haven and London: Yale University Press, 1972).

Westermann, Claus, *The Parables of Jesus in the Light of the Old Testament* [*Vergleiche und Gleichnisse im Alten und Neuen Testament* (Stuttgart: Calwer Verlag, 1984)], trans. and ed. Friedemann W. Golka and Alastair H.B. Logan (Edinburgh: T. & T. Clark, 1990).

White, Hayden, *Metahistory: The Historical Imagination in Nineteenth-Century Europe* (Baltimore and London: John Hopkins University Press, 1973).

– *Tropics of Discourse: Essays in Cultural Criticism* (Baltimore and London: John Hopkins University Press, 1978).

Wilder, Amos N., *Early Christian Rhetoric: The Language of the Gospel* (London: SCM, 1964).

– *Jesus' Parables and the War of Myths* (London: SPCK, 1982).

– *The Bible and the Literary Critic* (Minneapolis: Fortress Press, 1991).

Wiles, M.F., 'Early Exegesis of the Parables', *Scottish Journal of Theology* 11 (1958), 287-301.

Wimsatt, W.K., and Monroe C. Beardsley, 'The Intentional Fallacy' [1946], in David Lodge (ed.), *20th Century Literary Criticism: A Reader* (London: Longman, 1972), 334-45.

Wink, Walter, *The Bible in Human Transformation: Toward a New Paradigm for Biblical Study* (Philadelphia: Fortress Press, 1973).

Witherington III, Ben, *Jesus the Sage: The Pilgrimage of Wisdom* (Edinburgh: T. & T. Clark, 1994).

Wolterstorff, Nicholas, *Divine discourse: Philosophical reflections on the claim that God speaks* (Cambridge: Cambridge University Press, 1995).

Wright, N.T., *The Messiah and the People of God: A Study in Pauline Theology with Particular Reference to the Argument of the Epistle to the Romans* (D.Phil Thesis, University of Oxford, 1980).

– *The New Testament and the People of God*, Christian Origins and the Question of God I (London: SPCK, 1992).

– *Jesus and the Victory of God*, Christian Origins and the Question of God II (London: SPCK, 1996).

Wright, Stephen I., 'Parables on Poverty and Riches', in Richard N. Longenecker (ed.), *The Challenge of Jesus' Parables*, McMaster New Testament Studies 4 (Grand Rapids: Eerdmans, 2000), 217-39.

– 'An Experiment in Biblical Criticism: Aesthetic Encounter in Reading and Preaching Scripture', in Craig Bartholomew, Colin J.D. Greene and Karl Möller (eds.), *Renewing Biblical Interpretation* (Carlisle / Grand Rapids: Paternoster Press / Zondervan, forthcoming).

Young, Brad H., *Jesus and his Jewish Parables: Rediscovering the Roots of Jesus' Teaching* (Mahwah, New Jersey: Paulist Press, 1989).
- *The Parables: Jewish Tradition and Christian Interpretation* (Peabody, MA: Hendrickson, 1998).
Zerwick, Max, and Mary Grosvenor, *A Grammatical Analysis of the Greek New Testament*, 2 vols. (Rome: Biblical Institute Press, 1974/1979).
Ziesler, J., 'Luke and the Pharisees', *New Testament Studies* 25 (1978-1979), 146-57.

Index of Ancient Literature

Old Testament

Genesis
22 *188, 189*
37:5-11 *231*
37:18-28 *231*
39 - 45 *242*
42:21f. *232*
43:19-22 *232*
43:26-28 *232*
45:3-15 *232*
50:20 *232*

Leviticus
18:1 - 19:37 *233*
18:1 *179*
18:3 *233*
18:26 *233*
18:37 *233*
19:1 *233*
19:9f. *233*
19:13-18 *233*
19:15 *191*
19:18 *233*
19:34 *233*
19:35-37 *233*
23:13 *204*
23:39-43 **58**

Deuteronomy
1 - 3 *242*
1:17 *191, 226*
10:18f. *233*
21:15-21 *244*
30:15-20 *49*
31:15f. *242*
34 *244*

Judges
9:7-15 *242*

Ruth
54

2 Samuel
12:1-7 *242*

2 Kings
7 *216, 242*
17:7-18 *232*

2 Chronicles
28:14f. *242, 244*

Job
209, 245
19:13-19 *77*
26:2 *7-9, 13*
33:21 *191*

Psalms
7:11 *227*
9:1 *180*
51:1 *192*
68:5 *225*
73 *209*
80 *8*
82 *226*
89:4 *8*
89:26 *225*
96:13 *225*
103:13 *225*
105:6 *145*
105:43 *145*
118:22 *50, 60*

Proverbs
1:1 *231*
1:7 *242*
1:11ff. *77*
3:7f. *224*
8:13 *242*

8:22-31 *230*
8:35 *242*
15:1 *83*
15:17 *230*

Ecclesiastes
103

Song of Songs
101, 179

Isaiah
5:1-7 *8*
6:9f. *64*
42:1 *145*
43:20 *145*
63:16 *225*
65:9 *145*

Ezekiel
17:1-10 *242*
23 *242*

Hosea
6:4 *7, 78*
6:6 *204*

Amos
6:4-7 *234*
9:7f *234*

Jonah
54, 245
3 *216*

Micah
6:8 *217, 242*

Malachi
1:2f. *163*
1:6 *225*

Apocrypha and Pseudepigrapha

Wisdom of Solomon
6:7 *191*

Tobit
4:7 *78*

Sirach
128, 146, 226
4:22 *191*
33:19-23 *211*

35:13-18 *242*
35:18 *125*

Testament of Levi
17 *220*

New Testament

Matthew
3:9 *37*
6:12 *41, 57, 58*
8:11 *37*
8:32 *79*
10:28 *217*
13:33 *158*
15:22-28 *91*
18:24 *213*
22:34-40 *73*
25:8 *99*
25:14ff. *57*
25:15 *213*
25:31-46 *226*

Mark
4:11-20 *63*
4:11f. *63-64, 101*
4:34 *134*
8:31 *104*
10:17 *124*
10:21 *124*
10:24 *220*
10:26 *220*
10:30 *57*
10:45 *9-10, 194*
12:1-12 *179*
12:28-34 *73*
12:44 *40*

Luke
1:1-4 *30*
1:5f. *35*

1:5 *68*
1:6 *45*
1:14 *42*
1:38 *33*
1:46-55 *33*
1:50 *45, 217*
1:51-53 *33*
1:52 *50*
1:53 *38, 39*
1:54 *34, 45*
1:55 *36*
1:58 *45*
1:72 *45*
1:73 *36*
1:78 *45*
2:10 *42*
2:25 *45*
2:36ff. *35*
2:37 *47*
3:5 *50*
3:8 *37*
3:12f. *36*
4:4 *48*
4:18 *38*
4:21 *38*
4:25f. *35*
5:8 *37*
5:27 *36*
5:29 *36*
5:30 *37*
5:31 *49*
5:32 *45, 46, 59*
5:33ff. *47*

6:20 *39*
6:23 *42, 58*
6:24 *38*
6:32-35 *58*
6:34 *39*
6:35 *219*
7:10 *49*
7:13 *45, 59*
7:22 *39*
7:29 *47*
7:30 *36, 56*
7:32ff. *48*
7:34 *36, 37, 41*
7:35 *48*
7:36 *36*
7:37 *37*
7:39 *39*
7:41 *41*
8:13 *42, 43*
8:14 *39*
8:43 *39*
9:5 *43*
9:33 *58*
9:48 *43*
9:52f. *35*
9:53 *43*
10:5 *44*
10:8 *43*
10:10 *43*
10:15 *50*
10:20 *42*
10:25-37 *73*
10:25-29 *55*

10:25 *33, 48, 49, 208,*
209, 242
10:28 *49*
10:29-37 *110*
10:29 *33, 48, 225*
10:30-37 *196, 198, 200,*
233, 234
10:30 *50*
10:31 *35*
10:33 *35, 44, 59*
10:34f. *189*
10:34 *69*
10:35 *70*
10:36f. *77*
10:36 *33, 184*
10:37 *45, 194*
10:38-42 *222*
11:4 *41, 57, 58*
11:5-8 *43, 224, 242*
11:37 *36*
11:39 *46*
11:42 *47, 218*
12:4 *43*
12:5 *217*
12:15 *40, 48*
12:16-21 *118, 136, 216,*
218
12:16-20 *38*
12:16 *38*
12:18f. *39*
12:19 *41*
12:21 *38, 40*
12:33 *40*
12:42-44 *40, 57*
12:44 *40*
12:52 *44*
13:3 *49*
13:4 *58*
13:5 *49*
13:16 *37*
13:17 *42*
13:20f. *158*
13:28 *37*
13:31 *56*
13:32 *8*
13:35 *44*
14:1 *36, 44*

14:7-10 *50*
14:11 *50*
14:12-14 *39, 58*
14:12 *38, 43*
14:14 *45*
14:16-24 *214, 225*
14:21 *39*
14:23 *44*
14:33 *41*
15 *40, 60, 85, 104, 162-*
163, 171, 203
15:1f. *34, 37, 84*
15:1 *36, 81, 163*
15:2 *163*
15:3-7 *117*
15:4 *49*
15:5 *42*
15:6 *43, 49*
15:7 *42, 45, 59*
15:8-10 *222*
15:9 *43*
15:10 *42*
15:11-32 *36, 45, 59, 84,*
203, 215, 218, 220,
223, 224
15:12 *39*
15:13 *57, 221, 226*
15:15f. *79*
15:15 *51*
15:16 *73, 209*
15:17ff. *31*
15:17 *40, 49*
15:20 *44, 59, 189, 219,*
223
15:22 *189*
15:23 *41, 103, 209*
15:24 *41, 49, 81, 208*
15:25ff. *82*
15:25 *58*
15:27 *49*
15:29 *41, 42, 79, 112*
15:30 *39, 40*
15:31 *162, 220, 223*
15:32 *41, 42, 49, 209*
16 *85, 104, 203, 208*
16:1-13 *59*
16:1-9 *59, 90, 242*

16:1-8 *57, 153, 186, 216,*
218, 221, 224
16:1 *38, 40, 57, 190, 203,*
221
16:2 *88*
16:3f. *31*
16:3 *99, 124*
16:4-7 *40*
16:4 *43, 44, 226*
16:5ff. *86*
16:5 *41*
16:6f. *88*
16:7 *41*
16:8-13 *171*
16:8f. *184, 196, 208, 215*
16:8 *46, 59, 85, 122-123,*
152, 166, 190, 192,
208, 214, 219, 232
16:9 *42-43, 44, 46, 58,*
59, 85, 88, 108, 122,
124, 190, 209, 215,
226
16:10-13 *34, 55*
16:10 *46*
16:11 *46*
16:14 *40, 46*
16:15 *46, 48, 225*
16:16f. *46*
16:18 *46, 60*
16:19-31 *38, 39, 59, 99,*
118, 200, 203, 207,
215, 221
16:19-26 *124, 167*
16:19f. *208*
16:19 *38, 41, 99*
16:20 *38*
16:21 *38, 91, 209*
16:22 *38, 148*
16:22f. *36, 58*
16:23f. *93*
16:23 *199*
16:24 *37, 44, 45*
16:25 *36, 37, 39, 48, 94,*
220
16:27-31 *124, 167*
16:27f. *208*
16:27 *37, 44*

16:28 *90, 209*
16:29 *36, 56, 130*
16:30 *37, 56, 94, 208*
16:31 *56*
17:10 *41*
17:13 *45*
17:16 *35*
18:1-14 *223*
18:1-8 *35, 186, 204, 209,*
  226, 242
18:1-6 *224*
18:1 *34, 51, 55, 56, 95-*
  96
18:2-5 *125*
18:2 *191, 192*
18:3 *35, 48, 209, 219,*
  225
18:4-6 *214*
18:4f. *31, 192*
18:4 *191*
18:5 *192, 223, 225*
18:6-8 *125-126, 184*
18:6 *46, 51, 190, 191,*
  216
18:7f. *34, 209*
18:7 *48, 96, 125, 209*
18:8 *209*
18:9-14 *36, 37, 45, 50,*
  96, 118, 196, 197, 198,
  201, 203, 211, 220,
  234
18:9 *36, 45, 50, 55, 169,*
  192
18:10f. *35, 56*
18:10 *36*
18:11 *36, 46, 193*
18:12 *47*
18:13 *36, 37, 193, 199,*
  223
18:14 *44, 47, 50, 96, 169,*
  184, 192, 193, 209,
  211
18:18-23 *38*
18:18 *49*
18:20 *46, 47*
18:22 *39, 47, 49*
18:23 *38*

18:25 *38*
18:29f. *44*
18:30 *39*
18:38f. *45*
19:1-10 *56*
19:2-8 *38*
19:2 *36, 37*
19:5 *44*
19:6 *42*
19:7 *37*
19:8 *39, 41*
19:9 *37, 44, 56*
19:10 *49*
19:12ff. *57*
19:37 *42*
20:19 *164, 194*
20:20 *45*
20:47 *35, 40*
21:1-4 *38*
21:2f. *35*
21:3 *39*
21:4 *39, 40*
21:16 *43*
23:11 *50*
23:12 *43*
23:40 *217*
23:47 *45*
23:50 *45*
24:7 *37*
24:41 *42*
24:52 *42*

John
5:25 *74*
8:31 *7*
8:48 *7*
8:52 *7*
8:57 *7*
10:30 *121*
15:1 *8*
21:25 *8*

Acts
2:26 *42*
2:33 *50*
3:13 *36*
3:14 *45*

3:15 *48*
3:25 *36*
4:1 *35*
4:10 *49*
4:11 *50*
4:32 *41*
5:20 *48*
5:31 *50*
5:34 *62*
6:1 *35*
6:7 *35*
7:41 *42*
7:52 *45*
8:9-11 *35*
8:12-25 *35*
8:14 *44*
10:2 *217*
10:22 *45*
10:28 *51*
11:1 *44*
11:18 *48*
13:2f. *47*
13:16 *217*
13:17 *50*
13:26 *36, 217*
13:38f. *48*
13:46 *48*
13:48 *48*
14:23 *47*
15 *60*
15:7-31 *51*
16:23 *50*
16:32 *51*
16:33 *50, 91*
17:11 *44*
17:25 *48*
22:14 *45*
22:35 *217*
23:6 *56*

Romans
2:12-16 *107*
4:5 *218*
11:18ff. *96*
11:25f. *82*

1 Corinthians
1 - 4 *109*
1:28 *107*

2 Corinthians
10 - 12 *109*

Ephesians
2:19 *81*
4:17 *106*

James
2:5 *109*
5:4 *88*

1 Peter
2:12 *106*

Revelation
2:5 *88*
11:2 *106*
7:4-8 *107*

Parables

The Good Samaritan
(Luke 10:25-37)
18, 29, 33, 49, 50, 51, 63, 66, 70, 72, 75, 76-79, 87, 104, 105, 118-119, 123, 126, 129, 134, 135, 140, 157, 160-162, 184, 189, 195, 196, 199, 203, 205, 216, 222, 235, 240, 242, 243, 244

The Great Banquet
(Luke 14:16-24)
39, 214

The Judge and the Widow
(Luke 18:1-8)
18, 34, 48, 85, 95-96, 125-126, 168, 171, 187, 195, 196, 199, 222, 242

The Leaven
(Matthew 13:33 / Luke 13:20f.)
157, 158

The Lost Sheep
(Luke 15:3-7)
49

The Pharisee and the Customs Officer
(Luke 18:9-14)
18, 45, 50, 96-97, 126, 129, 136, 152, 157, 169-170, 172, 192, 195, 204, 221, 222, 235

The Prodigal Son
(Luke 15:11-32)
18, 29, 34, 36, 39, 40, 41, 42, 49, 51, 53, 58, 72, 73, 75, 79-84, 119-122, 158, 162-166, 171, 189, 195, 199, 203, 204, 205, 208, 209, 211, 217, 219, 221, 222, 223, 226, 231, 242

The Rich Fool
(Luke 12:13-21)
38, 219

The Rich Man and Lazarus
(Luke 16:19-31)
18, 34, 36, 39, 47, 90-95, 124-125, 133, 152, 167-168, 189, 193, 195, 199, 204, 206, 208, 211

The Shrewd Steward
(Luke 16:1-9)
18, 34, 41, 44, 85-90, 91, 122-124, 152, 157, 166, 171, 190, 195, 196, 199, 204, 242, 243

The Sower
(Matthew 13:3-9, 18-23 / Mark 4:2-9, 13-20 / Luke 8:4-8, 11-15)
39, 44, 63, 155, 178

Index of Greek Words

Ἀβραάμ 36
ἀγαθά 39
ἀδικίας 190, 191
ἄδικοι 46
αἰώνιον 209
ἁμαρτωλῷ 37
ἀνέζησεν 209
ἀπεδοκίμασαν 60
ἀποδεκατῶ 47
ἀπέλαβες 39
ἀπόλλυμαι 49
ἅρπαγες 46
ἀρχιτελώνης 36

βίον 39

δεδικαιωμένος 47, 209
δέξωνται 43, 226
διεβλήθη 190
διεσκόρπισεν 57
δίκαιοι 45
δικαιοῦν 46, 225
δικαιοῦντες 46

ἔθνη 81, 107
ἐκδίκησιν 48
ἐκδίκησον 48, 209, 225
ἐκολλήθη 51
ἔλεος 45
ἐλέησόν 45
ἐντρέπομαι 191
ἐξουθενοῦντας 50
ἐξυφαίνει 130
ἐπεθύμει 209

ἐπιθυμῶν 209
ἐσπλαγχνίσθη 45, 189
εὐφραίνεσθαι 41

ζωήν, 48, 209

ἱερεύς 35
ἵνα 64
ἱστορία 238

κατ᾿ ἰδίαν 134
καταφαγών 40
κατεφίλησεν 223
κληρονομήσω 49
κριτής 191

λόγος 44, 127, 139, 145

μακράν 199
μακρόθεν 199
μακροθυμεῖ 125
μοιχοί 46

νηστεύω 47
νόησιν 130

οἰκονόμον 190
οἴκους 44
ὀφειλέταις 41
ὀφείλειν 41
ὀφειλήματα 41

παραβολή 64, 116, 146
περισσεύονται 40

πληγάς 51
πλούσιος 38
πλουτεῖν 38
ποιήσις 238
ποιήσω 124
πτωχός 38

Σαμαρίτης 35
σκιρτήσατε 58
σκηνή 58
σπλάγχνα 45

ταπεινῶν 50
ταπεινωθήσεται 50
τέκνον 37, 220, 223
τελώνης 36

ὑγαίνοντα 49
ὕψης 49
ὑπάρχοντα 40
ὑπωπιάζῃ 223, 225
ὑψωθσεται 50
ὑψῶν 50

Φαρισαῖος 36
φίλος 42, 43

χαρά 42
χαρῆναι 42
χήρα 35
χορτασθῆναι 209
χορῶν 58
χρεοφειλετῶν 41

Index of Authors

Achtemeier, P J. 220
Alter, Robert 22, 26, 28, 61
Ambrose of Milan 67, 68-71, 75, 76, 77,
 79, 81, 84, 85, 87, 90-91, 92, 93, 98,
 99, 100, 102, 104, 105, 107, 109, 112,
 132, 133, 134, 135, 136, 219, 220
Amphoux, Christian-B. 250
Aquinas, Thomas 67, 72, 105, 148
Aristotle 23, 67, 71, 99, 110, 111, 116,
 117, 135
Armstrong, Robert P. 22, 25
Athanasius 29
Auerbach, Erich, 184, 188, 213, 216
Augustine of Hippo 63, 66, 67, 69, 85, 86,
 93, 100, 101, 102, 112, 134, 135

Bailey, Kenneth E. 22, 55, 56, 60, 212,
 214, 217, 219, 220, 221, 224, 242
Ball, M. 226
Barr, James 148
Barthes, Roland 6, 13, 14, 21, 26
Barton, John 22, 27
Basil 108
Baumann, Maurice 184, 212, 213, 214,
 216, 224
Baur, Ferdinand Christian 115, 142
Beardslee, W.A. 242, 243
Beardsley, Monroe C. 25
Bede 17, 28, 67, 68-71, 76, 80, 82, 85-87,
 89, 91-92, 96, 99, 100, 109, 110, 112,
 134, 135, 250
Bell, Michael 22
Beza, Theodore 103
Bindemann, Walther 212, 217
Binder, Hermann 143
Blomberg, Craig L. 57, 138, 143, 149,
 177, 219, 244
Bloom, Harold 7, 13, 14-17, 19, 23, 26,
 27, 28, 100, 139, 141, 177, 215, 228,
 229, 235-239, 240, 241, 242, 244, 245,
 247, 251

de Bolla, Peter 27, 241
Bonaventure 67, 71-73, 77, 78, 80, 83, 87,
 88, 89, 90, 91, 92, 94, 96, 99, 100, 102,
 103, 104, 105, 107, 109, 110, 111, 123,
 124, 134, 135, 148
Borg, Marcus J. 19, 174, 181, 182, 189,
 203, 212, 213, 220, 221, 225, 235, 244
Borsch, Frederick Houk 143, 213
Boucher, Madeleine 9, 12, 13, 17, 23, 101,
 143, 219, 224
Bruns, Gerald L. 28, 147, 251
Bucer, Martin 103, 130
Bullinger, E.W. 23
Bultmann, Rudolf 28, 154, 161, 180, 216,
 217, 220
Burke, Kenneth 24
Burke, Seán 13, 14, 25, 242

Caird, G.B. 23, 143, 215
Calvin, John 67, 73-74, 75, 78, 79, 80, 81,
 83, 84, 88-90, 91, 92-95, 96, 97, 98,
 99, 100, 103, 104, 113, 114, 123, 124,
 125, 130, 134, 216
von Campenhausen, Hans, 102, 104, 105,
 111
Cappadocian Fathers 130
Childs, Brevard S. 55
Chrysostom, John 108
Clement of Alexandria 28, 29, 74, 75, 104,
 108, 112, 130
Coleridge, Samuel Taylor 23, 149, 215
Cooper, David E. 24
Cranfield, C.E.B. 101
Crossan, John Dominic 13, 143, 149, 153-
 155, 177, 178, 180, 201, 214, 223, 236,
 237, 239, 244, 245, 248
Cyril of Alexandria 125, 130

Daube, David 57, 190, 216, 217, 224, 241,
 242
Dawsey, James 19, 22, 31, 55, 58

Delitzsch, Franz J. 243
Derrida, Jacques 13, 14, 26, 155
Dibelius, Martin 5, 16, 22
Dodd, C.H. 62-67, 74, 76, 101, 102, 118,
    137, 143, 149, 183, 194, 212, 241
Donahue, John R. 32, 49, 55, 56, 57, 59,
    60, 61, 213, 216, 219, 220, 221, 222,
    223, 224, 225, 226, 243, 244
Dormeyer, Detlev 241
Dorn, K. 29
Downing, F. Gerald 61
Drury, John 4, 19, 20, 22, 55, 56, 61, 101,
    149, 177, 203, 212, 213, 221, 223, 224,
    226, 228, 231, 239, 241, 242, 243, 244,
    245
Dumarsais 21
Dunn, James D.G. 26, 212, 220

Edersheim, Alfred 243
Eliot, T.S. 241
Ellis, E. Earle 23, 48, 190, 191
Erasmus 103, 130
Erlemann, Kurt 225, 226
Etchells, Ruth 20, 23, 24, 186, 187, 215
Evans, G.R. 58, 61, 111

Farrell, Thomas J. 251
Fearghail, Fearghus O. 98, 111
Fernandez, James W. 25
Fiebig, Paul 228
Finan, Thomas 101
Fitzmyer, Joseph 108, 145
Fletcher, Angus 11, 23, 56, 194, 215, 218,
    223
Fletcher, Donald R. 59
Fontanier, Pierre 3, 20, 21, 23, 55, 218
Foucault, Michel 13, 14, 26
Fowl, Stephen 20
Frei, Hans 26
Freud, Sigmund 139, 181
Fuchs, Ernst 218
Funk, Robert W. 1, 143, 160-161, 177,
    184, 199, 213, 214, 244

Gadamer, Hans-Georg 22, 25, 28
Gerhardsson, Birger 56, 177, 219
Gilbert of Poitiers 102

Göbel, S. 114
Goethe, Johann Wolfgang 23, 138
Green, Joel B. 30, 56, 58, 214, 244
Greene, T.M. 228
Gregory the Great 67, 91-92, 100, 109,
    135

Harnisch, Wolfgang 110, 178, 187, 195,
    212, 213, 219, 223, 224, 225
Hawkes, Terence 22, 23, 24, 61, 138, 149
Hayes, Charles 149, 214
Hays, Richard B 27, 55
Hedrick, Charles W. 2, 21, 22, 57, 59,
    101, 110, 180, 184, 188, 191-192, 193,
    212, 213, 214, 216, 217, 224, 225, 238
Heidegger, Martin 26, 28, 154
Heininger, Bernhard 23, 179, 213, 214,
    216, 221, 225
Herder, Johann Gottfried 138, 147
Herzog II, William R. 57, 58, 59, 60, 190,
    212, 216, 217, 218, 219, 220, 221, 222,
    224, 243
Hill, David 21, 57, 58
Hippolytus 125
Hirsch, E.D. 25, 100
Holgate, David A. 29
Holladay, Carl R. 101
Hollander, John 27, 228
Hooker, M.D. 20
Horsley, Richard 221
Hugh of St Victor 109
Huizinga, J. 105, 106
Hunter, A.M. 60, 102, 111, 143

Ignatius of Antioch 241
Irenaeus 65, 101, 108, 112
Iser, Wolfgang 174, 178

Jacobs, Louis 222
Jakobson, Roman 24, 215
Jeffrey, David Lyle 26, 107, 112, 224, 241
Jeremias, Joachim 1, 2, 19, 58, 59, 63, 64,
    94, 101, 143, 144, 149, 151-152, 177,
    212, 214, 217, 224, 245
Jerome 100, 112, 131, 134, 148
Johnson, Luke T. 22, 37, 38, 55, 56, 57,
    58, 59, 60, 216, 221

Jülicher, Adolf 1, 2, 11, 17, 18, 20, 21, 26, 29, 59, 62, 63, 65, 74, 76, 81, 92, 96, 102, 108, 110, 111, 113-150, 151-155, 156, 158, 159, 160, 161, 162, 171, 172, 173, 174, 175, 176, 177, 179, 183, 185, 195, 196, 203, 210, 212, 215, 219, 221, 243, 245, 248, 249

Jüngel, Eberhard 27, 177, 214

Kelber, Werner H. 250
Kermode, Frank 28, 29, 101, 148
Kim, Kyoung-Jin 29
Kissinger, Warren S. 65, 142, 143
Kjärgaard, Mogens Stiller 9, 10, 22, 24, 25, 143, 179, 197, 198, 205
van Koestveld, C.E. 142
Kümmel, W.G. 141, 142

Leibniz, Gottfried Wilhelm 24
Lentricchia, Frank 16, 27
Lindemann, Andreas 59
Linnemann, Eta 16, 26, 28, 59, 60, 144, 152, 177, 213, 217, 218, 220, 224, 243
Loader, William, 58
Lodge, David 215
Louth, Andrew 3, 20, 21, 22, 25, 28, 29, 65, 100, 105, 109, 110, 111, 112, 177, 251
Luther, Martin 60, 130, 146

Madsen, Iver K. 219
de Man, Paul 5, 13, 21
Marcion 112
Martin, Janet 5, 24, 143
McDonald, J. Ian H. 56, 112, 226
McEvoy, James 103
Milavec, Aaron A. 111
Milton, John, 27, 238
Minnis, A.J. 72, 102, 103, 104
Moberly, R.W.L. 226
Morgan, Robert 22, 23
Moxnes, Halvor 59

Neill, Stephen 5, 22, 142
Nietzsche, Friedrich 24, 181, 201
Novalis 138

Oakman, Douglas E. 58, 219, 223
Oesterley, W.E.O. 244
Ong, Walter J. 61
Origen 60, 94, 102, 103, 112, 130-131, 134, 135, 148
Owen, John 24

Parker, Andrew 60, 101, 177, 207, 214
Peristiany, J.G. 222
Philo 98, 111
Pittner, Bertram 29
Plummer, Alfred 67, 103, 148
Porter, Stanley E. 58, 215
Powell, Mark Allan 179, 216

Quick, Oliver Chase 212, 219, 225
Quintilian 23, 194, 218

Rau, Eckhard 224
Ricoeur, Paul 20, 21, 23, 24, 25, 26, 28, 55, 56, 119, 143, 154, 158, 178, 181, 202, 213, 218, 244
Rohrbaugh, Richard L. 222, 224, 225
Rollinson, Philip 109
Rousseau, Jean Jacques 138
Rowe, Arthur 101
Rupert of Deutz 103
Ryken, Leland 107

Sanders, E.P. 20, 25, 61, 183, 212
Sanders, James A. 58
de Saussure, Ferdinand 9,
Schaberg, Jane 205, 222, 223
Schlegel, Friedrich 24, 137, 149
Schleiermacher, Friedrich D.E. 6, 16, 17, 19, 22, 28, 149, 178
Schneiders, Sandra 223
Schweitzer, Albert 141, 143
Schweizer, Eduard 226
Scott, Bernard Brandon 1, 2, 11, 17, 20, 23, 24, 26, 29, 35, 36, 57, 143, 144, 151-181, 186, 191, 192, 201, 202, 205, 208, 212, 213, 214, 215, 217, 218, 220, 223, 224, 236, 242, 248, 249
Sellew, P. 55, 216
Sider, John W. 219, 221, 224
Siebald, Manfred 107

Smalley, Beryl 103, 111
Smith, C.W.F. 22
Snodgrass, Klyne R. 25, 225
Soskice, Janet Martin (see Martin, Janet)
Squires, John 57
Stegemann, Ekkehard W. 57, 212, 221
Stegemann, Wolfgang 57, 212, 221
Stein, Robert H. 21, 60, 105, 112, 148
St-Jacques, Raymond 112
Strauss, David Friedrich 115, 142
Stuhlmacher, Peter 105, 141, 142, 146
Swartley, Willard M. 58, 228, 241, 242
Swinburne, Richard 24

Tannehill, Robert C. 56, 57, 58, 59, 60
Tertullian 130, 147
TeSelle, Sallie McFague 24, 26, 176, 235
Theophylact 60
Thielman, Frank 31, 55, 58, 219
Thiselton, Anthony C. 6, 19, 22, 24, 28,
    102, 103, 104, 146, 147, 149, 220, 250,
    251
Tillich, Paul 24, 57
Tolbert, Mary Ann 13, 28, 53, 61
Torrance, Thomas F. 28, 29, 74, 101, 112
Trench, Richard Chenevix 60, 63, 102,
    131, 148
Trueblood, Elton 58
Tucker, Jeffrey T. 29

Via, Dan Otto 28, 152-153, 154, 177, 217
Vico, Giovanni Battista 138

Wailes, Stephen L. 29
Weder, H. 179, 226
Weder, Hans. 243
Weiss, Bernhard 117
Weiss, Johannes 129, 143
Welch, Claude 137, 138, 147, 149
Westermann, Claus 24, 228, 242
White, Hayden 22, 23, 25, 56, 106

Wilder, Amos N. 22, 25, 143, 226, 242
Wiles, M.F. 19
Wimsatt, W.K. 25
Wink, Walter 220
Witherington, Ben 23, 61, 242, 244
Wolterstorff, Nicholas 20, 22, 24, 26, 28,
    101, 102, 107, 109, 142, 165, 172, 181,
    242, 243, 245
Wordsworth, William 138, 149
Wright, N.T. 22, 60, 142, 212, 225, 243,
    245
Wright, Stephen I. 20, 57

Young, Brad H. 19, 29

Ziesler, J. 57

Index of Subjects

Abraham 36, 39, 44, 48, 59, 83, 90, 93, 94, 124, 167, 188, 199, 200, 211, 213, 220, 226, 238
Acca, Bishop 17, 100
Adam 238
aesthetic objects 152, 153, 177
allegorical interpretation 74, 83, 101
allegorizing 25
allegory 9, 11, 23, 40, 52, 66, 74, 76, 77, 81, 91, 94, 102, 105, 110, 115, 117, 125, 126, 127, 132, 133, 137, 138, 139, 141, 147, 149, 152, 170, 171, 175, 178, 218, 223, 228, 248
Arians 99
alliteration 7
analogy 116, 221
anthropology 25, 154, 205
anthropomorphism 24
anti-Judaism 111
aphorisms 213, 247

Beispielerzählung (see example story)

characters, characterization 31, 35-37, 51, 52, 75, 77, 78, 79, 97, 126, 161, 162, 184, 185-201, 204-207, 210-211, 213, 214, 216, 218, 219, 220, 226, 231-232, 234, 237
cliché 10
covenantal nomism 183, 206
customs officers 36, 37, 43, 48, 52, 120, 163, 201, 206
dead metaphors 9
debt 41, 57, 58, 100, 243
debt code 243

echo 15, 27, 53-54, 66, 100, 245
ellipsis 194, 238
enigma 116
Eve 238

example story 18, 118, 136, 160-161, 169, 195, 202, 221

Fabel 19, 116, 142
fiction 21, 106, 184, 185, 194, 214, 232, 238, 240, 245
figure of speech, definition of 3-4
Figurenlehre 214
form-criticism 1, 19, 155
Former Prophets 230
four senses of Scripture 76, 98, 105
friars 102, 111

Gleichnis 110, 116, 141, 142
Gleichiserzählung (see *Fabel*)
Haggadah 243
Halakah 243
Herod 8, 10, 24, 43, 50, 185
historical criticism 4, 6, 113-114
historiography 25, 31
holiness code 233, 243
hyperbole 8, 23, 187-193, 229, 237, 244

implied speaker 156, 157, 179
influence 12, 14-17 and passim
insight 12, 17-18 and passim
intention 12-14 and passim
irony 7-9, 13, 24, 58, 59-60, 187, 215, 229, 236

Jesus Seminar 1
John the Baptist 37
Judaism 20, 25, 49, 126, 163, 169, 175, 183, 198, 222, 224, 225, 226, 232, 238, 245

kingdom of God 19, 27, 29, 38, 44, 52, 63, 117, 128, 139, 158, 159, 161, 162, 166, 168, 169, 170, 171, 185, 214, 251

Lord's Prayer 41

mashal, meshalim 56, 116, 127, 153, 203, 219, 223, 230, 231, 240, 242
mendicant orders 67
metalepsis 8, 23, 24, 210-211, 215, 238-240, 245
metaphor 8-10, 75, 154-155, 158-160, 185-186, 238, 248 and passim
metonymy 8, 10, 23, 24, 31-33, 51-52, 75, 77, 168, 186-187, 215, 237, 247
Moses 238
mythology 213

narrative, metaphorical function of 158-159
Neo-Platonism 98
'new hermeneutic' 13, 16, 26-27, 152

Oedipus 113, 139

parody 188
patriarchy 182, 204-206, 223
Pentateuch 27, 242
persona 105-106, 186
Pharisees 36, 37, 40, 46, 47, 48, 50, 52, 53, 56, 59, 60, 84, 86, 120, 162, 163, 164, 165, 183, 198, 218, 233, 243
poetry 14-15, 23, 27, 137-138, 149, 207, 224, 228-229, 236, 241
post-structuralism 177
preaching 27, 56, 70, 102, 122, 216
priests 35, 56, 68, 78, 119, 164, 201, 220
prophecy 27, 229-230, 234-235
purity 51, 159, 204, 210, 222, 243, 247
purity code 243
realism 36, 41, 78, 88, 95, 106, 123, 125, 135, 183-184, 186, 191, 193, 195, 198, 205, 210, 213, 214, 216, 223, 231, 239, 246
redaction-criticism 155
Redefigur 21, 116

Renaissance humanism 99
rhetoric 5, 7, 23, 109, 116-117, 207, 219, 224, 230, 241
riddle 127, 128, 132, 141
Romanticism, Romantics 27, 137-139

Scharfsinn 17, 132, 140, 147
scholasticism 99, 130
sensus literalis 80
sermocinatio (see *Figurenlehre*)
simile 6, 7, 11, 23, 94, 102, 110, 115-118, 120, 123, 127, 129, 132, 133, 135, 137, 139, 141, 143, 145, 158, 175, 185, 248
source-criticism 1, 114-115, 128
stereotype 35, 47, 53, 96, 161, 165, 198, 201, 225
structuralism 154, 177
Sturm und Drang 138
symbol 23, 29, 138, 158, 166, 186, 215, 231
synecdoche 7-11, 75, 193-207, 230-235, 236-237, 246-247 and passim

Tabernacles, Feast of 58
Talmud 192, 220
Theophilus 30, 61
Torah 15, 52, 61, 158, 183, 191, 199, 222, 229, 232-234, 235, 236, 242, 243
Tosephta 192
trope, definition of 7
tropology 135
widows 35, 40, 197
wisdom 48, 55, 56, 58, 122-123, 127, 139, 157, 207-212, 224, 225, 226, 229-231, 235, 236, 237, 239, 240, 242, 243, 246
wisdom, 'common' or 'conventional' 2, 5, 20, 174-176, 235

Zacchaeus 36, 37, 38, 39, 41, 42, 44, 49, 56, 86

Paternoster Biblical Monographs

(All titles uniform with this volume)
Dates in bold are of projected publication

Joseph Abraham
Eve: Accused or Acquitted?
A Reconsideration of Feminist Readings of the Creation Narrative Texts in Genesis 1–3

Two contrary views dominate contemporary feminist biblical scholarship. One finds in the Bible an unequivocal equality between the sexes from the very creation of humanity, whilst the other sees the biblical text as irredeemably patriarchal and androcentric. Dr Abraham enters into dialogue with both camps as well as introducing his own method of approach. An invaluable tool for any one who is interested in this contemporary debate.

2002 / 0-85364-971-5 / xxiv + 272pp

Octavian D. Baban
Mimesis and Luke's on the Road Encounters in Luke-Acts
Luke's Theology of the Way and its Literary Representation

The book argues on theological and literary (mimetic) grounds that Luke's on-the-road encounters, especially those belonging to the post-Easter period, are part of his complex theology of the Way. Jesus' teaching and that of the apostles is presented by Luke as a challenging answer to the Hellenistic reader's thirst for adventure, good literature, and existential paradigms.

2005 */ 1-84227-253-5 / approx. 374pp*

Paul Barker
The Triumph of Grace in Deuteronomy

This book is a textual and theological analysis of the interaction between the sin and faithlessness of Israel and the grace of Yahweh in response, looking especially at Deuteronomy chapters 1–3, 8–10 and 29–30. The author argues that the grace of Yahweh is determinative for the ongoing relationship between Yahweh and Israel and that Deuteronomy anticipates and fully expects Israel to be faithless.

2004 / 1-84227-226-8 / xxii + 270pp

Jonathan F. Bayes
The Weakness of the Law
God's Law and the Christian in New Testament Perspective

A study of the four New Testament books which refer to the law as weak (Acts, Romans, Galatians, Hebrews) leads to a defence of the third use in the Reformed debate about the law in the life of the believer.

2000 / 0-85364-957-X / xii + 244pp

Mark Bonnington
The Antioch Episode of Galatians 2:11-14 in Historical and Cultural Context
The Galatians 2 'incident' in Antioch over table-fellowship suggests significant disagreement between the leading apostles. This book analyses the background to the disagreement by locating the incident within the dynamics of social interaction between Jews and Gentiles. It proposes a new way of understanding the relationship between the individuals and issues involved.
2005 / 1-84227-050-8 / approx. 350pp

David Bostock
A Portrayal of Trust
The Theme of Faith in the Hezekiah Narratives
This study provides detailed and sensitive readings of the Hezekiah narratives (2 Kings 18–20 and Isaiah 36–39) from a theological perspective. It concentrates on the theme of faith, using narrative criticism as its methodology. Attention is paid especially to setting, plot, point of view and characterization within the narratives. A largely positive portrayal of Hezekiah emerges that underlines the importance and relevance of scripture.
2005 / 1-84227-314-0 / approx. 300pp

Mark Bredin
Jesus, Revolutionary of Peace
A Non-violent Christology in the Book of Revelation
This book aims to demonstrate that the figure of Jesus in the Book of Revelation can best be understood as an active non-violent revolutionary.
2003 / 1-84227-153-9 / xviii + 262pp

Robinson Butarbutar
Paul and Conflict Resolution
An Exegetical Study of Paul's Apostolic Paradigm in 1 Corinthians 9
The author sees the apostolic paradigm in 1 Corinthians 9 as part of Paul's unified arguments in 1 Corinthians 8–10 in which he seeks to mediate in the dispute over the issue of food offered to idols. The book also sees its relevance for dispute-resolution today, taking the conflict within the author's church as an example.
2006 / 1-84227-315-9 / approx. 280pp

Daniel J-S Chae
Paul as Apostle to the Gentiles
*His Apostolic Self-awareness and its Influence on the Soteriological Argument
in Romans*
Opposing 'the post-Holocaust interpretation of Romans', Daniel Chae com-
petently demonstrates that Paul argues for the equality of Jew and Gentile in
Romans. Chae's fresh exegetical interpretation is academically outstanding and
spiritually encouraging.
1997 / 0-85364-829-8 / xiv + 378pp

Luke L. Cheung
The Genre, Composition and Hermeneutics of the Epistle of James
The present work examines the employment of the wisdom genre with a certain
compositional structure and the interpretation of the law through the Jesus
tradition of the double love command by the author of the Epistle of James to
serve his purpose in promoting perfection and warning against doubleness
among the eschatologically renewed people of God in the Diaspora.
2003 / 1-84227-062-1 / xvi + 372pp

Youngmo Cho
Spirit and Kingdom in the Writings of Luke and Paul
The relationship between Spirit and Kingdom is a relatively unexplored area in
Lukan and Pauline studies. This book offers a fresh perspective of two biblical
writers on the subject. It explores the difference between Luke's and Paul's
understanding of the Spirit by examining the specific question of the
relationship of the concept of the Spirit to the concept of the Kingdom of God in
each writer.
2005 / 1-84227-316-7 / approx. 270pp

Andrew C. Clark
Parallel Lives
The Relation of Paul to the Apostles in the Lucan Perspective
This study of the Peter-Paul parallels in Acts argues that their purpose was to
emphasize the themes of continuity in salvation history and the unity of the
Jewish and Gentile missions. New light is shed on Luke's literary techniques,
partly through a comparison with Plutarch.
2001 / 1-84227-035-4 / xviii + 386pp

Andrew D. Clarke
Secular and Christian Leadership in Corinth
A Socio-Historical and Exegetical Study of 1 Corinthians 1–6
This volume is an investigation into the leadership structures and dynamics of first-century Roman Corinth. These are compared with the practice of leadership in the Corinthian Christian community which are reflected in 1 Corinthians 1–6, and contrasted with Paul's own principles of Christian leadership.
2005 / 1-84227-229-2 / 200pp

Stephen Finamore
God, Order and Chaos
René Girard and the Apocalypse
Readers are often disturbed by the images of destruction in the book of Revelation and unsure why they are unleashed after the exaltation of Jesus. This book examines past approaches to these texts and uses René Girard's theories to revive some old ideas and propose some new ones.
2005 / 1-84227-197-0 / approx. 344pp

David G. Firth
Surrendering Retribution in the Psalms
Responses to Violence in the Individual Complaints
In *Surrendering Retribution in the Psalms*, David Firth examines the ways in which the book of Psalms inculcates a model response to violence through the repetition of standard patterns of prayer. Rather than seeking justification for retributive violence, Psalms encourages not only a surrender of the right of retribution to Yahweh, but also sets limits on the retribution that can be sought in imprecations. Arising initially from the author's experience in South Africa, the possibilities of this model to a particular context of violence is then briefly explored.
2005 / 1-84227-337-X / xviii + 154pp

Scott J. Hafemann
Suffering and Ministry in the Spirit
Paul's Defence of His Ministry in II Corinthians 2:14–3:3
Shedding new light on the way Paul defended his apostleship, the author offers a careful, detailed study of 2 Corinthians 2:14–3:3 linked with other key passages throughout 1 and 2 Corinthians. Demonstrating the unity and coherence of Paul's argument in this passage, the author shows that Paul's suffering served as the vehicle for revealing God's power and glory through the Spirit.
2000 / 0-85364-967-7 / xiv + 262pp

Scott J. Hafemann
Paul, Moses and the History of Israel
The Letter/Spirit Contrast and the Argument from Scripture in 2 Corinthians 3
An exegetical study of the call of Moses, the second giving of the Law (Exodus 32–34), the new covenant, and the prophetic understanding of the history of Israel in 2 Corinthians 3. Hafemann's work demonstrates Paul's contextual use of the Old Testament and the essential unity between the Law and the Gospel within the context of the distinctive ministries of Moses and Paul.
2005 / 1-84227-317-5 / xii + 498pp

Douglas S. McComiskey
Lukan Theology in the Light of the Gospel's Literary Structure
Luke's Gospel was purposefully written with theology embedded in its patterned literary structure. A critical analysis of this cyclical structure provides new windows into Luke's interpretation of the individual pericopes comprising the Gospel and illuminates several of his theological interests.
2004 / 1-84227-148-2 / xviii + 388pp

Stephen Motyer
Your Father the Devil?
A New Approach to John and 'The Jews'
Who are 'the Jews' in John's Gospel? Defending John against the charge of antisemitism, Motyer argues that, far from demonising the Jews, the Gospel seeks to present Jesus as 'Good News for Jews' in a late first century setting.
1997 / 0-85364-832-8 / xiv + 260pp

Esther Ng
Reconstructing Christian Origins?
The Feminist Theology of Elizabeth Schüssler Fiorenza: An Evaluation
In a detailed evaluation, the author challenges Elizabeth Schüssler Fiorenza's reconstruction of early Christian origins and her underlying presuppositions. The author also presents her own views on women's roles both then and now.
2002 / 1-84227-055-9 / xxiv + 468pp

Robin Parry
Old Testament Story and Christian Ethics
The Rape of Dinah as a Case Study
What is the role of story in ethics and, more particularly, what is the role of Old
Testament story in Christian ethics? This book, drawing on the work of
contemporary philosophers, argues that narrative is crucial in the ethical shaping
of people and, drawing on the work of contemporary Old Testament scholars,
that story plays a key role in Old Testament ethics. Parry then argues that when
situated in canonical context Old Testament stories can be reappropriated by
Christian readers in their own ethical formation. The shocking story of the rape
of Dinah and the massacre of the Shechemites provides a fascinating case study
for exploring the parameters within which Christian ethical appropriations of
Old Testament stories can live.
2004 / 1-84227-210-1 / xx + 350pp

Ian Paul
Power to See the World Anew
*The Value of Paul Ricoeur's Hermeneutic of Metaphor in Interpreting the
Symbolism of Revelation 12 and 13*
This book is a study of the hermeneutics of metaphor of Paul Ricoeur, one of the
most important writers on hermeneutics and metaphor of the last century. It sets
out the key points of his theory, important criticisms of his work, and how his
approach, modified in the light of these criticisms, offers a methodological
framework for reading apocalyptic texts.
2006 / 1-84227-056-7 / approx. 350pp

Robert L. Plummer
Paul's Understanding of the Church's Mission
Did the Apostle Paul Expect the Early Christian Communities to Evangelize?
This book engages in a careful study of Paul's letters to determine if the apostle
expected the communities to which he wrote to engage in missionary activity.
It helpfully summarizes the discussion on this debated issue, judiciously
handling contested texts, and provides a way forward in addressing this critical
question. While admitting that Paul rarely explicitly commands the
communities he founded to evangelize, Plummer amasses significant incidental
data to provide a convincing case that Paul did indeed expect his churches to
engage in mission activity. Throughout the study, Plummer progressively
builds a theological basis for the church's mission that is both distinctively
Pauline and compelling.
2006 / 1-84227-333-7 / approx. 324pp

David Powys
'Hell': A Hard Look at a Hard Question
The Fate of the Unrighteous in New Testament Thought
This comprehensive treatment seeks to unlock the original meaning of terms and phrases long thought to support the traditional doctrine of hell. It concludes that there is an alternative—one which is more biblical, and which can positively revive the rationale for Christian mission.

1997 / 0-85364-831-X / xxii + 478pp

Sorin Sabou
Between Horror and Hope
Paul's Metaphorical Language of Death in Romans 6.1-11
This book argues that Paul's metaphorical language of death in Romans 6.1-11 conveys two aspects: horror and hope. The 'horror' aspect is conveyed by the 'crucifixion' language, and the 'hope' aspect by 'burial' language. The life of the Christian believer is understood, as relationship with sin is concerned ('death to sin'), between these two realities: horror and hope.

2005 / 1-84227-322-1 / approx. 224pp

Rosalind Selby
The Comical Doctrine
The Epistemology of New Testament Hermeneutics
This book argues that the gospel breaks through postmodernity's critique of truth and the referential possibilities of textuality with its gift of grace. With a rigorous, philosophical challenge to modernist and postmodernist assumptions, Selby offers an alternative epistemology to all who would still read with faith *and* with academic credibility.

2005 / 1-84227-212-8 / approx. 350pp

Kiwoong Son
Zion Symbolism in Hebrews
Hebrews 12.18-24 as a Hermeneutical Key to the Epistle
This book challenges the general tendency of understanding the Epistle to the Hebrews against a Hellenistic background and suggests that the Epistle should be understood in the light of the Jewish apocalyptic tradition. The author especially argues for the importance of the theological symbolism of Sinai and Zion (Heb. 12:18-24) as it provides the Epistle's theological background as well as the rhetorical basis of the superiority motif of Jesus throughout the Epistle.

2005 / 1-84227-368-X / approx. 280pp

Kevin Walton
Thou Traveller Unknown
The Presence and Absence of God in the Jacob Narrative
The author offers a fresh reading of the story of Jacob in the book of Genesis
through the paradox of divine presence and absence. The work also seeks to
make a contribution to Pentateuchal studies by bringing together a close reading
of the final text with historical critical insights, doing justice to the text's
historical depth, final form and canonical status.
2003 / 1-84227-059-1 / xvi + 238pp

George M. Wieland
The Significance of Salvation
A Study of Salvation Language in the Pastoral Epistles
The language and ideas of salvation pervade the three Pastoral Epistles. This
study offers a close examination of their soteriological statements. In all three
letters the idea of salvation is found to play a vital paraenetic role, but each also
exhibits distinctive soteriological emphases. The results challenge common
assumptions about the Pastoral Epistles as a corpus.
2005 / 1-84227-257-8 / *approx. 324pp*

Alistair Wilson
When Will These Things Happen?
A Study of Jesus as Judge in Matthew 21–25
This study seeks to allow Matthew's carefully constructed presentation of Jesus
to be given full weight in the modern evaluation of Jesus' eschatology. Careful
analysis of the text of Matthew 21–25 reveals Jesus to be standing firmly in the
Jewish prophetic and wisdom traditions as he proclaims and enacts imminent
judgement on the Jewish authorities then boldly claims the central role in the
final and universal judgement.
2004 / 1-84227-146-6 / xxii + 272pp

Lindsay Wilson
Joseph Wise and Otherwise
The Intersection of Covenant and Wisdom in Genesis 37–50
This book offers a careful literary reading of Genesis 37–50 that argues that the
Joseph story contains both strong covenant themes and many wisdom-like
elements. The connections between the two helps to explore how covenant and
wisdom might intersect in an integrated biblical theology.
2004 / 1-84227-140-7 / xvi + 340pp

Stephen I. Wright
The Voice of Jesus
Studies in the Interpretation of Six Gospel Parables
This literary study considers how the 'voice' of Jesus has been heard in different
periods of parable interpretation, and how the categories of figure and trope may
help us towards a sensitive reading of the parables today.
2000 / 0-85364-975-8 / xiv + 280pp

Paternoster
9 Holdom Avenue,
Bletchley,
Milton Keynes MK1 1QR,
United Kingdom
Web: www.authenticmedia.co.uk/paternoster

July 2005

Paternoster Theological Monographs

(All titles uniform with this volume)
Dates in bold are of projected publication

Emil Bartos
Deification in Eastern Orthodox Theology
An Evaluation and Critique of the Theology of Dumitru Staniloae
Bartos studies a fundamental yet neglected aspect of Orthodox theology: deification. By examining the doctrines of anthropology, christology, soteriology and ecclesiology as they relate to deification, he provides an important contribution to contemporary dialogue between Eastern and Western theologians.

1999 / 0-85364-956-1 / xii + 370pp

Graham Buxton
The Trinity, Creation and Pastoral Ministry
Imaging the Perichoretic God
In this book the author proposes a three-way conversation between theology, science and pastoral ministry. His approach draws on a Trinitarian understanding of God as a relational being of love, whose life 'spills over' into all created reality, human and non-human. By locating human meaning and purpose within God's 'creation-community' this book offers the possibility of a transforming engagement between those in pastoral ministry and the scientific community.

2005 */ 1-84227-369-8 / approx. 380 pp*

Iain D. Campbell
Fixing the Indemnity
The Life and Work of George Adam Smith
When Old Testament scholar George Adam Smith (1856–1942) delivered the Lyman Beecher lectures at Yale University in 1899, he confidently declared that 'modern criticism has won its war against traditional theories. It only remains to fix the amount of the indemnity.' In this biography, Iain D. Campbell assesses Smith's critical approach to the Old Testament and evaluates its consequences, showing that Smith's life and work still raises questions about the relationship between biblical scholarship and evangelical faith.

2004 / 1-84227-228-4 / xx + 256pp

Tim Chester
Mission and the Coming of God
Eschatology, the Trinity and Mission in the Theology of Jürgen Moltmann
This book explores the theology and missiology of the influential contemporary theologian, Jürgen Moltmann. It highlights the important contribution Moltmann has made while offering a critique of his thought from an evangelical perspective. In so doing, it touches on pertinent issues for evangelical missiology. The conclusion takes Calvin as a starting point, proposing 'an eschatology of the cross' which offers a critique of the over-realised eschatologies in liberation theology and certain forms of evangelicalism.
2006 / 1-84227-320-5 / approx. 224pp

Sylvia Wilkey Collinson
Making Disciples
The Significance of Jesus' Educational Strategy for Today's Church
This study examines the biblical practice of discipling, formulates a definition, and makes comparisons with modern models of education. A recommendation is made for greater attention to its practice today.
2004 / 1-84227-116-4 / xiv + 278pp

Darrell Cosden
A Theology of Work
Work and the New Creation
Through dialogue with Moltmann, Pope John Paul II and others, this book develops a genitive 'theology of work', presenting a theological definition of work and a model for a theological ethics of work that shows work's nature, value and meaning now and eschatologically. Work is shown to be a transformative activity consisting of three dynamically inter-related dimensions: the instrumental, relational and ontological.
2005 / 1-84227-332-9 / xvi + 208pp

Stephen M. Dunning
The Crisis and the Quest
A Kierkegaardian Reading of Charles Williams
Employing Kierkegaardian categories and analysis, this study investigates both the central crisis in Charles Williams's authorship between hermetism and Christianity (Kierkegaard's Religions A and B), and the quest to resolve this crisis, a quest that ultimately presses the bounds of orthodoxy.
2000 / 0-85364-985-5 / xxiv + 254pp

Keith Ferdinando
The Triumph of Christ in African Perspective
A Study of Demonology and Redemption in the African Context
The book explores the implications of the gospel for traditional African fears of
occult aggression. It analyses such traditional approaches to suffering and
biblical responses to fears of demonic evil, concluding with an evaluation of
African beliefs from the perspective of the gospel.
1999 / 0-85364-830-1 / xviii + 450pp

Andrew Goddard
Living the Word, Resisting the World
The Life and Thought of Jacques Ellul
This work offers a definitive study of both the life and thought of the French
Reformed thinker Jacques Ellul (1912-1994). It will prove an indispensable
resource for those interested in this influential theologian and sociologist and for
Christian ethics and political thought generally.
2002 / 1-84227-053-2 / xxiv + 378pp

David Hilborn
The Words of our Lips
Language-Use in Free Church Worship
Studies of liturgical language have tended to focus on the written canons of
Roman Catholic and Anglican communities. By contrast, David Hilborn
analyses the more extemporary approach of English Nonconformity. Drawing
on recent developments in linguistic pragmatics, he explores similarities and
differences between 'fixed' and 'free' worship, and argues for the
interdependence of each.
2006 */ 0-85364-977-4 / approx. 350pp*

Roger Hitching
The Church and Deaf People
*A Study of Identity, Communication and Relationships with Special Reference to
the Ecclesiology of Jürgen Moltmann*
In *The Church and Deaf People* Roger Hitching sensitively examines the history
and present experience of deaf people and finds similarities between aspects of
sign language and Moltmann's theological method that 'open up' new ways of
understanding theological concepts.
2003 / 1-84227-222-5 / xxii + 236pp

John G. Kelly
One God, One People
The Differentiated Unity of the People of God in the Theology of
Jürgen Moltmann
The author expounds and critiques Moltmann's doctrine of God and highlights
the systematic connections between it and Moltmann's influential discussion of
Israel. He then proposes a fresh approach to Jewish–Christian relations building
on Moltmann's work using insights from Habermas and Rawls.
2005 / 0-85346-969-3 / approx. 350pp

Mark F.W. Lovatt
Confronting the Will-to-Power
A Reconsideration of the Theology of Reinhold Niebuhr
Confronting the Will-to-Power is an analysis of the theology of Reinhold
Niebuhr, arguing that his work is an attempt to identify, and provide a practical
theological answer to, the existence and nature of human evil.
2001 / 1-84227-054-0 / xviii + 216pp

Neil B. MacDonald
Karl Barth and the Strange New World within the Bible
Barth, Wittgenstein, and the Metadilemmas of the Enlightenment
Barth's discovery of the strange new world within the Bible is examined in the
context of Kant, Hume, Overbeck, and, most importantly, Wittgenstein.
MacDonald covers some fundamental issues in theology today: epistemology,
the final form of the text and biblical truth-claims.
2000 / 0-85364-970-7 / xxvi + 374pp

Keith A. Mascord
Alvin Plantinga and Christian Apologetics
This book draws together the contributions of the philosopher Alvin Plantinga to
the major contemporary challenges to Christian belief, highlighting in particular
his ground-breaking work in epistemology and the problem of evil. Plantinga's
theory that both theistic and Christian belief is warrantedly basic is explored and
critiqued, and an assessment offered as to the significance of his work for
apologetic theory and practice.
2005 / 1-84227-256-X / approx. 304pp

Gillian McCulloch
The Deconstruction of Dualism in Theology
With Reference to Ecofeminist Theology and New Age Spirituality
This book challenges eco-theological anti-dualism in Christian theology, arguing that dualism has a twofold function in Christian religious discourse. Firstly, it enables us to express the discontinuities and divisions that are part of the process of reality. Secondly, dualistic language allows us to express the mysteries of divine transcendence/immanence and the survival of the soul without collapsing into monism and materialism, both of which are problematic for Christian epistemology.
2002 / 1-84227-044-3 / xii + 282pp

Leslie McCurdy
Attributes and Atonement
The Holy Love of God in the Theology of P.T. Forsyth
Attributes and Atonement is an intriguing full-length study of P.T. Forsyth's doctrine of the cross as it relates particularly to God's holy love. It includes an unparalleled bibliography of both primary and secondary material relating to Forsyth.
1999 / 0-85364-833-6 / xiv + 328pp

Nozomu Miyahira
Towards a Theology of the Concord of God
A Japanese Perspective on the Trinity
This book introduces a new Japanese theology and a unique Trinitarian formula based on the Japanese intellectual climate: three betweennesses and one concord. It also presents a new interpretation of the Trinity, a co-subordinationism, which is in line with orthodox Trinitarianism; each single person of the Trinity is eternally and equally subordinate (or serviceable) to the other persons, so that they retain the mutual dynamic equality.
2000 / 0-85364-863-8 / xiv + 256pp

Eddy José Muskus
The Origins and Early Development of Liberation Theology in Latin America
With Particular Reference to Gustavo Gutiérrez
This work challenges the fundamental premise of Liberation Theology, 'opting for the poor', and its claim that Christ is found in them. It also argues that Liberation Theology emerged as a direct result of the failure of the Roman Catholic Church in Latin America.
2002 / 0-85364-974-X / xiv + 296pp

Jim Purves
The Triune God and the Charismatic Movement
A Critical Appraisal from a Scottish Perspective
All emotion and no theology? Or a fundamental challenge to reappraise and realign our trinitarian theology in the light of Christian experience? This study of charismatic renewal as it found expression within Scotland at the end of the twentieth century evaluates the use of Patristic, Reformed and contemporary models of the Trinity in explaining the workings of the Holy Spirit.
2004 / 1-84227-321-3 / xxiv + 246pp

Anna Robbins
Methods in the Madness
Diversity in Twentieth-Century Christian Social Ethics
The author compares the ethical methods of Walter Rauschenbusch, Reinhold Niebuhr and others. She argues that unless Christians are clear about the ways that theology and philosophy are expressed practically they may lose the ability to discuss social ethics across contexts, let alone reach effective agreements.
2004 / 1-84227-211-X / xx + 294pp

Ed Rybarczyk
Beyond Salvation
Eastern Orthodoxy and Classical Pentecostalism on Becoming Like Christ
At first glance eastern Orthodoxy and classical Pentecostalism seem quite distinct. This ground-breaking study shows they share much in common, especially as it concerns the experiential elements of following Christ. Both traditions assert that authentic Christianity transcends the wooden categories of modernism.
2004 / 1-84227-144-X / xii + 356pp

Signe Sandsmark
Is World View Neutral Education Possible and Desirable?
A Christian Response to Liberal Arguments
(Published jointly with The Stapleford Centre)
This book discusses reasons for belief in world view neutrality, and argues that 'neutral' education will have a hidden, but strong world view influence. It discusses the place for Christian education in the common school.
2000 / 0-85364-973-1 / xiv + 182pp

Hazel Sherman
Reading Zechariah
The Allegorical Tradition of Biblical Interpretation through the Commentary of Didymus the Blind and Theodore of Mopsuestia
A close reading of the commentary on Zechariah by Didymus the Blind alongside that of Theodore of Mopsuestia suggests that popular categorising of Antiochene and Alexandrian biblical exegesis as 'historical' or 'allegorical' is inadequate and misleading.
2005 / 1-84227-213-6 / approx. 280pp

Andrew Sloane
On Being a Christian in the Academy
Nicholas Wolterstorff and the Practice of Christian Scholarship
An exposition and critical appraisal of Nicholas Wolterstorff's epistemology in the light of the philosophy of science, and an application of his thought to the practice of Christian scholarship.
2003 / 1-84227-058-3 / xvi + 274pp

Damon W.K. So
Jesus' Revelation of His Father
A Narrative-Conceptual Study of the Trinity with Special Reference to Karl Barth
This book explores the trinitarian dynamics in the context of Jesus' revelation of his Father in his earthly ministry with references to key passages in Matthew's Gospel. It develops from the exegeses of these passages a non-linear concept of revelation which links Jesus' communion with his Father to his revelatory words and actions through a nuanced understanding of the Holy Spirit, with references to K. Barth, G.W.H. Lampe, J.D.G. Dunn and E. Irving.
2005 / 1-84227-323-X / approx. 380pp

Daniel Strange
The Possibility of Salvation Among the Unevangelised
An Analysis of Inclusivism in Recent Evangelical Theology
For evangelical theologians the 'fate of the unevangelised' impinges upon fundamental tenets of evangelical identity. The position known as 'inclusivism', defined by the belief that the unevangelised can be ontologically saved by Christ whilst being epistemologically unaware of him, has been defended most vigorously by the Canadian evangelical Clark H. Pinnock. Through a detailed analysis and critique of Pinnock's work, this book examines a cluster of issues surrounding the unevangelised and its implications for christology, soteriology and the doctrine of revelation.
2002 / 1-84227-047-8 / xviii + 362pp

Scott Swain
God According to the Gospel
Biblical Narrative and the Identity of God in the Theology of Robert W. Jenson
Robert W. Jenson is one of the leading voices in contemporary Trinitarian theology. His boldest contribution in this area concerns his use of biblical narrative both to ground and explicate the Christian doctrine of God. *God According to the Gospel* critically examines Jenson's proposal and suggests an alternative way of reading the biblical portrayal of the triune God.
2006 / 1-84227-258-6 / approx. 180pp

Justyn Terry
The Justifying Judgement of God
A Reassessment of the Place of Judgement in the Saving Work of Christ
The argument of this book is that judgement, understood as the whole process of bringing justice, is the primary metaphor of atonement, with others, such as victory, redemption and sacrifice, subordinate to it. Judgement also provides the proper context for understanding penal substitution and the call to repentance, baptism, eucharist and holiness.
2005 / 1-84227-370-1 / approx. 274 pp

Graham Tomlin
The Power of the Cross
Theology and the Death of Christ in Paul, Luther and Pascal
This book explores the theology of the cross in St Paul, Luther and Pascal. It offers new perspectives on the theology of each, and some implications for the nature of power, apologetics, theology and church life in a postmodern context.
1999 / 0-85364-984-7 / xiv + 344pp

Adonis Vidu
Postliberal Theological Method
A Critical Study
The postliberal theology of Hans Frei, George Lindbeck, Ronald Thiemann, John Milbank and others is one of the more influential contemporary options. This book focuses on several aspects pertaining to its theological method, specifically its understanding of background, hermeneutics, epistemic justification, ontology, the nature of doctrine and, finally, Christological method.
2005 / 1-84227-395-7 / approx. 324pp

Graham J. Watts
Revelation and the Spirit
*A Comparative Study of the Relationship between the Doctrine of Revelation
and Pneumatology in the Theology of Eberhard Jüngel and of
Wolfhart Pannenberg*
The relationship between revelation and pneumatology is relatively unexplored.
This approach offers a fresh angle on two important twentieth century
theologians and raises pneumatological questions which are theologically crucial
and relevant to mission in a postmodern culture.
2005 / 1-84227-104-0 / xxii + 232pp

Nigel G. Wright
Disavowing Constantine
*Mission, Church and the Social Order in the Theologies of John Howard Yoder
and Jürgen Moltmann*
This book is a timely restatement of a radical theology of church and state in the
Anabaptist and Baptist tradition. Dr Wright constructs his argument in dialogue
and debate with Yoder and Moltmann, major contributors to a free church
perspective.
2000 / 0-85364-978-2 / xvi + 252pp

Paternoster
9 Holdom Avenue,
Bletchley,
Milton Keynes MK1 1QR,
United Kingdom
Web: www.authenticmedia.co.uk/paternoster